Aid, Technology and Development

Over the last 50 years, Nepal has been considered an experiential model in determining the effectiveness and success of global human development strategies, both in theory and in practice. As such, it provides a rich array of in-depth case studies in both development success and failure. This edited collection examines these in order to propose a novel perspective on how human development occurs and how it can be aided and sustained.

Aid, Technology and Development: The lessons from Nepal champions plural rationality from both a theoretical and practical perspective in order to challenge and critique the status quo in human development understanding, while simultaneously presenting a concrete framework with which to aid citizen and governmental organisations in the galvanisation of human development.

Including contributions by leading international social scientists and development practitioners throughout Nepal, this book will be of great interest to students, scholars and practitioners working in the field of foreign aid and development studies.

Dipak Gyawali is a hydroelectric power engineer trained at the Moscow Energy Institute and a political economist trained at the Energy and Resources Group of the University of California at Berkeley and was Nepal's Minister of Water Resources in 2002/03. A *Pragya* (Academician) of the Nepal Academy of Science and Technology, he conducts interdisciplinary research at the interface of technology and society, mostly from the perspectives of cultural theory. He has been a visiting professor/research scholar as well as member of advisory boards throughout various universities and international organisations, including the UN University in Yokohama, Battelle Pacific Northwest National Lab and Mekong's MPower. Currently he is on the advisory committee of UNESCO's World Water Assessment Program, Stockholm International Water Institute's Scientific Program Committee and IDS Sussex STEPs Center' advisory board. He chairs the Nepal Water Conservation Foundation as well as Inter Disciplinary Analysts.

Michael Thompson has had a long association with Nepal: first as a teenage soldier in the Malayan 'emergency' (where he served in the British army's Gurkha Division), then as a Himalayan mountaineer and subsequently as an anthropologist-cum-policy analyst (*Uncertainty on a Himalayan Scale*, 2007). Trained at University College London (BSc, PhD) and Oxford (BLitt), he is currently a senior researcher at the International Institute for Applied Systems Analysis, a global change think tank in Austria. There he develops and applies the concept of 'plural rationality': people doing very different things and yet still behaving rationally, given their different sets of convictions as to how the world is and people are (*Cultural Theory*, 1990; *Organising and Disorganising*, 2008).

Marco Verweij is professor of political science at Jacobs University in Bremen, Germany. He holds a doctorate in social and political science from the European University Institute in Florence, Italy, and previously earned his keep at the Max Planck Institute for Research on Collective Goods in Bonn, Germany, and at the Singapore Management University. In his research, he attempts to understand how 'wicked' social and environmental problems can be resolved through the combined forces of (inter-)governmental action, entrepreneurship and technological innovation, as well as civil society engagement. He also explores the possible synergies between social and political theory, brain research and the analysis of human complex systems.

Science in Society Series

Series Editor: Steve Rayner
Institute for Science, Innovation and Society, University of Oxford

Editorial Board: Jason Blackstock, Bjorn Ola Linner, Susan Owens, Timothy O'Riordan, Arthur Petersen, Nick Pidgeon, Dan Sarewitz, Andy Sterling, Chris Tyler, Andrew Webster, Steve Yearley

The Earthscan Science in Society Series aims to publish new high-quality research, teaching, practical and policy-related books on topics that address the complex and vitally important interface between science and society.

Vaccine Anxieties:
Global Science, child health and society
Melissa Leach and James Fairhead

Democratizing Technology
Risk, responsibility and the Regulation of Chemicals
Anne Chapman

Genomics and Society
Legal, ethical and social dimensions
Edited by George Gaskell and Martin W. Bauer

A Web of Prevention
Biological weapons, life sciences and the governance of research
Edited by Brian Rappert and Caitríona McLeish

Nanotechnology
Risk, ethics and law
Edited by Geoffrey Hunt and Michael Mehta

Unnatural Selection
The challenges of engineering tomorrow's people
Edited by Peter Healey and Steve Rayner

Debating Climate Change
Pathways through argument to agreement
Elizabeth L. Malone

Business Planning for Turbulent Times
New methods for applying scenarios
Edited by Rafael Ramírez, John W. Selsky and Kees van der Heijden

'"Development" is one of those fields where technical-sounding terminology and dense bureaucratic jargon go along with multiple, conflicting and ever-shifting recipes for success, such as better-functioning markets, super-bureaucracies, strong "third sector" organizations. Focusing on the critical case of Nepal, this interesting book argues that the conflicting development recipes map onto four fundamental and conflicting forms of social organization. And it offers a distinctive recipe of its own, arguing that what is needed for effective development is not more money but better social organization in the form of a mixture of those four approaches. Everyone interested in understanding how development fails and how to avoid the pitfalls of the past should read this book.'

Christopher Hood, Oxford University, UK

Aid, Technology and Development

The lessons from Nepal

Edited by Dipak Gyawali,
Michael Thompson and
Marco Verweij

Routledge
Taylor & Francis Group

LONDON AND NEW YORK

from Routledge

First published 2017
by Routledge

2 Park Square, Milton Park, Abingdon, Oxfordshire OX14 4RN
711 Third Avenue, New York, NY 10017

Routledge is an imprint of the Taylor & Francis Group, an informa business

First issued in paperback 2018

British Library Cataloguing-in-Publication Data
A catalogue record for this book is available from the British Library

Library of Congress Cataloging-in-Publication Data
Names: Gyawali, Dipak, editor. | Thompson, M. (Michael), 1937– editor. |
Verweij, Marco, editor.
Title: Aid, technology and development : the lessons from Nepal /
edited by Dipak Gyawali, Michael Thompson and Marco Verweij.
Description: Abingdon, Oxon ; New York, NY : Routledge, 2017. |
Series: Earthscan science in society
Identifiers: LCCN 2016026338| ISBN 9781138656918 (hbk) |
ISBN 9781315621630 (ebk)
Subjects: LCSH: Economic assistance—Nepal. | Economic development—
Nepal. | Technological innovations—Nepal.
Classification: LCC HC425 .A69 2017 | DDC 338.95496—dc23
LC record available at https://lccn.loc.gov/2016026338

ISBN: 978-1-138-65691-8 (hbk)
ISBN: 978-1-138-61256-3 (pbk)

Typeset in Bembo
by Florence Production Ltd, Stoodleigh, Devon, UK

Contents

List of illustrations   ix
List of tables   x
About the authors   xi
Acknowledgements   xvi
IIASA   xviii

PART 1
THE *DHARMA* OF DEVELOPMENT: A CONCEPTUAL
FRAMEWORK   1

1 The *dharma* of development   3
   MICHAEL THOMPSON, DIPAK GYAWALI AND MARCO VERWEIJ

2 A cultural theory of how to aid development   13
   MARCO VERWEIJ

3 The arrested success of pro-poor initiatives in democratic Nepal   26
   BIHARI KRISHNA SHRESTHA

4 Trickle to torrent to irrelevance? Six decades of foreign aid
   in Nepal   54
   SUDHINDRA SHARMA

PART 2
THE CASE STUDIES   75

5 Bhattedanda Milkway: why a climate- and mountain-friendly
   technology continues to be ignored   77
   MADHUKAR UPADHYA

6 Whither electric vehicles?   95
   ASHOK RAJ PANDEY

 7 Micro and small hydro: serial leapfrogging to a braver new Nepal   113
    AJOY KARKI

 8 Large hydro: failures in financial engineering   132
    RATNA SANSAR SHRESTHA

 9 Biogas: buoyant or bust?   153
    SAROJ RAI

10 Water supply and sanitation: elusive targets and slippery means   167
    ANIL POKHREL

11 Community forestry: thwarting desertification and facing
    second-generation problems   185
    HEMANT R. OJHA

PART 3
BEYOND THE AGE OF AID   201

12 Nepal's experience of foreign aid, and how it can kick the habit   203
    PRAKASH CHANDRA LOHANI

13 Afterword: the lessons from Nepal   218
    DIPAK GYAWALI, MICHAEL THOMPSON AND MARCO VERWEIJ

    References   *222*
    Index   *236*

Illustrations

Figure 1.1   *Dharma* and its dynamics   7
Figure 5.1   Longitudinal profile of Bhattedanda ropeway   77
Map 5.1   *Khuwa*-producing areas of Lalitpur   78
Figure 5.2   The valleys in-between   83
Figure 9.1   Schematic design of a household biogas plant   156
Figure 12.1 National permutations and trajectories   207

Cover picture (by Madhukar Upadhya: author of Chapter 5): The ropeway at Bhattedanda, built with the help of the EU to transport milk to the urban market, opened avenues to the villagers to creatively export other goods and cottage industry skills as well. The picture shows *Amriso* brooms heading for Kathmandu's lucrative market. *Amriso* (botanical name: *Thysanolaena Maxima Graminaeae Poaceae Bambusecea*; in English: Broom Grass) is a cultivated fodder plant whose leaves are fed to domestic livestock and the hard stem with the flowering top is used to make the brooms that are traditionally widely used in Nepali households. Unlike industrial plastic-based brooms, *Amriso ko kucho* as it is called in Nepali is completely bio-degradable. Also visible in the picture is the deep valley between Bhattedanda and the road-head, much of it clad in healthy forest that is a vital component in the villagers' agro-forestry farming system: one of the 19,000 or so community forests that are the subject of Chapter 11.

Tables

2.1	Four perspectives on human development	22
3.1	Co-op versus bank share in investments	44
4.1	Remittance inflow to Nepal	55
4.2	Changes in Nepali government's spending over the years	68
5.1	Total of goods exported from and imported by the Milkway	80
5.2	Energy costs for diesel and hydro to operate the Milkway	87
7.1	Cost comparisons between hydropower projects implemented by various public- and private-sector arrangements	121
8.1	Estimated and actual costs of Kulekhani 1	135
8.2	Estimated and actual costs of Marsyangdi	136
8.3	Projects implemented between 1995 and 2015	137
8.4	Estimated and actual costs of Kali Gandaki-A	142
8.5	Estimated and actual costs of Middle Marsyangdi	143
8.6	Estimated costs of West Seti	144
9.1	Biogas plant construction trend after the establishment of BSP	158
10.1	Coverage of water supply and sanitation in some western, mid-western and far-western regions of Nepal	175
10.2	Cost analysis of drinking water supply and sanitation projects	177

About the authors

Dipak Gyawali (*editor; Chapters 1 and 13*), a hydroelectric power engineer trained at the Moscow Energy Institute and a political economist trained at the Energy and Resources Group of the University of California at Berkeley, was Nepal's Minister of Water Resources in 2002/03. A *Pragya* (Academician) of the Nepal Academy of Science and Technology, he conducts interdisciplinary research at the interface of technology and society, mostly from the perspectives of cultural theory. He has been a visiting professor/research scholar as well as member of advisory board in various universities and international organisations, including the UN University in Yokohama, Battelle Pacific Northwest National Lab as well as Mekong's MPower. Currently he is on the advisory committee of UNESCO's World Water Assessment Program, Stockholm International Water Institute's Scientific Program Committee and IDS Sussex STEPs Center' advisory board. He chairs the Nepal Water Conservation Foundation as well as Inter Disciplinary Analysts.

Ajoy Karki (*Chapter 7*) received his engineering degree from the University of Iowa in 1990 as well as his MSc in hydraulic engineering from IHE-UNESCO, the Netherlands, in 2000. He is currently the director of Sanima Hydro and Engineering P. Ltd, Nepal, which designed and commissioned the 22MW Mai and 7MW Mai Cascade hydropower plants and is currently designing two in-house projects: the 28.1MW Lower Likhu and the 54MW Middle Tamor hydropower projects. His early work was with Butwal Power Company and the German GIZ. Over the last decade he has worked with various national and international institutions including the Asian Development Bank, the World Bank, the International Finance Corporation and Winrock International in Nepal and in 15 countries in Asia and Africa, from Laos to Liberia and Rwanda to Afghanistan.

Prakash Chandra Lohani (*Chapter 12*), who has an MBA from Indiana University and a PhD in 1969 from University of California Los Angeles (UCLA), is a senior leader of Nepal's Rastriya Prajatantra Party. He was first elected to Nepal's parliament, the Rashtriya Panchayat, in 1971. He has served as the country's finance minister (1983–85 and 2003–04) and foreign minister (1994–95) and was also a member of the Constituent Assembly from 2008 to 2012, elected from his home district of Nuwakot. It was during his tenure as finance minister that Nepal saw financial liberalisation and the growth of private banking and financial institutions. He serves as chairman of the South Asian Institute of Management, affiliated to Pokhara University, and his interests include political economy and development issues.

Hemant R. Ojha (*Chapter 11*) received his PhD (2007) from the University of East Anglia. He conducts research blending critical social theory (with a focus on Habermas, Bourdieu and Gramsci) with practices of adaptive deliberative governance of natural resources. On the editorial board of various journals and a consultant to several international agencies including CIFOR, USAID, The Asia Foundation, IDRC and NORAD, he has made seminal contributions to Nepal's community forestry as a field worker, critical action researcher and policy analyst. Founder of ForestAction Nepal in 2000 and Southasia Institute of Advanced Studies in 2011, he is also advancing critical action research assisting activist intellectuals working to transform public policy through social learning and participatory development. He has been a senior fellow at the University of Melbourne and is a research fellow at the University of New South Wales.

Ashok Raj Pandey (*Chapter 6*) was trained as a mechanical engineer at the Indian Institute of Technology (IIT)-Kharagpur in 1972. He then worked at the Nepal government's industry promoting bank NIDC as well as its policy analysis and consultancy think tank (Industrial Services Center) before going on to Harvard, from where he received an MBA in 1982. After a few years of working at John Hancock Insurance of Boston and Montgomery Ward of Chicago, he returned to Nepal to set up a firm promoting the export of Nepalese garments to the American market. In 1998, he was instrumental in setting up the country's first electric vehicle company, Nepal Electric Vehicle Industry (NEVI), and currently serves as its managing director. He has been visiting faculty at the Kathmandu University School of Management and since 2007 has been a professor of finance at the South Asian Institute of Management, Pokhara University.

Anil Pokhrel (*Chapter 10*) was trained as a civil engineer at Kathmandu's Tribhuvan University and in environmental management at Yale University's School of Forestry and Environmental Studies under a Fulbright fellowship. Over the last 15 years, he has worked in community-led water supply systems and disaster risk reduction, as well as climate change adaptation with various Nepalese and international NGOs and bi- and multilateral international development agencies. He brings rich operational and research experiences into his professional work of environmental management in the Asia-Pacific region. His current interests are focused on disaster risk management, resilient infrastructure and climate change adaptation.

Saroj Rai (*Chapter 9*) holds a degree in chemical engineering from the Regional Engineering College of West Bengal and an MBA from Asian Institute of Management in Manila. He entered the energy sector in 2001 as a programme coordinator of a complex rural electrification scheme with solar photovoltaic systems funded by Denmark. In 2006, he became the executive director of BSP-Nepal, which implements Nepal's national Biogas Support Program. He streamlined the biogas programme, among other things, by improving the triangular interplay of government, private-sector and civil society interests. He was also successful in helping bring the programme into the Clean Development Mechanism of the Kyoto Protocol. He joined the SNV Netherlands Development Organisation in Nepal in 2011 as senior advisor and moved to SNV Ethiopia in 2014 as an energy sector leader, where, inter alia, he leads the technical assistance to the National Biogas Program of Ethiopia.

Sudhindra Sharma (*Chapter 4*) is executive director of Inter Disciplinary Analysts (IDA), a Kathmandu-based research and consulting organisation with which he has been associated since 1996. From 2004 onwards, he has focused on quantitative social sciences, primarily nationwide opinion polls as well as surveys on armed violence, police reform, business climate survey, voter registration etc. A sociologist by training, he received his master's degree in sociology from Ateneo de Manila University of the Philippines and completed his PhD at the University of Tampere, Finland, in 2001. He is the author of the book *Procuring Water: Foreign Aid and Rural Water Supply in Nepal* (2001) and a co-editor of the book *Aid Under Stress: Water, Forests and Finnish Support in Nepal* (2004). He is also an adjunct professor of sociology at the Nepā School of Social Sciences and Humanities and a docent at the Institute of Development Studies, University of Helsinki.

Bihari Krishna Shrestha (*Chapter 3*) is an anthropologist with an MA from Michigan State University (1967) who worked in Nepal's government until 1991 and pushed through several innovations, including Nepal's first rural development policy, The Integrated Panchayat Development Design (1978), the user groups as the institutional mainstay for development at the grass roots (1979), Nepal's first legislation on decentralisation, the Decentralization Act 1982 and the promotion of forest user groups (1988), as well as Mothers' Groups and Female Community Health Volunteers in the health sector (1988). Such measures have reversed Nepal's once-denuded forests and catapulted Nepal to becoming a top performer in achieving the UN's Millennium Development Goals (MDGs) in child survival and maternal mortality reduction. He remains a civil society activist, interested mainly in the empowerment of the people at the grass roots, and believes that government agencies should use more ethnographic methods to unveil data and ground realities that other methods do not yield.

Ratna Sansar Shrestha (*Chapter 8*), who is a Fellow Chartered Accountant (CPA/USA and FCA/ICAN) as well as a Nepal Bar Council-licensed advocate, specialises in financial/economic, managerial and legal aspects of water, hydropower projects, clean energy technologies, carbon trading etc. He has been visiting faculty at Kathmandu University's school of engineering since 2005, as well as its school of management (1998 to 2000). He also taught at the Institute of Management at Tribhuvan University (1974–84) and was a member of the National Development Council 2013, a member of the boards of directors of the Nepal Hydro & Electric Company (2009 to present), the Nepal Electricity Authority (2002–04), Everest Bank Ltd (2006–10) and the Butwal Power Company Ltd (2001–15), as well as a member of the Water Supply Tariff Fixation Commission (2007–11). He has been involved in policy formulation work in Nepal, Afghanistan, Bhutan and Pakistan.

Michael Thompson (*editor; Chapters 1 and 13*) has had a long association with Nepal: first as a teenage soldier in the Malayan 'emergency' (where he served in the British army's Gurkha Division), then as a Himalayan mountaineer (Annapurna South Face 1970; Everest Southwest Face 1975) and subsequently as an anthropologist-cum-policy analyst (*Uncertainty on a Himalayan Scale*, 2007). Trained at University College London (BSc, PhD) and Oxford (BLitt), he is currently a senior researcher at the International Institute for Applied Systems Analysis, a global change think tank in Austria. There he develops and applies the concept of 'plural rationality': people doing very different things and yet still behaving rationally, given their different sets of convictions as to how the world is and people are (*Cultural Theory*, 1990, West View; *Organising and Disorganising*, 2008, Triarchy).

Madhukar Upadhya (*Chapter 5*) graduated as an agriculturist in 1978 from Punjab Agriculture University in India and later received his master's degree in watershed science in 1986 from Utah State University in the USA. While working within the Nepal government's Department of Soil and Water Conservation, he managed the EU-funded Bagmati Watershed Project, which conceptualised and implemented the use of small-haul ropeways to save forests and reduce poverty among hill farmers. With over two decades of government service, he left to become research director at the Nepal Water Conservation Foundation and in 2002 was chair of the Institute for Social and Environmental Transition (ISET-Nepal). He also worked as a Poverty Environment Initiative Advisor to the National Planning Commission of Nepal, where he helped in integrating climate change into the national planning and budgeting processes. He teaches watershed science at the School of Environmental Management, University of Pokhara, Nepal.

Marco Verweij (*editor; Chapters 1, 4 and 13*) is professor of political science at Jacobs University in Bremen, Germany. He holds a doctorate in social and political science from the European University Institute in Florence, Italy, and previously earned his keep at the Max Planck Institute for Research on Collective Goods in Bonn, Germany, and at the Singapore Management University. In his research, he attempts to understand how 'wicked' social and environmental problems can be resolved through the combined forces of (inter-)governmental action, entrepreneurship and technological innovation, as well as civil society engagement. He also explores the possible synergies between social and political theory, brain research and the analysis of human complex systems.

Acknowledgements

This book is the result of a long journey that started in March 2007 when most of its authors, commentators, editors and others who were interested in reflecting on the problems of development gathered in Kathmandu for a three-day workshop and field visit sponsored by IIASA. Much help has been received from many individuals and institutions, families and friends along the way – with advice, time, understanding and support. A quick scan of the authors' bios would show the wide diversity of their experience and intellectual backgrounds, which circle the globe, starting from California's Pacific shores, traversing through the United States, Europe, Africa, the Middle East, South and East Asia before ending on Australia's eastern coast. Mercifully, most of them have limited their thanks to the institutions and colleagues they have been associated with and are mentioned in their bios. Additionally, Sudhindra Sharma (Chapter 4) would like to thank his students (and subsequent research assistants) from the Immersion Course on Contemporary Social Issues that he has been associated with since the mid-1990s; and Anil Pokhrel (Chapter 10) thanks the library of grey literature at the Nepal Water Conservation Foundation (NWCF). RS Shrestha (Chapter 8) has an unusual request: he wants to thank his unlettered mother – who herself grew up next to Nepal's second hydropower plant Sundarijal (1934 AD) – for whetting his life-long appetite for things hydro by explaining to him as a child how a bicycle dynamo worked and showing him how it was similar to the turbines of Sundarijal.

As editors, we have to thank first and foremost Joanne Linnerooth-Bayer and her risk studies team at the International Institute for Applied Systems Analysis (IIASA), Vienna. Its Adaptation and Mitigation project provided the original impetus for this publication, and allowed those making this journey to meet in Kathmandu in 2007. It also enabled Michael Thompson to return to Kathmandu for a month of editing in 2011. Steve Rayner of Oxford is sincerely thanked for encouraging us to submit this effort to Earthscan's Science and Society series for its consideration. Dipak Gyawali wishes to thank, in addition to the staff and colleagues at NWCF and Interdisciplinary Analysts (IDA) for logistical and other support, the Stockholm International Water Institute, the Institute for Development Studies' STEPS Center, as well as

Durham University's Low Carbon Energy for Development Network. While these excellent organisations have not been directly involved with this book, they have brought him over from Nepal to Europe on numerous occasions, thus also allowing him to work together with Mike Thompson in London and Bath, and with Marco Verweij in Amsterdam and Bremen.

September, 2016
Bath/UK, Bremen/Germany and Kathmandu/Nepal

IIASA

Founded in 1972, IIASA is an international scientific institute that conducts policy-oriented research into problems that are too large or too complex to be solved by a single country or academic discipline. The problems it studies include climate change, energy security, population ageing and sustainable development, which have a global reach and can be resolved only by international co-operation.

IIASA has a demonstrated track record of delivering global, regional and national impact through conducting excellent interdisciplinary research into real-world problems, often in collaboration with large international research networks, and working with policymakers to identify and assess possible solutions based on the results of that research. Funded by prestigious research funding agencies in Africa, the Americas, Asia, Europe and Oceania, IIASA is independent and unconstrained by political or national self-interest.

International Institute for
Applied Systems Analysis
IIASA www.iiasa.ac.at

Part 1

The *dharma* of development

A conceptual framework

1 The *dharma* of development

*Michael Thompson, Dipak Gyawali
and Marco Verweij*

In 1957 (six years after the overthrow of the 'feudal' Rana regime, the Nepalese historical equivalent of the Japanese *shoguns*) Nepal's forests were *nationalised*, a reform that resulted in massive deforestation and degradation. This outcome was then blamed on the victim: the 'ignorant and fecund peasant', and justified in terms of what is now called THED: the Theory of Himalayan Environmental Degradation.[1] This theory held that it was the mushrooming population that was forcing the farmers to fell more and more trees on steeper and steeper hillsides so as to create more terraced fields on which to grow the crops to feed all the extra mouths, while at the same time requiring them to extract more and more fuelwood from that ever-diminishing forest. The reduced cover, so the theory went, then increased erosion by the monsoon rains, while the ever-steeper new terraces increased the incidence of landslides, thereby propelling more and more precious topsoil into the mountain torrents, increasing the flooding down in the plains of India and Bangladesh, clogging the turbines in the downstream hydroelectric power stations and rapidly filling their dams with silt. And so it went, population increase leading to vicious circle piled upon vicious circle, a diagnosis that led, in the 1980s, to the General Assembly of the United Nations identifying the Himalayan region as one of the world's 'environmental hot-spots'. It was only at (and in the lead-up to) the Mohonk Mountain Conference in 1986 that THED was shown to be invalid and that the true cause – nationalisation – was identified (Thompson and Warburton 1985; Ives and Messerli 1989; Ives 2004; Thompson and Gyawali 2007).

Around a decade later, the development orthodoxy having swung to the other extreme, there was a major effort – the Finnish-funded Bara Forest Management Plan – to *privatise* the forest. The idea was that a Finnish private company, in partnership with some Nepalese business houses, would be given responsibility for the regeneration of the entire (47,000-hectare) forest, together with near-monopoly rights to its commercial exploitation. The aim, in line with the then-ascendant 'Washington Consensus',[2] was to introduce radical change in a sector that had not hitherto been oriented to market-led approaches. However, unbeknown to the aid providers – it was an 'unknown known' in Rumsfeld-speak[3] – the Bara Forest was already a complex mosaic of property rights: private, public and common-pool (often rather informally established rights, and at small social-scale levels, but rights nevertheless; see Sharma *et al.* 2004).[4] Unsurprisingly, this ambitious project eventually turned into a disaster so unmitigated, and so universally acknowledged, that the Finns swore never again to get involved in forestry in Nepal.

In the gap between these two abysmal initiatives there came what is now acknowledged to be Nepal's great development success story: the *communitisation* of the forests (see Ives 2004, especially Chapter 3). In this initiative (which grew, in large part, out of the Nepal–Australia Forestry Project in the late 1980s together with some Nepalese ethnographers 'in the right place',[5] and which is in many ways a re-discovery of the 'traditional' commons-managing arrangements that had been widespread in Nepal in the years before nationalisation) ownership of the forests was devolved to 'forest user groups', typically village-based though sometimes encompassing two or more smaller villages. To be precise, ultimate title remains with the state, with the new Forest Act of 1993 which enshrined the user rights as the inalienable property of the villagers (the old Forest Act of 1962, by contrast, had authorised Department of Forestry officials, under certain circumstances, even to shoot those villagers suspected of encroaching upon state property). There are now (as is explained in Chapter 11) in excess of 19,000 of these community forests – they take in a third of all the country's officially forested land and have visibly improved the crown cover of the Nepalese landscape – and this has been accompanied by the emergence of the discipline of *social forestry*; indeed, many university departments of forestry around the world are now headed by social scientists. One consequence of this process of 'social learning' is that this institutional arrangement has now been exported to other developing countries and, more remarkably, to some developed countries, most prominently Canada, where community forests are rapidly catching on (Gilmour and Fisher 1991; Gyawali and Koponen 2004; Ives 2004). Indeed, the 37th Session of the SAARC (South Asian Association for Regional Cooperation) Council of Ministers in March 2016 has proposed (albeit, at the time of writing, tentatively) community forestry as a worthwhile regional co-operation programme for all of South Asia.

There are, we suggest, some lessons that can be learnt from Nepal's half century of experience of being on the receiving end of development assistance. If we are right, then everything comes down to the question: what *are* those lessons? A clue can be found in the post-mortem on the Bara fiasco, which, to their credit, was commissioned by the aid-providing country's science academy and carried out by a team composed of Nepalis and Finns. They arrived at the following conclusion (Sharma *et al.* 2004: 241–2):

> As a villager in Nepal is apt to say, it is the *dharma* of the bureaucracy to regulate, of the markets to innovate and of activist groups to advise caution. The case of Bara was one in which *dharma* had gone wrong – a situation characterised by the bureaucracy assuming the role of the market and vice versa. It further showed that the hierarchical order that has broken down

is no instrument for the implementation of radical reforms, without first mending that order and restoring its legitimacy, or as the villager might say, restoring the *dharma*.

Dharma, especially in the West, is often equated with fate or mis-translated as 'religion', but it is much more than that. *Dharma*, from the Sanskrit root that means 'to uphold', is 'the correct way of life' or, more properly, 'the righteousness that underlies the law'. Hence the emphasis on legitimacy, and the accompanying consequence – breakdown – when, as in the case of Bara, that legitimacy is eroded. Legitimacy, moreover, cannot spring from the interaction of just markets and hierarchies: the only sort of interaction that was entertained by the Washington Consensus and several earlier development paradigms, such as the Nehruvian 'commanding heights' argument that justified the nationalisation, back in the 1950s and 60s, of those parts of the economy – Nepal's forests among them – that were seen as too important to be left to the mercy of the marketplace. Legitimacy requires a third institutional form – egalitarianism, as it is called by those (they have been dubbed 'the New Durkheimians', see 6 and Mars 2008) who venture beyond the dualisms that have long pervaded social science – and it is manifested here in Bara as the 'activist groups' whose *dharma* it is to advice caution.

If, however, *dharma* goes wrong, fatalism emerges, in the sense that more and more people will find themselves labouring under what has been called 'the double burden': increasingly impoverished and increasingly subject to social exclusion (Gurung *et al.* 2014).

Development has long been seen as very much an economic process. The interactions of the various actors – state, market, civil society and so on – have been put into a 'black box', into which aid is then fed in some way and the result – development if you are lucky – read off in terms of per capita gross national product. Increasingly, however, it has become evident that it is economic only in its consequences; it is something else – entitlements, democratisation, social capital – that makes development possible (Dasgupta 1993; Putnam 1993; Sen 1999). A new paradigm is therefore called for, one that goes inside the black box. And that, we will now show, is precisely what this conclusion from the Bara post-mortem enables us to do.

This deceptively simple diagnosis – in terms of '*dharma* gone wrong' and '*dharma* restored' – is the black box opened up: four ways of organising, perceiving and justifying social relations, or forms of 'social solidarity', to borrow from Émile Durkheim (1893) – *hierarchy* (e.g. state and local bureaucracy), *individualism* (e.g. markets, from the global to the local), *egalitarianism* (e.g. activist groups, home-grown and international) and *fatalism* (e.g. the double burden-carriers). Each of these, so the theory argues, is (or, rather, should be) in contentious (but potentially constructive) engagement with the other three: something that you are most unlikely to get if you are operating with a development paradigm that allows, at the most, for just hierarchies and markets. In other words, that twofold paradigm does not encompass the *requisite variety* (for the theory itself – it is called 'cultural theory', the 'theory of plural rationality' or 'neo-Durkheimian institutionalism' – see Thompson *et al.* 1990; Rayner 1992; Ney and Douglas 1998; Thompson 2008; 6 and Mars 2008; Ney 2009; Verweij and Thompson 2006; Thompson and Beck 2015).

On the rare occasions when the policy process *has* encompassed the requisite variety – Nepal's community forests are the prime example, but there are others (the Bhattedanda Milkway, for instance, and the partial communitisation of the electricity sector (see Thompson 2011/12 and Chapters 5 and 11 of this volume for the former and Gyawali 2013, Yadoo and Cruickshank 2010 and Chapter 7 of this volume for the latter) – which stand in such contrast to both the Bara fiasco and the earlier nationalisation of the forests, we find that each of the three contending 'voices' – the hierarchical, the individualistic and the egalitarian – is (a) able to make itself heard and (b) is then responded to (rather than dismissed by) the others (fatalistic actors tend not to have a voice; if they had they would not be fatalistic). In this 'clumsy' or 'polyrational' situation – *dharma* restored – none of the solidarities undermines its own distinctive morality (Verweij 2011). State actors (hierarchy) behave like Edmund Burke's (1790) 'trustees', focusing on the long-term general interest rather than on opportunistic and narrow claims; market actors (individualism) are guided by Adam Smith's (1776) 'invisible hand' and do well only when others also benefit, and civil society actors (egalitarianism), like Edmund Burke's (1790/1986) 'little platoons', are genuinely of the grass roots. But that, thanks to the over-'elegant' and voice-silencing way in which aid has been fed in, is not how things so often are in Nepal, or, we dare say, in many other aid-addicted countries in the Global South (Figure 1.1).

In '*dharma* gone wrong' – typified by Bara – government actors, forgetting all about Edmund Burke, direct their energies to what is euphemistically called 'rent-seeking'; market actors, thanks to what has been dubbed 'licence raj' (or 'crony capitalism'), increasingly deal in club goods that only look like private goods (in other words, they do well even when others do not benefit); and NGOs, though they may walk and quack like genuinely egalitarian actors, turn out on closer inspection to be BONGOs, GONGOs, DONGOs and PONGOs (business-organised, government-organised, donor-organised and political party-organised NGOs, respectively). Historians (e.g. Schama 1987) can show us that these distortions were largely absent in all those countries that we now label 'developed'. In other words, the proponents of old development paradigms have created a situation in which development is hard to achieve. That is why we need to shift across to this new, and requisite variety-ensuring, one (the old development paradigms, and the required shift, are explained in Chapter 2).

This book aims to effect that paradigm shift within the ongoing aid business: a business that lost its *elan vital* with the collapse of the Berlin Wall and is running on nothing more than inertia. In Nepal, for instance (and as explained in Chapter 3), the aid industry was caught on the hop by the emergence of the remittance economy (based on its citizens going to work, on short-term

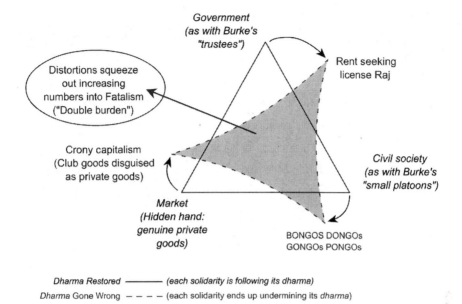

Figure 1.1 Dharma and its dynamics

contracts, in the Gulf States and elsewhere). These remittances, which now constitute about 30 per cent of the country's Gross Domestic Product (GDP), far exceed (by up to five times) the total amount of international aid that Nepal receives. And something similarly surprising has happened with electricity generation, where the combined capacity of diesel generating electric sets installed by shops, hotels and housing complexes now rivals that of the national grid's hydroelectricity provision (long the focus of aid providers, as we will see in Chapters 7 and 8).

In other words, lack of money is no longer the primary constraint on development. How could it be if the government's revenue (from indirect taxation on consumption from the inflow of remittances) is increasing at an annual rate that is even greater than China's much-vaunted growth? Clearly, with shops and housing complexes paying up to five times more for privately generated (diesel) electricity than official (mostly hydropower) utility rates, largely in order to avoid the regular and now long-standing fifteen-hour five-times-a-day outages, something is going on down there in the cities and villages that, while readily discernible to those who take the toad's eye view of things, is invisible to those – the global-level scientists and the international development agencies – who have opted for the eagle's eye view.[6]

While the cases of elegant failures (where one or more of the solidarities' 'voices' are excluded) and clumsy successes (where each of those voices is both heard and responded to by the others) in the following chapters may all be from Nepal, they are really international, in two ways. First, the aid-giving agencies involved in our case studies range from Australians 'down under' to Europeans and Americans 'up north'. Second, the development philosophies that guided, and are still guiding, these interventions have originated, for the most part, in the capital cities of these donor countries: in their universities, their government ministries, their think-tanks and their consultancies. And they have been applied to other countries across the Global South, though perhaps with less documentation and contestation than has been the case in Nepal.

Moreover, Nepal (as explained in Chapter 4) is unique in never having been a colony of any of the donor countries. While strongly influenced, as we will see, by development aid for much of the last half century, it has managed to retain sufficient indigeneity in its sociopolitical life to pose strong counter-approaches: the aforementioned community forestry and community electricity for instance, and also low-tech renewable-powered vehicles (Chapter 6) and biogas (Chapter 9). It has seen different development philosophies come and go – nationalisation, for instance, and then privatisation – and it has seen its own political system undergo some dramatic transitions: the king-led Panchayat system giving way in 1990 to a tumultuous multi-party democracy that was almost immediately challenged by a raging Maoist insurgency, which has now fizzled and fractured, leaving the country to muddle along in a kingless and constitutionally-challenged transition to something (but it is anyone's guess what) that has yet to come.

Nepal's first experience of aid (as is explained in Chapter 4) was courtesy of the United States: Harry Truman's '4H program' in the immediate aftermath of the Second World War (during which many Nepalese citizens saw service in the British army). It was then followed by India, Britain, China, the Soviet Union, Japan, various European countries (including even, as a rather late entrant, Finland) and, very feebly, Thailand (with its technical aid to Kathmandu Valley's Kodku water supply study). The donor development philosophy changed almost every decade, from import-substituted, to export-led, to integrated, to structural adjustment, to basic needs, to poverty alleviation, to that current flavour of the month: climate change. Remarkably, and this is often overlooked, the distinctive core of Nepal's social life – a rich composite of 124 caste and ethnic groups laced together by 103 languages – has adapted remarkably well in coping with these ever-changing development fads, along with myriad natural and geopolitical disasters.

For instance (and as discussed in our final chapter), when the April 2015 earthquake struck the Nepal Army and Nepal Police mobilised almost 90 per cent of their capacity within days and went on to successfully coordinate the rescue and relief operations with a host of international armies and civilian organisations. The rest of the government machinery, however, along with the political parties, were virtually absent (and when they did put in an appearance they were often chased away). Six months elapsed before the government even got around to forming an earthquake reconstruction authority, for which it has not yet been able to mobilise the international relief funds that have been committed. Social self-help groups, however, have been able to maintain peace and security, feed the homeless, rebuild collapsed houses and care for the injured. It is clear, therefore, that the 'failed state' concept can hardly be applied to Nepal. Rather, the contrast – between the abject failure at the higher level and the resourceful and innovative mobilisation at the lower level – tells us that *Nepal is a weak state but a strong society*. To misquote Molière's famous line about doctors, despite all the aid provider's efforts, Nepal (i.e. the patient) developed!

Those who take the toad's eye view will argue, quite understandably, that those who are soaring with the eagles are looking for development in the wrong place: up there among the projects cooked up by the aid agencies and the national ministries. But the successes, having been down there among the grass roots and largely in the informal sector, have remained invisible: unknown knowns in Rumsfeld-speak. In consequence, the high-level actors have gravitated towards technologies and development choices defined by bureaucratic (and over-elegant) hierarchism, and away from the multi-voiced and messy interactions that are actually taking the country in the desired direction. What is needed, we argue, is a pluralised (and clumsy) approach: an approach that recognises that, to the extent that development is infrastructure building – water supply and sanitation, in particular (see Chapter 10) – it cannot be left to the private sector alone: it needs the state's involvement, together with the critical observations of civil society: Edmund Burke's 'little platoons'. Unresponsive monologue has therefore to give way to a boisterous and, quite literally, uncontrollable engagement between the contradictory certainties that are inevitably generated by the various solidarities. If *dharma* is to be restored it must be conceded that technical innovations happen in the market realm, that behavioural innovations come primarily from arguments and debates in the civic realm and that (as argued in Chapter 12) the managerial methods must come from a bureaucracy that is led by enlightened statesmen and stateswomen.

Anyone who has wandered through rural Nepal (or similar places in the Global South) will have been struck by the contrast between the rusting remains of large-scale aid projects – Nepalis call them *Bikasey chihan*: 'development tombs' – and the exuberant small-scale activity that surrounds them: entire farms, for instance, that have sprung up on some hitherto barren hillside by taking advantage of the water leaking from a pipe that was intended to supply an irrigation scheme or drinking water tank. The formal sector all too often ends up like a whale that has beached itself on some sandy shore, with the informal sector resembling the lively little fishes that swim around in the pools the giant beast has inadvertently created.[7] By no means all aid projects (as we will see) end up as beached whales, of course, but those that do should alert us to a destructive interplay between the formal and the informal, with the formal all too often stifling the resilience that has been informally built up by local populations, often (as with the village forests prior to their nationalisation) over generations. For too long, the formal has been hailed as 'modern' and the informal stigmatised as 'traditional' (Douglas 2004). This bias – with the foregrounded formal sector having a major hierarchical component and the backgrounded informal sector being predominantly egalitarian and individual-istic – has then fed through into similarly biased choices of technology. It has been, for instance, the hierarchical commitment to 'big is best', and its over-riding of both the 'small is beautiful' egalitarian commitment and the more intermediate individualistic commitment to 'cheap and cheerful', that has led to all those development tombs. Technology, in other words, is never neutral, even though the proponents of development assistance have always tried to insist that it is. Rather, it is deeply political, and therefore sorely in need of democratisation (Schwarz and Thompson 1990; Douglas 1997; Thompson 2004).[8]

The post-monsoon brushwood dams that enabled farmers on the Tinau River to grow two (or even three) crops of rice a year, to give a well-documented example (Gyawali 2004),[9] were done away with by the Hattisunde Barrage, a massive aid-funded concrete structure that almost immediately became a development tomb when the river changed its course (that being what Himalayan rivers frequently do, once they have debouched onto the Gangetic Plain: an unknown known to the Indian aid providers). With the hierarchical solution no longer working, and the brushwood dams no longer an option (thanks to the grid of concrete canals that had been superimposed on the downstream pattern of natural drainage), the farmers then resorted to the newly available individualistic technology – boreholes and diesel-powered pumps – each cheaply and cheerfully installed on an individually owned plot.

In doing this, they reshaped the water that, with the community-built brushwood dams, was a common-pool good, and then, with the Hattisunde Barrage, a public good, into a private good. This switch to the individualist technology has now caught on across much of South Asia – there are estimated to be in excess of 30 million in India alone – and in many places it has led to a 'beggar my neighbour' lowering of the water table, with the water becoming a club good as it is captured by those farmers who have the resources and the ruthlessness sufficient for them to drill down further: 'competitive deepening' as it is called (Specter 2006). Those whose wells run dry, because they are no longer deep enough, then find themselves squeezed out into fatalism (see endnote 4).

If development aid projects are intended to promote resilience among beneficiary communities – resilience being something that is difficult to define but palpable when it is depleted – it must be recognised that it inheres in the skills, practices, knowledge and institutional arrangements by which com-munities relate themselves to, and in so doing continually transform, their physical surroundings.[10] And they do this, we argue in this book, in ways that are more pluralised – in terms of the constructive interplay of the formal and informal sectors, and in terms of the endless and similarly constructive interplay of contending technological commitments – than is attainable through just government and market efforts. And, in so doing, and often in spite of those official development efforts, they have strengthened their capacity to pick themselves up after they have been hit by some disaster. Disasters, therefore, need to be seen not as externalities that wing their way in and knock the carefully planned development process off course but as something that is internal to that process. Disasters, you could say (borrowing the tag-line of the South Asian NGO Duryog Nivaran: see Gyawali 2015a), are 'the unfinished business of development'.

Notes

1   It was, of course, the critics of THED who pointed out that this was how THED's proponents had characterised the victim. Around that time, for instance, an eminent forester famously declared that 'the only way to get a forest to grow in Nepal is to put a barbed wire fence around it and post armed sentries at 50-yard intervals'. Yet community forests, managed by those ignorant and fecund peasants, are now flourishing across Nepal, with no barbed wire and no armed guards.
2   In which policy actors, even if they are not themselves market actors, agree that market-like mechanisms (public–private partnerships, for instance, and carbon credits) are what are needed. The Washington Consensus was officially declared dead in 2008 (by the British prime minister, Gordon Brown, at the Gleneagles G20 meeting) but it still refuses to lie down.
3   Though Donald Rumsfeld omitted this fourth permutation from his famous list, perhaps because he thought no one could be *that* stupid. But, as Rayner (2012) has shown, it is important that it not be omitted.
4   Economists and political scientists have long recognised four kinds of goods, classifying them in terms of two distinctions: *jointness of consumption* (a lighthouse, for instance, scores high, being as bright for the nth user as for the first) and *exclusiveness of consumption* (a club, for instance, scores high, since it can readily exclude all those who are not members). In terms of our new framing (set out later in this chapter) the individualist solidarity tends to generate *private goods* (low jointness/high exclusiveness), the hierarchical solidarity *public goods* (high jointness/low exclusiveness), the egalitarian solidarity *common-pool goods* (low jointness/low exclusiveness), and the fatalist solidarity *club goods* (high jointness/high exclusiveness). Club goods are the odd ones out, in the sense that it is the ease with which fatalist actors can be excluded that makes them possible, as in 'It doesn't matter who you vote for, the government always gets in' (see Verweij 1999).
5   Bihari Krishna Shrestha (author of Chapter 3), who was at that time a joint secretary in the government, played an key role in persuading the World Bank to include community forestry in its aid plans for Nepal.
6   Our 'toad's eye view' is inspired by a couple of lines from Rudyard Kipling:

> *The toad beneath the harrow knows*
> *Where every separate tooth-point goes;*

The next two lines can perhaps be seen as sketching something that is closer to our 'eagle's eye view':

> *The butterfly upon the road*
> *Preaches contentment to that toad.'*

7   This example comes from near the rim of Kathmandu Valley, just above Bodhnath in a village towards Sundarijal which supplies bulk drinking water to Kathmandu. Perhaps the finest examples of development tombs are the Hattisunde Barrage (courtesy of Indian government aid) which was left high and dry, a year after it was built, when the Tinau

River changed its course (see Gyawali 2004). The Kulekhani 1 hydropower project (courtesy of the Japanese government, the World Bank and several other donors) now has a common-pool fishery established on its lake by the villagers who were displaced to make way for the project. Through wholly unanticipated (indeed there were attempts to evict the commoners), the harvesting of those 'lively little fishes' has turned out to be the only feature of the project that makes any economic sense (see Chapter 8 of this volume).

8 If there were only economies of scale then the scale:unit cost curve would be L-shaped, and big would be best. If there were only diseconomies of scale, however, the curve would be J-shaped, and small would be beautiful. And if there were both economies and diseconomies of scale then the two curves, when added together, would have a minimum somewhere between these two extremes. Trying to divine just where that minimum might be is the goal of those whose commitment is to 'cheap and cheerful': cheap enough to turn a profit, cheerful enough to attract the punters. Each, at times and in places, can be true, and that is why we need them all to be there, and in constructive engagement.

9 Something almost identical, in terms of contending technologies, also holds for farmers and water in Iran (Yazdanpanah *et al.* 2013; Yazdanpanah *et al.* 2014).

10 For a discussion of resilience, and of why it is much more than just 'bounce-back', see Thompson and Beck (2015, especially Box D). And for the ways in which a community can relate to and, in so doing transform its physical surroundings see Thompson (2002).

2 A cultural theory of how to aid development

Marco Verweij

A very short history of development aid paradigms

For decades, the practice and theory of development aid have lurched from one policy fashion to the next (Rist 2006). Although a plurality of aid paradigms has competed at any one point in time (Schuurman 2000), a single paradigm has usually dominated. From the launch of development assistance in the late 1940s (Frey *et al.* 2014) to the early 1980s, the notion held sway that 'development' could be measured by the annual growth of per capita national income. Moreover, it was believed that such growth could only 'take off' in developing countries if significant amounts of capital were transferred from the coffers of rich states to those of poor ones. This would allow the governments of those poor countries to increase spending on roads, canals, schools, electricity generation and distribution, irrigation schemes and other infrastructural projects, thus facilitating self-sustaining economic growth (Solow 1956; Rostow 1960; Chenery and Strout 1966).

A dent in the popularity of this development paradigm was made in the mid-1970s, when the UN General Assembly called for the establishment of a 'New International Economic Order', in which economic, health and other global inequities were going to be radically levelled (Tinbergen 1976; Cox 1979). Inspired by psychologist Abraham Maslow's 'hierarchy of needs' (Maslow 1943), and guided by work undertaken at the International Labor Organization (Emmerij 1976), the aid agencies operationalised this concern as a need to spend more money on meeting poor people's basic human needs, such as food, clothing, housing, education and public transportation (Streeten *et al.* 1981).

A more substantive paradigm shift occurred in the following decade, when the governments of US president Ronald Reagan and UK prime minister Margaret Thatcher made their continued support of international agencies (such as the World Bank and International Monetary Fund) dependent on the adoption of policies promoting the expansion of markets at the expense of states. The resulting 'structural adjustment policies', or 'Washington Consensus', made the receipt of development aid conditional upon governments reducing subsidies and other state expenses, deregulating their markets and opening them up to foreign competition, floating exchange rates, securing rights to private property, selling off of state assets and cutting budget deficits and inflation (Williamson 2009). Hence, throughout the 1980s and 1990s, a lack of development was mainly viewed as having been caused by the existence of a series of market 'imperfections' (i.e. deviations from the neoclassical model of economics) in poor countries (Stiglitz 1989; World Bank 1990a; Sachs 1996).

The pendulum of development swung again in the 2000s, which saw the emergence of the 'post-Washington Consensus', with its emphasis on 'good governance' and 'aid effectiveness' (World Bank 1997; Hulme and Fukuda-Parr 2009; Kaufman 2009). This latest paradigm has combined the following elements: (a) greater responsibility and accountability of recipient countries for their own development through the drawing up (preferably with the participation of civil society) of national 'Poverty Reduction Strategy Papers' with clear, quantified targets and timelines; (b) a renewed global commitment to helping developing countries reach these targets, especially through increased budget support; (c) a close (national and international) monitoring of the extent to which targets are being reached in a timely fashion; and (d) a harmonisation of the aid and trade policies of donor countries (Mawdsley *et al.* 2014). These principles were enshrined in the 2005 Paris Declaration on Aid Effectiveness by the OECD countries, and operationalised, first with eight UN 'Millennium Development Goals' (2000–15), and then with 17 UN 'Sustainable Development Goals' (2015–30) (Sachs and McArthur 2005; OECD 2008; United Nations 2015a).

The rationale for agreeing on 17 Sustainable Development Goals (and 169 associated targets) was that the previous adoption of eight Millennium Development Goals (and 22 related targets) was deemed to have been highly effective by policymakers (e.g. Sachs 2012; McArthur 2013; Fukuda *et al.* 2016). In the words of UN Secretary-General Ban Ki-Moon (United Nations 2015b: 3):

> The MDGs (Millennium Development Goals) helped to lift more than one billion people out of extreme poverty, to make inroads against hunger, to enable more girls to attend school than ever before and to protect our planet. They generated new and innovative partnerships, galvanised public opinion and showed the immense value of setting ambitious goals.

However, correlation is not causation. The flaw in the argument that the MDGs lifted more than a billion people out of extreme poverty between 2005 and 2015 is that this period also witnessed unprecedented economic growth, especially in China, India, Brazil and Indonesia, countries in which 44 per cent of the world's population, and the majority of people in extreme poverty, live (Cruz *et al.* 2015: 9). As the World Bank (2016) has noted,

> China alone accounted for most of the decline in extreme poverty over the past three decades. Between 1981 and 2011, 753 million people moved above the $1.90-a-day threshold. During the same time, the developing world as a whole saw a reduction in poverty of 1.1 billion.

And (Cruz *et al.* 2015: 7):

> From a broader historical perspective, the global poverty rate has fallen by approximately 1 percentage point a year since 1990, with rapid poverty reduction in China and India playing a central role in this outcome.

Unfortunately for those who have pushed the line that the MDGs have greatly reduced poverty, the economic rise of China, India, Brazil and Indonesia has had little, if anything, to do with these goals or with development assistance aimed at reaching them. For instance, the People's Republic of China 'has never shown any interest in MDGs' (*The Economist* 2013). In addition, the Chinese government has a long-standing policy of maintaining its autonomy by not accepting anything more than a trifle of development aid. In the past 10 years, India, China and Brazil have themselves become major aid donors (McCormick 2008), including to Nepal (Yang *et al.* 2014).

The efforts to achieve development by setting, and monitoring, quantifiable targets have also been criticised for being overly rigid and technocratic (Van Norren 2012; Fehling *et al.* 2013), corroding democracy and human rights (Christie 2015; Esser and Ha 2015; Fukuda-Parr and Yamin 2015; Reddy and Kvangraven 2015), taking up too many scarce administrative resources (Jerven 2014), relying too heavily on official development assistance as a means of transfer (Fukuda-Parr 2006) and not having led to any behavioural change (Caliari 2014). Sakiko Fukuda-Parr, Joshua Greenstein and David Stewart (2013: 22) conclude 'that there is no convincing evidence of a marked post-MDG acceleration of improvement in reducing human poverty for the world's countries as a whole'. This is somewhat surprising, given that Jan Vandemoortele (2011: 1) has found that 'statistics have been abused to fabricate evidence of success [of MDGs]'. In any case, it can be concluded that there is scant evidence that the aid effectiveness paradigm of the post-Washington Consensus has been effective (Dijkstra 2013). This paradigm may merely be the manifestation, in the field of development assistance, of the 'evaluatis' (Frey 2007) that has recently held sway in public management (Hood 2012). The impoverished character of the development paradigm of the post-Washington Consensus is especially poignant, as the academic debate on what development *is*, and how it can be aided, has grown increasingly rich and nuanced in the last 15 years.

The latest insights from academia

The study of development assistance has recently been enriched by the (re)emergence of at least four sets of insights. First, a broader conception of the social conditions that development efforts strive to overcome – usually labelled 'poverty' – has been advocated. Instead of narrowly defining poverty as low levels of GDP or the number of people who earn less than a certain amount of money per day, the recent Commission on the Measurement of Economic Performance and Social Progress (2009), chaired by economists

Joseph Stiglitz, Amartya Sen and Jean-Paul Fitoussi, has pleaded for an understanding of poverty that focuses on current and future human well-being. According to the Commission (2009: 14–15), measuring well-being involves simultaneously considering the following eight dimensions: material living standards (income, consumption and wealth); health; education; personal activities, including work; political voice and governance; social connections and relationships; the present and future state of the natural environment; and economic, as well as physical, insecurity. As such, the Commission builds on earlier publications by economist Partha Dasgupta (1993) and political scientist Robert Putnam (1993) that stress the importance of non-coerced social interactions for human well-being (cf. Sen 1999). With its 'Better Life Index', the OECD has followed up on the recommendations of the Stiglitz–Sen–Fitoussi Commission.

A second nascent insight is that poverty can only be defeated by the creative combination, at each level of analysis (from the local to the global), of different sets of institutions, embodied by the market, state and civil society (Rodrik 2007; Ostrom 2010; De Haan 2015). It has been emphasised that it is not possible to prescribe or predict which precise combinations of these institutional forms are most conducive for alleviating poverty (Ostrom *et al.* 2007; Forsyth and Walker 2008; Banerjee and Duflo 2011). Rather, any such combination needs to remain flexible, and be adjusted to the specifics of time and place. One promising way in which to do so is by making use of deliberative-democratic forums in which stakeholders defend, debate and justify their policy preferences (Dietz *et al.* 2003; Evans 2004).

Third, the view has emerged that in order to facilitate the institutional change through which poverty can be overcome it is imperative to focus on political power and how it is used to maintain the status quo (Hyden 2008; Hout 2012; Carothers and de Gramont 2013). The idea is that powerful elites, at both the domestic and international level, benefit from existing economic, political and social inequalities in poor countries, and will often seek to thwart institutional progress. Development cannot take place without circumventing, or even overcoming, this opposition. Aid should at least not enable it – as has happened far too often in the past.

Last, it has come to be realised (anew) that for development as institutional change to come about it is necessary to reflect critically on the daily activities and precise roles that aid agencies and their employees take on (Stirrat 2008; Mosse 2011; Fechter and Hindman 2014; cf. Hirschman 1967; for an application to development workers in Nepal, see Harper 2011). Far from being all-knowing guides on the path to development enlightenment, aid workers are enmeshed in their own social networks, are subject to professional and other biases, often wield significant power and are driven by a mix of motives that can range from altruistic to self-centred. Their interventions have at times been as responsible for major policy disasters as have the actions of domestic stakeholders.

These novel insights have enriched our understanding of what development *is* and what may be involved in bringing it about. Nevertheless, taken together, they at most constitute a mixed bag of loosely related concepts. In other words, these insights do not add up to a coherent, conceptual whole. They have, for instance, been drawn from such different, if not contradictory, theoretical and epistemological traditions as behavioural economics (Banerjee and Duflo 2011), post-structuralism (Fechter and Hindman 2014) and rational choice analysis (Ostrom 2010). This disjointedness may be one reason why these new insights have not been taken over, and implemented, by practitioners to any significant degree (Hout 2012). A theoretical synthesis of the various insights and viewpoints that have recently emerged would therefore be helpful, especially if this integration came with clear, practical implications for how to aid development.

It would be even better if such a theoretical synthesis also achieved another feat, namely to take into consideration the positive and negative roles that technological change can play in human development. How technological change comes about and how this can be regulated have been neglected by development theorists. This is regrettable given that technological progress has long been viewed as the ultimate driver of economic growth and social change (e.g. Rosenberg and Birdzell 1986). Below, I argue that the 'cultural theory' (short for 'theory of socio-cultural viability') pioneered by anthropologist Dame Mary Douglas incorporates and synthesises the four insights that have recently (re)emerged in the study of human development, while also including an account of technological change.

Cultural (or plural rationality) theory

After Douglas's ground-breaking work (Douglas 1966, 1978, 1982), cultural theory (nowadays also known as 'plural rationality theory') was further developed by other anthropologists, in tandem with a number of political scientists (Thompson *et al.* 1990; Rayner 1992; Hood 1998; Thompson 2008). As mentioned in Chapter 1, cultural theory distinguishes between four primary ways of organising, perceiving and justifying social relations (called 'ways of life' or 'social solidarities'): *egalitarianism, hierarchy, individualism* and *fatalism*. The theory postulates that these four ways of life emerge in contradistinction to each other in every conceivable domain of social life. Most such domains (say, the way in which a school operates or the manner in which an international regime functions) will consist of some dynamic combination of these pure forms. As many social domains can be distinguished within and between societies (and as many societies can be distinguished around the world), the theory allows one to perceive a wide and ever-changing cultural and social variety – while still enabling the formulation of general propositions about social and political life. These propositions include possible ways in which people understand what constitutes human development and how it can be aided. In order to explain this, I now have to set out plural rationality theory in some detail.

Each of the theory's four ways of life consists of a pattern of social relations as well as a supporting cast of perceptions, values and interests. The typology is derived from two dimensions of sociality that Douglas called 'grid' and 'group'. Grid measures the extent to which ranking and stratification constrain the behaviour of individuals. Group, by contrast, measures the extent to which an overriding commitment to a social unit constrains the thought and action of individuals. Assigning two values (high and low) to the two dimensions gives the four ways of organising social relations. Egalitarianism is associated with a low grid score (little stratification) and a high group score (strong group boundaries and solidarity). The combination of a high score on the grid dimension (lots of stratification) with a high score on the group dimension (much solidarity) gives hierarchy. The third way of life, individualism, is associated with low scores on both the grid and group scales. Last, fatalism is characterised by a high grid and a low group score.

According to cultural theory, each of these four ways of organising tends to induce, and be supported by, a particular way of perceiving nature, human nature, time, space, risk, technology, justice and governance. Since it was first formulated, this classification has helped illuminate the paradoxical and sometimes contradictory manners in which people approach a welter of contemporary public issues (Ney 2009; Hendriks 2010; Hartmann 2011; Verweij 2011; Swedlow 2014). Moreover, plural rationality theory posits that social domains and policy discourses are forever in flux due to the never-ending waxing and waning, splitting and merging, of its four ways of life. Adherents to a particular way of life constantly compare its truth claims (regarding nature, human nature, risk, technology, etc.) with perceived reality. When this distance becomes too large, they will start to adjust their views (and social relations).

The theory's classification can be usefully applied to the topic of economic and political development. In an egalitarian social setting, actors see nature as fragile and intricately interconnected, and man as essentially caring (until corrupted by coercive institutions such as markets and bureaucracies). We must all tread lightly on the earth, and it is not enough that people start off equal; justice demands that they end up equal as well. The good life is therefore spent in solidarity with others and in close harmony with nature. Technology should be funded and operated by locally organised collectives, and enable a modest, communal lifestyle. Human development consists of any steps towards this frugal, collectivist ideal. It can be aided through a levelling of the fundamental inequities that characterise the international system, the dismantling of international bureaucracies such as the IMF, World Trade Organization (WTO) and World Bank, the embracing of voluntary simplicity and economic localisation, and the spread of direct, grass-roots democracy. In this view, the commons should be promoted over private property, the market mechanism and bureaucratic regulation. Although global solidarity is demanded, official development assistance and even the charity of rich people are viewed with suspicion. In the global debates about how to aid development, these views have been advocated by such authors as E. F. Schumacher (1973), Naomi Klein (2007) and Slavoj Žižek (2009), as well as by the civil society groups that make up the global justice and alter-mondialisme movements (Bakker 2007; Della Porta

2016). These groups include the Fifty Years Is Enough campaign (Danaher 1994), the Development Group for Alternative Policies (www.developmentgap. org), ATTAC (www.attac.org) and the Occupy Now movement (Gitlin 2012), among others. Each year, many of these groups descend upon the World Social Forum.

In a hierarchical setting, actors see the world as controllable. Nature is stable until pushed beyond discoverable limits, and man is deeply flawed but redeemable by firm and long-lasting institutions. Fair distribution is by rank and station or, in the modern context, by need (with the level of need being determined by expert and dispassionate authority). Environmental management requires certified experts to determine nature's limits, and statutory regulation to ensure that human activity is kept within those limits. The same applies to economic growth, which is viewed as too complex and too much in need of public goods to be left to the free interplay of market forces or the wishes of civil society. Instead, it should be carefully planned by technocratic elites, who take into consideration the long-term interests of all social strata, as well as the imperatives of sustainability. The type of technology that most effectively ushers in economic progress consists of large infrastructure programmes (large dams, canalisation, nuclear plants, road and rail networks etc.) that are too expensive to be financed either through markets or by local communities. If democracy is unavoidable, then it should be an indirect, guardian model of democracy. Hierarchical actors are convinced that peace among nations requires expanding international and supranational organisations and strengthening international law. Human development, in their view, is a slow, but steady, improvement on many fronts, such as income per capita, longevity, literacy rates, child mortality, degree of biodiversity loss, crime rates, connection to electricity networks, number of schools and roads per region, agricultural productivity, Internet coverage and so on. Poor countries usually lack both the expertise and the financial means to kick-start development and therefore require the financial assistance and expert advice magnanimously offered by advanced nations. This perspective has often prevailed among aid agencies. It can be detected in the Millennium Development Goals and Sustainable Development Goals strategies, as well as in the development paradigm that reigned supreme from the 1950s to the 1980s. It has also been touted, in ever-changing versions, by a string of eminent development experts, including W. W. Rostow (1960), Jan Tinbergen (1976), Richard Jolly (Mehrotra and Jolly 2000), Jeffrey Sachs (2005) and Paul Collier (2008).

In an individualistic setting, actors view nature as resilient – able to recover from any exploitation – and man as inherently self-interested and atomistic. Trial and error, in self-organising ego-focused networks (unfettered markets), is the way to go, with Adam Smith's invisible hand ensuring that people only do well when others also benefit. Risks are opportunities to be exploited by the enterprising individual. The upholders of individualism see it as only fair that those who put the most in get the most out. They prefer policies and regulations that work with the grain of the market. Only these will ensure rapid economic progress. Technological development is a major motor of economic growth, but will only flourish if left untouched by technocratic fiat, taxes or subsidies. As they believe that everyone is eager to maximise their personal freedom of choice, a pluralist, Madisonian form of democracy – with checks and balances preventing a tyranny of the majority – is seen as the best way of organising the polity. In their view, international peace is promoted by the spread of pluralist democracy and global markets, as well as by restricting international bureaucracy. Human development is fundamentally the expansion of individual opportunity and private property. Official development assistance is frowned upon, as it distorts market incentives, creates moral hazard and lessens the dependence of poor states on the consent of their citizens (private charity initiatives and remittances are of course matters of individual choice). Instead of development aid, individualistic actors prescribe the opening of domestic markets to foreign banks, firms, labour and capital. This take on development has been voiced by the International Financial Institution Advisory (or Meltzer) Commission (2000), as well as by many libertarian organisations – from the Cato Institute (Ayodele *et al.* 2005) to the Adam Smith Institute (www.adam smith.org/blog/?tag=development). It also has a long pedigree in academia, having been advocated by, for instance, Peter Bauer (1972), Graham Hancock (1989), William Easterly (2006a), James Shikwati (2007) and Dambisa Moyo (2009).

In a fatalistic setting, actors find neither rhyme nor reason in nature and suppose that man is untrustworthy. Fairness is not to be found in this life, and there is no possibility of improving society. 'Defect first' – the winning strategy in the one-off prisoner's dilemma – makes sense to them, as does a ceaseless striving to achieve relative (rather than absolute) personal gain. Spreading democracy, peace and development around the world may be a lofty endeavour, but is not a realistic goal. The only forms of co-operation that temporarily emerge in a fatalistic setting is the banding together of the weak to thwart the emergence of a predominant actor, or to enable the collective plunder of a third party. For the rest, everyone has to fend for him or herself, while the devil will surely take the hindmost. As a result, there is no point wasting time over what development is or how it could be furthered. Official development assistance is at most deceptively used by stakeholders to promote their self-interests and clout at the expense of others. For obvious reasons, few academics and governments have openly advocated a fatalistic stance on human development – with one exception being the philosopher John Gray (2007). Nevertheless, it has been argued that such cynical power motives at least partially drove the aid strategies of the adversaries in the Cold War (Dunning 2004) and currently form part of the rationale of the Chinese government to offer international assistance (Tull 2006).

Hence, plural rationality theory's fourfold classification captures the perspectives and policies of many of the protagonists involved in the practice and study of development aid. Table 2.1 offers an overview. Not all protagonists have adhered to a single rationality. For instance, the basic human needs approach advocated in the 1970s combined hierarchical and egalitarian views. The Washington Consensus of the 1980s and 1990s mixed hierarchical traits with individualistic ones.

Cultural, or plural rationality, theory also has important normative and policy implications. These flow from the theory's premise that each of its four ways of life is not only different from (and in competition with), but also dependent on, all other ways of life. That is to say, each way of life contains blind spots and self-undermining features that can only be compensated for by the other ways of life. Hence, each way of life can only survive with the help of the others. From this premise, the following hypothesis can be derived: *Attempts to resolve pressing social and environmental problems that flexibly combine all ways of defining and resolving the issues at hand tend to be more successful than attempts that rely on fewer ways of life.* The latter will not only fail according to the goals, norms and values prioritised in the excluded ways of life, but they will also fail on their own terms – as each way of organising and perceiving is complementary to, and co-dependent on, the other three. These efforts have often been labelled 'clumsy solutions' (Verweij and Thompson 2006), although the term 'polyrational' (Davy 2012) has been used as well. They resemble legal scholar Cass Sunstein's (1995) notion of 'incompletely theorised agreements', as well as philosopher John Rawls's (1987) concept of 'overlapping moral consensus'. They are policy solutions that are acceptable to all stakeholders involved, albeit for divergent reasons and from alternative normative viewpoints. By now, a number of case studies (Rayner 1986; Hendriks 1999; Ney 2009; Franks 2010; Hartmann 2011; Verweij 2011; Bruggemann *et al.* 2012; Levin-Keitel, 2014; Scolobig *et al.* 2016) have confirmed the empirical validity of clumsy solutions.

Cultural theory has also been applied to development issues (Thompson and Warburton 1985; Wildavsky 1994; Gyawali 2003; Gasper 2006; Roe 2012; Yazdanpanah *et al.* 2013). According to cultural theory, human development only comes about when solutions to pressing social and environmental ills, at any level of analysis, reflect all four perspectives on how to define and resolve the issues at hand. As each of these perspectives favours a different allocation mechanism and a particular way of organising, human development proceeds through creatively and flexibly combining alternative sets of institutions. Human development is therefore pluralistic, reflexive and contested. By contrast, under- or non-development occurs when solutions to social and environmental issues are not based on all perspectives advocated, but have been dictated by the adherents of just one or two ways of organising, perceiving and justifying social relations. If that happens, or so cultural theory predicts, an increase in only one way of life – namely, fatalism – will result in the end. According to the approach, lack of development can therefore be equated with the spread of fatalism, and is the outcome of monolithic attempts to repress the diversity innate to social life. Unfortunately, far too often this characterises the impact that development aid has on poor countries or regions. Such aid frequently enables a set of stakeholders (often state officials), with a singular view on how to conceive of and resolve the problems at stake, to start dominating all other

Table 2.1 Four perspectives on human development

	Individualism	Egalitarianism	Hierarchy	Fatalism
View of human nature	Intelligent and informed, but egocentric and materialistic	Essentially altruistic and caring, but corruptible by money, status and power	Sinful without imposed guidance and restraints, as well as highly differentiated in terms of morals and intelligence	Unpredictable, deceitful and amoral
View of nature	Cornucopian, abundant	Ephemeral, fragile	Stable within boundaries that are knowable to experts	Unknowable
Domestic governance ideal	Pluralist, Madisonian democracy and a limited, 'night-watchman' state	Participatory, grass-roots democracy aimed at forging consensus among all those affected	Technocratic guidance and expertise; if democracy, then a guardian democracy	A (hopefully somewhat) benevolent dictatorship
International governance ideal	The spread of unfettered, global markets and Madisonian democracy	Global solidarity between small, autonomous political units; if not yet feasible, then rule by global civil society	Extensive international and supranational institutions and treaties (if not world government)	Short-term alliances to maintain balance of power; or a (hopefully) benevolent hegemony of one state
Economic ideal	Unfettered, competitive markets	Local production and consumption, collectively decided upon	Centrally planned production, allocation and consumption	Getting rich at the expense of others (mercantilism; kleptocracy)

Favourite type of technology	Whatever proves most efficient (and profitable)	Locally constructed, small-scale and simple (requiring little investment or expertise)	Capital- and knowledge-intensive (complicated and large-scale)	Whatever gives an edge over rivals
Attitude towards economic, technological and environmental risks	Risk is opportunity	Risk needs to be minimised	Risk needs to be managed	Risk cannot be eradicated; therefore, it needs to be shed unto others
Justice	Equality of opportunity	Equality of condition	Those at the top aiding those at the bottom	Whatever is necessary for survival (amoralism)
Preferred allocation mechanism	Markets	Civil society/the commons	The bureaucracy	Rule from the shadows
Perception of the poor	Inventive, self-reliant, entrepreneurial	Oppressed, excluded and marginalised	Deserving of a firm, but helping hand	Unreliable
Official development assistance	Distorts private incentives and facilitates corruption	Is a fig leaf for the unwillingness to redress global inequities, if not a tool for capitalist exploitation	Is a global public good and a moral imperative	Makes the rich and powerful richer and more powerful
Human development	Entails expanding individual opportunities and private property	Consists of living in solidarity with fellow community members and in harmony with nature	Involves ever more people moving up a hierarchy of needs	Is not to be had in this life

Source: Adapted from Thompson and Wildavsky (1986) and Verweij (2011: 56–7).

actors. As a result, the inflow of significant amounts of aid money tends to promote one type of institutions (such as the state or the market) at the expense of others. Yet, as all types of institutions are co-dependent, this eventually only leads to institutional eutrophication, social decay and economic and technological stagnation – fatalism, in one word.

Developing *dharma*, according to cultural theory

Cultural theory not only captures rather well, and criticises, the competing perspectives on how to aid development that have long been advocated and practised. It also encapsulates the four theoretical desiderata that have recently been emphasised. A broader conception of poverty, rooted in social relations, has long been central to Douglas's theoretical project (Douglas and Isherwood 1996). As she explains in a World Bank publication (Douglas 2004: 90–91),

> A tentative definition of poverty should start from the fact that human persons are social beings who interact and exchange. From this basis social life can be defined as a system of exchanges (market or gift) between individuals and between groups. Culture is the series of local debates which thrash out the definition of a well-functioning person. The causes of poverty are various disablements from entry into the exchanges that define a social being.

Although this is a broader understanding of poverty than the long-dominant materialistic ones, it is easily measurable as it equates to prevailing levels of fatalism (i.e. social relations characterised by low collectivity and high stratification). Moreover, this conceptualisation immediately highlights the need to focus on the impacts of power and politics in poverty alleviation. As Douglas (2004: 91) continues,

> Working with this definition, discussions of poverty should incorporate political culture because it exerts control on distribution, and it should obviously attend to exclusionary behavior, both local and international.

Indeed, cultural theory has paid close attention to what constitutes political power and how it can be exerted (Tansey 2004; Richards 2011). Furthermore, the approach is fully in line with the insight that economic and political development requires a flexible and resilient combination of different institutional forms, and especially the market, bureaucracy and civil society. It can even be argued that cultural theory's version of this insight is more complete than other variants, as the approach also spells out the perceptions (of nature, human nature, time, space, risk, technology etc. – see Table 2.1) that undergird these institutional patterns. Finally, cultural theory lends itself well to analysing how the biases of aid workers and their agencies influence the process of development. This is the case as:

It is individuals as social creatures that, not only being molded by but actively molding their social context – shaping the maze as well as running it – that are the focus of cultural theory.

(Wildavsky 1987: 7)

As cultural theory presumes that actors and social structures are co-constituted (Douglas 1987), it facilitates analysis of the collective impact of stakeholders' daily activities. Thus, it has informed ethnographies of social exclusion among high school students in Berlin (Wellgraf 2014), workplace cheating in Britain (Mars 1994), and the ways in which Belgian police officers interact with the public (Loyens and Maesschalck 2014), to give just a few examples.

Hence, cultural theory constitutes a single, coherent framework, with falsifiable (but empirically supported) predictions and clear policy implications, that makes use of all the four insights that have recently been highlighted in the academic debate about development assistance. Moreover, it made an early, important contribution to the analysis of how technology is socially constructed and sounded the call to democratise technological choice (e.g. Schwarz and Thompson 1990). By now, the approach has elucidated why some emerging technologies, such as the Internet or residential green buildings (Tranvik and Thompson 2006; Wilkinson *et al.* 2014), have been widely endorsed, while others, including nanosilver and the Korean National Educational Information System (Foss Hansen and Baun 2015; Kim and Kim 2010), have met with fierce resistance. In other words, cultural theory also deepens our understanding of how technological progress comes about – unlike many approaches that have thus far informed the study and practice of development aid. Hence, it is high time to empirically and systematically explore the contributions that cultural theory can make to our understanding of poverty alleviation and human development. That is what this volume does.

3 The arrested success of pro-poor initiatives in democratic Nepal

Bihari Krishna Shrestha

Resham Bhattarai (a pseudonym), together with five other small farmers in Sri Antu (in the far east of Nepal), formed a co-operative group in 1986 under the Small Farmer Development Project, an initiative of Nepal's Agricultural Development Bank, with funding being provided as a loan from a foreign donor, the International Fund for Agriculture Development. His total asset when he joined the group was 2.5 ropani (0.12 hectares) of agricultural land, against which he was able to borrow 15,000 rupees. 4,000 rupees went towards the purchase of a horse and he used the rest as trading capital, buying ginger and *amleso* (the shrub from which the ubiquitous brooms are made) locally. These he and his horse then transported to India (or sometimes to Fikal Bazaar in Ilam District), importing various Indian goods on the return journeys. While doing this, as he himself stressed, he remained a disciplined member of his group under the close and benign supervision of his sub-project office's group organiser.

His first break came when he planted ginger himself while still carrying on with his trading trips, and by 1990 his annual income had climbed to 100,000 rupees (roughly 1,000 euros[1]). In 1992 he was able to buy 20 ropani of land for 200,000 rupees from a neighbour who was migrating to the Terai, and by 1997 he had 22 ropani under large cardamom. Finding that he no longer had the time for his trading trips, he sold the horse. Shortly afterwards he was able to buy another 40 ropani for 450,000 rupees, including a loan of 40,000 rupees from the Small Farmer Co-operative Limited (as the Small Farmer Development Project had by then become). At present he has a total holding of 62 ropani, of which 30 are under tea, 10 under ginger and 22 under cardamom. He has also resumed his export business, taking broomsticks and ginger to Silgudi in India and cardamom to Fikal Bazaar. In another five years or so he sees himself selling tea for about 300,000 rupees a year, on top of what he is earning from his ginger and cardamom. The Bhattarais have two children who are at boarding school in Ilam and, by their own assessment, are now worth in excess of four million rupees.

This impressive progress, far from being exceptional, has been matched by all but one of the members of his six-person group. This single failure, Resham explained, was 'because he had two wives'. Nor is there anything exceptional about this particular group. The 80 or so per cent success rate holds for all the other small farmer members he knows (and this, as we will see, is confirmed by the overall statistics for the small farmer co-operatives). 'Before the programme', Resham recalls, 'a quarter of the small farmers had to go to the moneylenders each year to borrow for rice', and those who lagged behind, once the programme was up and running, were 'those who were too lazy to work according to the credit plan and had too many children'. He attributes his own success to the credit extended by the programme, to the 60 per cent subsidy on irrigation that it made available, and to strong supervision from its sub-project office (where his local group organiser is located).

So, from a situation, back in 1986, where, with their tiny landholding and the likelihood of having to resort to the moneylenders every year just to get enough rice, Resham and his wife have crashed straight through that 'one dollar a day' poverty line, way past the point at which they have become rupee millionaires, and are now sufficiently well off to be able to send their children to a private boarding school. Nor, now that they are producing high-value crops – tea, cardamom and ginger – that are quite easily transported to India, where demand is already strong and can only get stronger as its economy grows and grows, is there much chance that their fortunes will go into reverse. In other words, Resham and his wife and all those 80 or so per cent of small farmer members like them, are shining examples of an aid-assisted development initiative, something that, one might suppose, would by now have been latched on to by the entire donor community, given a salient position in the government's strategy and rolled out and replicated across the entire rural landscape of Nepal. In fact, the exact opposite has happened.

The Small Farmer Development Programme has been in retreat for some years now, neither the government nor the donors have much interest in it and the level of rural poverty remains staggeringly high, even as Nepal reels under the twin burdens of social unrest and an ever-ballooning foreign debt. The reason, as we will see (and as is confirmed in many of the subsequent case studies) is the chronically erratic nature of foreign aid management, by both the donors and the recipients. We should also point the finger of blame at those – the academic community, civil society organisations, public intellectuals, the media and so on – who have stood silently by instead of weighing in so as to deprive these complacent development players of the impunity that they have, for far too long, enjoyed.

The socio-economic context of small farmer co-operatives

Though democracy was restored to Nepal in 1990, it has failed to translate into socio-economic benefits for the poor in general and, in particular, for the small farmers who constitute a majority within this predominantly agrarian country (and of course that failure is not unrelated to the emergence of, and quite strong popular sympathy with, the Maoist insurgency).

While 85 per cent of the population is rural and 78.5 per cent of the workforce is dependent on agriculture, the terrain is so mountainous that only 18 per cent of Nepal's land area is available. Cultivable land, even with the remarkable terracing skills of the country's inhabitants, is therefore scarce and landholdings tend to be small. In 1998, it was estimated that 70 per cent of all agricultural landholdings were below one hectare, with 40 per cent being below 0.5 hectare (NSAC 1998). Resham Bhattarai, of course, started off in the latter category, a fact that can be seized on, by those who take a zero-sum view of man–land interactions, to argue that Resham's success has been at the impoverishment of others. Only if the game was, or has become, positive-sum, would the small farmer co-operatives be delivering development. Resham's first land purchase, from a neighbour who was migrating to newly available farmland in the Terai, was clearly not at the expense of others' holdings. And the same must also be true of land that has more recently become available as people have migrated to Kathmandu and other urban centres (for the economic opportunities, or to escape from the Maoists, or both) and of those who have been able to de-intensify their farming efforts, thanks to remittances from family members working in the Gulf States and elsewhere. In addition, it is difficult to maintain the zero-sum view when subsistence farmers are shifting to cash crops of such high value that they can buy in their rice and still be much better off. So Nepal, it would seem, is currently undergoing the sort of shift from the countryside to the city that occurred in the now-developed countries a couple of centuries or so ago, in the course of the Industrial Revolution.

Population growth, particularly over the second half of the twentieth century (when the game was not sufficiently positive-sum to fully compensate) has exacerbated this scarcity. It has been estimated that land availability in 1954 was 0.6 hectare per capita and that, by 1990, it had declined to 0.24 (World Bank 1997b). By 1997 it was estimated to have fallen to 0.15 (NSAC 1998).

These statistics, however, because of the averaging they involve, do not tell the full story, since land ownership is very unevenly distributed. It has been estimated that in 1997 the top 5 per cent of the population owned 40 per cent of the land, with the bottom 60 per cent having only 20 per cent of it (World Bank 1990b). By 1997, only half of all rural households were deemed to be food secure, while underemployment was pervasive: 47 per cent nationally and 47.5 per cent in rural areas (NSAC 1998). Seven years later these rates remained largely unchanged (CBS 2004). On top of all that, and despite the large proportion of the workforce being engaged in agriculture, the sector (according to a 2001 estimate) contributes only 39 per cent to the country's Gross Domestic Product.

Despite agriculture being overcrowded and underemployment rife, the possibilities for the surplus workforce to shift across to the non-agriculture sectors have remained chronically limited, with only 10 per cent of the annual increased workforce finding employment outside of agriculture (NSAC 1998: 100). In the manufacturing sector – the biggest employer of labour, but with traditionally sluggish growth – only about 20 per cent of jobs are unskilled, which means that most of the largely illiterate and unskilled workforce cannot be absorbed into it. Those who cannot be absorbed have therefore been forced to seek income and employment opportunities in agriculture itself, even as they also go on seasonal and longer-term out-migration, mainly to India. This is the traditional coping strategy, a way of generating much-needed supplementary income through mostly menial and low-paid work.

In recent years, however, there have been some dramatic changes within this strategy, with the out-migrants now overflying India (literally) to take up employment in the Gulf States and other overseas countries. Nepalese international migrants reached three million in 2010, where it had only been 10,000 in the early 1990s (Devkota 2014: 36). In 2010, the households receiving remittances reached 55.8 per cent, whereas it was only 23.4 per cent in 1995. Nominal average remittances per household also increased to 80,436 rupees in 2010, while it was 15,160 rupees in 1995 (Devkota 2014: 37). If the unrecorded amount from India to Nepal is added, then the contribution of remittances could be as high as 30 per cent of GDP (Devkota 2014: 36–7). This has led to a massive reduction in poverty: from 42 per cent in 1995 to 31 per cent in 2004 and to 25 per cent in 2010 (Devkota 2014: 37). This despite the country being embroiled in civil war, and it is a trend that continues unabated. Nepalis, of course, may not be willing to keep this up for generations but, at this rate of poverty reduction, they may well not need to. To gain some further understanding of how this traditional coping strategy has suddenly had such a transformative effect, it may be helpful to provide a brief description of the 'structural' poverty to which it has long been the response.

Systemic inequality

Poverty in Nepal has been strongly associated with the exclusionary nature of its social structure. It is much more than just the inevitable consequence of a competitive struggle on a level playing field. Orthodox Hinduism has been the basis of the Nepalese polity for centuries, with the two high caste groups – Brahmans and Chhetris – having been politically the most powerful while also enjoying priority in land grants from the state. In the fourfold vertical caste classification, the artisans (blacksmiths, butchers and so on) came at the bottom and were defined as the 'serving castes'. Stigmatised as untouchable, they were precluded from land ownership, and to this day they render labour and caste-specific occupational services to higher-caste households in the traditionally self-perpetuating patron–client relationship, under which they receive seasonal payments and other occasional largesse towards their subsistence from the former. It is this historical legacy that makes the occupational caste groups – now generically referred to as Dalits (the oppressed) – the poorest and most deprived in the country.

The cultural landscape of Nepal also includes a large population of casteless, and mutually distinct, Tibet–Burman ethnic groups, now generically referred to as Janjati (ethnic – i.e. non-Hindu – people). These ethnic groups, each of which is indigenous to a specific geographical region, number over 60, and together they make up around 40 per cent of the country's population. However, due to the all-pervasive nature of the Hindu caste system, these ethnic groups have found themselves drawn into the vortex of the caste hierarchy, where they have been assigned a status just above that of the Dalits. Only the Newars – indigenous to the fertile Kathmandu Valley (and thus prosperous, both agriculturally and in connection with trade up into Tibet and down into India) share in the affluence and influence of the two Hindu high caste groups. In 1998, these three groups, together accounting for some 20 per cent of the population, had the highest Human Development Indices: Brahman 0.441, Chhetri 0.348 and Newar 0.457 (all considerably higher than the national average of 0.325). The rest of the Janjati groups have remained at the margins of this 'Hindu core', with the result that poverty is most pronounced among them and the Dalits. This is also true of the Terai region, where the Dalits are relatively more numerous, but even more disadvantaged and stigmatised, than in the hills.

Women too find themselves the victims of the exclusionary nature of orthodox Hinduism, which relegates them to inferior status across all the caste, class and ethnic categories (with the exception, many would argue, of the poly-androus and trade-focused Tibetan Buddhist communities such as the Sherpas).[2] Serving men has been defined as their highest calling in life, and as a con-sequence female illiteracy is rampant. In most households they bear the brunt of both domestic and farm work, putting in many more hours of work than do their menfolk. At the same time, they own fewer assets, receive less food and are less attended to during sickness. Their mobility tends to be restricted, and household decisions involving money and external contacts remain the man's prerogative. Much of this has resulted from the discriminatory laws on marriage and inheritance, which, in their turn, are manifestations of the low status accorded to women by orthodox Hinduism.

Non-systemic inequality, neoclassical economics would argue, will be responsive to incremental 'changes at the margin', and most efforts to alleviate poverty in Nepal have been based on that assumption. But, with systemic inequality, such changes will be ineffective; it will take an 'optimal perturbation' – a major jolt – to overcome the lock-in that the system has generated. The recent flood of remittances by Nepalis working outside the country seems to have provided precisely that jolt.

While successive national development plans have, in various forms, continued to lay emphasis on alleviating poverty in Nepal, no significant progress has materialised. The Tenth Plan (2002–07), for instance, acknow-ledged that the annual rate of economic growth had 'hovered around 4 per cent for the last three decades as against the annual population growth rate of 2.5 per cent during the same period', leading to, it conceded 'very minimal per capita income increments'. Under these conditions – conditions that had persisted for at least 30 years – there could be no percolation of benefits to the poor, and thus no way to prevent the perpetuation of poverty in the country. The Plan further recognised that what growth had taken place had been in the non-agricultural sector and in the urban areas. It had thus 'sidestepped the rural areas where most people live'.

In recent years, however, and as has been indicated above, the incidence of poverty has fallen from 41.8 per cent in 1995/06 to 30.8 per cent in 2003/04. This dramatic shift (in the midst of a civil war, moreover) was almost entirely due to a significant increase in remittances. It has been estimated that in 2007 more than one million Nepalis were working abroad and remitting the equivalent of more than one billion US dollars annually. In addition, the average remittance increased from Rs 15,000 in 1998 to Rs 23,900 in 2006, even after allowing for inflation. Over the same time, the proportion of households receiving remittances has increased from 23 per cent to around 32 per cent (New Era 2006: 62). The future, this suggests, is no longer what it used to be.

None of this is to say that all is now rosy on the poverty front, only that there seems to have been a transformative change: the inequality, it would seem, is no longer systemic, and thus self-perpetuating, in the way it has long been. Poverty is still mainly rural, and still fairly directly related to the amount of land owned. And low caste people, having been marginal land-owners (at best) and (at worst) landless, are still seriously disadvantaged. According to a World Bank source, the incidence of poverty among those owning less than 0.2ha of land is 39 per cent, falling to just 24 per cent for those owning more than 0.2ha (quoted in New Era 2006: 61). The ethnic people, likewise, are still disadvantaged but with creamy layers of various depths, thanks to their traditional engagements in trade and tourism or with service in foreign armies: British, Indian and, most recently, private ones in places like Iraq and Afghanistan.

Tenacious poverty and unresponsive democratic governance

Despite the numerous examples from around the world of a positive association between democratic governance and the betterment of people's living conditions, the correlation in Nepal's case is mixed. It is negative at the national level and strongly positive among the primary stakeholders at the grass-roots level, community forests (see Chapter 11), small farmer co-operatives (this chapter) and the Bhattedanda Milkway (Chapter 5) being prime examples.

Nepal's village communities are generally composed of several caste/ethnic groups, including Dalits (Bhattedanda, for instance, comprises Brahmans and Tamangs, the former being high caste, the latter just above Dalit status). Despite the advent of a democratic ideology favouring equality and human rights, the vertically stratified power structure that is defined by the convergence of high caste and economic advantage has remained more or less intact. Thus, in most rural communities, a select club of competing high caste elites lords it over the rest. For the village poor, politically and economically unable to challenge this hegemony, allegiance to one or other faction within these local power centres is an inescapable necessity.

While multi-party democracy was restored to the country in 1990, the local chapters of the various political parties are generally led by the very same traditional elites, with rivals joining opposing parties not for reasons of ideology but in response to their historic and competitive relationships. There is therefore something illusionary about the idea that elections based on adult franchise will give people the power to choose their representatives. For the village poor, the option is limited to choosing between rival elites. In consequence, they generally cast their votes on the basis of their traditional allegiance to a specific power centre in the community. Likewise, in elections to the national legislature, votes are cast according to the behests of their traditional leaders: their patrons. Getting democracy to take hold in a largely agrarian society is not easy, as many political scientists have pointed out. Fortunately, Nepal is now much less agrarian than it was, not least because so many Nepalis are now working in the Gulf States, not on the land.

Money comes into this picture in a big way, because illiterate and poor voters are easily swayed by it. For instance, in a village in Jumla during the 1991 general election one low caste family with several adult members was approached by several of the competing parties and was given money by all of them for their votes. It was inconceivable for these poor villagers not to accept the money; to do so would have amounted to an act of hostility – defiance, even – towards the local elites, and that was something they could not afford. When the election came, these villagers resorted to the safest option and divided their votes equally among all the competing parties. The elites, for their part, could not fault these poor voters for having fallen for their pecuniary inducements. This is not an isolated case but an instance of a widespread pattern, and the result is that the democratic process is subordinated to the pre-existing and systemic inequality.

Widespread vote-buying then inevitably enhances the corruptibility of elected officials, thereby generating the main paradox of Nepalese democracy: political leaders promising the people good governance and prosperity and then ensuring through the process of getting themselves elected, that those promises are the very first casualties. They have to recoup their election-time investments (and more) and that can only be done through corruption; the practice is now so blatant and widespread that accusing politicians of corruption has entirely lost its sting. A successful politician, it is generally assumed, is a corrupt person. Unlike the occasional 'rotten apple' in stable democracies, Nepalese politicians are all at it, and the two critical elements of good governance – transparency of decision-making and accountability of leaders – are systematically compromised. While the different parties may profess different ideologies – social democracy, dialectical materialism and so on – they share a single and overriding motivation: the pursuit of money and power. In consequence, Nepal's democratic journey, restarted in 1990 after a 30-year hiatus, has been characterised by a steady deterioration in public trust and consent, thereby making room for the Maoist armed insurgency that quickly engulfed the nation. This deterioration is also evident at more local levels; while billions of rupees have passed through the hands of local bodies at village, district and town levels, both before and after 1990, there has been no improvement in the living conditions of those in the rural communities (until, that is, the remittances have started to flood in).

While bureaucracies are renowned for corruption, the expectation was that a democratically elected government would quickly reform the bureaucratic rules so as to minimise it, or even eliminate it altogether. But, with the elected leaders up to their ears in corruption, the bureaucrats have become handy tools for the purpose. The bureaucracy, in consequence, has become highly politicised and now lacks any measure of professionalism and sense of accountability to the public. Staff absenteeism in the districts and villages is often high and, even when officials are in their offices, their presence does not necessarily mean that they will be doing anything to help the villagers.

So the Nepal paradox is that people are alienated from the state in a democratic set-up. Just 10 years after the restoration of democracy, a study (in two districts: one in the hills, the other in the Terai) concluded (Shrestha 2000: 104):

> The people could not be more alienated from the government and the political parties than what they have been in the two districts. . . . Poor governance is pervasive and people at the grass roots are still waiting to be empowered despite the re-advent of the 'government of the people' a full decade ago.

Nepal's ostensibly democratic political system, we can now see, is a reflection of a social order that is no longer there. At any rate, it is nowhere near as 'there' as it used to be! Foreign aid is not neutral in relation to this unstable state of affairs. Though most people would expect it to act in a way that helps bring the political system into line with the changed social order, the evidence from the small farmers' co-operatives experience is that it does the reverse.

The Small Farmers' Co-operatives Programme

The programme was initiated in 1988 but had its roots in the Small Farmer Development Project that was implemented by the Agricultural Development Bank of Nepal. This project had been piloted in 1975 in two villages: one in the Middle Hills, the other in the Terai. Sponsored by the United Nations Food and Agriculture Organization and led by two field officers from the bank, both pilots were resounding successes and were quickly replicated across the country.

The Small Farmer Development Project was carried out by the district branches of the by then renamed Agricultural Development Bank Ltd. A sub-project office was set up in each village development council under the leadership of a group organiser (but with some officers acting for more than one village). Each group organiser, on the basis of a socio-economic survey of the community, then promoted groups of five to seven mutually trusting small farmers. These were farmers whose incomes fell below the then 'poverty threshold' of 2,500 rupees per capita per annum. To qualify, they also had to come from a common locality and be in possession of citizenship certificates. The tendency, in mixed groups, for men to dominate the project promoted separate groups (with the same requirements) for women. Members made redeemable monthly contributions to their group savings and undertook other co-operative activities.

The original philosophy was to make credit accessible to even the poorest by extending collateral-free lending on the basis of the joint liability of all group members ('social capital', as it is now called). The bank gave loans to individual members, on the basis of the group's assessment of the credit needs and capabilities of its members. In the event of a borrower defaulting the whole group was held responsible for the repayment (of both principal and interest) and further lending to group members was suspended until these dues were cleared.

The groups, it turned out, were not as sufficiently 'socially capitalised' as had been hoped, and the frequent defaults by individual members rendered the original provisions untenable. So, in 1978, a collateral system was introduced 'for those who had it', with members who had no collateral still being eligible, in theory, for loans. In practice, however, this new provision, thanks to the joint liability rule that was still in place, quickly led to those who were landless being unable to join new groups or to access loans within existing ones. Though landless farmers are not numerous in Nepal (making up, it has been estimated, just 4 per cent), the new provision ended up hurting precisely that portion of the small farmer community which was most in need of this supposedly pro-poor initiative.

A decade or so later, the Maoist insurgency, its ranks swollen by these 'excludees', instituted its own rough-and-ready form of project evaluation, destroying those it assessed to be of no assistance to the poorest of the poor and supporting those it assessed to be beneficial. It is therefore difficult to avoid the conclusion that those who imposed this collateral provision, while managing not to see that it was undermining the whole purpose of the programme, must bear some of the blame for the civil war that eventually broke out. And why, one can reasonably demand, was this 'Maoist perspective' not included in the elaborate and expensive exercises in *project evaluation* to which donors and aid agencies are so addicted?

The providers of foreign aid, inspired by the initial success of this whole approach, and oblivious to the new provision having undermined its explicit aim, then pitched in in order to help its rapid expansion across the country. The International Fund for Agricultural Development extended a loan of over two billion rupees, arranged in three phases across the years 1982–93, with the Asian Development Bank chipping in too during the final phase. With this impetus, the number of sub-project offices reached 455 by 1990, covering a total of 622 village development committees. This represented 15 per cent of the 4,000 village development committees in Nepal and catered to a total of 200,000 small farmer households, spread across 73 of the country's 75 districts.

With this influx of foreign aid, the emphasis shifted away from group organisation (the nurturing of 'social capital') and towards the disbursement of loans. The quality of the programme (which is what had made it successful in the first place) began to suffer, with inflated lending targets being handed down to the sub-project offices. Where, in the past, credits were apportioned according to the needs and capacities of individual members, lending became increasingly indiscriminate; loans were pushed without due consideration, thereby increasing both the risk of default and the opportunities for corruption.

The way was then open for further distortions; the politically inspired recruitment of an excessive number of staff (resulting in unsustainable overhead costs), the politically instigated disbursement of loans, mounting and deliberate defaults and a rapid and alarming decline in recovery rates. The once highly rated programme suddenly found itself fighting for its survival. In 1990, with the restoration of multi-party democracy, a large number of non-governmental organisations moved into the fields of micro-finance and local development. These new players, inspired by the achievements of the Grameen Bank in Bangladesh, provided donors with new and viable alternatives for small-scale lending; at the same time, the performance of the Small Farmer Development Programme was going from bad to worse. Unsurprisingly, the donors withdrew from the programme in the early 1990s. This sorry tale serves to reveal a breathtaking lack of responsibility on the part of the providers of foreign aid. Yes, they pulled out of a programme that was no longer working, but they somehow managed to ignore the fact that it was not working because they themselves had destroyed it. Where, the unfortunate victims of all this might reasonably ask, is the aid in that?

Rebirth as the Small Farmers' Co-operative Limited

By the late 1980s, the Small Farmer Development Programme, having become a liability, was faced with the prospect of collapse. Even so, it was at that time the only significant poverty alleviation initiative in the country. German Technical Cooperation (GTZ) therefore came to the rescue, extending assistance to the Agricultural Development Bank of Nepal in order to effect the transformation of the village sub-project offices into farmer-managed co-operatives. To that end, it funded a five-year programme of 'action research in institutional transformation'. This was based in Dhading District and led to the creation and formal registration of four small farmer co-operatives.

The basic units, as with its predecessor, the Small Farmer Development Programme, are the small farmer groups (each composed of some five to eight members). These are then federated, at the ward level, into inter-groups, each composed of between three and 15 small farmer groups. These inter-groups, in their turn, are federated, at the village development committee level, into main committees (each encompassing between nine and 15 inter-groups).

Each inter-group is then supported by a volunteer facilitator (*Sahayogi Karyakarta*), who liaises with the small farmer groups and their individual members and also promotes the formation of new groups. The main committee is made up of the representatives (generally the chairs) of the constituent inter-groups. Where the Small Farmer Development Programme had had bank-appointed group organisers (and other staff), each co-op has a small team of professional staff (at least one manager and one female worker) that is hired and paid for by the co-op itself.

These small farmer co-operatives, unlike regular co-ops (which are comprised of shareholders and a board of directors elected by them) are three-tiered organisations that mirror the lowermost levels of local government. This means that, in order to be elected to the main committee, a member of a small farmer group has first to prove his worth as an inter-group member. And, once elected to the main committee, he has to remain accountable to the inter-group to which he belongs. This provision, by tapping into local spatial and face-to-face relationships, has minimised, if not prevented, the politicisation of leadership within the co-ops as well as protected the professional nature of their management.

It is the main committee, with the aid of its professional staff, which manages the disbursement and repayment of loans, together with a range of other development activities that a small farmer co-op is expected to implement. It is aided in this by a separate three-member accounts committee, elected by the general assembly, which keeps track of the co-op's multitudinous transactions. A small farmer group member who wishes to obtain a loan first presents his land ownership certificate to the main committee as collateral. The co-op then asks the Land Revenue Office to 'block' the land, so that its ownership cannot be transferred to a third party until the loan has been cleared and the co-op authorises its 'unblocking' (this can involve a little greasing of palms in the Land Revenue Office, amounting to as much as 60 rupees in the case of one co-op in the Terai).

The conversion of a sub-project office into a small farmer co-operative limited company is not straightforward. It requires a two to three-year phase of institutional development, during which the inter-groups and main committee are formed and trained in the managing of the co-op, including the maintenance of its accounts.

It is clear from the above that Small Farmer Co-operatives Limited is very different from the Small Farmer Development Programme that preceded it. In particular, it is much more 'of the grass roots' and much less imposed 'from on high'. However, the rate of conversion has been rather slow, with just 73 sub-project offices (spread across 29 districts) being converted between 1993 and 1998. With the small farmer co-op programme being only a small part of the bank's activities, it did not receive the priority it deserved. Even so, the pace of conversion did pick up, with 19 new co-ops in 2001, 16 in 2002 and

20 in 2003, the total reaching 161 by July 2004. In 2012 the total across the country was 220. Though 22 of these 220 co-ops were established in non-sub-project office villages, thanks to the efforts of neighbouring and well-established co-ops, their creation depended, for the most part, on the conversion of already existing sub-project offices. In the 1990s, there were 445 of these, catering to 622 village development committees, but most of these were disbanded by the bank before they could be converted. That they were no longer performing well was part of the reason for this lapse into de-development, compounded by the Maoist armed conflict which made it ever more difficult to keep field-based officers functioning. As a result, the small farmer co-ops have largely been a programme in retreat.

The evolution, over nearly 40 years, of efforts based on small farmer groups has been typical of the development experience in Nepal: a roller coaster ride. When there is foreign aid around it surges; when that aid is withdrawn it slumps. That, as we have seen, is what happened with the Small Farmer Development Programme. In the case of its successor – the Small Farmer Co-operatives Limited – the original donor (German Technical Cooperation) is still engaged, but the support it is providing is nominal in relation to what is needed. It has made no effort to rescue this vital programme from stagnation, even though the vast majority of small farmers remain sunk in poverty. And the recent dramatic reduction in poverty across the country has nothing to do with foreign aid; households have done it themselves by finding work outside the country. Even so, and as is evident from Resham Bhattarai's remarkable transition from rags to riches, the small farmer co-ops have made an enormous difference in those areas where they have been put in place. This success, as we will now explain, has stemmed mainly from the same source as that which lies at the heart of the enterprising exodus to the Gulf: self-help.

The governance lessons from the small farmer co-ops

'Self-help' can be usefully unpacked with the aid of the typology of solidarities that were set out in Chapters 1 and 2. Much of the impetus – be it Resham Bhattarai on his native heath or the planeloads of poor Nepalis winging their way to Doha – is clearly from the individualist solidarity, but with a strong dose of egalitarianism too. This latter is the solidarity that is being mobilised in all those small farmer groups that are successful, and it is also what enables the workers in the Gulf to live together, cheaply, peaceably and in a mutually supportive way, while they are on their prolonged forays away from home. Nor is hierarchy absent; the three-tier structure of the co-ops depends on the country's administrative structure, and loans could not be extended without the legal framework – the local Land Revenue Office, in particular – that clarifies and upholds the property rights of those who are intent on bettering themselves. What *is* largely absent, however, is fatalism; there is little sign of the sort of 'beggar my neighbour' attitude characteristic of those who see things in a zero-sum way and are therefore distrustful of their fellows. But this is not to say that those solidarities, mutually complementary though they are, are in some sort of stable equilibrium; there is always contention. With some pushing for more autonomy, others for more mutual support, others for more authority and control and others crying 'What's the point?', and with endless disagreement as to just how much of each is appropriate to this or that transactional context, it is vital that there be forums within which all this clumsiness-enabling deliberation can take place. The three tiers, complicated though they may appear to those who want the market to do it all, or the collectivity, or the 'powers that be', or Lady Luck, can therefore be seen as providing those vital arenas. Most of the problems, as we will see, stem, not from the programme itself, but from its patchiness: from it not being made available to small farmers everywhere.

Once it has been handed over to them by the Agricultural Development Bank, the members of a small farmer co-op know that it is they who now own the organisation, an organisation that is managed by their own staff, recruited and paid for by themselves. They receive no grant or subsidy from the government or the donor for the purpose of management. Transactions, under these circumstances, are more efficiently conducted than was the case with the Small Farmer Development Programme, and loan disbursements and re-collections are similarly improved. Apart from those instances where there has been Maoist interference or intrusions by local political parties, there is a spirit of competition among the co-ops, with many of them consistently maintaining a 100 per cent recovery rate. The same has happened with the size and number of disbursements: an indication that the co-ops are vying with one another in their poverty-alleviating efforts. For instance, in each of the four original co-ops – handed over in Dhading District in 1993 – the average fresh loan disbursement increased from 1.5 million rupees in 1993/04 to three million in 1998.

Co-ops, once they have been handed over, tend to multiply, bringing ever more of the poor in their 'catchments' into the fold. The Naktajheel co-op in Dhanusha District, for instance, which was handed over in 2000 after 17 years as a sub-project office, had added 38 groups to its original 40 by 2002, dramatically increasing membership from 346 to 509 (Shrestha 2004). And Fatehpur in Bara District, where 57.4 per cent of its small farmers are already co-op members, is committed (in its annual report) to bringing in the remaining 523 households so as to achieve 100 per cent coverage (Fatehpur SFCL, 2006). However, the legal requirements for citizenship certificates and land ownership mean that, in many villages, 100 per cent membership is unattainable. But, even here, as we will see, ways around this unfortunate and 'poorest of the poor'-excluding obstacle have been found.

The 'richest of the poor' can also present problems. In Prithvinager in Jhapa District, for instance, where membership (at 1,557) is already rather large, the management is selective in its induction of new members. In view of their limited credit capabilities, they have chosen to protect their poorer members by denying membership to a rather large number of technically eligible aspirants on the grounds of their better economic status. These included 170 households that were already dealing directly with various banks, 360 ex-servicemen who were in receipt of fairly large pensions and a number of locals with regular jobs in government or other offices (Shrestha 2004).

Another problem has arisen with 'latecomers'. In Sri Antu (Resham Bhattarai's village), for instance, 502 out of the 873 households were co-op members in 2002. Since then, many of the non-members have been attracted to join but some of them have found that they cannot. Being spread out across all the wards, there turn out to be too few aspirants in some wards for them to form a new group. And the alternative – joining existing groups – is difficult because they require new members to make down payments equal to the savings each of their members has made.

Landless farmers, likewise, pose problems because the loans from the Agricultural Development Bank are extended only against collateral, which is invariably land. So, as happened with the Small Farmer Development Programme, it is these 'poorest of the poor' who find themselves excluded. However (and this is a crucial difference from that earlier programme, which was not 'owned' by the farmers themselves), co-op members do feel concerned about this and (especially in the Terai, where landless farmers are most numerous) have introduced a policy of 'supervised credit', lending the co-op's own money without collateral to a few landless farmers at a time. The income-generating activities that are made possible by these loans are then closely monitored by fellow co-op members. The co-op in the village of Prithivinagar, for instance, extends collateral-free credit up to a maximum of 5,000 rupees to each such member, subsequently raising the ceiling to a maximum of 10,000 rupees if their performance is satisfactory. They have found that after around three years of such supervised borrowing the borrowers are normally able to buy some land of their own (which, of course, is then available as collateral).

The great advantage of the Small Farmer Co-operatives Limited, we can now see, lies in their being effectively organised and self-sustaining entities owned by the people themselves. Moreover, now that they have demonstrably succeeded in bringing in the poorest of the poor, the elusive goal of hard-core poverty eradication is clearly achievable. There is therefore no need for fresh initiatives, such as those in which direct cash transfers are made to selected households (with all the problems inherent in their selection). What *is* needed, however, is that central authorities and donors recognise this, monitor the spread and performance of the co-ops and extend their support in such a way that the co-ops reach full countrywide coverage as quickly as possible. Before considering how that might best be done, however, we need to look at how the co-ops have got to grips with that other great divide: *gender inequality.*

While the Agricultural Development Bank insists that women make up at least 10 per cent of co-op membership, the proportion has actually been much higher. In a study of four co-ops (Shrestha 2004) female membership ranged between 36 per cent (in Prithvinagar) and 45 per cent (in Naktajheel). The Naktajheel example reveals that women's participation is positively linked to local accountability; in 2000, when it was transferred to local management, women made up just 20 per cent of the co-op membership but this rapidly increased to 45 per cent, thanks to all 38 of the incremental groups being composed exclusively of women. The reasoning of the co-op's (male) leadership had two strands; first, this prioritisation was justified because (as with the landless farmers) women were socially disadvantaged and, second, that they deserve this prioritisation because they tend to be disciplined borrowers and responsible homemakers. Unlike men, it was stressed, women are available in the village all the time, turn up for meetings, are little involved in politics and are true to their word. They are also more interested than men are in social activities and tend to be more committed to their income-generating activities (Shrestha 2004).

However, because the emphasis on women's participation back in the sub-project office days was largely cosmetic, their involvement across the co-ops is not uniform. If membership of a co-op was largely male at the time of conversion, and if the co-op was already large (as in Prithvinagar) or already had substantial small farmer coverage (as in Sri Antu), then women's participation would tend to remain small (unless membership policy was relaxed so as to allow more than one member per household).

Participation is attractive to women for two main reasons. First, it gives them the opportunity to earn their own income within their households: by setting up a village shop, for instance, or investing in cattle-, goat- or pig-rearing. Many, with accumulating experience, have now invested heavily in such activities and report that their lives have improved both financially and socially. They send their children (boys *and* girls) to school, have an optimistic view of the future and contribute to further group savings so as to be able to embark on further and more ambitious income-generating activities. In Sri Antu, for instance, four of the five members in a group that was formed in 1988 have each obtained credit 12 times; while the initial credits were around 1,500–5,000 rupees, three of them now have outstanding loans of 20,000–22,000 rupees each. And in just two years the initial saving rate of 10 rupees per month per member has risen to 50, a reflection of their rapidly enhanced resource capacity. One has borrowed as much as 65,000 rupees, investing it in tea, a cow and goats. Successful women such as these are seen as role models that others can realistically emulate.

The second attraction is the opportunity that co-op membership provides for social developments: learning to read and write, for instance, and acquiring various skills. Also, as earning members of the family, they participate in household decisions on a par with their menfolk and they do not face any restrictions on their participation in public activities, such as village- and district-wide meetings. Increasingly they draw the line at two children (though a son is still preferred) and four of the five in the Sri Antu group mentioned above say they would like to be born women again. And, when a male member of a mixed group remarked that having women as members was a bit inconvenient for the households concerned, he was bluntly told that that held true only for men like himself.

The operational details of the programme

The overall approach comprises three main components – *saving, credit* and *income-generating activities* – which, together, are significantly bolstered by the programme's access to the Agricultural Development Bank's *bulk lending facility*. While monthly individual (and redeemable) contributions to group savings are the primary requirement for membership, the programme has developed a range of savings portfolios so as to help co-ops to maximise their resource bases. The rates of monthly savings are decided by each small farmer group and generally range between five and 20 rupees (though some groups go even higher).

A further source of funds is the share capital that each group member must buy (though some elect to buy more than one share). While the shares are generally priced at a standard 100 rupees each, some ambitious co-ops have raised the price so as to generate capital more quickly. Naktajheel, for instance, raised its share price to 500 rupees, with the result that, while in 2004 the seven-year-old Prithvinagar (with 1,557 members) had a total share capital collection of some 700,000 rupees, the two-year-old Naktajheel (with just 509 members) had already made it to 500,000 rupees.

Another saving instrument is the Loan Security Fund, into which the Agricultural Development Bank requires each borrower to deposit a minimum of 2 per cent (redeemable) of the loan amount. This fund, as well as augmenting individual savings, provides a liquid means for the borrower to make timely interest payments on the loan, thereby making himself or herself eligible for a rebate. Since this saving is made immediately on receipt of a fresh loan, members are often willing to deposit more than the mandatory two per cent. In Naktajheel, for instance, they have gone for 10 per cent. In the aforementioned study, the four co-ops, with a total membership of 2,846, had, in 2002, a cumulative deposit of 3,755,000 rupees. This averages out at 1,319 rupees per member.

Yet another source of saving is the self-managed Livestock Insurance Scheme. This evolved out of the bank's credit programme as a means of protecting small farmers who took out livestock loans and then went bust when the animal died. The co-op charges a non-refundable annual premium of 5 per cent, which is then matched by the government. The premium decreases by one percentage point per year and is closed at the end of the third year, by which time the loan will have been repaid. The co-op's Livestock Insurance Committee determines the value of the livestock on the basis of prevailing market prices and, in the event of an animal's death, the policy holder receives 80 per cent of the insured value. The scheme is popular with members because, as well as covering against a serious risk, their premium payments remain in the co-op and are used to provide credit to other members. Furthermore, the co-ops, in order to lessen the mortality rate of the insured livestock (thereby reducing their payouts) provide support through their own veterinarians. Though they receive only two weeks' training by the district veterinary office; these veterinarians inoculate and treat the insured animals with considerable effectiveness. While most co-ops want further training for their vets (and are even willing to share the cost), this rudimentary veterinary support has already made the scheme a profitable proposition. In 2004, the four co-ops had together earned a total of 5,142,000 rupees from this insurance business, which averages out at 1,807 rupees per member.

Finally, in recent years, a further source of capital – limited banking – has become available to some co-ops. Limited banking – an initiative of Nepal's Central Bank – has been piloted by issuing licences to a number of local micro-finance organisations, including a few small farmer co-ops. Under this, co-ops run a limited range of banking services which enable their members to open savings and fixed deposit accounts, paying interest at 8 per cent, much higher than the 3–4 per cent paid by the commercial banks. Since this interest is free of income tax, and since commercial banks have a poor coverage of rural areas, limited banking has been attractive, making it an important source for local savings mobilisation. However, despite (or perhaps because of) this popular demand, the Central Bank has now stopped issuing further licences. In 2002, of the four co-ops studied, two – Prithvinagar and Sri Antu – held licences and had together mobilised 2,556,000 rupees in savings deposits and 439,000 rupees in fixed deposits. The co-ops themselves lend at higher rates and enjoy a comfortable interest spread of 8–9 per cent. Maoist rebels at that time were robbing money from these local finance centres with impunity, but the Sri Antu centre maintained that if the security situation were to improve (as it now has) it alone could mobilise up to four million rupees a year from this source.

Bulk borrowing facilities

Access to bulk loans – now channelled through the Small Farmer Development Bank – has its origins in the sub-project office days, when the Agricultural Development Bank lent to small farmer groups through its own staff, the group organisers. The bulk lending facility, coupled with the ever-increasing savings of their members, enables the co-ops to make relatively large loans towards the income-generating undertakings of their members. This unique facility, as well as distinguishing the co-ops from other micro-finance initiatives, points the way for commercial banks to invest profitably in rural areas, thereby helping to eradicate poverty without any recourse to foreign grants or loans. This is all the more feasible now that Nepal's banking sector is awash with remittances, adding up to hundreds of billions of rupees, even as it suffers from a chronic lack of evenness for investment.

Bulk loans to the co-ops are collateral-free, while the onward lending to co-op members is only against collateral (apart from the exceptions – landless farmers etc – mentioned earlier), which is almost always in the form of land ownership certificates. The Agricultural Development Bank's interest rate has been coming down over the years and currently stands between 9 and 12 per cent per year, the lower rate being applicable to borrowers who make timely repayments. While the co-ops are free to fix their own interest rates, the bank expects then to add at least 4–5 per cent so as to allow a 'margin' to meet their overhead costs. The co-ops, thanks to this income, are able to run their organisations with their own resources and they receive no grants or subsidies for the purpose from any quarter.

Some co-ops, in their zeal to expand their capital bases, have at times fixed their onward lending rates even higher. And frugal Naktajheel, while levying one of the highest interest rates (20 per cent) made do with just two paid staff, relying on volunteers from its board of directors as and when necessary. However, Prithvinagar, which is bigger and longer-established, runs an extensive range of services for its members and has a complement of 10 salaried staff. And Dumrawana, whose services extend to milk collection, packaging and marketing, along with livestock insurance, agricultural extension and a school, has a total of 52 staff on its payroll, of whom 38 are permanent.

Credit management

While the small farmer groups disburse credits from their own savings directly to their applying members, they also function as the primary level for their co-op's *annual credit plan*, which it has to submit to the Agricultural Development Bank as the basis for the bank's bulk lending to it. A group's allocation of a loan is based on the members' collective assessment of the applicant's prior credit performance in relation to the present request. Loans from the group's own savings are restricted to group members and are transacted at its regular meetings that are usually held several times a month. While the group loans are collateral-free, the main committee loans (which are larger) are made only against collateral. For instance, a five-member women's group in Prithvinagar, which in November 2002 had savings of just over 44,000 rupees, distributed that entire pot among all its members in loans that ranged from 5,000 to 20,000 rupees. However, when there are undistributed savings the money is deposited with the main committee, which then pays interest on it.

A major attraction for co-op members is the availability of cheap credit in relatively large sums; interest rates range between 16 and 17 per cent per year, compared with the 36 to 60 per cent charged by private moneylenders. While the co-ops are increasing their resources through their own internal savings portfolios, these resources remain somewhat limited in relation to member needs. The Agricultural Development Bank's bulk borrowing facility eases this bottleneck, making it possible for small farmers to invest relatively large sums in their income-generating ventures. Table 3.1 shows how this split pans out in the four co-ops that were studied.

The four co-ops, as we can see, disbursed an impressive 2.8 million rupees from their own savings, together with more than 17 million rupees through bulk lending from the Agricultural Development Bank. However, this imbalance – own savings just 16.3 per cent of bulk landing – does not reflect the savings that the small farmer groups handle on their own, that information

Table 3.1 Co-op versus bank share in investments

	Lending from coop own source (thousands of rupees)	Lending from ADBN bulk loan (thousands of rupees)	Own source as percentage of ADBN bulk loan	Total loans disbursed (thousands of rupees)	Per member credit (thousandth of rupees)
Naktajheej	1,153	5,145	22.4	6,298	13.2
Prithvinagar	649	5,549	11.7	6,198	4.0
Sri Antu	493	4,155	11.9	4,648	9.3
Samaalbung	525	2,430	21.6	2,955	9.1

Source: Shrestha (2004: 33). ADBN stands for Agricultural Development Bank Nepal.

not being available within the co-ops. Also, not all members, particularly those members who have outstanding loans, borrow in any given year. So actual loan sizes are generally larger than the averages given in the table.

In marked contrast to the Small Farmer Development Programme days, this self-management of credit by the co-ops has ensured that credit is 'properly' used: used, that is, for the stated income-generating purposes. Under the previous regime, credit was tied to the annual cycle of agricultural activities. Small farmers, in consequence, quickly learnt how to exploit this seasonality, borrowing for an activity that fitted the current 'credit season' and then using the loan for something else. Bank officials, because they were under foreign aid pressure to make inflated lending (the 'disburse or die' mantra that we have encountered in earlier chapters), readily went along with this, even though they often suspected the loans would not be used for their stated purposes.

This behaviour was then further fuelled by the generally widespread temptations towards rent-seeking. Indeed, bank officials, when they look back, concede that only about 10 per cent of the lending in those days was used for its stated purpose, and this despite their being required to regularly supervise their clients' projects. The oft-recounted joke about those field visits was that the borrower would take the official to the village pasture and point out to him, at a good distance, his neighbour's livestock contentedly grazing, assuring him that they were his own and had been bought with the credit that had been extended to him.

This situation has been completely reversed; at least 90 per cent of credit is now used for the stated purposes. The reason, of course, is that members now have a stake in the proper use of credit and in the proper functioning of their co-op. Indeed, a borrower's loan request is now scrutinised at three levels: small farmer group, inter-group and main committee. For instance, in Samaalbung – a village in Ilam District that borders India – cross-border trading (comprising the export of brooms, potatoes, cardamom, ginger, peas and chilli and the import of rice, salt, oil, kerosene and livestock feed) has proved so profitable that the co-op decided to allocate 373,000 rupees of its own money to further promote it. This was lent to 12 members, the largest loan being 100,000 rupees and the smallest 14,000, the allocation being based on the recipients' demonstrated creditworthiness. Initially there were 25 applicants (from among the 57 small farmer groups, totalling 362 members). This was shortlisted at the inter-group level to just 15 and further reduced to 12 by the main committee. Personal recommendations were not entertained, and even the chairman of the village development council, realising his ineffectiveness, stopped backing any individual loan-seekers.

The credit system, thanks to its devolution, has become more versatile and better able to address the wide-ranging needs and priorities of co-op members. And where the bank's rules still cannot accommodate investment for certain portfolios the co-ops now use their own resources. In Naktajheel, for instance, sugar cane is a major cash crop and is crushed to produce unrefined sugar (*sakkar* or *gnund*), for which there is a good market. But it takes 50,000 rupees to install a crusher and the bank's rules set a ceiling of 40,000. The co-op therefore lent the additional 10,000 rupees from its own internal sources. Similarly, in Prithvinagar, where going to work in the Gulf States has become quite popular, the co-op has created a special portfolio, lending up to 100,000 rupees, to enable its members to cover their up-front costs without having to go to the moneylenders (who charge around 60 per cent interest).

Co-op autonomy has also helped members in the valuation of their collateral. Under the previous regime the bank's policy on valuation was very conservative, and borrowers often found themselves with less credit than they wanted. Now, with local autonomy and local knowledge, valuations can reflect market prices, enabling larger loans without any accompanying increases in risk.

Increased autonomy has also made it possible for co-ops to make allocations to members at times of misfortune. Most small farmer groups, for instance, have a standing rule for extending interest-free credit to members with personal crises, such a death in the family. And one seven-member group in Prithvinagar has generously provided a non-refundable grant of 5,000 rupees to tide over funeral expenses.

The Prithvinagar co-op has further used its autonomy to encourage better performance. It has distinguished four categories of members: the landless, who (as explained earlier) can borrow up to 10,000 rupees on 'supervised credit', those eligible to borrow up to just 30,000 rupees, those eligible for 50,000, and tea-growers, who can borrow up to 90,000. Graduation to higher categories is then permitted for those whose credit utilisation and repayment records are good enough. Since such promotions have to be recommended by the inter-group and approved by the main committee, this sharpens and intensifies supervision within the overall system.

This partial devolution of authority to the co-ops has also been beneficial to the 'devolvee', the Agricultural Development Bank, particularly in relation to the recovery of the delinquent loans – dubbed 'handover loans' – that it inherited from the previous regime. In Prithvinagar, for instance, such loans amounted in 1995 to 12,722,000 rupees but, by 2002, they had been reduced to just 461,000 rupees. Naktajheel, which in 2000 inherited a total of 29 million rupees in handover loans, did even better, reducing them to zero by 2003. This easy re-collection stems, of course, from the intimate and intense webs of relationships that exist between the co-ops' management and their borrower members, a phenomenon that was largely absent under the previous regime. Bank staff attribute this surge in 'social capital', in large part, to their paid employees now being able to draw constructively on an extensive contingent of unpaid (but reliable and knowledgeable) officials located at the inter-group and main committee levels. However, for all these impressive successes, not everything in the small farmer co-operative garden is lovely.

The current problems

The co-ops' credit management is still beset by difficulties, some of which, it is fair to say, are beyond its control; others, to some extent, are self-inflicted. A major headache in recent years has been the worsening of the recovery rate on loans from the Agricultural Development Bank source (in contrast with the repayment rate on loans from 'own savings', which has always remained at 100 per cent). The additional 2 per cent interest that co-ops slap onto loan defaults has proved to be an insufficient deterrent, for two reasons. First, since the market rate of interest is even higher, it is in the borrower's interest to delay repayment as long as possible. Second, borrower defaulting is inadvertently encouraged by the bank's long-standing practice of writing off parts of the principal and interest on bad loans in the hope of salvaging what it can. Although this facility is available only to the bank's direct borrowers, and not to autonomous bodies such as the co-ops, it *was* available during the sub-project office days, and this has encouraged a lingering hope – 'one day we too will make it' – among current borrowers. In Sri Antu, for instance, only 84 out of its 434 borrowers (19 per cent) repay on time. And neighbouring Samaalbung, with 50 regular repayers out of 326 borrowers, things are only slightly better. The feeling among the co-op management is that only a stronger disincentive will deter the defaulters, who, it seems, are mostly from among the better off co-op members.[3]

Until quite recently, the Maoist insurgency has taken its toll on the co-ops. The Maoists, in their efforts to paralyse the government, instructed the co-op members not to repay their loans, under threat of 'physical action' (i.e. maiming). These were unpleasant and trust-destroying days, but most co-ops managed to escape the rebels' attentions by keeping a low profile.

A perennial problem has been the lack of government and donor interest. This has severely retarded replication across the country and also prevented the existing co-ops from accessing the technical support of government agencies in rural areas. In Naktajheel, for instance, the local District Agricultural Development Office had to be shamed into providing support, World Food Day in 2002 having provided the co-op's president with the opportunity to lash out at a senior agricultural official who had been specially invited to the village (in recognition of his organisation's performance there!). And in Prithvinagar, which is the pioneer of small farmer tea-planting, the technical support for this difficult-to-grow crop came not from the government's tea agency but from a chance visit by an Indian professor, who subsequently arranged for visits by various Indian experts who trained the co-op members in the requisite skills (particularly pruning, which is the trickiest aspect of tea cultivation and can make a big difference to the yield).

Ideally, as the programme expands, the bulk borrowing facility should not remain an Agricultural Development Bank monopoly; co-ops should be able to 'shop around' among the regular commercial banks. However, because of the Agricultural Development Bank's long association with the co-ops, it has been happy to go along with the arrangement whereby the collateral for loans – the land ownership certificates – are lodged with the co-ops, and this is not something that is congenial to the commercial banks. A solution, in the form of a supplementary document – a 'second charge' – should be possible, but it is not yet in place.

Finally, there is a 'second-generation' problem. An increasing number of successful borrowers, who are now intent on taking out longer loans, wish to deal directly with the Agricultural Development Bank, rather than through their co-op. In Sri Antu, for instance, following the switch into tea-growing, there has been a major spurt in the demand for credit. As the co-op manager explained, 'people whose credit need was limited to 5,000 rupees only a few years ago now seek a loan of more than 100,000 rupees'. Because the small farmer group and inter-group levels often do not endorse these requests for large loans, the successful farmers are starting to feel suffocated by a system that previously had breathed new life into them. Group cohesiveness is being threatened and the co-ops are in danger of becoming institutions that are in conflict with themselves.

Various options have been proposed for dealing with the second-generation problem – co-ops in conflict with themselves – and some are already being tried. In Sri Antu, for instance, some 60 co-op members now transact directly with the bank for their larger loans. In other villages those seeking larger loans have been able to persuade less ambitious fellow members to let them use their share of their Agricultural Development Bank loans. Even so, it is evident that the wealth-generating success of the co-ops has to some extent eroded the 'social capital' that made that wealth-generation possible. In terms of the typology set out in Chapters 1 and 2, individualism is beginning to supplement egalitarianism. But that is part and parcel of the process of development, and the game is still 'positive-sum'. Only if things become so unbalanced that they reverted to the sort of 'zero-sum' and 'beggar my neighbour' (i.e. fatalist) state of affairs that characterised so much of rural life in Nepal in the pre-co-op days would there be cause for alarm. In order to ascertain whether there is any real likelihood of that reversion to fatalism happening we need to look at all the other desirable things, besides income-generation, that have been achieved by the co-ops.

From income-generation to community development

Co-op members, as we have seen, can borrow only for their stated income-generating purposes, which are then implemented under the watchful eyes of fellow members, leaving virtually no scope for any jiggery-pokery. Those activities range from livestock-rearing, through vegetable-growing, orchard-planting, sugarcane cultivation and cereal crop production, to blacksmithing, rice-milling and so on, all dependent on the local terrain and the market potential. The women's groups tend more towards small livestock (e.g. goats and poultry), retail shopkeeping and vegetable-growing.

Trading is often a major activity too. In Naktajheel, for instance, 115 of the co-op members used their loans for trading during 2001–02, importing goods from outside to sell in the village and its surroundings and exporting local goods and produce. In Sri Antu and Samaalbung, cash crops have proved highly profitable, particularly large cardamoms, *amleso* (for brooms) and potatoes. The micro-climate favours these crops, with the large cardamom being particularly attractive because it grows on poor-quality land and needs little labour. *Amleso* finds a ready market, in both Nepal and India, and fetches a decent price, while the leaves make good fodder for the livestock. And the various 'specialist' potatoes from Nepal's hill regions (*Godar aloo* being the most prized) are also highly profitable.

Moreover, the co-ops, as well as promoting the desirable, have shown that, thanks to their organised strength, they can also prevent the undesirable. In Jhapa and Ilam Districts, for instance, the large tea estates were creating adverse conditions for the crops in the adjoining fields of small farmers, who then found themselves forced to sell their meagre holdings to these large commercial concerns. The Prithvinagar co-op was able to put an end to this creeping dispossession by mounting a sustained lobbying campaign with the government, eventually succeeding in getting tea included in the small farmer lending portfolio of the Agricultural Development Bank. Tea-growing is now a major and lucrative income-generating activity in many of the co-ops in this area. In Sri Antu, for instance, one 60-ropani (three-hectare) farm has tea on 35 ropani, forest on 10, *amleso* on five and a kitchen garden (maize, potatoes etc) on another five, with the remaining five ropani left as fallow slope. Another farmer, with 120 ropani, has tea on 50, forest (for fuelwood and fodder) on 30, maize, potatoes and ginger on 20 and cardamom on the remaining 20.

The choice of income-generating activities lies with the individual farmer and is based on his or her personal experience and sense of confidence in managing them. So the resources are always tailored to the needs and capacities of the individual farmers, and these then change over the years with increased experience and confidence. The small farmer groups, in consequence, function as 'clearing houses', where members are continually learning from both their own and one another's experiences. While the credit-induced emphasis on income-generation turns poor farmers into active entrepreneurs, they are never left to fend for themselves; the group members, since they are not in direct competition with one another, are fellow travellers on the development road.

Indeed, the co-ops often provide credit for 'group projects'. These are usually undertakings requiring a large initial investment, for which the group members pool their resources, including credit. In Naktajheel, for instance, four group members pooled their land (totalling 0.3 hectare) and credits (amounting to 20,000 rupees) in order to establish a horticultural nursery. Two years later they were turning a net profit of 250,000 rupees. They market their produce in local centres and villages, and buyers from India often come to them. They would be doing even better, they say, if they had been able to receive technical support from the relevant government agencies.

Individualised but not isolated

Confident entrepreneurs who are also learning from one another and, when it makes sense, pooling their resources are far from being like those ruthless go-it-alone egomaniacs who populate so much of capitalist mythology ('Don't get mad, get even', 'Nice guys come last' or 'How I turned Chrysler around'). So it is not surprising to find that the co-ops also contribute significantly to the general development of their communities, providing (or helping to provide) a wide range of public (or common-pool) goods: drinking water, sanitation, child-care centres, track and trail construction, forest conservation and so on.

In Naktajheel they have grouped the various development activities under three headings: 'collective', 'social' and 'community'. The 'collective' activities include savings, irrigation, afforestation, forest nursery, a 'service centre' area in the village, fisheries promotion, livestock insurance and a school. To encourage fruit cultivation, for instance, it once bought a full truckload of assorted fruit saplings and sold them to individual members. 'Social' activities consist of latrine construction and the installation of drinking water tube wells, while 'community' activities take in health care (including immunisation against diphtheria, pertussis and tetanus), veterinary services, cultural activities, women's development and family planning.

Prithvinagar's co-op has promoted a '10 plus 2' school in its area, and also created a special 'unit' within its organisational structure for education, health and community development activities. This unit is responsible for women's literacy, women's empowerment, kitchen garden promotion, health camps, afforestation, environmental protection and child development. In 2001 and 2002, for instance, the unit, with the help of two international non-governmental organisations, provided legal education and empowerment training for 492 of its women members. And it has gone on to organise free health clinics and child development (in conjunction with the local schools and the district administrative office). It has distributed vegetable seeds to its members so as to encourage vegetable-growing and it has formed some 20 women's groups to fight polygamy, extend support to vulnerable women and, above all, to curb drinking and gambling in the community. They once organised a rally of 4,000 women against drinking in the village.

All in all, these are impressive achievements, efforts that should enable these communities to reach the Millennium Development Goals (and more) from the 'bottom up', rather than just sitting there just waiting (probably for a very long time) for them to be provided from on high. Economic improvement, access to services and an enhanced sense of confidence, small farmers report, have been the major gains from the co-op programme. Most members are now able to send their children (boys *and* girls) to school, their living conditions have improved and they can now afford better food, clothing and shoes. Most co-ops have a provision for interest-free loans in the event of a death in the family, and there is now a widespread awareness of the need for family planning (with most opting for temporary devices). The preferred number of children is two, which, if held to, would soon put Nepal in the 'demographic transition' (a stable or falling population). A son, however, is still a priority in most families.

The best gain of all, in the opinion of both male and female members, is their new-found ability to speak in front of other people. In the past, they recall, their very presence was not tolerated by the rich and powerful, let alone their venturing an opinion! Now that has totally changed; a small farmer from Naktajheel, for instance, has become an elected member of the district-level assembly. Literacy levels – traditionally low, especially among women – have risen, thanks to the need for co-op members to keep track of their finances. In Naktajheel the co-op requires its members to at least be able to sign their names. Out of 125 adult women in one of its villages, Sripur, 25 can now do · this.

While many young men in Prithvinagar still want to go to the Gulf States to work, migration to India has been reduced to a trickle: from 25 per cent in the past to a mere 5 per cent now in Sri Antu. In Samaalbung, which adjoins India, relatives visiting from across the (open) border find it more prosperous (and this despite the fact that India provides many subsidised commodities for its low-income people). Co-op members expect that things will get even better. In Prithvinagar they feel that, 10 years down the road, they will have more than 300 hectares under tea, all small farmer-owned, sufficient for them to run a big (i.e. commercial tea estate-sized) factory of their own. The co-op leadership anticipates that, once they have this factory, each member household will have at least one *pucca* (brick-built) house and a motorbike. Even the poorest in Naktajheel have enjoyed a transformation of sorts in their economy. They no longer need to make ends meet by felling trees in the fragile Churia Range to sell firewood in the markets, and many of them have been able to expand their holdings by buying land from local absentee landlords.

In Sri Antu and Samaalbung the economic transformation has now shifted development priorities towards infrastructural improvements – roads, electricity, telecommunications – and free labour is readily mobilised to that end. All of the electricity poles in the area were carried in, by co-op members, from Fikal Bazaar, a good two hours' walk. And the co-op official, noting the distressingly low voltage in the area, said they would gladly go to Fikal to carry a new transformer on their shoulders if it were to be provided for the village. Other needs include a high school, an expanded drinking water system, more tea factories, agricultural technicians and the black-topping of the 15km road from Pashupati Nagar to Sri Antu. According to the former president of the Sri Antu District Council, the changes that have already come to Sri Antu have rendered the place 'nothing less than a paradise'.

Conclusion: unresponsive government and self-centred donors

An external review of Small Farmer Co-operatives Limited, conducted in 2003 by a team of German and Nepalese experts (Koch *et al.* 2003), pronounced it to be 'probably one of the most successful – if not the most successful – poverty alleviation programmes in Nepal'. They judged it to be 'sustainable, cost-efficient and owned by the target group'. Furthermore, referring to the Maoist insurgency raging at that time, the report noted that 'despite the crisis, some financial figures improved, such as deposits, paid-up capital and outstanding loans, a clear sign for trust on the side of the members'. The co-ops function, it observed, 'as important and effective forums for social and economic development among their members in the communities' and further confirmed that, since the days of the previous regime, 'the fortunes of many small farmer members have dramatically changed for the better'. Noting that, 'for bureaucratic reasons, its progress is held back', it asserted that the programme 'has the potential of becoming one of the most effective and self-sustainable institutional mechanisms for poverty reduction and good governance in Nepal'. The programme, it continued, 'should be liberated from bureaucratic hurdles' and its 'replication should become one of the core products of RUFIN' (the branch of GTZ – German aid in Nepal – responsible for the programme). It specifically recommended that there should be 'at least 400 SFCL (co-ops) with 400,000 households in four years ('four – four – four'); at least 30 percent female membership; at least 30 percent of disadvantaged households'.

These recommendations, despite their forcefulness, fell on deaf ears, on both sides of the aid aisle: government and donors. The national planning system has not even acknowledged the existence of the co-op programme, as is evident from the lack of reference to it in its successive Five-Year Plan documents. Instead, the planners have chosen to parrot what has been handed down to them by the donors, the latest instance of which has been the IMF/World Bank's Poverty Reduction Strategy Paper (IMF/World Bank 2003), which became the framework for Nepal's Tenth Five-Year-Plan (2002–07). This handed-down framework subsequently triggered a multimillion-dollar loan to the government to launch an adaptation of the micro-finance initiatives that were being widely implemented by various non-governmental organisations. The Poverty Reduction Strategy Paper makes no mention of the decade-old and home-grown co-op programme.

Despite all the pious rhetoric around poverty reduction – not least the United Nations' much-vaunted Millennium Development Goals – there has been little effort, nationally or internationally, to address poverty on an effective and measurable basis (as is evident, for instance, in the plucked-out-of-thin-air estimates of safe drinking water provision; see Chapter 10). Nepal's governance may be democratic in form but it has proved to be remarkably unresponsive to the needs and aspirations of the people, especially the poor.[4]

While the volume of foreign aid has been increasing in recent years, and while the stated purpose of most of that aid has been poverty reduction, it has been remarkably ineffective. Nepal has been receiving foreign aid since 1949 and yet it is still chronically poor. Its foreign debt in 2005 was 233 billion rupees, more than 49 per cent of its annual Gross Domestic Product, and required 17 billion rupees of principal and interest payments per year. Its per capita Gross Domestic Product is 271 US dollars a year – one of the lowest in the world – and the Gini Coefficient of income distribution, at 0.41, is the highest in South Asia. All of which suggests that aid provision and poverty are positively related.

Key to this positive relationship is *donor* hegemony. Nepal's development agenda has always been donor-driven and donor-defined, and it is the donors' officials who exercise the decisive power in its allocation (as exemplified by the World Bank's Poverty Reduction Strategy Paper and its translation into Nepal's Tenth Five-Year Plan). These officials, as they touch down briefly in Nepal in their stately progress through the world's impoverished regions, constitute an unaccountable über-caste: the Lords of Poverty, as they have been called. Inadequately informed about the country's development experience and the factors that underlie that challenge,[5] and preoccupied with their personal ambitions, they climb the career ladder by foisting their self-defined agenda onto the receiving country. A harsh judgement, some may object, but how else can we explain the German neglect, following its change of guard in the relevant section, of the small farmer co-ops, or the World Bank's failure to acknowledge the programme's existence?

The reason these officials have such an easy time with their counterparts in the national government – able to push anything they feel like pushing – is the 'democratic deficit': the aforementioned lack of accountability among the country's political and bureaucratic decision makers (compounded, of course, by a matching unaccountability among the über-caste). Donors always want to hear the word 'yes' in response to their proposals, and their government counterparts are largely unprepared to say 'no' (because, in most cases, they are unable to explain 'why'; that would require them to understand the concerns and aspirations of the supposed beneficiaries, and to then be responsive to them). No surprise, therefore, that foreign aid has been ineffective for more than half a century, and that this sustained unresponsiveness has eventually ended up provoking a murderous 'People's War'.

For the poor of Nepal, and for its small farmers in particular, the situation, if we assume that development can come only from the donor-national government hegemony, is one of stalemate: in excess of 50 years of stalemate, in fact. But, if we look at what has happened once the small farmer co-ops became largely autonomous, or at the social and economic transformations that have been set in train by all those enterprising citizens who have gone off to work in the Gulf (not that they are unconnected; each, as we have seen, is involved in funding the other), then that continuing stalemate becomes increasingly irrelevant.

Notes

1 At the current exchange rate. A direct comparison, however, would be misleading. Anyone in Nepal making 100,000 rupees a year is doing well. And European visitors to Nepal are astonished by how cheap everything seems to be.
2 See von Furer-Haimendorf (1975). A Sherpa woman would likely marry two or more brothers – a set-up that facilitated the mix of subsistence agriculture and trade – but many women also engaged in trading (and nowadays in all sorts of tourism-related business).
3 This is supported by the small farmer group experience, where peer pressure to repay has led to the rates on potential defaulters being raised as high as 60 per cent: the market (i.e. moneylenders') rate.
4 The Paris Declaration on Aid Effectiveness (OECD 2008) explicitly charges donors and partner countries to work 'in a spirit of mutual accountability', the assumption being that saying this will make it happen. But that would require a marked softening of donor hegemony, and of that there is no sign. Indeed, the declaration emerged from a meeting of 'Ministers and officials from developed and developing countries, as well as senior officials from bilateral and multi-lateral development institutions': from a meeting, that is, of the hegemons.
5 As is abundantly clear from the Bara Forest fiasco described in Chapter 1, augmented by numerous instances (such as the unawareness of the 'khuwa line' that was responsible for Bhattedanda's unfortunate predicament) in the subsequent case study chapters.

4 Trickle to torrent to irrelevance?

Six decades of foreign aid in Nepal

Sudhindra Sharma

The Nepalese state, because of its dependence on foreign aid, has to take donor preferences and expectations into consideration and cannot act entirely on its own. In so far as these forces are beyond its control, foreign aid sets out structures that limit the Nepalese state's space to manoeuvre. Aid thus constitutes the invisible ceiling, so to speak, beyond which the Nepalese state cannot go. Foreign aid, however, is not the only structural constraint faced by the Nepalese state. It has always had to contend with the constraints posed by whoever happens to be the hegemonic powers to the north and to the south: in China and India.[1] From its earliest nation-building days, Nepal has had to reckon with this particular geopolitical constraint: 'a yam between two boulders', as Prithvi Narayan Shah, the King of Gorkha – who unified Nepal towards the end of the eighteenth century – so aptly put it.

Indeed, it was only with the dawning of the Age of Aid (at Bretton Woods in 1945) that Nepal became subject to the second structural constraint, a constraint that then became ever more pronounced as the country became ever more dependent on aid to finance what is euphemistically called its 'development'. While the first constraint did not disappear, it was absorbed into the second, to some considerable extent, as both India and China became prominent players within Nepal's 'donor community'. This partial absorption has made it difficult to tell just what is happening to these two sets of constraints. While many may feel that the second set – the aid constraints – has created something of a one-way process, with both the volume of external assistance and Nepal's dependence on it becoming ever greater, there are, as we will show, some signs that it has recently gone into reverse. What matters, we will argue, is not the absolute volume of aid but its volume relative to the size of Nepal's economy, and that, in turn very much depends on how you measure it.

If you use just official GNP (Gross National Product) – the economy, that is, as it shows up in terms of the things the government is able to measure – then there is little sign of any reversal. But if you include remittances from all the Nepalese citizens who are temporarily working overseas – a sum that is difficult to estimate but which has certainly burgeoned in recent years – then ODA (Official Development Aid) becomes of less and less significance. And if the 'home-grown' informal economy is also included – again, it is not easy

Table 4.1 Remittance inflow to Nepal

	2009/10	2010/11	2011/12	2012/13	2013/14	2014/15*
Remittance inflow (in billion NRs)	231.7	253.6	359.6	434.6	543.3	371.0
Percentage change	10.5	9.4	41.8	20.9	25.0	4.0
Ratio to GDP	19.4	18.5	23.5	25.7	28.0	–
Share of remittance income in current transfer income	80.5	81.5	84.0	87.3	86.0	88.2

Source: Nepal Rashtra Bank, quoted in MoF (2015).
Note: *First eight months

to measure and even more difficult if you add in the illegal and the 'grey' economies – then the decline becomes even more pronounced (see Table 4.1) It is a bit like iceberg-weighing; do you calculate its mass from what you can see of it or from what you know is there?

Nor is the partial absorption fixed. Development aid is increasingly being subordinated to climate change concerns: 'mainstreaming' (in terms of the twin goals of mitigation and adaptation) is the word that is used. Quite what the structural constraints that are being generated by international negotiations over climate change are is by no means clear, but what is certain is that the members of Nepal's donor community are finding themselves increasingly subject to them. Moreover, since Nepal has a miniscule carbon footprint compared to those of its donor community, and since it is almost unaffected by the deep technological lock-ins to fossil fuels that, to varying degrees, afflict all its donors, it is all set to float free of these latest constraints. This, perhaps, is how the Age of Aid is ending: not with a bang, with a whimper.

The first two decades: the 1950s and 1960s

Nepal's Rana regime – often characterised as isolationist (which it was) and feudal (which it was not) – emerged virtually overnight in 1846, in the wake of the spectacular Kot (courtyard) Massacre in the Royal Palace. The regime, which soon became symbiotic with the southern 'boulder' – the British Raj in India – finally collapsed in February 1951, just four years after India had gained its independence (and its partition from West and East Pakistan, with the latter eventually becoming Bangladesh). Foreign aid had made its way into Nepal just before these momentous regional transformations, in the form of a gesture of support from the United States Office Mission (or USOM, as USAID was then called) to the tottering Rana regime. This largely symbolic transfer stemmed directly from the United States' strategic concerns to support Nepal as a 'front-line state', Communist China – the northern 'boulder' – having occupied Tibet (another yam-like little country) in 1949 and subsequently consolidated its rule there.[2] Since the Ranas, though certainly authoritarian, were quite development-minded,[3] we can see that development aid was really something of a misnomer from day one. Far from meshing constructively with existing Rana development policy, it was just one of the first shots in the Cold War.[4]

Newly independent India, under its Indian National Congress government, was not as sympathetic towards the Ranas as the imperial British had been. The Nepali Congress Party, which had been sheltering in India, had already initiated a campaign against the regime, and in 1950 it launched an armed revolt against it in parts of the Terai (the low-lying strip of Nepal along its open southern border with India). These insurrectionary activities, along with Britain's withdrawal from India and an alliance with King Tribuvan – Nepal's ceremonial but powerless monarch – were all that was needed to cause the century-old regime's collapse. With mediation from India, a settlement – it was called the Delhi Compromise – was then worked out between the king, the Ranas and the Nepalese Congress. In 1951, the powers of the monarchy (which had been eclipsed for a century and a half) were restored, an interim government was formed and the Ranas were out in the cold. A legitimate but powerless king, so the popular narrative went, had risked his throne for the common people and enabled Nepal to finally emerge 'from beneath the carapace of feudal despotism'.[5]

Post-colonial India's role in the events of 1950 and 1951 brought two institutions centre stage in Nepal: assertive monarchy and political parties. These two institutions soon became rivals and, over the next 60 or so years, have existed in an uneasy and unstable tension. Constitutional monarchy and multi-party democracy were seen as Nepal's twin pillars and supported by the international community (including India but not China), but *assertive* monarchy, and the parties' resistance to it, have from the outset undermined this 'Westminster-on-Bagmati' ideal. These political changes, as we have already seen, also coincided with the beginnings of the Age of Aid. Those Nepalis who had fought for political change, as well as being energised by their encounters with the anti-colonial and democratic movement in India, were much impressed by the modern amenities that had been introduced to India by the British. Nepal's new rulers were therefore eager to modernise their country and, as luck would have it, the resources that they saw as vital to the achievement of that goal had just become available, in the shape of US president Harry Truman's Four Point Program, (the fourth point of which was the addressing of the huge problems of underdeveloped nations).[6]

The 1951 revolution had abruptly terminated the seclusion of Nepal that the Ranas had painstakingly enforced for more than a century. The country thus found itself opened up to a host of novel political, social and economic influences, a transition that has been characterised as Nepal's first encounter with modernity (Khanal 1977). The forces of tradition, however, were still quite strong, among them the Rana clan itself, whose members were later to stage a comeback, regrouping, after King Tribuvan's death in 1955, around

King Mahendra, who did not share his father's democratic convictions. Politics throughout the 1950s were therefore far from stable. It was a period of experimentation with democracy, with cabinets being formed and dissolved, advisory assemblies being established, disbanded and re-established and parties being created and fragmented (Blaikie *et al.* 1980). Inevitably, all this instability strengthened the monarchy's hand, eventually to the point where the king was able to sweep the political parties aside.

When a long-overdue parliamentary election was held in February 1959, the Nepali Congress Party won by a two-thirds majority and formed a government headed by Bisheswar Prasad Koirala, 'B. P.', as he was popularly known. Such a decisive outcome was a threat to an assertive monarchy and, in December 1960, King Mahendra, using the emergency powers vested in him by the then constitution, arrested BP, dissolved parliament and assumed executive control.[7] The Nepalese Congress challenged the king's move, on the grounds that, there being no discernible emergency, it was unwarranted, and an insurrection, with tacit Indian support, soon got under way in the Terai. Things might well have swung back, and away from the king, had there not been some dramatic geopolitical developments. In 1962 China launched a massive attack on India's Himalayan territories, to both the east and west of Nepal. With India's security suddenly vulnerable across its extensive northern borders, the Nepalese Congress's insurrection had to be curtailed in the interest of India's security within the entire region, a switch that worked very much in the king's favour, ushering in 30 years of 'guided' (i.e. party-less) democracy.[8] It was during these long years, when contesting voices were unable to make themselves heard, that foreign aid really got going in Nepal. Of course, most of Nepal's donor countries had plenty of contesting voices 'back home', but in Nepal (and as is spelt out in Chapters 1 and 3) they could not be heard.[9]

Though the United States was the first country to sign an agreement of co-operation, it was projects supported by India that were the first to get under way, in the wake of the first visit to Kathmandu, just four months after the overthrow of Rana rule, by Prime Minister Jawaharlal Nehru. Later that year (1951) an Indian military mission arrived to modernise Kathmandu's airport and built a road up to the capital from the border with India (the few cars in the city, up to that time, having been laboriously carried up through the jungle-clad Himalayan foothills by teams of porters). Initially, Indian aid was concentrated on administrative reform, transport and communication, and was shaped, first, by its security concerns over China and, second, by its desire to counterbalance the USA's growing influence in what it saw as its 'back yard'.

Following King Mahendra's assertive move (1960), Nepal's relationship with India chilled, with Nepal seeing its dependence on India as inimical to its national interests. King Mahendra therefore sought to establish diplomatic and economic relations with other countries, thereby lessening its giant southern neighbour's hold over it (Panday 1999). Various international and regional initiatives then facilitated Nepal's move in this direction:

- Nepal became one of the 29 countries to attend the Afro-Asian Conference in Bandung, where China and India were two of the principal actors.
- Nepal had finally become a member of the United Nations in 1955, establishing diplomatic relations with China later that same year and with the Soviet Union the year after.[10]
- In 1960 Nepal established diplomatic relations with Pakistan, a step that simultaneously completed the framework for the conduct of its international relations and symbolised its independence from India (India and Pakistan having been to war with each other three times in the past 60 years).

From that moment on, the flow of aid into Nepal steadily swelled from a trickle into a torrent, its mainstream further boosted by an ever-increasing number of tributaries. The USA initially granted $15 million to the B. P. Koirala government (the finance minister having written to the US mission about the financial crisis faced by the newly elected Congress administration) and, though it disapproved of King Mahendra's actions, it did not turn off the tap, that decision being much influenced by its desire to keep Nepal free from communist infiltration. India, not to be outdone, and despite its grievance about the king's actions, also continued its aid programme, which by then was involved with forestry, mineral exploitation, local development, maternity care, airfield construction, irrigation and drinking water supply (Mihaly 2003).

China, which, back in 1956, had granted Nepal cash and commodities to the value of $12.6 million (along with the freedom to use it in whatever way it pleased), was fairly unconcerned about the king's actions and therefore saw no reason not to continue. Chinese aid was broadly spread but with some focusing on transportation and industry (especially import substitution so that Nepal could become less dependent on Indian consumer goods). Chinese aid was strategic in nature: a goodwill gesture for Nepal's support of its position in Tibet and for not engaging in activities that could be construed as interfering in China's internal affairs. Post-1962, the goodwill further extended to Nepal's strict neutrality during the Sino-Indian border conflicts.

The Soviet Union, anxious not to be left out, signed an agreement with Nepal in 1959. This was for $7.5 million worth of free economic and technical assistance for a range of projects: the 2.4 MW Pananti hydroelectric installation, a 1,000-ton daily capacity sugar factory and a survey for the Simara–Janakpur section of the East–West Highway. There was also $100,000 towards a 50-bed hospital in Kathmandu and a grant of 15 scholarships for Nepalese students (the latter coming as an unofficial birthday present to the king during his visit to Moscow). According to Mihaly (2003), Russian aid had the immediate aim of securing King Mahendra's friendship and the longer-term aim of supporting Nepal's non-alignment initiatives. These gestures were portrayed as alternatives to economic reliance on the West for Nepal's modernisation (Khadka 1997).

Though British influence was minimal in the aftermath of the 1951 revolution, the bond between the two countries was kept intact through the long-established arrangement whereby Nepalese volunteers were recruited into Britain's Gurkha regiments. A combination of sentiment about Gurkha soldiers' past exploits and the desirability of keeping them in the British army (especially in connection with the 'emergency' in Malaya) formed the initial basis for Britain's aid programme (Mihaly 2003). From a modest scholarship scheme for undergraduate training in 1952, things had expanded to a grant of $2.8 million for the period 1961–66. Australian and New Zealand aid also began, in a small way, through contributions to the Colombo Plan.

Israel, which was to go on to become a major aid player, introduced a scholarship programme for Nepalese students in the early 1960s (Mihaly 2003), while Swiss aid, initially cheese-focused, began a little earlier and was founded on feelings of affinity (topography, yumminess . . . high regard for cows) between the two countries. Finally, United Nations agencies, eventually to become major players, also entered the scene around this time, with the earliest – a World Health Organization-led malaria eradication programme – dating from the mid-1950s.

We can summarise these first two decades as follows. The 1944 Bretton Woods settlement was soon made evident by, among many other things, President Truman's Four Point Plan. The subsequent and largely unanticipated wave of decolonisations then provoked a host of regional and geopolitical adjustments – the collapse of Nepal's Rana regime among them – one result of which was to widen (and increase the visibility of) the gulf between the rich countries and 'the rest', and to provoke among the rich a feeling that something should be done about it. Foreign aid was that something, and it had only just got going when the Cold War set it, piggybacking, in Nepal's case, on the pre-existing tensions between its northern and southern 'boulders': China and India. Nepal then became a cockpit within which the strange dynamics of the Cold War were played out. This was strange because, though India, China, the USA, Russia, Britain and the others were all incomparably richer and more powerful than Nepal, they found themselves powerless in the face of actions, such as those by the king in 1960, of which some of them strongly disapproved.

The third and fourth decades: the 1970s and 1980s

The 1962 constitution had introduced 'guided democracy': the Panchayat system, as it was called.[11] Political parties were banned, with both sovereignty and the powers of the state being vested in the person of the king, rendering him both the guardian of the constitution and the key political actor within it. This constitution, together with its 'guided democracy' and its Panchayat system (but with some major amendments in 1971 and again in 1980), then lasted for almost three decades until, in 1990, a popular people's movement – *Jana-andolan* – forced King Birendra (King Mahendra's elder son) to abrogate it. The nation may have had a different hand on the tiller but, perhaps surprisingly, King Mahendra and his son held to pretty much the same course as had been set by B. P. Koirala, the first elected prime minister of Nepal, in

1959. As well as land reform, a new civil code, the abolition of vassal princelings and states and the decentralisation of the administration, these monarchs pushed on with BP's programme of planned economic development, relying on a bureaucracy that was manned by a new and forward-looking elite, many of whom had received their education in India. This long period of assertive monarchy, it is probably fair to say, ushered in Nepal's modernisation, exemplified by the capital's transformation from a small medieval city, whose 200,000 inhabitants could walk through paddy fields to their Hindu and Buddhist temples, to a traffic-crammed conurbation of almost three million souls and an Internet café on every corner.

This internal modernisation went hand in hand with some major shifts in Nepal's external relations, 'hand in hand' because these shifts too were largely in the bureaucratising, modernising and planning direction. The result was the sustained ascendancy of an uncontested technocracy, exemplified by the only permitted (state-controlled and excruciatingly boring) broadsheet, *Gorkhapatra* (in Nepali since the Rana days) and *The Rising Nepal* (in English later under King Birendra).

The USA's rapprochement with China – the famous Nixon doctrine – altered its relationship with Nepal, since the perceived threat of communist aggression from the north receded. Economic support to Nepal continued, however, but US interest in the whole region declined. India, by contrast, was on the up-and-up. In the 1960s it had been attacked, and in places overrun, by China along its Himalayan frontier, but its defeat of Pakistan in 1971 (and the subsequent India-assisted war between Pakistan's two halves, with the eastern one becoming Bangladesh) cemented India's position as a regional power. Nepal, however, had by then largely reduced its dependence on its southern 'boulder', thanks to King Mahendra having made his move while India was at its most vulnerable. Furthermore, the 1970s saw a marked increase in West German and Japanese aid, even as the Soviet Union, the USA and (to a lesser extent) India maintained their presence. Canada, the Netherlands and Denmark also joined Nepal's donor community around this time, along with Norway and Finland, both of which were to become prominent players by the 1990s.

King Birendra, who came to the throne in 1972 on the death of his father, continued the policy of trying to keep Nepal equidistant from both China and India. In India's case this was not easy, and relations waxed and waned markedly, reaching a low when Nepal sought to disassociate itself from India's informal security umbrella by proposing that the 'yam' be declared a 'zone of peace'. This was given short shrift by India, even though more than 100 nations around the world, the USA among them, had given their support. Another low came in March 1989 when India blockaded Nepal in reprisal for it having done an arms deal with China. This, as we will see in the next section, contributed to some dramatic changes in Nepal and to some unwelcome surprises for its donor community.

Throughout these Mahendra/Birenda decades, the Nepalese state construed its dependence on India as undermining its independence, and therefore sought, wherever possible, to reduce that dependence. This it did (as we have already seen) by establishing extensive diplomatic relationships and plugging itself into multiple channels of aid. It also instigated a policy of trade diversification and, over the years, was able to significantly increase its imports from and exports to 'third nations'. Even back in the 1960s, for instance, Nepal's exports to countries other than India increased from US$313,000 to nearly US$10 million in just five years (1962/63–1967/68). And Nepal's dependence on trade with India declined from more than 95 per cent at the beginning of the 1960s to 82 per cent by 1974/75 and to just 50 per cent by the start of the 1980s. In 1989/90, helped by India's blockade, it sank to 22 per cent (Panday 1999). Foreign aid, and particularly its making available of 'hard currency', greatly facilitated this diversification of trade (even though that was not what it was intended to do).

The United Nations agencies (as we have already seen) began their assistance as early as the 1950s, and they were joined in the early 1970s by international loan-disbursing agencies such as the Asian Development Bank and the World Bank. The main thrusts of the United Nations Development Programme and of the Food and Agriculture Organization were towards natural resource management (forestry, irrigation, agricultural extension and so on) while United Nation's Children's Emergency Fund (UNICEF) focused on child education and welfare (but also drinking water and sanitation). The International Labour Organization concentrated on labour-intensive public works programmes. The World Bank's priorities were irrigation and agriculture, followed by power, telecommunications, drinking water supply and sewerage, while the Asian Development Bank concentrated its early efforts on agriculture, industry and transport. The influence of these multilateral donors, though initially slight, became increasingly significant from the mid-1980s onwards. So too did their turf wars, given the considerable areas of overlap in their self-appointed remits.

The European Commission began its assistance programme in 1977 (notwithstanding the fact that pretty well all of its member countries were already involved) and other non-DAC (Development Assistance Committee) multilateral donors – the Organization of the Petroleum Exporting Countries (OPEC) and the International Fund for Agricultural Development (IFAD) among them – also joined in (Acharya and Acharya 2004).

Finally, all this bilateral and multilateral proliferation led, in 1976, to the formation of the Nepal Aid Group. Members included Australia, Austria, Canada, Finland, France, Germany, Japan, the Netherlands, Switzerland, the United States, Britain, the United Nations Development Programme and the World Bank. The aim of this aptly named NAG is to cajole its members into providing development assistance in a more systematic and coordinated manner.

India's economic blockade of Nepal in 1989 resulted in widespread scarcity, along with rapidly rising prices for everyday consumption items such as fuel (not just for vehicles but for cooking too). With the people facing all these hardships, and with the government unable to reach any sort of agreement with India, the political parties saw this as the right moment to mount a movement against the Panchayat system. The long-established antipathy between the Nepalese Congress and the various communist parties had largely evaporated in the face of India's unneighbourly actions and, by late 1989, these two wings were able to formally ally themselves in the struggle to restore parliamentary democracy and get rid of the system that, by that time, had been in place for three decades. In April 1990, that regime was toppled and an interim government, with Krishna Prasad Bhattarai of the Nepalese Congress as its prime minister, was formed. That interim government was given two important mandates: to hold a parliamentary election and to draft a new constitution. Easily said (and the Bhattarai government did manage to fulfil its mandate) but, as tumultuous events over the next two decades have made clear, not easily sustained.

For the donors too this was a time of momentous change: the fall of the Berlin Wall and, very shortly afterwards, the collapse of the Soviet Union. Though none of the donors had threatened to suspend aid when, back in 1960, King Mahendra had snuffed out parliamentary democracy, nor had they spoken out in support of the parties and their struggles during the 30 years of 'guided democracy' that followed, the end of the Cold War was to change all that. Both the donor community and the recipient were, you could say, altered almost beyond recognition.

The fifth decade: the 1990s

During the transition of 1989/90 Western donors became more vocal in spheres that they had earlier deemed as pertaining to Nepal's domestic affairs. Increasingly they made their preferences known to the Nepalese government, airing their concerns about its handling of the people's movement and pressing for the protection of human rights and for the restoration of democracy (multi-party, that is, not 'guided'). Having been content for 30 years to operate on what is called an 'uncontested terrain', they were suddenly all clamouring for changes that (though perhaps they did not realise this) would allow 'other voices' to challenge their cosy conversations with their counterparts in the Nepalese administration. The most famous instance was the eleventh-hour cancellation, by the World Bank, of the huge and long-planned Arun 3 hydroelectric project, an event that upset the other donors who were to have been the World Bank's partners in this project and did not please many of those in the ranks of Nepal's hydrocracy.

The restoration of multi-party democracy (which, as we will see, did not go smoothly) also coincided with the moment when *liberalisation*, as a particular orientation towards the economy and society, came into the ascendant the world over. The Nepalese state, in line with the almost unquestioned assumption that the capitalist West had 'won' (most famously enunciated in Francis Fukuyama's (1989) *The End of History*) opted for a much more open and market-oriented economy. The new strategy that guided Nepal's political, economic and social reforms throughout the 1990s was therefore aimed at creating an open economy that was integrated with the wider regional and global trading system. This, among other things, entailed the meshing of Nepal's economic, commercial and industrial policies with those of India. The country's dependence on its southern 'boulder' was no longer seen as a hindrance to its development and a threat to its independence. With 30 years of policy reversed overnight, with donors speaking up where they had long kept silent and with foreign aid switched away from the far-sighted planners so that the always-myopic market could do the deciding, the restored multi-party democracy clearly had a lot on its plate.

Unsurprisingly, it fell short of what was needed. Between November 1994 and May 1999, Nepal saw eight coalition governments, covering every possible permutation of left, right and centre. This instability inevitably resulted in extensive and, so far as the electorate was concerned, unedifying horse-trading among the political parties. The regard in which Members of Parliament were held was further eroded by their self-serving behaviour. The eagerness with which they voted themselves ever more perks and facilities was highlighted by the 'Pajero Scandal' (Pajeros being Japanese 4x4s that MPs entitled themselves to import – one per MP – free of customs duty and then promptly sold or rented out to travel agencies at a large profit).

Worse still, there were many, especially in the poorer and remoter districts of Nepal, who had not heard the news about the capitalist West having won. These were the members and supporters of the Communist Party of Nepal (Maoist). The Maoists, right from the outset, had rejected the 1990 constitution and had set about consolidating themselves in the hinterland (and establishing links with kindred revolutionary groups in India; China, by contrast, afforded them no support whatsoever). However, it took several more years before they emerged as a formidable and disruptive force in Nepal's politics. On 4 February 1996 the Maoists submitted a list of 40 demands to the then prime minister, Sher Bahadur Deuba, along with the stipulation that if 'positive indications' were not seen by 17 February (just 13 days later) they would be compelled to initiate an armed struggle against the state. The prime minister and his government, spectacularly misjudging the situation, ignored the demands, dismissing the Maoists as 'a small group of radical leftists'.[12]

Civil War – the Maoists called it the 'People's War' – was formally declared on 13 February (four days ahead of the deadline) and was almost immediately followed by attacks on police posts in Rolpa and Rukan districts and by assaults on factories, a bank and police posts elsewhere across the country. The Maoists had evidently been planning their People's War – a war that was to eventually result in over 15,000 deaths in this hitherto impressively peaceful nation – for quite some time.

Between 1996 and 1998 the country went through four more coalition governments, most of which took a positive decisive position regarding the Maoists. As these short-lived governments were making their entries and exits, the Maoists were making full use of the confusion and instability by, for instance, obstructing the 1997 local elections in 87 constituencies. Later that year, an attempt by one of the coalition governments to introduce an Act of Parliament under which the Maoists would have been classed as 'terrorists' was called off amid protests from the media, the general public and the international community. In April 1997, the government led by the Nepalese Congress finally bit the bullet and launched a 'search and kill' operation spread across most of the Maoist-affected areas. However, this attempt to use armed force to crush the insurgency, in the absence of complementary programmes to win the hearts and minds of the people, did not yield positive results. In May 1999, a general election was held with the Nepali Congress Party under Krishna Prasad Bhattarai winning a simple majority. One of its first acts was the formation of a 'high-level committee to provide suggestions to solve the Maoist problem'. Contact with the Maoist leaders was then established but, before any substantive progress could be made, the government fell and a rival faction of the Nepali Congress Party, led by G. P. Koirala, formed the new government. A few months later, between September 2000 and April 2001, the Maoists carried out two devastating attacks on the security forces, all the while refusing to hold talks with the Koirala government. Koirala's attempt to deploy the Royal Nepal Army (at that time largely ceremonial and averse to killing fellow Nepalis) was turned down by the chief of the army.

All through these unrests, Nepal's donor community, in line with the ever-new thinking on development, prioritised support for poverty reduction, governance reform and the strengthening of parliamentary democracy. Awkward cusses will wonder whether there might be some causal connection between the ever-increasing amount of aid being directed towards these three explicit priorities and their ever more marked non-materialisation. Indeed, there is a hypothesis – we have elaborated, in a previous chapter, in terms of the contrast between '*dharma* restored' and '*dharma* gone wrong' (Figure 1.1) – that aid that is distorting the triangular interplay between market, state and civil society will simultaneously be turning Nepal into an 'aid junkie' while urging it to kick the habit. Certainly, and as will be even more evident when we come to the sixth decade, things have got worse and worse on those three priority fronts as the volume of aid targeted at them has got larger and larger.

Aid, as well as being re-focused on these three priorities, increased in volume throughout the 1990s, and by 1999 it made up just under half of the development expenditure, constituting 6.7 per cent of Nepal's gross national income and amounting, were it to spread evenly, to US$18 for every man, woman and child in the country.[13] The level of foreign aid that Nepal receives is the highest (in GNI and per capita terms) in South Asia and one of the highest in the world. Over this fifth decade, Nepal has received an average of some US$400 million annually (in both grants and loans)[14] and its external debt at the start of the sixth decade stood at US$2.82 billion. Japan was, by this time, the biggest provider of aid to Nepal, followed by the United States and Britain. Japan's contribution was 20.2 per cent of total aid, the Asian Development Bank's 18 per cent, the World Bank's 15.4 per cent and the United Nations agencies' 10.7 per cent. It was during this decade that 'small' European countries – Norway, Finland, the Netherlands and Denmark – emerged as important donors, with their combined aid exceeding that of 'large' donors such as the United States. Other traditional European donors, such as Switzerland and Germany, continued their levels of allocation. Multilateral agencies – notably the Asian Development Bank and the World Bank – significantly increased their lending, equalling if not exceeding the amounts granted by the bilateral donors. The 1990s also saw a sharp rise in the number of INGOs (international non-governmental organisations) operating in Nepal, and a steady increase in their disbursements over the years.[15] India and China have been providing fixed amounts of aid to the 'yam' since the mid-1990s: 80 million yuan (equivalent to US$10 million) annually from China since 1995, and 50 million rupees (about US$11 million) from India since 1997.

Though Nepal had been receiving aid for more than 50 years, it had no aid policy: no position regarding what to expect from aid, how to channel it and how to supervise it. It was only in 2000 that a draft policy on foreign aid was produced and, after some discussions within the country, formally adopted in 2002. Unsurprisingly, this policy does not overtly criticise aid or the aid givers and is primarily concerned with the regulation and control of aid flows. The goal, again unsurprisingly, is self-sustaining: high economic growth and self-reliance through the mobilisation of the resources required to finance development, a goal, we would note, that assumes that development is essentially an economic process, rather than (as we have argued in Chapter 1) a sociopolitical process that is economic only in its consequences. However, the document does go on to list a number of 'problems' that, taken together, *do* add up to a fairly strident critique of foreign aid.

Nepal's preference, it states, is for receiving grants, making judicious selection and use of loans and reducing reliance on technical assistance. Yet it notes that aid has been donor-driven, that aid resources are not reflected in the government's budgets, that its debt burden is increasing and that aid has led to an excessive dependence on technical assistance. Concern is also raised over aid not flowing to priority sectors but rather being directed to non-governmental sectors. This can be read as a complaint about aid being increasingly fed into the market and civil society apices of our 'triangular interplay' rather than just into the state apex as used to be the case. There is, we would say, a certain validity to this, in that if nothing is being done to remedy the distortion of the triangle – restore the *dharma*, that is – then changing the points at which aid is fed in will not make much of a difference.

The sixth decade: the 2000s

On 1 June 2001, the entire royal family, except for King Birendra's younger brother, who happened to be out of town, was massacred by an emotionally disturbed Crown Prince, who then shot himself. This is the official version of what happened, and it is not easily disputed with many witnesses who survived (some with bullet wounds) and who have deposed before the inquiry commission consisting of the Chief Justice and the Speaker of Parliament. Nevertheless, it *is* disputed, with various conspiracy theories being elaborated around the fortuitous absence of Gyanendra, who succeeded to the throne a couple of days later,[16] and being lent credibility by the marked and eerie similarities with the Kot Massacre a century and a half earlier.

A week later, Maoists killed 41 policemen when they attacked security outposts in Gulmi, Lamjung and Nuwakot, and a few days after that abducted 69 policemen from their post at Holari in Rolpa District. Prime Minister Koirala's attempt to deploy the Royal Nepal Army without first going through the Security Council as required by the constitution was rejected once more, and he resigned. His replacement, Sher Bahadur Deuba was regarded by the Maoists as more 'liberal' than Koirala (whom they labelled 'fascist')[17] and they readily accepted his invitation to peace talks. The first round of these was held a few weeks later and, on 30 August 2001, a ceasefire was agreed. The ceasefire, however, did not hold. At the second round of peace talks the Maoists put forward their demands for a constituent assembly, an interim government and a republic. The government made some concessions but insisted that a constituent assembly was out of the question. The peace talks broke down and, on 23 November, the Maoists resumed their armed struggle. Three days later, the Deuba government declared the Maoists to be a 'terrorist organisation' and publicly announced bounties on their leaders' heads.

King Gyanendra, in his capacity as commander-in-chief of the Royal Nepal Army, then authorised its deployment against this terrorist organisation, a move that further hardened the Maoists in their republican resolve (the monarchy, from the very earliest days of nation-building, had always been viewed as the repository of Nepalese nationalism, including even among the Maoists). More extensive operations against them were then mounted in the wake of a declaration of a state of emergency. Then, in May 2002, Prime Minister Deuba dissolved the House of Representatives in preparation for a mid-term election within the next six months. When he failed to hold that election, the country was plunged into a constitutional crisis, the eventual upshot of which was that the king, using the 'residual powers' vested in the head of state through Article 127 of the constitution, dismissed the prime minister and appointed the first of several caretaker governments. None of these, however, succeeded in holding an election, on account of the armed insurrection having by then engulfed large parts of the country. Finally, on 1 February 2005, the king dismissed the coalition government of the Nepali Congress Party and the Nepal Communist Party (UML), led by Prime Minister Deuba (who, this time around, had been nominated by the king himself), declared another state of emergency, took executive power and formed a cabinet under his own chairmanship. Assertive monarchy was back once more but only, as it turned out, for 14 months.

Dramatic though this move by the king appeared, it was in fact just the culmination of the long series of events that accompanied the progressive overshadowing of the political scene by the Maoist insurrection that had started almost a decade earlier. Even as Kathmandu became embroiled in the 2002 constitutional crisis, a political crisis was unfolding across the entire country, large tracts of which had by then fallen under the control of the Maoist political-party-turned-guerrilla-force.[18] With the state's monopoly over coercive power now seriously challenged, sovereignty itself was no longer assured, a wobbly state of affairs that was then further compounded by the unresolved constitutional crisis. This, once apprehended, generated consternation within the international community, with many of its members fearing that Nepal was (or was about to become) a 'fragile state', just one stop short of a 'failed state' (on a par, that is, with countries like Afghanistan and Somalia, which had recently become breeding grounds for terrorist movements such as al-Qaeda).

The donors at last began to pay serious attention to the insurgency, most of them becoming preoccupied with 'identifying the root causes of the conflict' (though with little consideration that they themselves might be among those root causes).[19] Social exclusion, inequality and the lack of good governance were then identified as the country's main problems, and these, along with an emphasis on 'the poorest of the poor', soon became the catchphrases in the new development discourse. Fix those, so the argument went, and the conflict will disappear. Even so, some donors toyed with the idea of withdrawing from the country altogether.[20] Some did downsize their programmes (or had them downsized for them by the Maoists) but all eventually continued their engagement, albeit with a now much-altered strategy. In particular, the country assistance plans of all donors, especially those formulated after 2000, began to include the issue of conflict as well as attempts to respond to it through development strategies.

The Nepalese government's reading of the situation also converged, to some extent, with that of the donors. The government was already instituting a poverty reduction strategy programme (PRSP) and some of the donors' concerns, especially those dealing with the alleged root causes of the conflict, made their way into it. Indeed, the PRSP was broadened so as to become the country's Tenth Five-Year Plan (2002–07) and centred on four objectives: broad-based and sustainable economic growth, social sector development, social inclusion and good governance. It also introduced a medium-term expenditure framework and was further influenced in its priority-setting by that global paradigm: the Millennium Development Goals. No mention, as yet, of climate change, though it was presaged by the insertion of the term 'sustainable' in front of 'economic growth'.

While the Nepalese state concurred with the donors' reading of the insurgency, it also pressed ahead with the military option, allocating more and more funds of security-related personnel and equipment. A consequence of this was an increased proclivity on the part of the Nepalese state towards siphoning resources from development into security. This can be detected from the anomaly between regular and development expenditure, the state procuring arms from the former and donors allocating funds to the latter.[21] As can be seen in Table 4.2, before the Maoist insurgency and until financial year 1995/96 there was a steady increase in social and economic expenditure and

Table 4.2 Changes in Nepali government's spending over the years (in million NRs)

Particulars	1999/00	2000/01	2001/02	2002/03
Total expenditure	66,273	79,835	80,072	94,006
Annual change in percentage	–	20.5	0.3	4.9
Regular	34,523	42,769	48,590	54,973
Annual change in percentage	–	23.9	13.6	13.1
Development	31,749	37,066	31,482	29,033
Annual change in percentage	–	16.7	−15.1	−7.8
Royal palace expenses	88	93	116	388
Annual change in percentage	–	5.8	25.1	233.8
Total security expenses	6,750	9,009	11,987	13,619
Annual change in percentage	–	33.5	33.1	13.6
Defence (military) expenses	3,482	3,813	5,860	7,382
Annual change in percentage	–	9.5	57.3	26.0
Police (civilian and armed)	3,268	5,195	6,128	6,237
Annual change in percentage	–	59.0	17.9	1.8
Total foreign aid inflow (budgetary)	17,528	18,757	14,385	15,885
Annual change in percentage	–	7.0	−23.3	10.4
Grant	5,721	6,753	6,686	11,339
Annual change in percentage	–	18.2	−1.0	69.6
Loan	11,812	12,004	7,699	4,546
Annual change in percentage	–	1.6	−35.9	−41.0

Source: Economic Survey 2003/04 and 2004/05, His Majesty's Government of Nepal, Ministry of Finance.

a marginal increase in security expenditure, whereas after financial year 2000/01 there has been a decline in economic sector expenditure while security spending has increased.

The donors' understanding of the conflict as stemming from existing poverty and inequality and from the failure of past governments to address the socio-economic conditions of the people – an understanding that was largely shared by the government – overlooked the *agency* of the Maoists: their ability to mobilise people on the basis of ideology. Since this mobilisation was then reinforced by the actions of the state and its security forces against them, the remedying of these root causes (assuming they had been correctly identified) will not, in itself, resolve the conflict; that would require some sort of counter-agency: demobilisation. Hence all the fraught (and still unsatisfactory) efforts, later in this sixth decade, to transfer the now-no-longer-armed insurgents from their UN-supervised camps to either their home villages or into the national army.[22]

Thanks to this overlooking of the Maoists' agency, the 2000s turned out to be a decade of two halves. In the latter half of the decade, as a flood of experts in conflict resolution disembarked in Kathmandu, the donors' focus shifted yet again: from the remedying of what were seen to be the root causes of the insurgency to the demobilisation of the insurgents themselves. At the same time, and in international forums remote from Nepal, a new 'totalising discourse'[23] – climate change – was transforming the donors' idea of what foreign aid should be trying to do. The latter transition has been particularly marked in the European Union, the part of the developed world from which the majority of Nepal's donor community hails. This shift has been made operational in terms of *mainstreaming*: the subsuming of development assistance into global efforts to mitigate and adapt to the climate consequences of global warming.[24]

However, these shifts have been problematic for Nepal for two reasons. First, the set of aid officials and consultants coming to Nepal who were well versed on poverty, equity or governance issues was not as equipped to deal with conflict resolution and vice versa.[25] Second, while the European Union (and most of its member countries) are now well versed in both the science of climate change and its policy implications, such concerns are barely on the radar in Nepal, as is evident from interviews (discussed in Chapter 13) with both 'elite' actors (government ministers, university vice-chancellors etc.) and 'ordinary folk' (shopkeepers, farmers etc.). These two sets of transitions, as we go from the first to the second half of the sixth decade, were also accompanied by a host of turbulent events within Nepal, which means that we will now have to try to tease out what has been happening as the country and its donors have together bumped along the bottom that they reached in 2005.

As the emergency escalated, donors adopted various specific approaches in order to maintain their operations in the conflict-affected areas. They sought to increase 'transparency' by being more explicit about what they were doing and why, and they made efforts to employ more staff from the regions in which they were involved. They also conceded that the conflict was having an adverse effect on development co-operation, and some donors even set about realigning their future assistance strategies with the rapidly evolving political and socio-economic changes in the country. Increasingly, for donors to continue working effectively in this conflict situation, the 'acceptability' of their programmes to both the Maoists and the government became the dominant concern.

Along with these strategic shifts, donors found themselves operating in 'grey areas' between relief and development activities, and increasingly sought to align their community-based approaches with humanitarian principles. As early as 2002, for instance, Britain's DfID and Germany's GTZ established a joint risk management office which, drawing on concepts that are generally associated with humanitarian work, developed a 'Safe and Effective in Conflict' approach. Another group of donors adopted a set of 'Basic Operating Guidelines' (with the unfortunate acronym BOG).[26] As early as 2001, the government had sought to take 'development' to the core Maoist areas and had increased its spending considerably. But, by 2003, almost half of the country's development projects had come to a halt. The media carried ever more frequent reports of the Maoists asking donors to sign up with them, along with extorting money from them and threatening their staffs, and by the end of 2004 donors began to actually pull out of those parts of Nepal most severely affected by the rebellion.

Just as there was a rift among the legitimate (i.e. non-Maoist) political actors in Nepal from October 2002 onwards, so there was a growing difference of opinion among Nepal's donors, a rift that came to a head at the Nepal Development Forum meeting in May 2004. The donors split into two camps: the multilaterals and the Americans in one, the remaining bilaterals in the other. The first camp favoured the schedule for the meeting that had been set out by the government; the second camp pressed for a consensus between the palace and the political parties before proceeding with the meeting itself. A 'pre-consultation' was indeed held (at the Norwegian Embassy),[27] with the members of the second camp requesting the political parties and the king to come up with a suitable prime ministerial candidate: a far cry from those Cold War days when the donors were careful to stay out of Nepal's domestic affairs. Yet, despite all this dissension and political turmoil, and despite some disagreements over how the aid was to be disbursed, both camps agreed that aid to Nepal would continue. Indeed, most of the bilateral donors actually increased their aid commitments. Overall, the donors (bi- and multilateral) pledged to provide $560 million a year as assistance under the new poverty reduction strategy that had been endorsed in 2003. The great foreign aid juggernaut was evidently not for turning!

However, the king's actions on 1 February 2005 forced all these donors to rethink their positions in Nepal. This was particularly so when, in his 28-minute-long royal proclamation, the king criticised the political parties for misusing their parliamentary privilege and placed most of the political elite, including former prime ministers (with whom, of course, the donors had long been used to working), under house arrest. Each donor, having originally entered into a partnership with the Nepalese government of the day, was now in the awkward predicament of having to decide whether the current government was legitimate. All, of course, were free to withdraw but all decided to stay put and to then try to influence events, each in the way it saw fit. Most of them then opted for rapprochement: for doing whatever they could to get the two 'constitutional forces' – the monarchy and the political parties – to settle their differences. This was a strategy that, as well as flying in the face of more than half a century of recent history, left out the Maoists (with whom, it subsequently turned out, some of the donors were in regular and amicable contact).

Many donors took a common line, opting to continue those programmes that had already been agreed while refraining from signing any new agreements. But the Asian Development Bank signed its US$19 million loan the day after the royal proclamation, and Japan went ahead with two projects, totalling US$17 million, on the grounds that the money had already been allocated. The World Bank postponed its US$70 million (for anti-poverty budgetary support) but argued that this had been decided before the royal assertion, because of the newly dismissed government's failure to meet reform targets. The responses of India and China to the royal moves were strikingly different. India (which had been giving tacit support and safe haven to the Maoists) suspended its arms deliveries to the Royal Nepal Army, but later resumed 'non-lethal' military aid. China (which had consistently distanced itself from the Maoists) said that the whole thing was Nepal's internal matter. However, after the king's action it began to aid Nepal in a variety of ways, including direct budgetary support.

It is clear from all of the above that the donor community was by this time in considerable disarray and therefore not at all well prepared for the deluge of political, and increasingly violent, events that this stand-off between the monarchy and the political parties, compounded by the Maoist insurgency, was about to unleash. However, we will delay covering this until the last chapter, because it is focused on climate change and because it was at around this time that the donor community began, seriously and systematically, to subsume the delivery of foreign aid into the much wider and international efforts to deal with the consequences of human-made global warming. Development was suddenly no longer enough; it had to be *sustainable*.[28]

A final point is that, though we have so far covered only five and a half out the of six decades of foreign aid, it is glaringly obvious that, with the donors being all the time caught up in Nepal's political transitions and instabilities (and vice versa), there has been precious little attention paid to the question of whether all (or indeed any) of this development aid is aiding development (be it sustainable or unsustainable)! That seriously unexamined question has been opened up in the preceding chapter and will be further delved into in the seven case studies that form Part 2 of this book.

Notes

1   Britain was the hegemonic power in India for the Nepalese state's first century and a half, with India gaining its independence in 1947, and with West and East Pakistan (later Bangladesh) being partitioned off. To the north there was a marked lack of hegemony until the defeat of the nationalist forces by Mao's Red Army (with Tibet – Nepal's immediate neighbour to the north, with whom Nepal has had relations going back almost two millennia, especially with the marriage of Princess Bhrikuti to the Tibetan king in the seventh century AD – coming under China in 1949). Northern and southern constraints have thus fluctuated wildly and have seldom been in balance.

2   Another yam-like country – Sikkim, immediately to the east of Nepal – was annexed by India between 1973 and 1975.

3   Which helps explain why, even to this day, you will hear little criticism of them in the countryside.

4   For a succinct account of the Ranas, and of what preceded them, see Rose and Scholz (1980).

5 This phrase, which is best declaimed in a Scottish accent, was coined by the eminent geographer and also cabinet minister Harka Gurung, who gained a doctorate from the Department of Geography, University of Edinburgh.

6 In his presidential address on 20 January 1949, President Harry Truman spelt out the four points that would guide American policies in the years to come. The first related to the interests of the United States, the second to the functioning of liberal market economies, the third to resistance against communism and the fourth to the problems of the world's underdeveloped areas.

7 Even as early as 1951, some groups in Nepal, including King Tribuvan himself in his famous proclamation upon return to Nepal from exile in Delhi, were toying with the idea of a constituent assembly that would draft a new constitution. Though it did not happen then, this, as we will see, was an idea that has been taken up with a vengeance in recent years.

8 The monarchy, once it had asserted itself, was able to rope in a wide range of disparate actors and interests. Among these were the displaced Ranas, disgruntled factions within the Nepalese Congress (along with the leaders of some of the smaller parties), leading figures from among the Madheshi (Tarai) and Janajati (non-Hindu) communities and the Rana-dominated Royal Nepal Army. Though King Mahendra retained the top leadership position, the regime was in fact a fairly broad coalition of societal and class interests, which probably explains why it was able to last for three decades.

9 The question then arises as to whether foreign aid and 'guided democracy', rather than just coinciding, actually reinforced one another, rather in the way that the British Raj in India was symbiotic with Nepal's Rana regime. And, beyond that, there is the question of whether this is what foreign aid has done elsewhere in the world. Certainly, in sub-Saharan Africa, where aid is almost ubiquitous, there are few if any regimes that have not been suppressive of contesting voices. If there is something to this hypothesis then we will need to explain why, in countries like Nepal (and also in South and Central America), contestation – we could term it 'unguided democracy' – has been able to break out. The end of the Age of Aid (circa 1989, if we take the collapse of the Soviet Union as the 'break point') could be one plausible answer.

10 Nepal had first applied for UN membership in 1949, but had been opposed by some members on the grounds that its status as an independent sovereign state was at best ambiguous. Ukraine had raised this objection and the Soviet Union had vetoed Nepal's membership to the United Nations in 1949. Objections were raised as to the fact that there was no adequate information on the status of the government and constitution of Nepal and that it was fully dependent on the United Kingdom as well as India. The treaties that Nepal had signed with India in 1950, namely the Treaty of Peace and Friendship and the Treaty of Trade and Commerce, were to underscore its existence as an independent, sovereign country and its 1955 application to the United Nations sailed through (Gyawali 2000).

11 The word 'Panchayat' comes from the traditional concept of a village council of five (from Sanskrit 'panch', meaning 'five' in most Indic languages) respected ones, called to decide on cases of dispute. Although the term was removed after the restoration of multi-party democracy in 1990, the term now describes the main form of village governance in India.

12 The then prime minister of the Nepalese Congress, Sher Bahadur Deuba, ignored these demands and went to Delhi to cement relations with India, primarily to ink the infamous Mahakali Treaty on the eponymous border river. The Maoist's 'People's War' was launched the day after the inking of this agreement.

13 One would have to be cautious in reading these numbers because not all sources provide the same figures. The Economic Survey of the Government of Nepal, World Development Reports by the World Bank, Development Cooperation Report and Human Development Report by the UNDP and individual authors all cite different figures.

The figure cited in the preceding section is from World Development Reports. Kotilainen and Kaitila (2002), Finnish authors who examine the impact of globalisation in Nepal also cite these figures.

14 The figure is derived from *Development Cooperation Nepal 2000 Report*, p. 11. This has been computed by taking into account all of the Overseas Development Assistance.

15 The sources are not unanimous regarding the disbursements from INGOs. For instance, according to UNDP's Development Cooperation Report, in 1999 INGOs disbursed around US$24 million while the Social Welfare Council shows INGOs committing some US$20 million for the year 2000. While the UNDP lists only 21 INGOs providing assistance to Nepal, the SWC shows 96. The SWC should, therefore, show a larger disbursement from INGOs, but that is not the case. Acharya (2002) rightly notes that these figures cannot be taken at face value. See also Panday (1999).

16 Royal succession protocol required that the Crown Prince, if alive, be made king, and this was quickly done even though he was in a coma. He died two days later, so Gyanendra, who was regent during the interim, did not directly succeed his brother.

17 Strangely, and as happened more often than not in the wonder that Nepal's convoluted politics, it was with Koirala that the Maoists eventually signed the India-brokered 12-point Delhi Deal in November 2005 (after Deuba had launched a full scale military attack on them) to start the process of ending the People's War and sidelining the monarchy.

18 The Maoists, in general, were able to take territory almost at will but were not then able to hold it. However, in those places and at those times when their control was not challenged, they established administrative systems of 'people's government' in place of those of the state.

19 However, there was a general concession that past development efforts had failed to benefit all the people and that this, along with the existing poor socio-economic conditions, the rising expectations that had been generated by the restoration of democracy and the rampant corruption (especially among politicians), had fuelled the insurgency.

20 The US Peace Corps packed up and left Nepal in 2004, after nearly 42 years of service. The German Technical Grant (GTZ) terminated its green road project in Gorkha, Danida suspended a rural electrification project in Kailali and the Swiss halted some of its field-level projects (as reported in *The Nepali Times*, 21–27 January 2005).

21 Recently the nomenclature has changed. The regular budget is now known as recurrent costs and development budget is known as capital costs.

22 On 10 April 2012, fearing revolt in the disgruntled Maoist cantonments, the government of Prime Minister Babu Ram Bhattarai (led by the Maoist party and with the concurrence of its supremo Prachanda) instructed the Nepal Army to take over the cantonments in a surprise swoop – which it did gladly – leading to further dissatisfaction in the Maoist ranks and to the splitting off of the Vaidya faction (called 'Dash Maoists', as opposed to the 'Cash Maoists' of Prachanda and Baburam, the popular Nepalese appellations being self-explanatory).

23 Totalising discourses, as Rayner (2010) has pointed out, block alternative modes of inquiry. They create an unconstructive state of affairs in which TINA (There Is No Alternative) holds sway when, in fact, there are alternatives aplenty. In cultural theory terms, this is the imposition of elegance – just one 'voice' drowning out the others – when what is wanted is clumsiness: each of the voices heard, and responded to, by the others.

24 Indeed this book has its origins in some major European Union-funded research – the ADAM (ADaptation And Mitigation strategies) Project – that sets out specifically to address the mainstreaming of climate change in development co-operation (see Gupta and van der Grijp 2010).

25 There is a similar disjuncture as evidenced by the oft-predicted break-out of 'water wars', between water conflict consultants who come to Nepal and the ones who deal with irrigation, drinking water or hydropower.

26 Basic Operating Guidelines (BOG) are a code of conduct adopted by international agencies in Nepal to carry out programmes and to set standards for their programmes and staff at the field level. BOG prohibits using development and humanitarian assistance for political, military or sectarian purpose, refuses to make forced contribution in cash or kind for activities other than development and humanitarian areas and asserts the right to withdraw from areas where staff and project safety are threatened.

27 Among these bilateral donors were Norway (the host), Denmark, Finland, Canada, Britain, the Netherlands, Switzerland, Germany, France and Canada (Khadka 2004).

28 Sustainable development, of course, had hit the headlines much earlier, most notably in the 1987 Bruntland Commission Report (World Commission on Environment and Development 1987). But it took a number of years before it acquired its mainstream status, and it was only then that Nepal and its donor community found themselves forced to pay attention.

Part 2

The case studies

5 Bhattedanda Milkway

Why a climate- and mountain-friendly technology continues to be ignored

Madhukar Upadhya

Every morning, high on the mountainous rim of the Kathmandu Valley, an Austrian cable system moves metal carriers containing fresh milk across a deep ravine to a truck waiting on the nearest road. Given the rugged topography, this three-mile link is a simple, cheap and efficient way of getting milk to market in the capital city before it spoils. This system – it is called the Bhattedanda Milkway and was funded by the European Union – is an interesting solution to a problem that, given Nepal's remarkably crumpled terrain, is always cropping up. However, it was a solution that was lucky to see the light of day. It was, for a start, the first of its kind[1] and there was much concern, within both the donor community and the various ministries, as to whether the local users would be able to manage its operation and maintenance without outside support. And the only way to discover whether such ropeways would work, as one of its champions, the British ambassador Barney Smith, observed, was 'to build one and see'.[2]

The ropeway, as we will see, went through more than a few wobbly moments during its early years, but has been functioning well for 15 or so years now. It has provided the farmers on Bhattedanda (*dandas* are high rounded

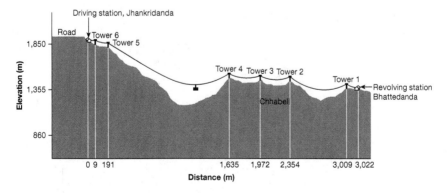

Figure 5.1 Longitudinal profile of Bhattedanda ropeway

ridges) with access to market for their dairy produce and helped to conserve the forest – these being the original and explicit aims of the project – but it has also enabled other developments that were not anticipated: diversification into market gardening (including organic produce), for instance, and substantial flows of goods up to the *danda* at rates much cheaper than would have obtained before. It was even able to save two lives when a woman who was experiencing serious childbirth difficulties was quickly transported (in contravention of all the rules) to a waiting vehicle at the roadhead.

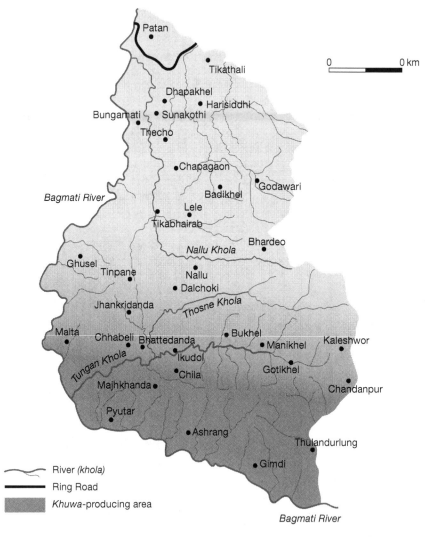

Map 5.1 Khuwa-producing areas of Lalitpur

The villages on Bhattedanda are located about 20 kilometres south of Kathmandu and are separated from the nearest road by a deep valley, an all too common predicament in the steep and rugged terrain of the Mahabharat (Map 5.1). The main crops are corn and millet but, with very little land on the steep slopes suitable for cultivation, most farmers produce only enough food for between three and six months of the year. Animal husbandry is the main source of their income, and it is this that has enabled them to pull through the six- to nine-month deficit period. Villagers elsewhere, who could reach the road within three hours, were able to sell fresh milk but, with the nearest Bhattedanda village a gruelling five-hour walk away, there has been no option but to boil the milk down into *khuwa*, a cottage cheese-like dehydrated milk paste.

Khuwa, though it can be stored for up to a week and, as well as being less bulky than milk, can be transported without going sour, has some major drawbacks. First, it requires huge amounts of firewood, the cutting and carrying of which is arduous and time-consuming and wreaks havoc on surrounding forests. Second, it is labour-intensive, both to make and transport to the road-head. Third, thanks to all the smoke that is entailed, its production is both unpleasant and unhealthy (especially for the women and children in the house). Fourth, *khuwa* sells for almost a third less than milk, the difference being due to the government-owned Dairy Corporation buying fresh milk at a regulated price while the price of *khuwa* is fixed by private middlemen.

What has the Milkway done?

The Milkway has reduced the village to roadhead collection centre travel time for the milk from five hours to less than 20 minutes. Since it now arrives at the road in ample time for the truck to take it to the chilling plant, there is no longer any need to boil it down into *khuwa*. Though the benefit of a 'milk-only' installation appeared to be of little consequence to many development practitioners and politicians, it has led to a host of improvements in terms of what is now called sustainable development: some anticipated, most not foreseen at all.

The most direct benefit, evident from the day the Milkway was commissioned, has been an increase in farmers' income of around 30 per cent. Increasing incomes in remote villages by any other means, as is evident from a host of development projects, is, to put it mildly, difficult. In this sense, it is a major step towards the achievement of those elusive MDGs: Millennium Development Goals.[3] Moreover, it has reduced the drudgery of the menfolk (if they were the ones who carried the *khuwa* to the road) and particularly of the womenfolk, who no longer have to go to the forest to collect the additional firewood, nor do they have to sit in front of the hearth for two to four hours extra every night after putting the children to bed, boiling the milk and suffocating the house with smoke. It also has massively reduced the pressure on the forest, thereby justifying its promotion as a *conservation* milkway.

To convert four litres of milk into *khuwa* requires about five kilograms of firewood, and each household was converting between five and ten litres every day. This gives a saving of around 300 tonnes of firewood a year in the area served by the Milkway.

There are some less direct benefits as well. Household members, especially the women and children, had to inhale the smoke while *khuwa* was being made. Now the indoor air is much cleaner. Young plants are no longer damaged by the feet of the hundreds of firewood collectors who used to roam the forest every day. This has reversed the loss of biodiversity, improved the health of the forest and given a considerable boost to the production of what are called 'non-timber forest products'.

Furthermore, once transportation became available, farmers realised that they could export perishable farm produce to market (and import supplementary feed to increase the fat content, and thus the price, of their milk). They have now diversified into tomatoes, green vegetables and beans (which command a premium in the capital, where they are marketed as organic and coming from Bhattedanda). Family incomes have thus risen still further, enabling them to enjoy better healthcare, send their children to school, provide themselves with a better and more varied diet, improve their living conditions (e.g. corrugated iron roofs instead of thatch that may be picturesque but is leaky, labour-intensive and prone to fire hazards) and to refurbish their temples and gompas (the villagers are a mixture of Brahmins and Tamangs). The scale and rapidity of these less direct benefits are evident in the amounts of goods exported and imported, which have risen constantly year-on-year since 1996 (see Table 5.1).

Benefits that are even less direct have also materialised: the conversion of the Milkway from fossil fuel to renewable energy (diesel-generated electricity to hydroelectricity from the national grid supplied by the local community electricity distribution co-operative) and the possible 'cross-over' of the technology to the construction of small to medium-sized hydropower installations (thereby circumventing two troublesome obstacles: the high cost of constructing a road to the site and the frequent reluctance of the Department of Forests to give permission for such road construction). Since these benefits are generic, with important ramifications far beyond Bhattedanda and its villagers, we will deal with them later in this chapter.

The spin-offs from and unintended benefits of development initiatives are sometimes more attractive than the intended use, and this is certainly the case

Table 5.1 Total of goods exported from and imported by the Milkway

Year	Annual import (tons)	Annual export (tons)
1995/96	55	158
2003/04	344	711
2004/05	320	273
2005/06	361	342

with the Milkway. These unintended benefits have, moreover, had a beneficial secondary impact. Financial flows into Nepalese villages generally originate from local moneylenders, who charge extremely high rates of interest (sometimes as much as 60 per cent per annum). Banks do provide cheaper loans but various administrative complications discourage farmers from accessing their services. However, the Milkway Committee has now started to use its savings to provide loans, both to its users and to local merchants. Interest is in the range of 8 to 15 per cent – far below other sources – and loans are disbursed on a first-come-first-served basis, provided the borrower can assure repayment, with the committee giving preference to members over non-members. The ropeway has thus become not only a transport system but a community-wide benefit provider, thanks to the 'social capital' that it has itself generated.

One major worry, as the ropeway was being established, was whether it would be 'sustainable'. As well as its novelty (in Nepal) as an engineering artefact, nothing so technologically sophisticated had ever been tried in a rural community. There were many questions asked: would the farmers switch from exporting *khuwa* to milk? Would they be able to operate the machinery without a qualified technician? What would happen if it broke down? Could they continue to operate as a group that made decisions in a democratic way? How would they resolve disputes? . . . and on and on. Above all, would the ropeway earn enough to keep itself going? These were hair-raising questions, because so much would depend on government (and donor) policy as well as on local politics, and we (i.e. the team advising the Bagmati Watershed Project) had no control over those. What we did have were some simple convictions that revolved around the economic and technological aspects of the transport system and very little around politics and policy.

Transport systems and the economy, we knew, are always interdependent. If economic growth is to be initiated and kept going transport systems will have to be efficient, cheap and reliable. A transport system can help build the economy, but it takes a strong economy to support a transport system. Our simple conviction was that if the ropeway could be operated, with some back-up support for a few years, then the economy would be improved to the point where it would itself contribute to the upkeep of the ropeway.

Nepalese farmers, we also knew, are familiar with simple river-crossing devices – such as *ghirlings* and *khit-khites*[4] – that are manufactured locally, but moving higher up the technological ladder would require more specialist skills and a level of training that was not at that time available at the local level. Villagers were fully competent with water mills and with diesel-powered rice mills, but a ropeway called for a considerably higher level of technological sophistication. That, after all, is why it had to come from Austria and have its installation supervised by an Austrian technician. Yet, after 15 or so years of operation it has become clear that Nepalese farmers have a remarkable capability to manage, operate and maintain ropeways. Such capability requires capital generation and skill development, and both these have been forthcoming. The ropeway has generated enough capital for its operation and maintenance to be carried out without any outside support. Its locally recruited operators have proved themselves to be fully up to the task of keeping it running, while collecting sufficient revenue to ensure its regular maintenance and its daily operation (except for a 14-month period around 2001, which we will explain later). It has not had to depend on outside support for its upkeep and the system has been operated, managed and maintained entirely by local users.

Even more remarkably, they have modified some of the ropeway's features to better suit their needs: most impressively in their converting its power from fossil fuel to renewables. This has ensured, even more firmly, that this undertaking is not only good for poverty alleviation, but also protects the environment (in contrast to the 'development tombs' listed in Chapter 1, which are neither conducive to poverty alleviation nor environmentally friendly). We say 'even more firmly' because right from the outset it was conceived as a *conservation* ropeway. The forest has indeed been conserved, thanks to the major reduction in firewood use, and its biodiversity has also been enhanced.

On the management side, the committee has been reformed six times over the first 12 years, all the time consistently pursuing and strengthening the democratic nature of the decision-making process. It is perhaps for this reason that the Maoist insurgents, who destroyed most of the rural infrastructure (including bridges and communication towers) across the country, did not harm the Bhattedanda Milkway.

How did it all begin?

In 1985 the Nepalese government, in partnership with one of its donors, the European Union, set about implementing the Bagmati Watershed Project. This was in response to the floods and landslides that had occurred four years earlier, and Bhattedanda, being one of the affected areas, was the focus of a number of efforts to conserve natural resources, reduce erosion and improve the living standards of the local people. The results, after five years of tree planting, landslide stabilisation, gully control, terracing and so on, were disappointing, especially in relation to the project's third aim: the improvement of the locals' living conditions. Clearly, there were some awkward questions that needed to be asked. How, exactly, does tree planting or forest protection improve living conditions? Does the stabilising of a gully enhance the economy; indeed, does it do anything to keep the village trail operational? Would the community be in a better position to cope with disasters, should the massive cloudburst, flooding and landslide events of 1981 be repeated (as they very likely will)? These sorts of questions, moreover, were being asked all across Nepal by those who found themselves on the receiving end of foreign aid.

Accordingly, in 1990, a team (of which I was a member) from the EU-funded Bagmati Watershed Project set about answering these awkward questions by looking into the basic features of the livelihoods of the people on Bhattedanda. *Khuwa*, we found, played a major part in the local economy, a part, however, that was not without its downside. *Khuwa* production requires large quantities of firewood, imposes drudgery (on women especially) in firewood collecting and in boiling the milk, and generates indoor smoke that is detrimental to health (especially that of the women and children). On top of all that, the finished product sells for roughly a third less than the fresh milk would have sold for, had it been possible to get it to market. As a result, many of those who were locked into *khuwa* production found themselves moving into a downward economic spiral. Indeed, *khuwa* producers were steadily becoming poorer and poorer. The activities of the Bagmati Watershed Project, we realised, were simply no match for the realities of resource utilisation on this hilltop. The goal of the project, it became increasingly evident, would not be achieved.

We also discovered that the downward spiral became steeper as we went from Bhattedanda to the successive (and increasingly remote) ridges, and that the attitude to the state became ever more negative. From this we deduced that it is the valleys between the villages that are the major cause of poverty and environmental problems in the Bhattedanda area (Figure 5.2).

So, if it is the valleys that are at the bottom of it all, is there anything that can be done about them? Between 1991 and 1993 we explored various ways in which the valleys could be 'missed out', so that milk could be taken from crest hamlet to crest hamlet quickly and without curdling and spoiling in the process as it went down the ridge, along the sub-tropical valley bottom and up again another ridge. Stretching a plastic pipe across the valley, through which the milk could then be poured, was one possibility; a tensioned cable, down which the milk churns could be slid, was another. All, however, had inherent problems (cleaning the tube, getting the churns over the uphill sections, getting

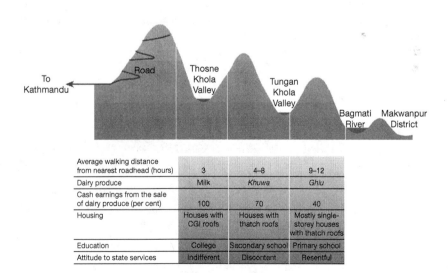

Average walking distance from nearest roadhead (hours)	3	4–8	9–12
Dairy produce	Milk	*Khuwa*	*Ghiu*
Cash earnings from the sale of dairy produce (per cent)	100	70	40
Housing	Houses with CGI roofs	Houses with thatch roofs	Mostly single-storey houses with thatch roofs
Education	College	Secondary school	Primary school
Attitude to state services	Indifferent	Discontent	Resentful

Figure 5.2 The valleys in-between

the empty churns back up and so on) and had to be rejected. Eventually, we ended up proposing a motor-powered ropeway, only to be met with a wave of objections:

- A ropeway was not a part of the Forest Ministry's Bagmati Watershed Project but something that belonged to the Transport Ministry; and there was no policy within the Forest Ministry to implement anything that had to do with transportation.
- It would be more expensive than the activities that were already planned or being undertaken, while the associated uncertainties made a ropeway much more risky than tree planting or landslide stabilisation.
- There was no local expertise, and the local communities would be in no position to render any opinion because the whole thing was unheard of.

These objections, taken together, sketch a caricature of a silo-focused hierarchy that is not far short of the way it often finds itself depicted by its market-oriented critics: 'A camel is a horse designed by a committee', 'Hierarchy isn't working: we need more hierarchy' . . . 'A committee is a group of people who individually can do nothing, but can come together in order to decide that nothing can be done'. And perhaps it was precisely because things had got this bad that there were some within the seemingly rejectionist ranks who were prepared to listen.

Certainly, continued discussions helped to muster some support for this outlandish scheme from a few officials in the government, and also from some in the European Union (not least, the European Commissioner Chris Patten). Some of those were even ready to bend the rules, if need be, to help with the purchase of equipment, and the government stepped out of line to help us by converting cash to commodity aid. The result, cutting a long story short, was that the ropeway was completed in June 1995. Songs of praise were sung at the opening ceremony, and for months thereafter, and government officials (ministers included) confirmed their appreciation by committing themselves to the Milkway's extension to the next ridgetop.

What made the Milkway's construction possible?

The period from 1990 to 1995 (as we have seen in Chapter 4) ushered in all kinds of changes on the development front. Multi-party democracy had just been restored, political parties that had been banned for 30 years found themselves in and out of power (often in a dazzling range of coalitional permutations) and an exuberant free press submerged the state-controlled media. With 'other voices' suddenly able to make themselves heard, development became a 'contested terrain' and many long-nurtured projects (most famously, Arun-3, which is discussed in some of chapters that follow) bit the dust. And the continuing political instability meant that no government was able to set and hold to a fixed development agenda.

In the wider world, the Earth Summit of 1992 had propelled 'the environment' to the top of the list of development priorities and every Nepalese minister (their stay in office was usually just a few months) wanted to help with these new ideas. On top of all that, donor support was overwhelming; the idea of introducing a ropeway so as to simultaneously improve farmers' economic conditions and protect the environment from further degradation simply could not have come at a better time. Once convinced – and that happened surprisingly quickly – both the Nepalese government and the European Union strongly supported the Milkway's construction.

Within just a couple of years the ropeway showed remarkable results. There was a marked increase in the volume and value of exports from the village, the number of buffaloes had increased and any houses in the area that had been thatched were re-roofed with corrugated galvanised iron sheets: a sign of rising incomes. These impressive changes then contributed to new ways of looking at problems in watershed management projects. The Bagmati Watershed Project was duly extended, with three times more money being allocated for the construction of three new ropeways in other locations within the project area. How, you might wonder, could anything possibly go wrong?

The new project – Bagmati Watershed Project Phase II – had a different management team, with different priorities. Emphasis was now given to biodiversity conservation. 'Social mobilisation' became central to the project and the promise to extend the ropeway beyond Bhattedanda was not kept.[5] The people across the next valley waited and waited but the extension never materialised and, in 2003, Phase II ended. The Bagmati Watershed Project perished, and with it all hopes of the government providing the ropeway's extension. The money that had been allocated to extend the ropeway lapsed back to the European Union.

Meanwhile, back on Bhattedanda . . .

When the ropeway first came into operation in 1995, there were some who, for a variety of reasons, did not like it. Some felt that, if the ropeway were operating effectively, they would not be able to ask the government to provide funds for the maintenance of the road. Then there were those political leaders who, not having been part of the ropeway project, could not take the credit for it. These people therefore set about fixing the road to Chhabeli. This road, which had been excavated four decades earlier but had (for a variety of reasons) never been brought into operation, was finally opened in 1998, thereby providing the milk producers with the option of the road or the ropeway. The milk producers split into two roughly equal groups, some sticking with the ropeway, the other opting for the road. The advantage of putting their milk (and other produce) in a truck was that farmers could then send their goods all the way to Chhabeli without having to pay the extra costs from Jhankridanda. Local politics further hindered the operation of the ropeway, because politically biased committee members had a vested interest in only benefitting their clients, thereby undermining the ropeway's democratic management. The Committee tried to ensure that there were enough farmers using the ropeway to keep it economically viable, but failed to do so. The road to Chhabeli had made the ropeway redundant and it ceased operation.[6]

In 2002, just four years after it was opened, the road to Chhabeli was washed away by heavy rain. That same downpour, however, did not affect the ropeway. The area, of course, had suffered similar rain-triggered landslides back in 1981 (and in the intervening years, and in subsequent years). Indeed, since these mountains are composed of highly weathered rock that cannot withstand heavy rainfall events, such destructive episodes need to be seen as the norm, something to be expected and lived with. With the road swept away, the milk trucks could no longer reach Chhabeli and, with milk exports stopped, the farmers were suddenly faced with huge losses. They had to continue feeding expensive animals and paying the high rates of interest on the loans they had only recently taken out to buy more buffaloes. On top of that, they had changed to a rice-based diet and that demanded a good income. They had no option but to revert to *khuwa*, losing 30 per cent of their income. The impacts were felt almost immediately and imports of rice (and other merchandise) ceased completely. Unable to withstand the economic loss, the farmers were forced to put their political differences aside and unite against this serious threat that afflicted them all. With some minor repairs and maintenance, they reopened the Bhattedanda Milkway, reformed the committee and elected a new chairperson.

The saying 'necessity is the mother of invention' certainly holds true for the Bhattedanda Milkway. The newly reconstituted management committee explored ways of improving efficiency: by maintaining bookkeeping, by reducing the tariff for the transport of goods and by laying off some staff. They then turned their attention to the technology itself. The ropeway was powered by electricity that was generated by a diesel engine. This was proving both expensive and unreliable, with the fluctuating power supply via the diesel generator causing frequent faults on the ropeway itself. Once they had connected the ropeway directly to the electricity grid, the frequency of the faults declined substantially, but there was a new problem: the grid electricity, because of the high demand and low supply, had low frequency and voltage and was far from optimal for the machinery that drove the ropeway. So the villagers bought and installed a heavy-duty voltage stabiliser: a fairly esoteric piece of equipment that they located at a trade exhibition in Kathmandu. With the machinery now powered by hydroelectricity and operating at its optimal voltage, the energy costs have decreased by 55 per cent, a massive boost to the ropeway's profitability (Table 5.2).

Then, attempting to further improve the economics of the ropeway, its extension was carried out beyond Bhattedanda to the next ridge at Majhkhanda. The financial support to this extension was provided by the Poverty Alleviation Fund (a semi-autonomous outfit established by the government with funding from major donors, including the World Bank, to fund poverty reduction

Table 5.2 Energy costs for diesel and hydro to operate the Milkway (in Nepalese rupees)

	Diesel	Electricity	Cost reduction (%)
Max	8500	3899	55
Min	6100	2400	60

related projects) and the District Development Committee of Lalitpur. The original design of the extension was made by the Austrian company at the request of the Nepal Water Conservation Foundation, but the construction of the ropeway was done by Nepalese engineers – a significant advance in terms of capacity-building. The design was an improvement on the original Milkway and provided an intervening middle station, between Bhattedanda and Majhkhanda, so that villagers there could also send their products through the ropeway. With this extension, the Milkway's influence reached beyond Majhkhanda. However, the Milkway stopped operating in 2012, when the road to Chhabeli was improved, with substantial investment, in order to enable the operation of regular transport services. The Majhkhanda extension continued to operate until 2013 and stopped when it too was connected into the road system. Regular maintenance and lack of spare parts, such as the rubber linings of the pulleys, was also a major problem in both the Milkway and its extended section.

The growth and decline of the Bhattedanda Milkway makes two things clear. First, it reveals an astonishing capacity within Nepalese communities to embrace and 'localise' novel and challenging technology in order to improve their conditions of life while also dramatically lessening the pressures on their environment. Second, it shows just how easy it is for things to fall way short of that capacity:

- Had the slew of objections to the ropeway proposal carried the day, the ropeway would never have seen the light of day.
- Had the villagers, responding to a massive flood and landslide disaster, not persevered with their technological modifications and their multiple reforms of the management system, the ropeway would have become just one more rusting relic from a failed and forgotten project.
- Had the weather event that destroyed the road to Chhabeli come a few years later, the ropeway would probably have deteriorated beyond the point where it could be brought back into operation.
- Had the villagers not found themselves forced to turn their milk into *khuwa*, their environment would not have deteriorated and, in the absence of any evidence of deterioration, the team from the Bagmati Watershed Project would probably never have realised that, across the whole of the Mahabharat, it is the valleys that are the insurmountable problem in transporting goods for hamlets on ridgetops.

Those aid providers who identify a set of goals and then assume that development will be the automatic result if funds are committed to the achievement of those goals are almost always going to be surprised. There is, as the saying goes, many a slip twixt cup and lip, and if that is how things are then it is the slips that should command most of our attention.

Roads: technical fix or technical fixation?

In its Tenth Development Plan (2002–07) the Nepalese government identified two key indicators for its goal of lessening the country's pervasive poverty: *access to market* and *time to reach the nearest roadhead*. Ever since the overthrow of the Rana regime (in 1951) planners have taken roads to be the means by which access to markets is to be improved.[7] By 2000, Nepal had built more than 16,000 kilometres of roads of various types. The average road density in the lowlands is eight kilometres per 100 square kilometres, and in the hills it drops to two kilometres per 100 square kilometres. Repairing and maintaining this road network and, at the same time, expanding it (with a priority on ensuring that all district headquarters are connected into it) have been seen as the major challenge for the transport sector.

In a Green Economy Development Dialogue – organised by the Himalayan Climate Initiative and the Confederation of Nepalese Industries in Kathmandu in 2012 – a representative from the ministry of local development revealed that, while 50,000 kilometres of local roads have been constructed, less than 10,000 kilometres are in serviceable condition, with around 40,000 kilometres damaged by monsoon rain every year. At the same time, more than 70 per cent of the more than 45 billion rupees earmarked for the local level are spent on infrastructure, especially roads. Out of that, more than 90 per cent are spent on 'non-engineering type' road construction. The maintenance cost of such infrastructures is thus almost equal to that required for its construction.

There are two assumptions built into this sort of transport policy. First, that their relative inaccessibility is a major barrier to the development of communities in the Middle Hills and highlands of Nepal. Second, that getting their agricultural produce to market is the key to the development of these communities. While both are valid for our villagers on Bhattedanda, they do not hold true everywhere.

The Sherpas in the Khumbu area below Mount Everest are a very long way from the nearest roadhead and yet they have become impressively prosperous through their involvement in mountaineering and tourism, helped by their education in the Edmund Hillary schools and by the construction of an airstrip at nearby Lukla. Moreover, since farming in the hills and mountains has always been of the subsistence variety, a pretty massive boost in productivity will be needed if farmers are to avail themselves of the access to market that has been made possible by an extended road network. (This does seem to have happened in the villages described in Chapter 3, where roads have facilitated access to India and farmers, thanks to their co-operatives, have been able to make the shift away from subsistence agriculture). In consequence, the uptake – the quantity of goods transported – might sometimes be far short of the level needed for the road connection to be economically viable, especially when the trucks that ply those roads are controlled not by the villagers but by cartels of traders. Finally, across the whole of Nepal (as we have seen in the preceding chapters) many families have adopted the strategy of getting at least one member into paid work outside the country (especially in the Gulf States). With their substantial remittances, they have been able to de-intensify their farming, with the result that, even if the roadhead were right at their front doors, they would have almost nothing to send to market.[8]

None of this is to say that there is no development point in improving access to markets, only that it cannot be assumed to hold true across the board. It certainly holds for Bhattedanda (and, it seems, for the villages described in Chapter 3), but there are likely to be many places where it does not. Nor, as we will argue in a moment, should it be assumed that, in these places where it does hold true, roads are always the answer. The transport planner therefore needs to gain a feel, first, for where these different sorts of places are located and, second, for how trunk roads and branch-off ropeways can best be combined so as to complement the strengths of both for an overall 'multi-modal' transport system.

Rethinking roads and poverty

The 'across the board' thinking has been that a major (perhaps *the* major) obstacle to development in the hills and mountains of Nepal is their poor accessibility. With mobility widely limited to the long-established network of trails and tracks, people can only get about by walking, and goods must be transported by pack animal (with that, in many instances, being the human porter). This, in general, is both slow and expensive; perishables (such as fresh milk and some vegetables) go sour or rotten before reaching the market, and goods with a low value-to-weight ratio have only a short range beyond which the time and labour involved will have eaten up the amount they can be sold for. This, of course, was how things were in Bhattedanda: a situation that was dramatically transformed by a combination of road and ropeway. Since the poor, in general, are disproportionately located in the remote rural areas, are primarily engaged in agriculture, are more likely to be women and children and are often concentrated among minority ethnic groups (e.g. Dalits) and indigenous peoples (e.g. Tamangs), the thinking has been, first, that resources need to be directed towards rural development in general and the agricultural sector in particular and, second, that this needs to go hand in hand with improved access to markets (i.e. with a well-planned and expanding road network).

And yet there are flaws to this long-established development orthodoxy:

- Roads, in hilly and mountainous terrains, are expensive to build and expensive to maintain. Because the volume of traffic in these areas is typically low – less than 20 to 30 vehicles per day – most hill roads are economically unproductive; their under-utilisation makes them a liability rather than an asset. Put another way, they are public bads, not public goods; if your aim were to lessen people's poverty then it would make more economic sense to forget the road and just share the money out among the poor instead! If they are to become public goods, the volume of traffic on these roads will have to be substantially increased.[9] This could be done, perhaps, by developing a feeder-road system that connected into networks of smaller farm roads, thereby increasing the 'area of influence' of a main highway and so promoting its viability. Alternatively (and this, of course, is the novel bit of thinking) you could leave the present road network as it is and, wherever it is separated from nearby villages by deep valleys, build ropeways. An even more novel thought is that, as Bhattedanda has shown, such ropeways, being some mix of common-pool and private goods, might be quite capable of connecting themselves (with the government and its aid partners doing nothing more than helping those communities that reckon it would be worth their while to have a ropeway to secure the capital to meet the front-end costs).[10]

- An additional advantage of ropeways, especially when we entertain the likelihood that many roads are public bads, is that they do not entail excessive *sunk costs*. If you realise you have built a road in the wrong place you cannot say 'Oops, I'll cancel it and have the money back'. But ropeways are designed to be moved around. Of course, there are *some* sunk costs (those involved in foundation piles, dismantling the ropeway, transporting it to its new location, re-erecting it etc.) but these are small in relation to the cost of the ropeway itself. Moreover, clipping these flexible transport systems onto roads that have turned out to be public bads can, in many instances, transform them into public goods by substantially increasing their 'areas of influence'.

- Road-building, especially in the geologically troublesome Himalayan terrain, usually has considerable environmental costs. Roads in Nepal are extensively damaged by landslides every monsoon; moreover, roads often 'cause' landslides, as well as providing 'growth points' for erosion. Vehicles have to be imported (a partial exception being electric vehicles; see Chapter 6) and so too does the fuel for them, the price of which has been rising fairly consistently. This combination of environmental damage and carbon dioxide emissions from the fossil-fuelled vehicles means that even roads that are not at present in the public bads category are likely to be heading that way.

- If roads are to be public goods, rather than bads, they will have to be transforming local economies by an amount that is greater than they are costing. This, it seems, is often not the case (Sharma 1991). The introduction of roads in the hills and mountains, according to Blaikie *et al.* (1980) has not created the price-led stimulus in demand for imported goods that was anticipated. Much of the area was (and still is) effectively served by human porters and pack animals, using the existing network of paths, and the direct involvement of rural households in the market has remained slight. And, with incomes low and sometimes falling, there has been little demand for imported goods.

The reason why the government has persisted in giving priority to roads, Blaikie *et al.* suggests, is because it obtains benefits from them (or, at any rate, from the vehicles that use them). There is customs duty and surcharge on imported vehicles, on fuel and on spare parts; and there are licensing and registration fees, vehicle taxes, route operation taxes (per passenger carried) and tolls. Public choice theory (which fits rather well with the sorts of institutional distortions – '*dharma* gone wrong' in our Figure 1.1 – that accompany the 'licence raj') predicts that politicians, bureaucrats and other state actors will use (or, rather, misuse) resources so as to consolidate and maintain their power and authority and, given half a chance, will use their positions to extract cuts and kickbacks. Twenty years later, Seddon and Hussein (2002) found that roads had not profoundly transformed farming systems, even in the plains of the Terai, where road-building is many times cheaper than in the hills. Nevertheless, roads still remain at the centre of the government's and their donor community's efforts to provide access for farmers across Nepal.

Is there any hope?

From all of the above, we could reasonably conclude that government and donor actors have got more important things on their minds than improving the livelihoods, and the supporting environments, of those at whom their projects are purportedly targeted. Roads, as we have seen, tie in nicely with these important things; ropeways do not. This conclusion is given further support when we look at that crucial step in the process of development: the replication of those projects that have proved themselves to be successful. Why, we should ask, has the Bhattedanda Milkway – a success if ever there were one – not been replicated?

It is difficult to give a straight answer to this question, but we can draw some inferences by looking at the types of projects that *have* been replicated and then comparing them with those that have not:

- Projects that tie in smoothly with 'distorted hierarchy' – projects, that is, that conform to the unflattering self-interest rationality that is assumed by public choice theory – have enjoyed replication throughout the Age of Aid (as is evident in this chapter and in the ones that follow).
- Some projects – roads are the prime example – start off under government responsibility and then remain under it (at best, as with some roads, they may be devolved to local government). Others start off within the ambit of the intended users, and with the government eventually bowing out, as it were, with responsibility then passing to the users themselves.

We find many instances of replication in each of these categories: roads (first category), irrigation (first category), water supply projects (both categories), poultry farming (second category), tree planting (second category, usually) and so on. Ropeways (at any rate, at the time of Bhattedanda) fall between these two categories: the users lack the capability to raise the funds and assemble the technical expertise needed for the design and construction of another ropeway, while the existing ropeway has already passed out of government responsibility (and, on top of that, ropeways are not high on the government's list of priorities). The government, therefore, did not go on to build any more ropeways, even though it already had the money and the programme to build three more in the immediate vicinity of Bhattedanda. The money, which was actually in Nepal, was refunded to the European Union.[11]

With all these factors working against them, the chances for ropeways in Nepal appear to be on a par with those of the proverbial snowball in hell. There are, however, some signs that things may not be quite so hopeless. First, the way in which the villagers on Bhattedanda acquired the technical skills, not just to operate the ropeway but to extensively modify and improve it, shows that, rather than falling between the two categories, ropeways are now very much within the second one. And this is confirmed when we look at the way they have repeatedly reformed the management system until they got it right (right, that is, for the sort of public-cum-common-pool good that they need).

Furthermore, ropeways may still not be near the top of the government's list of priorities, but roads are now very much on their way down that list. It is increasingly apparent that many of them are public bads, not public goods, and this is even more the case when, as has also been happening thanks to the focus on climate change, the environmental costs are taken into account. Of course, there may be ways in which roads could be eased across from badness to goodness: clipping ropeways onto them, as we have seen, is one such way. And, since it is fossil-fuelled vehicles that are the problem, not vehicles *per se*, locally produced biofuels and/or vehicles powered by hydroelectricity (with hydrogen as the energy 'carrier') offer another transitional pathway.

At the same time, the long-established network of tracks and footbridges has not gone away, and it is (and always has been) environmentally friendly. Ropeways offer a constructive way of harnessing the long-neglected synergies of these supposedly rivalrous transport systems: roads and footpaths. The Ranas did wonders for the network of footpaths by throwing what are, in effect, crude ropeways – suspension bridges and *ghirlings* – across the raging torrents in the bottoms of the deep valleys, and that good work could readily be continued by throwing more sophisticated versions right across the valleys themselves. In other words, ropeways do not have to be connected to a road. Portering – a crucial source of income, especially for the poorest of the rural inhabitants – would get a substantial boost while, at the same time, having the worst of its associated drudgery – the long and gruelling ascents and descents – removed.

A final, and in many ways paradigm-shifting, point – a point that is reiterated in our final chapter – is that the new framing in terms of climate change brings with it a mass of uncertainties (or, rather, *contradictory certainties*) that can neither be resolved nor denied.[12] The uncontested terrain that has long been the dominant institutional characteristic of the Age of Aid has gone. Other voices (besides the hierarchical one, that is) are being increasingly heard, even by those who would dearly like to silence them, and clumsy solutions are set to become increasingly prevalent. The Bhattedanda Milkway is a fine exemplar of that rosier (but messier, noisier and more argumentative) future.

Notes

1 Very different, that is, from the long, trans-district ropeways, from the Terai up to Kathmandu of the type built by the Ranas in 1924 and USAID in 1964. These are short-haul ones: about three kilometres as the crow flies.

2 L. Barnaby (Barney) Smith, in marked contrast to most aid providers, was explicitly committed to the idea that risk-taking is crucial to development. He was writing about the Barpak ropeway that benefited greatly from the Ambassador's Special Fund, enabling the promotors to import a second-hand Swiss army ropeway to be installed between the valley bottom settlement of Rangrung to the hamlet of Barpak some five hours' climb uphill, which the ropeway took only 20 minutes to negotiate. (Barpak was also the epicentre of the April 2015 Gorkha earthquake, which devastated central Nepal.) See Barney's preface in Gyawali *et al.* (2004).

3 Out of 8 MDGs, Goal 1 (Eradicate Extreme Poverty and Hunger) and Goal 7 (Ensure Environmental Sustainability) were relevant to this project. Halving the poverty by 2015 was nearly achieved by Nepal, not by development projects but by remittance income. Similarly, reducing biodiversity loss is likely to be achieved because hills are getting depopulated with out-migration and substantial reduction in livestock keeping by those that remain behind.

4 *Khit-Khites* and *ghirlings* are cables with some sort of trolley sliding along them. A *khit-khite* is just a wooden seat hanging from a pulley wheel; *ghirlings* are more sophisticated, having a carriage and secondary cables to pull it back and forth. See Gyawali *et al.* (2004).

5 'Social mobilisation' was seen as the way to involve communities in planning and implementing projects and also in their monitoring. It mainly focused on the already-proven forest users group approach in biodiversity, which was completely different from what was needed to replicate ropeways.

6 One system killing off another is something that quite often happens with transport technology, and this is always going to be a possibility with ropeways. Sachs (1984) describes in great detail how and why the automobile won the competition against the railways. It is important, therefore, to give this adequate consideration when assessing the economic viability of a proposed ropeway. First, since roads in Nepal are always at risk of being destroyed, ropeways can have a belt-and-braces value (as turned out to be the case with the Bhattedanda ropeway). Second, ropeways, unlike roads, can easily be dismantled and installed somewhere else (the Swiss army can do this in less than 24 hours). This means that, as long as there is somewhere else that needs one, the cost incurred in ropeway becoming redundant is quite small (and therefore can be allowed for in the initial costing of a particular installation).

7 Air travel, and the associated construction of airports and airstrips, is a partial exception. Partial, because air transport, being expensive, is appropriate only for high-value goods – tourists, for instance – and very few agricultural products have a sufficiently high

value-to-weight ratio. Interestingly, though the Ranas were very fond of their cars and built roads for them to run on in the Kathmandu Valley, their not inconsiderable development efforts beyond the valley were concentrated on measures to improve the speed, safety and reliability of pedestrian travel, mostly in the form of well-engineered suspension bridges (many of which are still in place, some with the words 'made in Aberdeen' sunk into the cast iron) across the Himalayan torrents that had long been such obstacles to travel (especially against the grain of the country).

8 Though they might well wish to import various goods: foodstuffs, for instance, to make good the deficit caused by their detensification. This sort of shift, combined with out-migration to towns and cities, is what happened in the more marginal rural areas of Europe during the Industrial Revolution.

9 Nepal already imports petroleum fuel worth 35 per cent more than its total export earnings. Increasing vehicular road traffic will add further pressure on its forex reserve.

10 The similarities here are with the establishing of community forests (see Chapter 11) and with more recent ventures in community electricity. For an explanation of the four kinds of goods – *public, private, common-pool* and *club* – see Verweij (1999).

11 After the ropeway's closure, in 2001, a number of site visits and investigations showed why the replication did not happen. The ropeway had been operating smoothly until the Jhakridanda/Chhabeli road was re-opened in 2001, but political and personal clashes within the ropeway's management committee had already started becoming manifest. It was also found that the users had lost interest in restarting the ropeway because it had become cheaper to use the small trucks that plied the reopened road. At the same time, the ropeway committee lost interest because the ropeway had not been transferred to them; and it was learned that most of the committee members had other political and business interests and were not giving enough time and attention to the ropeway. Indeed, they did not know how much revenue had been collected or even the name of the bank (and its branch) into which the funds had been paid. All this changed, however, in the wake of the road's destruction in 2002 and the reopening of the ropeway.

12 For an explanation of the important distinction between the long-recognised *decision-making under uncertainty* and the largely ignored *decision-making under contradictory certainties* see Thompson and Gyawali (2007) and Beck *et al.* (2011).

6   Whither electric vehicles?

Ashok Raj Pandey

In 1986, after a sojourn of six years in the United States, I returned to Nepal for a brief visit. It was wintertime, and the fresh clean air was so refreshing that I had to ask myself what I was doing living in America. I resolved to return to Nepal more often and, over the next few years, I noticed that breathing the air of my home country was no longer as pleasant as it had been. Indeed, the air quality in the Kathmandu Valley quickly became as bad – worse, even – as the worst that the States could offer. Then, in 1989, India blockaded Nepal, Nepal having done something – an arms deal with China – of which it did not approve. Nepal, at that time, was totally dependent on India for petroleum products, and the embargo soon began to hurt. Stockpiles within Nepal were quickly depleted and there were soon long queues for kerosene, liquefied petroleum gas (LPG), petrol and diesel. Traffic was grinding to a halt and households across the country were finding it ever more difficult to cook their food. Desperate times call for desperate measures, and a group of engineers, together with a local financier, set about developing a four-wheel electric vehicle that would be able to run on the hydroelectricity that is generated entirely within Nepal.

They began by converting a Volkswagen 'Beetle' and, within a year, had it running on the streets of Kathmandu. Since nothing like this had ever been attempted in Nepal, it was a considerable achievement. However, as with so many prototypes, it was far from trouble-free. It had a range of just 12 to 15 kilometres, and there turned out to be serious problems with recharging the batteries. Even so, it was of great symbolic value: a vehicle that, in running without imported fossil fuel, brought the promise of a Nepal that could be truly independent of India: a long-nurtured hope of many Nepalis and (as we have seen in Chapter 4) an explicit policy aim during the country's 30 years of 'guided democracy'. The vehicle was slow and, as it drove silently around the capital, people were able to have a good look at it, marvelling at the absence of exhaust fumes and, at times, cursing it for giving them no warning of its approach. But it was not just independence from India that this promised; it also brought the possibility of doing something about Kathmandu's ever-deteriorating air quality, a major threat to the health and quality of life of the residents and an effective deterrent to the tourists who are so large a component of the country's economy. Indeed, the increasingly thick photo-chemical smog often prevented the planes carrying those tourists who *were* prepared to brave the toxic air from landing, the airport not being equipped for landing by instrument and some fatal crashes having prompted strict rules about visibility. So, if only the technology could be made to work, there were two glorious prospects: independence from India and an end to our pollution. To these, of course, now that climate change has risen to the top of the development agenda, can be added a third: the transition from fossil fuels to renewables.

The case of the dirty white shirt

By the early 1990s, pollution in the Kathmandu Valley – a fertile 30 kilometre-diameter basin containing no fewer than seven UNESCO-designated World Heritage Sites – was becoming unbearable. Ward chairpersons (the city is divided into wards, a ward being the lowest administrative level) began complaining that their white shirts, after being worn for just a couple of hours, were becoming black and smutty because of the smoke emitted by the ubiquitous *tempos*: three-wheeler diesel-powered taxis. Older people, especially those suffering from bronchial complaints, were finding it more difficult to breathe, and government statistics showed that asthma among children was on the rise. Tourists arriving in 'Shangri-La' from Los Angeles encountered air pollution even worse than that which they had left behind. That was if their planes had managed to land overcoming the visibility hurdle. With tourism a major, and growing, component of the country's economy, this was serious. While disgruntled tourists may not have had much clout, ward chairpersons who were having to change their white shirts twice a day did. Something would have to be done, and doing something about the *tempos* seemed the obvious first step on the way to a pollution-free Kathmandu Valley.

These three-wheeler vehicles – Bikram Tempos, to give them their proper name – were, it was rumoured, powered by the same diesel engine as is popularly used to pump water for irrigation. Though not a highly efficient engine, it has the merit of being 'cheap and cheerful'. Nor is such a 'cross-over' unique. In Rajasthan, in India, much larger diesel engines that power irrigation pumps are disconnected and mounted on carts during the season when there are no crops in the fields so as to provide an effective (if slow, polluting and illegal) form of transport for both goods and people (DST 2008).[1] With the vehicle itself being inexpensive, the Bikram Tempo quickly became the transport of choice in the Valley, especially among its poorer inhabitants working in carpet and garment factories, and they were soon plying their trade along an even more dense network of routes connecting the outlying towns, suburbs and villages with the city centre. Despite the occasional accident, their popularity rose steadily and as the fleet grew ever larger and more over-packed so did the pollution, with the smoke being particularly dense wherever there were slight inclines. The ward chairpersons' shirts were getting blacker and blacker and the declining air quality could no longer be ignored.

It was at around this time that the deputy mayor of Kathmandu, while on a visit to Portland, Oregon, discussed the pollution-cum-transport problem with Peter Moulton, the founder of an INGO (international non-governmental organisation) called the Global Resources Institute. Moulton then visited Kathmandu, where he enlisted USAID's support for a project to develop an alternative to the diesel-powered vehicles and established an office in the city. The idea, which, in the light of the failure (in all but symbolic terms) of the electric VW beetle four years before, was clearly not without risk. It was, however, well-intentioned to kick-start Nepal's electric vehicle industry.

The Global Resources Institute staff quickly established that the main source of the pollution, as suspected, was the 600-strong fleet of diesel-powered *tempos*, and that that was therefore where the initial effort should be concentrated. Before turning to the electric vehicle path, however, they looked into the less radical possibility of switching the fleet from diesel to LPG (liquefied petroleum gas). Together with the director general of Nepal's Department of Transport Management, Mohan Bir Singh Tuladhar, they visited Bangkok, where LPG-powered vehicles were already widely used for public transportation. The director of Thailand's Department of Transport told them that there were some safety concerns associated with their LPG-powered *tempos*. Some had exploded and lives had been lost. He further explained that LPG was, at best a stopgap solution, since the level of carbon dioxide emissions, though much less than with diesel, was still considerably higher than is permitted in many cities around the world. For Kathmandu, with its particularly smog-prone atmospheric conditions, LPG imported from India was clearly a non-starter, a decision particularly vindicated during another economic blockade by India since October 2015, when it stopped all LPG and other petroleum products from entering Nepal.

With LPG out of the reckoning, electric vehicles were indeed the only alternative. Since electric vehicles had never been tried (let alone used) for public transportation, it seemed sensible, as a first step, to import two different three-wheeler chassis from Indian manufacturers: one a Sitara, the other from a company in Lucknow called Scooters India. Their development started in 1994, with technical assistance from two experts who were themselves working on an electric vehicle project in Sacramento, California. One concentrated on the basic technology suitable for conditions in Nepal, while the other focused on the development of a charging technology that would prolong battery life (battery life having been identified as crucial to the economic viability of the enterprise). By 1995, eight vehicles had been built and street-tested along several *tempo* routes. The designs were further improved and, by the middle of that year, they were ready for full trials on the city's streets.

Breaking into the market

Getting the product fully street-tested is, however, only half the battle; it then, assuming it has proved itself technologically, has to break into the market.

That it eliminates the ward chairpersons' dirty white shirts and undercuts the unit costs of the competition is no guarantee of acceptance if those who, one way or another, have invested in the competition are intent on sabotaging the new technology. These vested interests, it turned out, were formidable, comprising not just the owners and operators of the 600 diesel-powered *tempos*, along with the dealers and importers of the vehicles, but also all those in the government bureaucracy who were the recipients of kickbacks and other rent-seeking benefits of the 'licence raj'.

The Global Resources Institute, alert to all these obstacles to market entry, elected to follow the line of least resistance:

- In order to avoid any direct confrontation with the diesel-powered vehicles, a new route – one that did not interfere in any way with the existing routes – was established. This enabled the street-testing to go ahead largely unnoticed, and was a wise move in that it avoided ruffling the feathers of the 'transport mafia' – petroleum dealers, Bikram owners and operators. The new and unobtrusive route started in August 1995 and ran for a trial period of six months.
- A brand name – SAFA Tempo – was chosen for the new vehicle, in the hope that this would make it easier for people to realise that it was completely different form the existing diesel three-wheeler. SAFA means 'clean' in Nepali and *tempo* was, by now, a household name. They were also painted white so as to clearly differentiate them from the diesel *tempos*, all of which were blue.
- Advertising and other forms of publicity were avoided so as not to stoke up resistance to the new technology, with the result that many commuters did not hear about these mysterious machines. Nor, if they happened to see them – empty and silently sliding by – did they realise that they were intended for public transportation.

Even so, the news gradually spread by word of mouth, and at the end of the six-month trial the seven vehicles were handed over to a private operating company – the Nepal Electric Vehicle Industry (NEVI) – after a sealed-bid auction. It had been formed when the news spread that the Global Resources Institute was planning to auction the vehicles and the charging station, and it commenced commercial operation on 21 February 1996.

It was also in 1996 that *Newsweek* magazine published an aptly titled article, 'Goodbye, Shangri-La', which highlighted the bad air quality and environmental degradation in Kathmandu. It caused a furore, prompting tourism entrepreneurs onto a warpath and forcing the government to announce 1998 as the 'Visit Nepal Year'. The tourist trade industry began a campaign to reduce water pollution, ban plastic bags and better manage the city's solid wastes, conserve heritage sites and clean up air pollution. Among them, Bharat Basnet of the Explore Nepal Group, a private tour operator, began the campaign in 1997 to displace Bikram *tempos* from Kathmandu Valley by collecting 100,000 signatures, including that of Prime Minister Krishna Prasad Bhattarai and his well-regarded minister for environment Bhakta Bahadur Balayar. In 1998 this forced the government to prohibit the import and registration of any more Bikram *tempos*, thereby simultaneously preventing the pollution from getting any worse and sounding the death-knell for this popular mode of transportation.[2]

The SAFA *Tempo*'s technology

A crucial prerequisite (as in Chapter 5 with Bhattedanda's Milkway) is that the technology can be understood, operated and maintained with the technical capabilities of the indigenous mechanics. The Global Resources Institute had therefore kept the technology simple; though more sophisticated technology already existed in other countries – Singapore, for example – they opted for a DC (direct current) motor, which, being cheaper and more straightforward, was more easily handled in the Nepal context. Deep cycle lead/acid batteries were chosen, both for their cheapness and for ease of maintaining and charging (other batteries were considered but proved to be prohibitively expensive). To provide enough power for the normal daily run, a 72-volt system, using 12 six-volt batteries, was chosen, with the initial batteries (T-105s, developed by the US-based Trojan Battery Company) providing a 20-hour capacity of 215Ah. On the fairly level routes that were being considered, this was sufficient to give a daily range of about 60 kilometres.

The DC motor had a rated power of 6KW (or 8.5HP), with a maximum capacity of 15KW (or 22HP) and the speed controller had a maximum capacity of 275A and 72–120V. A DC/DC converter was fitted so as to convert the 72V battery system to 12V in order to power the lights and horns (but there was also a cheaper version in which the converter was omitted). The chassis came with a clutch and gearbox (five gears including reverse) but, in order to keep things as simple as possible, only the second gear was used, thereby doing away with the need for the clutch. Reverse was then achieved by means of a switch that reversed the flow of the current, thereby causing the armature to rotate in the opposite direction.

Battery lifespan was absolutely crucial, since, along with the daily costs incurred in charging them, this was the principal running cost (battery lifespan being very much shorter than the lifespan of the vehicle itself). With the batteries being the most expensive part of the operation, much hinged on the battery-charging technology, since poor charging could greatly reduce battery lifespan. Initially, the project relied on chargers developed in Denmark. These were electronically controlled automatic chargers which were exactly matched to the charging profile that was required by the Trojan batteries. Charging took about 15 hours and this meant that each vehicle, to remain continuously operational, needed three sets of batteries: a considerable capital outlay. A few years after the handover, a higher-capacity charger, capable of charging the batteries in about 10 hours, was installed, and this meant that each vehicle could be reduced from three to just two sets of batteries (three sets of batteries were still needed, however, in those cases where the required range was in the 120–180km bracket).

Since these were lead/acid batteries, the question of their disposal (at the end of their useful life) came up soon after the handover. The technology could not be said to be environmentally friendly if (as is famously the case with nuclear waste) there were no possibility of recycling (or upcycling). Since each battery contained almost 20 kilograms of lead, and since more than 96 per cent of the entire world's lead is recycled, there were scrap dealers who would readily buy the spent batteries and take them to India for recycling. Indeed, the demand for the spent batteries was so strong that they never entered the waste realm; even when no longer of any use for powering the *tempos* they were still a valuable resource.

The first years after the handover

By the time NEVI took over, it was clear that the electric vehicles had indeed broken into the market; at the very least, a niche had been created within which the new technology was viable. The problems that then cropped up, while serious, were therefore not in any way concerned with the social acceptability of this novel mode of transportation.

The Global Resources Institute, it turned out, had been paying its drivers wages that were far in excess of the market rate as foreign donor agencies and international INGOs often do, and NEVI was in no position to continue with that. The drivers, however, were not prepared to take a pay cut and walked out of the job, leaving NEVI with no option but to recruit from the large labour pool of diesel tempo drivers and quickly retrain them for the electric versions. This resulted in a financially damaging loss of service which, fortunately, lasted only a few days.

As summer came around, the speed controllers on some of the vehicles started overheating, a fault that had gone undetected due to the street-testing having taken place during the winter months. The supplier generously replaced two controllers free of cost, but NEVI had to pay for the rest. NEVI was able to bear that expense, but was seriously concerned about its financial survival should there turn out to be any further teething problems. The technology's viability, at this early stage, was evidently precarious – a quite common state of affairs with products that are markedly different from what has preceded them – and NEVI just had to hope that they would not be hit by any other 'bolts from the blue'. Unfortunately, there was a rather large 'bolt' out there in the form of the Nepalese government bureaucracy.

Governments, it is now generally recognised, are not very apt at innovation; it is market actors – often small, risk-taking firms or almost 'stand-alone' auto-nomous units (such as Lockheed's famous Skunk Works)[3] within large firms – that are best at coming up with something new that works. But this is not to say that there is no role for government in the innovation process; governments need to act as 'enablers', giving clear, consistent and long-lived signals as to the sort of direction in which things need to go – away from fossil fuels and towards renewables, for instance – and to ensure, at the very least, that they do not provide incentives (hidden subsidies, for instance) for things to go in the opposite direction. The Nepalese government had done exactly this when it prohibited the further importation of the diesel-powered *tempos* that were clogging the lungs of Kathmandu's citizens and smudging the white shirts of its ward chairpersons. And it was this clear signal that had provided the initial impetus for the development of the electric vehicles that were now up and running on the city's streets. What was lacking, however, were the consistency and the long timescale of that signal.

The Global Resources Institute, being part-funded by USAID, had no difficulty in registering its electric vehicles in its name. This was thanks to donors having a special clout with the Nepalese government (just one of the ultimately debilitating features of aid dependency). Indeed, Peter Moulton was able to gain a host of concessions: low customs duty and rebates on other taxes for the imported chassis and for the various components, all justified on the grounds that the unit costs were high because of the small number of vehicles being produced and that taxes and duties at the rates levied on the diesel-powered competition would kill the technology off before it could get going. However, after handover the government ruled that these concessions did not apply to private companies, and registration in NEVI's name was no longer straightforward. Indeed, the law was applied so strictly that registration was denied, on the grounds that the importation of all three-wheeled vehicles (and not just the polluting diesel-powered ones) had been prohibited. It took NEVI more than six months to find a way around this self-defeating interpretation of the law and get its vehicles registered.

With that obstacle resolved, NEVI set about increasing production and, over the summer of 1996, manufactured a further eight vehicles. On the basis of its experience, NEVI altered the technology, using a different chassis and switching from a 250A to a 400A speed controller. These were street-tested on a completely new route and, by February 1997, a total of 15 electric vehicles were in operation on two routes.

The 'Catch 22' situation, however, was that the electric vehicles were considerably more expensive than the diesel ones, because of the small numbers being produced, while the banks were unwilling to provide the finance needed to increase the number and drive down the cost. It was at this moment that another member of the donor community – the Danish agency, Danida – came to the rescue by purchasing seven of NEVI's vehicles and handing them over to the Ministry of Population and Environment for regular work. Without that intervention, NEVI (and, quite possibly, the whole of Nepal's electric vehicle industry) might well have collapsed. Just a few months after NEVI had been set up, another company, with a number of prominent Nepalese businessmen as shareholders – the Electric Vehicle Company (EVCO) – entered the field. It too ran into the same problems as NEVI, and Danida, with admirable even-handedness, rescued it too by buying some of its vehicles.

So we see a two-stage donor involvement: the Global Resources Institute (plus USAID) helping to get the technology going, and then Danida stepping in when, thanks in large part to Nepal government's lack of consistency, the technology faltered. It was, as the Duke of Wellington said of the Battle of Waterloo, a 'close-run thing'.[4] Danida, using its donor clout, then approached the Nepalese government with a proposal for converting all the existing diesel-powered *tempos* (there were more than 600 of them) across to electricity. This, of course, was the logical next step in the direction that had been so clearly signalled by the government, just a few years before, when it responded to the capital's ever-worsening air pollution by prohibiting any further importation of the diesel-powered *tempos*.

The proposal was not well-received, thanks to a strong mutuality of interest (of which both Danida and NEVI were unaware) between the Federation of Nepalese Transport Entrepreneurs and the automobile importers. The government backed down in the face of this formidable alliance, and the whole idea of conversion had to be shelved. Danida then used the funds that it had available for conversion to finance the purchase of a further 48 electric vehicles for public transportation. This was at the behest of the Ministry of Population and Environment and was regularised in the form of a public loan. However, this step may not have been necessary, since the fiscal year 1999/2000 witnessed a surge in demand for, and sales of, electric vehicles. This was largely due to changes, back in 1998, when the Agriculture Development Bank and the Rastriya Banijya Bank – both owned by the Nepalese government – came up with financing schemes for the purchase of electric vehicles. At last, with the market broken into and with the obstacles to financing removed, the technology was not just filling its niche but widening it as well.

At the time of handover from the Global Resources Institute (February 1996), the only electric vehicles in Nepal were the ones that NEVI took over, and the only charging station in operation was owned by them too. Manufacturer, charging station owner and fleet-owner were thus all rolled into one, but within just four years all that had changed. NEVI's fleet of 15 vehicles was but a fraction of the 600 that were by then on the road, and its charging stations were just three among a total of 36. Three more manufacturers had entered the market, with EVCO the largest, followed closely by NEVI. By 2000, NEVI's share of fleet ownership was only 2.5 per cent, its share of charging stations (in terms of the total number of vehicles charged) was 16 per cent and its market share in vehicle production had fallen to around 38 per cent. And vehicle operation had expanded from the original two routes to 20.

On the technical side, the chargers (initially imported from Denmark and subsequently from India) were completely replaced by ones manufactured in Nepal: some manually operated; others designed with microprocessors. The forward/reverse switch, which had done away with the need for a gearbox and had been imported from India, was replaced by a more compact unit that was developed in Nepal. There were also great strides in terms of the 'know-how' needed to maximise battery life, that being a crucial factor, given that the cost of a set of 12 batteries, in a poor country like Nepal, was more than the year's income of most electric vehicle owners. At the time of the handover in 1996, the battery life was expected to be 12 months but NEVI was able to achieve an average battery life of 21 months and many batteries even lasted as long as 24 months.

With the niche becoming wider and wider, and with design and production almost completely 'indigenised', Nepal was well on its way to being the world leader in low-tech and inherently green electric vehicle technology. But, just as things were at last looking rosy, the signals from the government became inconsistent once more. The Department of Transport Management, it turned out, had been working behind the scenes to permit the import of LPG vehicles from Thailand, a step that would, as we have already seen, directly contradict the advice, over both safety and environmental concerns, that had been given by Thailand's Director of Transport. Despite this, permission was granted (and, as so often happens with the 'licence raj', to just one company) for the importation of 10 LPG-powered *tempos*, on a 'trial basis'. The Department of Transport Management did not conduct any emission tests on the carbon monoxide emissions on the *tempos*. Instead they manipulated the tests conducted on an old Japanese four-wheel vehicle that had been imported into Nepal and converted to a LPG-powered vehicle.

Overall, four emission tests were conducted on the converted four-wheeler. The first three tests had indicated that the carbon monoxide emissions while idling were 0.5 per cent above the mandatory 3 per cent limit; some of the parts were then replaced and, on the strength of just one test conducted immediately after replacement of the parts (which indicated emissions of 1.25 per cent) permission was granted. On the basis of this one test, the vehicles were classified as 'non-polluting' and could therefore be imported with a 99 per cent exemption of customs duty.

The ultimate recommendation for import was made to the Ministry of Finance by the Ministry of Population and Environment, based on the recommendation of the Department of Transport Management. 'Non-polluting', we should note, as well as being based on just the one test, refers only to carbon monoxide – a toxic component of the emissions – and takes no account whatsoever of the carbon dioxide, the greenhouse gas that is the inevitable accompaniment of all fossil fuels and that is completely eliminated in the switch to hydroelectric-powered vehicles.

The report by the Institute of Engineering, which had carried out the tests, went on to state, categorically, that these were not non-polluting vehicles because, if they were to operate for mass transportation, they would need at least one LPG filling station. The Department of Transport Management dismissed this objection (on the grounds that, since no such filling station currently existed, permission could not be withheld) and gave the go-ahead for 650 *tempos* to be imported.

The government requires that emissions tests be carried out, each year, on all vehicles with internal combustion engines operating in the city of

Kathmandu. Vehicles are then given stickers: green for emissions below the mandated limit, yellow for those that are borderline (with another test required within a month) and red for those that are over the limit. Vehicles with red stickers are banned from the central area of the city. However, the Department of Transport Management exempted the LPG *tempos* from any such tests for a period of two years, thereby ensuring that, by the time the polluting effects had been recognised through the emission tests, the vehicles would be fully entrenched in the system. So the government was giving signals that were not just contradictory; they were the exact reverse of the ones they had given during the period when the desired, and genuinely non-polluting, technology was being developed. Winrock – an environmental INGO – came to the aid of NEVI (and the other electric vehicle companies) and filed a lawsuit in the Supreme Court, but its ruling was that the decision could not be reversed.

An unfortunate policy for the new millennium

The government's remarkable lack of consistency, it is tempting to conclude, reveals that it really has nothing that could be called a policy. That, however, is not the case. There *is* a policy, and it is short-term and revenue-driven, which is to stay un-green whatever the environmental costs. In consequence, it is oblivious of anything long-term and necessarily green. That is why consistency is of no concern, and why actors – such as NEVI, the Global Resources Institute and Danida – who, while not unaware of the day-to-day necessity of not going bust, are banking on a long-term transition from fossil fuels to renewables, have been getting such a rough ride. But, by the turn of the millennium, when they had broken into the market and were rapidly expanding the niche they had created, these actors should (according to the orthodox 'Austrian' economic theory) have found themselves being swept along by a Schumpeterian gale of destruction: a runaway process in which the old technology is quickly replaced by the new.[5] That this did not happen is down to the government's revenue-driven policy, and that, in turn, has its origin in the government's long-term relationship with its donor community.

I will conclude by briefly setting out the key instances of this policy, as it has impacted the electric vehicle sector over the first decade of the new millennium. This far-from-happy experience is also driven home in Box 6.1, which chronicles how one green-minded and forward-looking Nepalese citizen paid dearly for his valiant efforts to do 'the right thing'.

In 1998 the Nepalese government, in what looked like a fit of consistency, decreed that Kathmandu was to be free of diesel-powered *tempos* within just two years. Unsurprisingly, this gave a major boost to the fledgling industry, with 105 electric vehicles being produced in 1998–99, accelerating to 380 in 1999–2000. The wind of technological change, it was evident, was building up to gale force, aided and abetted by the direct action of a home-grown tour operator – the Explore Nepal Group and its intrepid campaigner Bharat Basnet described above – that blocked the operation of the diesel-powered

BOX 6.1 SAVING THE PLANET ONE CAR AT A TIME

When I first bought an electric car ten years ago, it was to make a statement. As the price of petrol doubled in that time, and Nepal was hit by regular fuel shortages and climaxed with the five-month Indian blockade in 2015, having an electric car became more than a statement – it was a necessity. With 0.01 ton of carbon per capita per year, whatever we do in Nepal is not going to make a difference on saving the planet. But switching to renewables can save our economy and perhaps even our country. Nepal has harnessed less than 800MW of its hydropower potential, and currently suffers 12-hour power cuts a day. Diesel and petrol generators provide up to 700MW of captive power to homes and businesses. Nepal's import of diesel from India had tripled in the past five years. The overwhelming dependence on energy imports has made Nepal not just economically dependent on India, but also politically, as the blockade proved.

Before I became a journalist I was a science graduate and had done my master's thesis on methanogenic thermophilic bacteria. I had helped my mother build a biogas plant back in 1980. The digester has seen three generations of cows, and still supplies methane to our kitchen. I started writing about environmental issues, linking them to development and politics, but I felt it was hypocritical to be pontificating away about global warming and have a large carbon footprint myself. I used to commute by bicycle, but Kathmandu's pollution meant it was like smoking two packs of cigarettes a day. So, when a pioneering Kathmandu-based renewable energy company called Eco-Vision decided to import small Indian-made electric cars called Reva in 2000 I was immediately interested. I didn't expect it to be so difficult, and didn't realise that the Nepalese government actually made it expensive for citizens to go green. The first four cars were ordered in 1999 after a written government directive that electric vehicles would only have to pay 10 per cent excise. But when the cars arrived, Eco-Vision was told it had to pay 150 per cent tax like all petrol cars. So the cars rotted in a customs shed at the border for six years.

Finally, Eco-Vision bought the cars back at a government auction for scrap. The vehicles were rebuilt from scratch at the company garage in Kathmandu, they got new seats, new batteries, a new motor and new tyres. In August 2006, expecting that my Reva would be ready, I sold my Maruti WagonR. No such luck. A cabinet meeting presided over by none other than the prime minister had to approve the registration of the four tiny refurbished electric cars. At a time when the country couldn't afford to import petroleum because it couldn't cut subsidies for political reasons, the government wasn't willing to announce a tax rebate on electric cars. Calculations show that even by cutting the import tax, the government would more than make up for the loss in five years just from savings on the petrol it wouldn't have to import for one car. When I asked our learned finance minister how come the government didn't cut taxes for electric vehicles, his reply was: "If everyone starts importing electric cars where is the government going to get its revenue?"

It took the cabinet six months to reluctantly sign the registration for four measly cars. But that wasn't the end of the story: Eco-Vision had to work another six months to work the files through the transportation and tax bureaucracy. World Environment Day on 5 June 2006 came and went, but the Revas were still grounded. Finally, on 20 August my little green Reva finally had its red licence plates but not before I had to shell out another Rs150,000 for VAT. All in all, the car cost 18,000 dollars, 70 per cent of which went to the government in taxes.

Since then, I have been the launch customer in Nepal for the new model Reva, and then since Reva was sold to Mahindra in India I have been driving the e2O since 2013. The electric cars have blown holes in my pocket, I have to rummage to pay my car loan at the end of every month. But all of this is more than compensated by the experience. In the decade that I started driving electric in Kathmandu, the petroleum shortage has got worse, there are lines at the gas stations sometimes 4km long.

From September 2015 to January 2016, during the Indian blockade, there was no petrol or diesel, and if it was available it cost five times more in the black market. LPG gas cylinders were selling for 10 times the price. But I was insulated because we had biogas for the home kitchen and an electric car for transportation. There are other benefits to driving a small electric vehicle in a city where might is right, I feel absolutely benign and harmless. I don't suffer from road rage anymore; I don't roll down the window to shout obscenities at bus drivers and motorcyclists. Because I'm small, I can't afford to show the dirty finger at anyone. I've learnt to go with the flow. Since the car is so quiet, pedestrians can't hear it coming so I have fitted a siren-type horn to warn people to get out of the way along Kathmandu's sidewalk-less roads.

I have to keep an eye on the charge gauge, although the e2O needs to be charged only once every three days for my average daily 20km commute. The car can do 100km on a full charge that takes about five hours and costs Rs 40. Yes, it's a bit cramped inside and my wife says I look like Mr Bean. People on the road point at the car and laugh. Kids wave at me from school buses, and I wave back. Traffic police at intersections smile and give me priority. Three years ago, the government it its wisdom finally cut the excise duty by half on electric vehicles and we don't have to pay the Rs27,000 annual road tax. But that still means the cars cost Rs2.4 million – much above the other smaller Indian petrol cars in the market. The real priority now should be to bring the tax on electric public transport down to zero, give rebates to large diesel buses for urban commutes, and prepare the rebates for the next generation of electric vehicles so that we can finally say we have done our bit to save ourselves and the planet.

– Kunda Dixit, editor of the *Nepali Times*, Kathmandu

tempos in many areas of Kathmandu.[6] Indeed, this egalitarian-cum-individualist intervention forced the government's hand still further, causing it to set a two-month deadline for the removal of the remaining diesel-powered *tempos*.

However, instead of allowing the gale of destruction to do its work by replacing all the diesel-powered popular transport with the electric alternative, the government opted for the importation, 99 per cent free of both customs duty and value-added tax, of expensive microbuses with ICEs (internal combustion engines) from Japan and Indonesia. The electric vehicles, given their already impressive and accelerating production rate, were clearly fully able to fill the transport vacuum created by the two-month deadline, but the politicians, bureaucrats and vehicle importers had other ideas and were not prepared to forego the considerable profits they could make from the importation of close to 650 microbuses. Moreover, with government actors within their ranks, they were able to halt the gale of destruction by deploying a host of hierarchical instruments – permits, licences, tax exemptions and so on – in such a way that the market forces that were responsible for the gale were effectively overridden.

The government had stipulated that the microbuses' seating capacity should not exceed 12–14 and that their emissions should comply with the Euro-1 standard (as specified by the European Union in 1991 and later embodied in the Nepal 2056 standard). These standards are normally verified within the importing country but Nepal, not having the technical facilities for verification, should have relied on the next best sources. These are either the certifications of trustworthy manufacturers (such as Toyota) or those of government-recognised 'third parties' in the vehicles' country of origin. The Nepalese government, though it has elaborate rules for such matters, had none that applied to 'next best' certification and therefore left it to its Department of Transport Management (DOTM), which, of course, should have gone for one of the 'next best' options but chose instead to accept the certification that was provided by the importing agents in Nepal. And, of course, it was in the agents' interest to provide an acceptable certification, as long as they could be confident that there would be no punitive action in the event of that certification being found to be false. They were therefore much reassured when the government exempted the microbuses from pollution tests for two years.

This jiggery-pokery was then compounded when, on it emerging that the imported microbuses had 15 seats, the DOTM categorised them as 12-seaters, on the grounds that three of these seats were removable and therefore did not count. These seats, however, were not actually removed and all the imported diesel-powered microbuses are still operating with their full complement of 15 seats and, one might add, extra passengers standing crouched in the aisle space.

A lack of consistency as spectacular as this cannot have arisen just by accident (or even by 'cock-up'); it has to have its origin in well-entrenched corruption at all levels of government and within the political parties whose leaders were able to extract their shares from the under-the-table payments from the importers of the vehicles. Indeed, it seems likely that this entire scheme for importing the fossil-fuelled fleet of microbuses was hatched back at the time when the government was giving its signals in support of the long-term transition to renewable-powered popular transport. Since some of the electric vehicle entrepreneurs, encouraged by those government signals, had already turned their attention to the development of both renewable-powered four-wheeler cars and microbuses, this sudden reversal was a devastating blow, killing off this promising line of technological development while it was still in its embryonic stage. Worse, however, was to come, in the form of signal-reversals that threatened the lives of the electric three-wheelers that had so triumphantly broken into the market.

The imported microbuses were put into operation on all of the routes that were being plied by the three-wheeler *tempos*: both diesel and electric. Where, before, the electric *tempos* had been steadily replacing the diesel ones (their operating costs being similar but with the electric vehicles having a great advantage when it came to pollution, health and white shirts), both now had to compete with the microbuses which, as well as being more comfortable and aesthetically pleasing than the *tempos*, also had a cost advantage. With the un-green environmental costs of this competition no longer a consideration (the microbuses having been classified as 'non-polluting'), and with the sudden and massive increase in the supply of public transport, the income from the electric vehicles fell by more than 25 per cent. This fall then had a 'ripple effect' that spread to all the sectors of the electric vehicle industry: production, development and the charging stations (many more of which had been built in anticipation of steadily increasing demand for the electric *tempos*). This – a powerful actor conniving with the authorities to kill off the competition and create a monopoly for itself – is not 'fair competition', nor is it how, as Adam Smith explained long ago, markets are supposed to work. Indeed, in many countries (quite a few of which are members of Nepal's donor community) it would result in criminal proceedings against the perpetrators.

There being no criminal proceedings, a member of the donor community – Denmark – stepped in with a large and ambitious project – Environment Sector Programme Support (ESPS) – of which electric vehicles were a small part of the fifth component. The first step was the creation of a 'stakeholder organisation' – Electric Vehicles Association of Nepal (EVAN) – that brought together the vehicle owners, the manufacturers and the operators of the charging stations. Danida (the Danish aid agency) then funded EVAN through their project's somewhat brief life – around four years – helping in the establishment of two new routes, supporting some technical studies and providing subsidies for the production of 45 new electric vehicles (this latter, which was promoted by a Danish expert, was then sabotaged by rival manufacturers who, understandably, resented the unfair competition inherent in the subsidies going to only two of their numbers). Unfortunately, the ESPS's approval process was so demanding that very little else gained approval during its four years in existence.

In 2000, just after the microbuses had been imported, the Department of Transport Management came up with a proposal to import a fleet of 24-seater diesel-powered buses from China, arguing that, since these buses could each carry more commuters, they would be less polluting than their smaller competitors. And, in order to ease the introduction of these buses, the registration of new electric vehicles was banned. Evidently, the unexcised tumour had just grown larger.

EVAN, which, with Danida's assistance, was in the process of building 30 new electric vehicles, was understandably alarmed and was able to secure a meeting of its delegation with the prime minister, who reversed the ban. This meeting, and the ban-reversal, were not unconnected with the very public embarrassment the prime minister had suffered when, in the celebrations to mark World Environment Day, the Resident Representative of the United Nations, Henry Karcher, had turned to him and described the ban as 'a ridiculous decision'.

Not that that was the end of it. Shortly afterwards, on the basis of a study by the Ministry of Transport, the registration of electric vehicles was again banned, this time for a period of just under two years. Eventually, Danida, working through the Ministry of Labour and Transport (MOLT), was able to get the registration channel for electric vehicles opened up again. By that time, however, the electric vehicle industry was virtually dead.[7] While Danida's intervention certainly gave some life support to the electric vehicle industry during this difficult period, it was powerless in the face of a deeper cause: the government's scandalous approval of the importation of the microbuses.

For the electric vehicle industry to stay dead, however, its diesel-powered competition had to remain cost-effective (in terms of the costs it actually had to bear, that is, it having managed to wriggle out of the environmental costs, the consideration of which had, all those years before, provided the initial opening for the electric vehicle industry). By 2006, however, petrol and diesel prices had risen by 71 per cent and the price of LPG by 60 per cent. The operating costs of the fossil-fuelled vehicles therefore rose sharply; those for electric vehicles were largely unchanged. The result was that the incomes generated by those electric vehicles that were still in service rose markedly. Second-hand vehicles, antiques if not already marked for the scrap heap, started fetching prices considerably above what had been paid for them, back in 1999, when they had been new. One single manufacturer that was able to survive all along, and a new manufacturer which had just entered the market started to devise production plans so as to meet the new demand. Time, it would seem, to think!

Whither electric vehicles? Whither air pollution?

Kathmandu, and the valley in which it sits, provide what is probably a unique combination of opportunities for these low-tech and indigenous electric vehicles:

- Distances are short, and speeds (thanks to the narrow roads and streets and the variety of vehicles, humans and animals with which they are thronged) are low: circumstances that are well matched to the inherent properties of the electric *tempos*.
- Hydroelectricity is (or, rather, can be) produced almost everywhere within Nepal; it is cheap and its supply is potentially almost unlimited (how to actually realise that potential being the question that is explored in the next two chapters).
- The temperature in the city and its immediate surroundings, being neither too hot nor too cold, is nicely matched for satisfactory battery performance throughout the year (climate change may increase or decrease these temperatures, but not by enough to make any significant different to battery performance).
- The valley's atmospheric properties, being similar to those that prevail in Los Angeles, render it particularly prone to photo-chemical smog, and this means that the environmental costs that can be avoided by switching from diesel-powered to electric *tempos* are both high and readily appreciated. Indeed (as we have seen), tourist planes being unable to land, and ward chairpersons' white shirts having to be changed at distressingly short intervals, were among the early drivers of this new technology. That these costs have still not gone away is evident from the high proportion of citizens who routinely wear face-masks when they venture out (indeed, traffic policemen and women wear breathing apparatus and specially fitted goggles).

So Kathmandu has a host of comparative advantages when it comes to this novel technology: a novel technology, moreover, that has already broken into the market (only to later find itself squeezed out as a result of wholly unwarranted interventions in and distortions of that market). However, even if these interventions and distortions were removed, Nepal's home-grown electric vehicle technology might not be able to hold its own against the global competition. Most of the major car manufacturers around the world are now seriously into the development and production of electric and hybrid vehicles (though not, unlike Nepal, into the supply of electricity from renewable sources) and these may soon flood into Kathmandu as their diesel and petrol-powered models have done. So the electric *tempos* may not endure. Nevertheless, the very fact that they exist, and have proven themselves to be economically viable, is of immense significance because it reveals just how well-placed Nepal is in relation to the technologies of the future.

However, the three-wheeler electric vehicles that ran successfully in Kathmandu for much of the last two decades has continued to survive. Although production has not picked up because of the problem of route permits, a mandatory document required in order to operate a public vehicle in a particular route, some electric vehicles have been produced and sold but they were for special use and not for public transportation. The government is now considering permitting the production and route allocation of about 150 more electric vehicles for public transportation in Kathmandu, the capital city. This is an important development in the last year prompted by yet another Indian blockade for five months, when fossil fuel arrived in Nepal at a trickle far less than what was required for transportation. While this is a positive aspect that has evolved recently, the collapse of oil prices worldwide may create a damper once again on the electric vehicle industry in Nepal.

Electric vehicles in Nepal are however finding new applications in many spheres that were unthinkable many years back. Most of the areas in the southern plains or the Terai areas were served by *rickshaws* – human-operated three-wheel carts that ran like taxis and accommodated two passengers. These are being replaced by a three-wheel electric battery operated vehicle with capacity for four to five passengers. There were merely about 500 such vehicles towards the end of 2014, but today there are over 8,000 such vehicles running in different parts of the country, especially in the flat Terai. In addition, the Indian blockade has motivated many a family to purchase electric four-wheelers imported largely from India as an alternative to fossil fuel-based transportation. The range of modern electric vehicles is sufficient for commutes in Kathmandu and many electric cars are now seen on its streets. There are now plans in the Lumbini Development Project area (Buddha's birthplace) to use 10–14-seater electric buses for transportation inside the Lumbini world heritage site and the project is already taking steps to promote these buses for transportation. Electric vehicle transportation may have taken time to take off after a rather impressive beginning in Nepal, and overcome many hurdles that should not even have been there in normal development planning, but it may now slowly be turning the corner.

Notes

1 *Jugad* literally translates from several Indic languages as 'to make do with'. This 'toad's eye' innovation is the result of farmers (often illiterate) doing better economics than engineers and economists in the hydrocracies who insist that government procedures for subsidised loans for irrigation pumps be limited to three horsepower (HP). That would pump water alright, but do only that for, say, 2,000 hours a year (out of the total 8,760 hours). Adding their own resources and buying a 10HP pump would allow smart farmers, during the non-irrigation days, to fit it on a chassis and have a perfectly functioning (even if questionably legal) truck to transport their goods for another three to four thousand hours, thus earning a lot more money and preventing their 'sunk capital' from rusting for much of the year in a godown. See DST (2008), p. 79 for a view of *Jugad*.

2 Based on interview with Bharat Basnet. There is a not so happy ending to this environmental feel-good success story as will be described further below: K. P. Bhattarai was ousted as prime minister by his own party leader, G. P. Koirala, who succeeded him. Following the interests of vehicle importers, he allowed the displaced three-wheeler Bikrams to be replaced, not by less polluting electric vehicles but by microvans.

3 Wikipedia (https://en.wikipedia.org/wiki/Skunk_Works): The designation 'skunk works' is widely used in business, engineering and technical fields to describe a group within an organisation given a high degree of autonomy and unhampered by bureaucracy,

tasked with working on advanced or secret projects. The management approach is defined by founder Kelly Johnson's 'Kelly's Rules', still in use today, which empower small teams with streamlined processes and the culture that values the lessons learnt when you are bold enough to attempt something that hasn't been done before: (see: www.lockheed martin.com/us/aeronautics/skunkworks.html).

4 The battle was in 1815, a month before the end of the Anglo-Nepal hostilities that culminated in the December 1815 Treaty of Sugauli, which opened the way a few more decades later for Nepalis to begin their legendary service as Gurkhas in the British Army. Had they been there with Wellington, it might not have been a so 'close-run thing'.

5 A process – Schumpeter called it 'creative destruction' – that tends to be uncongenial to hierarchical actors who like to feel that it is they, and not these sorts of runaway market forces, that are in control (see Schumpeter (1942), also Arthur (2009)).

6 This is also another conceptual disjuncture in Nepal: the tour operator outfit that did this direct, Greenpeace-like mass action (the Explore Nepal Group) is registered as a private limited company but finally got so fed up of pollution that it morphed to become increasingly egalitarian. It is continuing its campaign to make Kathmandu pollution-free (and more hospitable to tourists and bring more profit to the tourism sector).

7 To confuse things further, DOTM is a department of the government of Nepal under the Ministry of Transport. The Ministry of Labour and Transport, or MOLT, was the combined ministry before the Ministry of Labour and the Ministry of Transport were broken up into individual ministries, a game that continues into the second decade of the twenty-first century, with more ministries being broken up to accommodate more coalition party ministers: the Ministry of Water Resources into the Ministry of Irrigation and the Ministry of Energy; the Ministry of Agriculture into the Ministry of Livestock and the Ministry of Agriculture etc.

7   Micro and small hydro

Serial leapfrogging to a braver new Nepal

Ajoy Karki

My fascination with renewable energy started as a young boy, during school holidays, when my father would take me to rural areas of Nepal to oversee biogas plants being installed. Dr Amrit Bahadur Karki was a microbiologist and soil scientist assigned in those days by the government to promote household biogas plants in the country; and for his efforts he is now recognised as the 'Father of Biogas in Nepal'. With this imprint of rural development, and after completing my engineering studies, hydropower and specifically small and micro hydropower became the obvious professional choice I gravitated towards.

Nepal's small hydropower sector has now attracted, and is being significantly transformed by, the modern social entrepreneur. But Nepalese social entrepreneurship, in itself, is nothing new. Traditionally, the village entrepreneur, seeing the potential in falling streams, set up the *pani ghatta*: the water-harnessing technology that has long been used to grind flour and, in the Buddhist regions, to power eternally revolving prayer-wheels as well. Their ingenuity relieved the village women of much of their daily drudgery; hence the validity of the term 'social entrepreneur', in contrast to the more individualistically motivated characters − 'entrepreneurs' − who are conventionally credited with driving capitalism.[1] Then came various improvements, with the water being captured into a tube with a turbine at its lower end that could be used to drive a flourmill or mustard oil press during the day and, when also fitted with a generator, provide light for after-dark operation and also for a few houses as well. These, in turn, were gradually improved upon, giving birth to an indigenous micro hydropower technology that now provides household lighting and larger-scale agro-processing services to remote hill and mountain communities that are unlikely to be reached by the national electricity grid for years, if not decades. Indeed, with the national grid now in retreat − in the sense that even the capital, Kathmandu, is subject to electricity outages of 16 hours a day − they may never be reached with grid expansion orthodoxy.

The modern social entrepreneur now sees this indigenous technology extending from agro-processing and village lighting to ropeways (as at Bhattedanda: see Chapter 5), to lift irrigation, to a variety of rural ('cottage industry') enterprises and also, wherever a surplus can be generated, the sale of electricity into the national grid. His, or her, rewards, as all this technological enterprise takes hold, are, of course, likely to become greater. This raises the crucial question of how these inherently individualised benefits might be shared in some way with the communities that reside within the watersheds that are the initial generators of the falling water that these social entrepreneurs are increasingly finding new ways of harnessing.[2]

Small hydro, clearly, is very much a 'bottom-up' technology, and therefore very different from the 'top-down' (and usually large) hydro that is distributed – to some, and when outages allow – by the national grid. They are, at present, separate from one another but they are destined to meet up, once the social entrepreneurs have got things to the stage where there are surpluses that can be fed into the national grid. Conventional economic theory, with its faith in what are called 'economies of scale', is not much help here, since it simply tells us that, when the two meet up, the large-scale technology will drive out its smaller-scale competitor, a conclusion that is not easily reconciled with the fact that, in Nepal (and as will be fully set out in a moment), electricity from the large-scale production units has consistently been much more expensive than that from the smaller-scale ones. However, as Bela Gold (1981) has pointed out, there is no empirical support whatsoever for the economies of scale argument, even though you will read it in all the economics textbooks and hear it banged down, like a trump card, in many a debate on development assistance. The fact is that big is not always best or efficient, and small is not always beautiful; the optimum usually lies somewhere in between and, often enough, there can be more than one optimum. Differently scaled production units, this means, can often co-exist, like symbiotic species in their respective ecological niches, without one of them ever being able to drive out the others (Arthur 1996).[3]

Nepal's hydropower species

The general consensus in Nepal is that hydropower plants up to 100kW are considered to be *micro hydro* and those between 100kW and 10MW are *small hydro*, with anything above 10MW being *large hydro* (although this categorisation varies between various institutions in Nepal, with some placing the 10 to 100MW range in the *medium hydro* category).[4] Hydropower development in Nepal started in 1911, when the 500kW Pharping plant was constructed to supply electricity to parts of the Kathmandu Valley: those parts of it that were occupied by the palaces of the Ranas, the ruling elite at that time. The country has come a long way since then in the hydropower sector but, even so, only about 40 per cent of the population enjoys access to electricity (and, even then, at time of writing, for just eight hours a day).[5] In Nepal, and in line with the early stages of development in many industrialised countries, the business of providing electricity services, especially through the national grid, was assumed to be the sole responsibility of the state.[6] Until the early 1990s the generation, transmission and distribution of electricity were entirely in the hands of a state-owned corporation: the Nepal Electricity Authority (or its predecessor, the

Nepal Electricity Corporation).[7] As the Nepal Electricity Authority was expanding its supply to urban areas and to those rural areas that were relatively accessible, many remote communities in the hills and mountains were installing micro hydro plants and managing their supply (including for agro-processing) on their own. In this way, 'top-down' and 'bottom-up' were both expanding and now have come face to face, often contentiously, in certain areas.[8]

Micro hydropower

The micro hydropower plants that were introduced across the hills of Nepal in the 1960s, together with the locally developed turbines, steadily replaced the diesel engines that were being used for agro-processing. Until then, with the power from the abundant nearby streams going untapped, the villagers had had to carry imported diesel fuel on their backs from town centres that were often several days' walk away. With the new technology demonstrably successful, the state-owned Agricultural Development Bank made credit facilities available, thereby making it easier for all those village entrepreneurs who wanted to set up agro-processing businesses – rice mills, oil expellers and grinders being the most prevalent applications – to actually do it.

By the early 1980s the technology had developed to the point where it became practicable to fit small dynamos to the turbine mills so as to generate electricity that would provide light for night-time operation of the machinery, with the surplus going to light a few nearby houses. This potential was then demonstrated, rather forcefully, when the small town of Malekhu, on the Prithvi Highway, was electrified from a turbine mill owned by a local entrepreneur. The Agricultural Development Bank, convinced once more, began promoting electricity generation from turbine mills by providing a 50 per cent subsidy on the cost of the electrical components for the micro hydro plants. Electricity generation (along with the boon of lighting in the villages) was thus an 'unanticipated consequence' of a small-scale technology that set out just to provide agro-processing, and it is this 'dual use' that has been the secret of its success. Government-initiated small hydroelectricity plants, which were being built around the same time, but which (being the responsibility of the Nepal Electricity Authority) were 'single use', never really took off, being unable to raise enough revenue for their operation and maintenance.

So it was the private sector-led and 'dual use' micro hydro plants, with the villagers in remote areas as their driving force, which flourished. These 'stand-alone' – that is, non-grid-connected – micro hydropower plants quickly came to be coveted in areas as remote as Mustang, a mountain community (once a semi-autonomous kingdom) that, in the 1980s, was four days' walk from the nearest roadhead. Once a village glowed with electric light, neighbouring villages could no longer bear to live in darkness, and this is how micro hydro spread: by word of mouth, by people power or by the ability of villagers to organise themselves: *social capital*, as it is now called. The government-initiated small hydropower plants, by contrast, had no such social capital that they could tap into.

There is a lesson here that must surely be of immense importance, and it is not the simple-minded idea that government/bureaucracy can do nothing and market individualism can do it all. The social entrepreneurs would have soon run into difficulties if it had not been for the subsidies and credit facilities provided by the government in the form of the Agricultural Development Bank. Nor could those two sets of actors have made a success of it without the common-pool good-based social capital of the communities with which they were working. And there is a scale lesson here too, in the sense that the technology's production units slotted neatly into the watersheds that, in providing the falling water, largely defined the *relevant* community and thereby enabled it to develop its social capital. In terms of the framework we set out in Chapters 1 and 2, this is very much a clumsy solution; the government-initiated power plants were much too elegant.

As a result of four decades of concerted effort and rapid 'organisational learning', by government, by financing institutions, by donors and by rural social entrepreneurs, Nepal now has a micro hydro sector, based on an indigenously developed technology, that is clearly up and running: an exemplar, when it comes to the problems that beset other areas of the country's development, and something that other mountainous countries can learn from. Nepal is now in a position to transfer this technology to other countries in much the same way that Austria transferred the ropeway technology to it. In other words, Nepal is all set to be a donor country.[9]

Micro hydro's penetration and potential

By around the start of the twenty-first century there were a total of 1,760 micro hydro plants in Nepal. The Alternative Energy Promotion Center (AEPC) was established in 1996 as a central body of the government to promote alternative energy, especially in the rural areas. Essentially, the AEPC took the role of the Agricultural Development Bank and started providing subsidies to isolated micro hydropower plants (and other renewable energy technologies) and using these subsidies as a leverage to ensure quality standards. Since the establishment of the AEPC, around 1,400 micro hydropower plants with over 25MW of aggregate installed capacity have been built and are now providing off-grid electricity to more than 400,000 rural houses (World Bank 2015).

Micro hydro, as well as having displaced fossil fuels (diesel) in agro-processing, has provided household lighting (which is the primary domestic electricity demand) to many remote villages in the hills and mountains of the country: areas that the national grid is unlikely to reach. The low (and decreasing) population density, together with the low commercial:domestic demand ratio, renders grid-connected rural electrification in remote areas financially unattractive. As well as meeting lighting requirements, micro hydro technology brings a multiplicity of other benefits – some tangible, others less so – to the rural population. The range of agro-processing services that it provides massively reduces the traditional time and labour inputs. Women, who are predominantly involved in these activities, are relieved of much drudgery, and men, who were predominantly involved in the porterage of the diesel fuel, are similarly unburdened. And their households, of course, benefit financially from the large reduction in costs that (as we have seen in Chapter 5 with the Bhattedanda Milkway) is entailed in this switch from fossil fuels to renewables. On top of all that, access to electricity is also access to information from TV, radio and mobile phones. The electric light gives the chance of longer study hours for children and the possibility of additional income-generation activities for their parents; and the health status of them all is considerably improved once the traditional kerosene lamps (*tuki*), the fumes of which irritate the eyes and lungs, are no longer needed.

However, though micro hydro technology has brought all these social benefits to these poorer parts of the country, it has yet to become commercially viable. It has been kept going by a range of government/donor subsidies which is around 50 per cent of the implementation costs (US$700/kW to US$1,300/kW depending on the remoteness of the community plus US$250/ household as subsidy but limited to maximum US$2550/kW). While these subsidies can readily be justified – on the grounds, for instance, that they provide, at a fraction of the cost, the same benefits as are enjoyed by those in urban areas who are served by a real physical infrastructure: the national grid – a technology that was commercially viable without subsidies would obviously be preferable. Small hydro might be that technology.

Micro hydro's low installed capacity (which prevents it from enjoying certain economies of scale) together with its low load factor (a consequence of it not being used to the full at certain times of the day) work rather strongly against its financial viability. Grid-connected small hydropower, on the other hand, would (in principle, at any rate) have a round-the-clock market for the electricity it generates. Of course, it would have to be close enough to the grid for it to be able to connect into it, and that is not at present feasible in all areas. Even so, many of the social entrepreneurs who have cut their teeth on micro hydro are now considering investing (indeed, some have already invested) in grid-connected small hydropower plants. And their years spent in implementing micro hydro all across the country have ensured that the skills, technical capacities and human resources that are needed for the design, construction and management of small hydro plants are already in place.

Small hydro

The Hydropower Development Policy, announced by the government in 1992, paved the way for private-sector participation (including foreign investment) in hydropower plants. Close on the heels of this announcement (and also of the revisions of the Electricity Act and Regulation so as to reflect these policy measures), two relatively large small hydro plants were implemented, both with foreign investment:

- The 60MW Khimti 1 plant, commissioned in 2000, with major investment from the Norwegian Statkraft, a state-owned private company.
- The 36MW Bhote Kosi plant, also commissioned in 2000, with major investment from the American private sector.[10]

There has been much debate, in the wake of these two plants, with wide and still-persisting divergences of opinion regarding the desirability of foreign private investment in the hydroelectric sector, but there can be no argument over their timeliness. They came on line remarkably quickly, just as the country was suffering a chronic power shortage and electricity rationing (by means of regular and pre-announced outages) was becoming a daily routine. Without these two plants, the power shortage – brought on by the World Bank's cancellation of the 201MW Arun 3 project in August 1995, which it had been pursuing single-mindedly since the mid-1980s, and by the notorious 'flood–drought' syndrome in Nepal's energy planning[11] – would have been even more acute. Something, clearly, has collided with something else: the challenge is to work out what these somethings are.

An assertive monarchy versus a multi-party democracy is one possibility; an arthritic and hierarchical state-cum-international donor community versus a supple and individualistic global market is another; a large-scale, high-cost, expert-dominated and inflexible technology versus a smaller-scale, cheap-and-cheerful and flexible one is yet another. But simple dualistic distinctions such as these, while certainly capturing something of what is going on, do not, as we will see, capture it all.

Arun 3 and after

Throughout the Age of Aid, Nepal and its donor community gave priority to the building of large power plants, on the basis of careful and centralised planning, in order to meet the ever-increasing demand for electrical energy as a result of urbanisation and, to some extent, industrialisation. That that demand was increasing was not in doubt, but this planned approach required the accurate prediction, a considerable number of years ahead, of the exact amount of that increase: something that, if it turns out to be wide of the mark, can easily lead to the flood–drought syndrome – periods of excess capacity alternating with periods of under-capacity (and, the longer the lead times of the production units, the larger the amplitude of those fluctuations is likely to be).[12]

Priority in the aid-funded projects by which these production units were installed was given to the achievement of quality standards, including international competitive bidding for both the design and implementation work, with these latter generally being awarded to European, Japanese and North American firms. These priorities may have resulted in high-quality plants, but the unit costs have been astronomical. Kulekhani 1 and 2, Marsyangdi, Kali Gandaki and the recently completed Middle Marsyangdi (see Table 7.1) exemplify the high unit costs of the large-scale projects that have been consistently promoted by the policymakers and the donor community. Given the Nepal Electricity Authority's mandate from the government that it should operate as a commercial entity, these costs have been passed directly to the end users.

These unremittingly high unit costs, combined with the outbreak, in 1990, of democracy, resulted in the World Bank-funded Arun 3 project (which at that time was all ready to go) becoming highly controversial. Civil society organisations – the egalitarian solidarity, that is, whose voice had been silenced during the preceding and undemocratic decades – began asking whether the country could afford to continue along this high-cost technological path. The government-cum-donor community, it then turned out, had got their sums seriously wrong and the ensuing debate and mounting public opposition resulted, in the mid-1990s, in the World Bank dropping Arun 3, to its great embarrassment and to the dismay of its partners. Unsurprisingly, this sudden 'discontinuity' opened much wider the way for small hydro and for the private sector. But, of course, a precondition for that opening of the way was the entry of what we could call a 'third player' – civil society – and that is why the aforementioned dualistic explanatory schemes are inadequate.

Prior to the mid-1990s, when Arun 3 was dropped, little attention had been given to the goal of enhancing the country's own capabilities – human, technical and financial – in the hydropower sector.[13] Although there were some impressive achievements by the Butwal Power Company (established by an INGO, the Norway-based United Mission to Nepal, and described further in the next chapter) smaller projects utilising Nepalese resources and enhancing local capabilities were sidelined by the government and its donor community. The big boys, it seems, naturally gravitated to the big technology and then, firm in their faith in the economies of scale argument, failed to consider whether they might have something to learn from these smaller-scale efforts.

The Butwal Power Company's first venture, in 1967, was the 500kW Tinau hydropower plant. This plant, which was later upgraded to 1.0MW, enabled the electrification of the town of Butwal and the promotion of industrial development in its immediate vicinity. Next, moving up scale on the basis of what had been learnt from Tinau, came the 5.1MW Andhi Khola (1991), closely followed by 12MW Jhimruk plant (1994). Both were financed by way of the Norwegian government's grant assistance to Nepal, with the Nepal government then handing over both plants to the Butwal Power Company in exchange for a share in the company. In this way, the Nepal government became a major shareholder in the company, with the company itself remaining in the private sector: an early example of what later came to be known as public–private partnerships (PPPs).

In 1993, the Butwal Power Company, together with the Norwegian companies Stratkraft SF and Alstrom Power, set up Himal Power Ltd to implement the 60MW Khimti 1. The design and construction management of Andhi Khola, Jhimruk and (to some extent) Khimti 1 were undertaken by United Mission expatriates and Nepalese engineers (see the next chapter for some insight into how this actually worked). The Butwal Power Company currently has about a 15 per cent shareholding in Khimti 1, with the Nepalese government having sold its share in the Butwal Power Company to the private and public sectors in 2003. The company now operates as a public limited company designing, constructing and investing in hydropower plants. In 2006 it confirmed its commitment to 'appropriate' scale (rather than what might have appeared to be ever-larger scale) technology by commissioning the 4.5MW Khudi plant, with the design, investment and construction management being carried out by the local Khudi Hydropower Company, in which the Butwal Power Company is a major shareholder.

With the sudden and unexpected cancellation of Arun 3, the 'hydrocracy' (the nickname given to the Nepal government/donor community's actors in this sector) found itself in considerable disarray. No longer able to continue on its long-established large-scale technological path, it started on an urgent search for alternatives, one of which was the previously disdained implementation of small hydro, using indigenous resources. Thus the Butwal Power Company model was revisited, some 30 years after it had first been demonstrated. Inevitably, given this slow pace of organisational learning, the idea that the Nepalese private sector could develop hydropower was met with much scepticism. Nevertheless, the evidence to the contrary was all in place (in Tinau, Andhi Khola, Jhimruk and on and on) and there were plenty of experienced entrepreneurs willing to take the risks, provided the appropriate policy measures were put in place. This, to some considerable extent, has now happened.

In 1990 the government withdrew its licensing requirements for new private-sector projects up to 1,000kW (up from the 100kW limit that was set in 1986). And this was followed, in 1998, by the commitment by the Nepal Electricity Authority to purchase all the power generated by independent producers (for projects up to 5MW) at a pre-announced standard price, and all the power from plants in the 5–10MW range at a negotiated price.[14] As a result of such policy changes, at the time of writing this chapter over 45 hydro power plants, with an aggregate capacity of about 320MW, are owned and operated by the private sector. This is about 35 per cent of the total grid capacity available. Furthermore, by December 2016, the private sector will add around 220MW of new plants. Investment in the hydro sector since 1998 has now reached over US$82 million (US$76 million invested, with a further US$6 million committed for projects under construction). Most of this is through in-country (i.e. rupee rather than foreign exchange) financing. Furthermore, since it is Nepalese companies and personnel who undertake the engineering and construction works in the domestic hydro sector, national capacity – technical, human and financial – is also being enhanced.

How, then, do these two technological paths – the large-scale one that hit the buffers with the cancellation of Arun 3 (or the really mega ones with India such as the 6,480MW Pancheshwar on the Mahakali stuck in impasse since the last two decades) and the hitherto-neglected small-scale alternative – compare? This comparison, in 'bottom line' (i.e. unit cost) terms, is set out in Table 7.1.

Table 7.1 Cost comparisons between hydropower projects implemented by various public- and private-sector arrangements

Types of project	Project name (installed capacity)	Total project cost, million US$ (year of price)	Cost per kW	PPA offered Rs/unit (US cents/unit)
Public-sector projects with donor financing	Kulekhani I (60MW)	120 (1982)	$2,000	Not applicable since generation is also NEA's responsibility
	Marsyangdi (69MW)	276 (1989)	$4,000	
	Middle Marsyangdi (70MW)	400 (2008)	$5,714	
	Kali Gandaki (144MW)	450 (2002)	$3,125	
	Weighted average		**$3,623**	
International private. Sector financed through international commercial banks	Khimti (60MW)	140 (2000)	$2,333	(5.95 in 1995 level and continuous escalation based on Consumer Price Index of New York) (7.16 with 3% escalation for 12 years) Note: PPA for both plants are in USD
	Bhote Koshi (36MW)	96 (2000)	$2,667	
	Weighted average		**$2,610**	
Nepalese private sector with national financing in Nepalese Rupees	Chilime (22MW)	30.9 (2003)	$1,405	3.90 (5.44) during wet season[1] 5.52 (7.70) during dry season
	Piluwa (3MW)	4.35 (2003)	$1,450	
	Rairang Khola (0.5MW)	1.0 (2004)	$2,000	
	Indrawati –III (7.5MW)	23.3 (2002)	$3,107	
	Syange (0.183MW)	0.3 (2001)	$1,639	
	Sun Koshi (2.5MW)	5.3 (2005)	$2,120	
	Chaku Khola (3MW)	4.2 (2005)	$1,400	
	Khudi (3.45MW)	7.57 (2007)	$2,194	
	Baramchi (1MW)	2.58 (2007)	$2,580	
	Weighted average		**$1,832**	

Note:

1 Nepalese Independent Power Producers (IPPs) are offered these standard rates for all energy generated from their power plants. Dry season includes mid-December to mid-May and the rest of the period is considered wet season. PPA rates in US Cents are based on 2005 mid-year values.

A visiting economist from Mars, on perusing this table, would assume that electricity production in Nepal will now have shifted, in its entirety, to the small hydro path, with those large-scale plants, into which so much capital has been irreversibly sunk, sitting there like white elephants patiently waiting for someone to write off the bad debts with which they are saddled. The reality, however, is much less clear cut, with many powerful actors, both within and outside the country, still pushing for the mega-dams that are envisioned in the sorts of international agreements – the stalled and much-disputed Mahakali Treaty between India and Nepal being the prime example – that are the prerequisites for their construction. It is therefore worth pausing here for a moment to spell out what this table is saying:

- Small hydropower plants, developed by the Nepal private sector, have been built at markedly lower unit cost (cost per kW) than those with international commercial financing and those with public-sector and donor financing.
- Far and away the most expensive are the public-sector projects that are supported by donor concessionary financing. Their protagonists routinely seek to excuse this by pointing to the sizeable investments in infrastructure (particularly roads and bridges but also power lines) that have been included in the projects' costs, but it is difficult to argue that this justifies a doubling of unit costs relative to the small-scale private-sector projects. For example, in the aborted Arun 3 project, the estimated cost of the access road was less than 16 per cent of the estimated overall cost, yet its unit cost is more than double that of the small hydro projects (which, moreover, have been rupee-financed).[15]
- Nepal's private sector has now clearly demonstrated its ability to design, implement and manage small-scale hydropower projects and beyond. Now some Nepalese private-sector developers are seeking financial closure for hydro projects larger than 50MW. Within a period of around seven years (see Table 7.1), the private sector added just short of 40MW of capacity: an average addition of 5.7MW per year. Moreover, this has been achieved on an adversely tilted 'playing field', in that (as is evident in the final column of Table 7.1) the power purchasing rates available to the Nepal private sector are considerably lower than those available to the other two sectors. That is a market distortion that can easily be remedied. For the Nepal Electricity Authority, the least cost option, especially when account is taken of the 'dollar-denominated' electricity from the large-scale power plants that have been constructed with donor assistance, is clearly the electricity that is generated by Nepal's private sector, but that clarity is currently somewhat obscured by the unwarranted tilting of the playing field.[16]

Some, however, will argue that this 100 per cent switch to the small hydro sector and its distinctive technology simply is not on. They will point out that small hydro alone will not be able to cater to the increasing demand for electricity, which is estimated at over 100MW per year. A first response to this is that, even now, when all the sectors – large and small, in-country and donor-aided, dollar and rupee – are able to pitch in, that demand is not being met (as is glaringly evident in Kathmandu's routine 15 hours per day of outages). The crucial figure is not what Nepal's private sector is currently adding to capacity but what it *could* add.

The second response is that during the last 10 years the Nepalese private sector has come out as a strong player in the hydro sector. The private sector now owns around 35 per cent of the national grid's generation capacity and is constructing over 30 projects, with aggregate installed capacity of 500MW. It seems that the massive earthquake of April 2015 was only a temporary setback for the Nepalese hydro developers. Five operating power plants were partially damaged by the earthquake and four of them have already been put back into operation. A few under-construction hydro projects came to a halt temporarily, mainly due to damaged access roads. Construction activities have now resumed at these sites. The private sector now is capable of adding more than 50MW of capacity into the national grid per year. The final response is that the Nepalese private sector has graduated from small hydro to medium hydro. A number of private-sector companies are constructing hydropower plants between 25MW and 100MW.

Since there is no shortage of suitable sites[17], no shortage of rupee finance, no shortage of indigenous skills and capabilities, no shortage of local entrepreneurs and no shortage of village-level social capital, the sky, it would seem, is the only limit when it comes to increasing the supply of electricity. There is, however, a marked absence of a shortage of rent-seeking: of the sort of '*dharma* gone wrong' (see Chapter 1) that has its roots deep in the Age of Aid.

Moving forward under a smokescreen of paradigm confusion

The 'development paradigm' that has dominated and sustained the Age of Aid since its inception, at the end of the Second World War, was knocked sideways (in Nepal, at least) by the cancellation of Arun 3. The result (at least as far as Nepal's hydropower sector is concerned) has been a period of what the philosopher of science Thomas Kuhn (1962) famously called *paradigm (or model) crisis*. Old certainties are smashed (or, at the very least rendered shaky by the challenges mounted by 'other voices': voices that seem to have come out of nowhere), long-cherished dogmas (such as the economies of scale argument) start to fall apart, despite all the shoring-up efforts on the part of the faithful, and all sorts of hitherto calm, authoritative and trustworthy characters are suddenly running around like headless chickens. This, unkind and a little exaggerated though it may be, is the current reality. Like spilt milk, there is nothing to be gained by crying about it; more to the point, there *is* nothing to cry about, because periods of paradigm crisis are exciting: change is in the air, all sorts of things that were unthinkable when the old paradigm was firmly in place become thinkable and a whole multitude of possible futures becomes discernible. Of course, given all the confusion, it is not easy to say exactly what all these new thoughts and possible futures are, but we can conclude by listing some of those that loom large from where we stand in the midst of this current chaos.

First, a major shift within the past decade has been the growing realisation, among policymakers, the donor community and Nepal's private sector, that there are adequate technical, managerial and financial resources within the country for the implementing of not only small hydropower plants but also medium ones. Various investment models are now being experimented with, such as the community members and local institutions themselves investing in hydropower plants along with the entrepreneurs. Recent major achievements in the Nepalese independent hydro sector are:

- Sanima Mai Hydropower Ltd has successfully commissioned the 22MW Mai Hydropower Plant in December 2015 and the 7.0MW Mai Cascade Hydropower Plant in March 2016. Sanima Group is currently negotiating a power purchase agreement with Nepal Electricity Authority for the 28MW Lower Likhu and 54MW Middle Tamor hydropower projects. Sanima Group aims to start construction of these projects by early 2017. In parallel, this group is also carrying out detailed engineering design for 62MW Jum Khola hydropower project.
- Other relatively large private sector-led hydropower projects under construction are: 82MW Lower Solu, 27MW Dordi, 22MW upper Dordi, 50MW Upper Marsyangdi A and 42MW Mistri Khola.
- The Power Development Fund (supported by the World Bank) is financing the 30MW Kabeli project: a major change of course for the World Bank when set against Arun 3! And if the competitive bidding requirements are drafted so that Asian contractors are able to take part the costs are likely to be even lower, Indian and Chinese contractors now being as competent as their more expensive European and North American counterparts. With this sort of investment model we see the donor community supporting the private sector rather than, as has so often been the case, squeezing it out.
- The 22MW Chilime hydropower project uses a somewhat different investment model, which works in the same private sector-supporting way. Design, construction and supervision were carried out internally by the Nepal Electricity Authority's major shareholding company, Chilime Hydropower Ltd. Using the Chilime model, Nepal Electricity Authority is currently constructing the 102MW Middle Bhotekoshi, 14.8MW Upper Sanjen, 42.5MW Sanjen and 111MW Rasuwa Gadi hydropower projects.

Second, international private-sector participants will need to make as much use as possible of local (that is, rupee) financing, keeping hard currency investment to a minimum. This will reduce their risks in future projects, since they will still receive good returns on their investments, even with a large proportion of the negotiated power purchase agreement being in local currency. The commercial banks in Nepal at present are willing to provide loans for a payback period of about eight to 12 years; returns on investment would increase, making many schemes viable that are currently marginal, if the payback period could be extended to 15 years.

BOX 7.1 HYDRO POWERED EDUCATION AND COMMUNITY ELECTRICITY

Nepal has seen innovations in the electricity sector that are home-grown and without any external donor support. They have the potential to redefine rural development if only they could be 'mainstreamed' into development programmes of both the national government and the international development agencies: unfortunately, some kind of institutional filter prevents such inspiring initiatives from percolating into the higher reaches of policymaking and aiding the rethinking and rejuvenation of development itself.

The 250 kW Khandbari small hydropower plant in eastern Nepal had been bombed by the Maoist insurgents in December 2001. The government did not have the money to rebuild it, and even if they had, the plant could be the target for more bombing. To break this impasse, along came Hari Bairagi Dahal in early 2003, with an outlandish proposal to the Nepal Electricity Authority (NEA): if the government were to give a long-term lease to operate it and the right to sell the generated electrical energy to the national electricity grid, he could get three campuses of the district and a few others to rehabilitate the power plant at their own cost. Such a bizarre idea had never been suggested, let alone tried, before; but the NEA decided to try it.

Dahal with his campus colleagues formed the Community Education Development Electric Company, and rehabilitated the power plant in July 2006 at a cost of about US$169,000 (NRs10,800,000). A year later, their gross income was US$93,800, out of which they paid US$20,400 to NEA as lease charge and US$15,800 as tax to the government of Nepal, the rest being income for the three campuses. The company currently sells electricity to the grid at NRs3.40/kWh and pays a lease charge to NEA based on NRs0.60/kWh of energy sold plus NRs1,000 per kW of installed capacity.

Apart from fees collected from the students (which is less than $100/year per student), the income from the sales of electricity is the only other source of revenue for the three campuses in this remote Sankhuwasabha district. They no longer have to plead with the government for uncertain grants, and have taken other initiatives on their own: they now award scholarships to students that are handicapped, poor families and disadvantaged ethnic groups on a regular basis.

In the eastern Nepal village of Baluwadi in Jhapa District, Diptara Thamsuhang chairs a cooperative run entirely by women, which also manages the village's electricity distribution. She buys power in bulk from the NEA and then retails it in the village, allowing her cooperative to run a sustainable microcredit programme that finances small agro-processing concerns. Meena Khadga chairs a centre for mother and child development in Katari of Udayapur District, which manages electricity distribution for 532 households and maintains a policy of training and employing only women for meter reading, wiring and repairs. Her centre is planning to invest the profit it earns from its electricity business in a small hydroelectric plant. The surplus energy that is generated is to fund campaigns for child health, among other things.

Progresses such as these became possible after the monopoly NEA was partially reformed in 2003 through a set of by-laws on community electricity that allows any organised village group to buy electricity in bulk from the NEA and retail by themselves at a profit through possibilities that they themselves could foresee. If these women were still atomised and fatalised customers of the national monopoly utility, the NEA, beholden to diktats from distant managers, the initiatives in which they are involved would be unthinkable.

Today, a dozen years after its initiation, 257 communities and cooperatives in 49 districts of Nepal such as those of Diptara and Meena are managing their own electricity distribution system for over 350,000 rural households (with an additional 150,000 expected to be added in the coming year). They have raised over a billion rupees to invest in their distribution systems and run cottage industries that give jobs in the village itself obviating the need to migrate to cities. To the national electricity managers and experts of the development agencies they pose the following challenges: how is it that the community system is able to expand rural electrification at an average cost of $99 per household while projects run by the government and international agencies average $300; and how is it that in community run systems theft of electricity is zero while loss in cities and villages operated by the NEA is as high as sixty per cent and highly resistant to any improvement? And why don't you support such community efforts?

– based on discussions with Hari Bairagi Dahal, hydro entrepreneur and former MP of Sankhuwasabha as well as Dilli Ghimire, former chair of the National Association of Community Electricity Users – Nepal (NACEUN: www.naceun.org.np). See also Gyawali (2014), Batra (2010) and Dixit (2002)

Third, from a national perspective, there are two overriding priorities, both of which have been lost sight of over the past six decades. These are, first, to ensure that the consumer end tariff is affordable and, second, to increase the general public's access to that affordable electricity. If the government and its donor community are to enshrine these priorities (and many an ordinary Ram Bahadur will wonder how on earth they ever managed to become dis-enshrined) they will have to be jolted out of their 'cost-plus pricing' mindset. In other words, they will have to shift across to mechanisms that reward efficiency.

One option is to initiate competitive bidding for electric power (kW) and energy (kWh). The Nepal Electricity Authority would call for quotes from independent power producers of the price at which they are willing to sell the electricity from their proposed plants, the Authority having first announced its electricity requirements in the short and intermediate terms (the next 10 years, say). The Authority would then have the option to buy electricity (both power and energy) from those producers, on a least cost basis, to meet the growing demand.

Another option (which could also be reached by way of the first) would be to promote competition by creating an environment in which a multiplicity of generators and distributors can operate in a free internal national market, instead of having to operate with a monopolistic and dominant player. At present, the private sector is investing in the generation sector while the distribution sector is entirely owned by the Nepal Electricity Authority, and this means that each private producer has to sign a power purchasing agreement with the single distributor if it is to sell its electricity (into the national grid, that is, not when, as is often the case with micro and small hydro, there is no grid connection).[18] With the monopolistic barrier removed, prices could be brought down and Nepal could move towards the establishment of a spot market in electricity similar to that which has recently been initiated in India. The government has been considering unbundling the Nepal Electricity Authority into generation, transmission and distribution entities, and that, if carried out, would be a large first step on the way to the securing of these two priorities.

Fourth, simplifying and shortening the bureaucratic processes in relation to the small hydro sector would make an enormous and positive difference. The licence-processing time could certainly be shortened, and power purchasing agreements could easily be standardised (rather than, as happens at present, each independent producer having to negotiate each of its plants separately with the Nepal Electricity Authority). The 1992 Hydropower Development Policy, which (as we have seen) paved the way for small hydro, was revised in 2001 but the corresponding Act and Regulation was not updated in line with it. That needs to be done, otherwise the weak legal basis will result in investments in this sector not accelerating as strongly as they otherwise would.

Fifth, many of the best sites for small hydro lie in the mountainous far north of the country, where the streams have steep gradients and stable flows (thanks to the melting snow and ice), but their harnessing is hampered by a lack of transmission lines and roads. If infrastructure – in the form of grid-extensions and roads (or, in the light of the Bhattedanda experience – see Chapter 5 – ropeways) – could be extended northwards, these best (and therefore lower unit cost) sites could be brought on line ahead of those that are less good.

Sixth, turning to the micro hydro front, there is much that can be done to extend its penetration while, at the same time, lessening the level of donor support that is needed to keep it viable. Along with increasing the number and capacity of micro hydro plants, it is important to ensure that they can operate resiliently (cope, that is, with breakdowns and natural interruptions: landslides, glacier lake outburst floods and so on) and even commercially. Isolated micro hydro plants that happen to be quite close to one another can easily be linked into a mini-grid so that their consumers can be more reliably catered to. For example, if one plant shuts down, the others may be able to help out, and it may also be possible to meet fluctuations in demand (as long as they do not all occur simultaneously) without having to add extra capacity to each plant. Mini-grids would also help ensure standardised quality, since plants would have to be able to link up (a constant frequency of 50Hz, voltage level, for instance). The entrepreneurs' managerial capabilities would likewise be enhanced (through, for instance, the modalities of power exchange between and among the different producers). Power purchasing agreements would likely also have to be arranged, thereby preparing communities for the arrival of the national grid and for the sale of their electricity into it. A mini-grid pilot project that interconnects 6 micro hydro plants with total power capacity of 107kW through an 8km-long 11kV transmission line in Rangkhani, near Kushmishera in Baglung district (mid-western Nepal), was established in 2012 with support from AEPC and is managed by a local community named Urja Upatyaka Mini Grid Co-Operative, who, however, are having difficulties negotiating grid connection with a reluctant NEA. The interconnection of these small plants immediately resulted in: 24-hour power supply to villages that could previously operate their isolated plants only for a few hours at night; 10kW demand from a mobile operator to set up a telecom tower (resulting in better phone connection in this remote area of Nepal than even in parts of capital Kathmandu); and the setting up of several milk chilling centres.

Seventh, micro and hydro plants become more viable economically the more they are used; if (as is often the case at present) they are used only for household lighting (i.e. four to five hours a day) they may not be able to generate enough funds to meet repair, maintenance and replacement costs. Many plants, of course, are already extended to agro-processing, bakeries and cottage industries, but more technology promotion, entrepreneur training and end-use diversification is needed. One obvious extension is across to information technology (IT), with the electricity then being used for high-value activities. Micro hydro can readily power computers, fax machines and other electronic devices, thereby contributing to the education and IT sectors. Indeed, some are already doing this: the Selleri Chalsa Electricity Company's 400kW plant, which used to be two days' walk from the roadhead at Jiri until a few years ago, is enabling computer use as well as meeting part of the remote community's rural energy and lighting needs.

Finally, lurking behind the above seven points are some intriguing possibilities for leapfrogging: for Nepal getting way out ahead of all those developed countries that it has long lagged so far behind. The whole of hydropower – micro, small, medium and large – is, of course, renewable energy and (as has been stressed in Chapters 5 and 6) Nepal, with some its renewable energy already much cheaper than that from fossil fuel, is extremely well placed to leapfrog ahead in terms of the much longed-for transition to renewables. But there is something else – we could call it a 'serial leapfrog' – that might be possible for Nepal, and that is to miss out the entire centralised production/ national grid distribution phase of technological development that so much of the rest of the world, thanks to its reliance on fossil fuels, has got itself locked into.

Rather than insisting that a national grid, together with its key nodes (the power-generating centres), is the prerequisite for a country's electrification, we can start from the opposite extreme: the idea that electricity generation, instead of being centralised, can be 'distributed' – every house building its own power station, as it were.[19] That, after all, is not too far away from how things now are in Nepal with both micro, small hydro and photovoltaic solar. And, even in grid-connected places like Kathmandu, most buildings are generating at least a fraction of their energy: rooftop panels for solar water-heating, for instance, and, increasingly, photovoltaic panels too. Starting from this 'distributed' state of affairs, you can then think in terms of allowing mini-grids, and even meso-grids, to crystallise out, as and when it makes sense for those distributed producers to link themselves together in this way.[20] Again, that – the opposite of the technological configuration that the rest of the world is locked into – is pretty much how things currently are in Nepal: the micro hydro mini-grids, for instance, and the stand-alone 'island grids' that naturally form themselves around those small hydro projects that are not national grid-connected.

The one major exception, of course, is the national grid, and much of the current development debate (as we have seen) is focused on how this might be extended so as to supply all those parts of the country (India too, perhaps) that are beyond its present reach: a goal that is ever-receding in the sense that the national grid, with all its outages, is reaching (in terms of hours connected) fewer and fewer customers and is currently also importing power from India. But all this 'grid shrinkage' begins to look different once we adopt the 'serial leapfrogging' viewpoint. The current retreat of the national grid, far from being something to lament, is something to celebrate, since it helps shift the entire national picture much closer to the 'distributed' goal. Centralised production certainly makes sense when the fuels – coal and oil – are concentrated in pockets, but it makes no sense with renewables: the sun shines down on every square metre of the earth's surface and, even when its energy has been transferred to the water cycle, the streams cascade down (in Nepal, at least, and that is its great blessing) close to every human settlement.

Notes

1 However, there is now considerable interest, within what would normally be considered to be capitalist countries, in social entrepreneurship.
2 The idea here is that the falling water is (in part, at least) a *common-pool* good and that this means that the local community should be a shareholder in the individualistic (i.e. *private good*) business of extracting energy from it.

3 Breweries, in Europe and America, moved strongly up scale during the 1960s and 70s, with many of the middle-sized ones, often located close to city centres, becoming redundant. Yet, as this was happening, hundreds of very small production units – 'boutique breweries', as they are sometimes called – were opening up. Very large and very small units now co-exist: something that, according to the orthodox economic argument, is simply not possible.

4 Sometimes, however, those between 100kW and 1MW are also referred to as mini hydro, and those even smaller as pico, but we will not follow that usage here. As we will see, these categories sometimes do not match the different 'socio-technical' systems very well.

5 This – 40 per cent access – is the figure quoted in Nepal's 2001 census.

6 There were, however, some exceptions, among them Morang Hydro (in eastern Nepal) and Bageshwari Electrics, in Nepalgunj (in mid-western Nepal), the former started during the closing years of Rana rule and the latter during the Panchayat system (1960–90), when after the promulgation of land reform large landlords began to feel that electricity was a safer business than large land ownership.

7 This was apart from the distribution of electricity from the isolated (i.e. non-grid-connected) micro hydropower plants (which were limited to 100kW) and a few small private companies.

8 According to a study by the Alternative Energy Promotion Centre (AEPC), around 90 micro hydro plants, with net capacity of 2.7 MW, have been affected by the grid extension as of 2015 and this number is steadily increasing. NEA is very reluctant to allow the micro hydros to connect to the grid, happy to see them rust into scrap, and the AEPC's role in micro hydro is further discussed in the later parts of this chapter.

9 Peru, the Philippines, Cyprus and Armenia are among the countries that have recently opened embassies in Kathmandu, citing tourism and hydropower as high on their list of interests. (As reported in *The Himalayan Times*, Kathmandu, 19 March 2011).

10 A few years ago the American private sector sold its shares to Nepalese private parties, primarily the owners of the Soaltee Hotel group.

11 'Flood–drought syndrome' resulted from Nepal's official generation planning since the 1970s, of which Arun 3 was the prime example, not 'following the demand curve' but pushing a single, very large (in terms of the overall Nepalese power system) project, having a huge surplus when it came on line, and then, when that was quickly absorbed by a growing developing economy, having chronic shortage until another big project was built many years later. This 'creation of scarcity' by an unbridled hierarchy, the Nepal Electricity Authority, in order to 'manage' it and keep things under its control is discussed in Gyawali and Dixit (2010).

12 The rule in Nepal has always been that the larger the production unit the longer the lead time. In the case of Arun 3 the estimated lead time was at least eight years, without considering inevitable time overruns. Small hydro projects come in around half that time.

13 An interesting exception was the training, since 1980, of some 250 Nepalese engineers for five years in batches of 50 in India's premier engineering institute at Roorkee (founded by British India in 1847 to produce the manpower to build the Ganga Canal and other engineering works), primarily to build the 10,800MW Karnali Chisapani High Dam.

14 The current Nepal Electricity Authority policy is to purchase all power generated by independent power producers at a pre-announced standard price (NPR8:40/unit during dry season and NPR4:80 during wet season) along with provision for price escalation for the first five years of plant operation.

15 Interestingly, this justificatory argument is invoking a *diseconomy of scale*, since it is only as the scale of the production unit gets larger that these infrastructure costs pile up. This, of course, directly contradicts the economies of scale argument that justified these

projects in the first place. Nobody said it *had* to be built in the remote and pristine Arun Valley; only if you set off by insisting that it be large do you end up putting it in a place like that! And the six small hydro projects that, taken together, have quickly and cheaply filled the gap left by Arun 3's cancellation have emphatically driven this point home (more details in the next chapter on large hydro).

16 This least cost option becomes even more attractive if we allow for the likelihood of the Nepalese rupee's continuing devaluation vis-à-vis the donor currencies, making civil engineering construction a 'declining cost industry'.

17 Especially if the Forest Department's concerns can be allayed by the use of ropeways instead of roads (see Chapter 5).

18 Some movement towards 'pluralising the grid' began in 2003 with the initiation of community electricity. Today there are over 270 large and small community electricity users in Nepal who buy electricity in bulk from the NEA and retail by themselves (see the website of the National Association of Community Electricity Users-Nepal: www.naceun.org.np). Electricity grids are usually assumed to be *natural monopolies* (only in Lubbock, Texas, for rather bizarre historical reasons, do we find two of them) but that does not mean that the distribution of electricity through those grids has to be monopolistic, as is evident, in Europe and elsewhere, where multiple suppliers sell electricity to their customers over the single network. Such regimes enable competitive markets but only if there is also carefully designed and enforced regulation.

19 This extreme (which we are not proposing to go all the way to) is the egalitarian goal, just as the fully centralised system is the hierarchical goal.

20 And here, of course, we see the individualist goal coming into the picture. Things, in other words are moving away from elegance and towards clumsiness.

8 Large hydro

Failures in financial engineering

Ratna Sansar Shrestha

Missionaries, under Nepalese law, are allowed to work in the country but they are not permitted to proselytise and convert people to other faiths. This helps explain why the Norwegian constituent of the United Mission to Nepal has become such a key player in the country's hydropower development. Many missionaries, of course, turn their hands to medicine or education but Odd Hoftun, who arrived in Nepal on 8 January 1958, was an electrical engineer, and by 1965 he had single-handedly set up the Butwal Power Company and brought it to the point where its first venture – the 50kW Tinau plant[1] – was fully operationalised on 17 December 1970 (see Svalheim 2015, NEA 2015 and Chapter 7). The United Mission to Nepal, unlike most of the other actors in the hydropower sector, is a non-governmental organisation (an NGO)[2] and the way in which I came to work for the Butwal Power Company reveals much about the sort of approach – to technology, to the people it aims to serve and to its employees – that Odd Hoftun, its driving force, made sure it took.

The company's mission was (and still is) to develop hydropower projects using appropriate training, technology transfer and human resources development. During his long tenure as general manager of the company, Odd became highly respected and admired by his staff. He was undoubtedly a towering personality – though physically more like a wiry little Nepali than a hulking great Viking – and so I was more than a little apprehensive when, in January 1988, he sent for me to assist him in his work. To make matters worse, I was not in any way a technical person; I am a management professional, a chartered accountant and a corporate lawyer. At that time, I couldn't distinguish a kilowatt from a kilowatt-hour; and electricity, for me, manifested itself as nothing more than the light from an incandescent bulb.

Because he was himself working as a volunteer, he insisted on living like a poor Nepali: riding a bicycle when even his middle-level employees were cruising around on motorcycles. He was, however, offering to remunerate me for my services. Not handsomely, I might add, but such was the strength of his personality and example that I found myself unable to initiate any negotiations: I just accepted. The long and the short of it is that he has now retired (sort of) and lives in his homeland and I, as one of his dedicated pupils, am carrying a small part of his mantle. That small part can be labelled *financial engineering*, and of course it was because Odd had discerned the need for such a seemingly strange trade that he had sent for me in the first place.

My association with Odd transformed me into a student of the water resource sector and whetted my appetite for looking closely at the financial, legal and managerial aspects of projects in that sector. I came to realise that, when it comes to these projects, their financial engineering is every bit as important (more important, even) as are the kinds of engineering – civil, electrical and mechanical (including the application of sciences such as geology and hydrology) that normally command all the attention. Projects, as well as being sound from all these technical perspectives, have to be soundly engineered financially so as to ensure that, on the macro-hand, they do not have an adverse effect on Nepal's overall economy and, on the micro-hand, that the ultimate users of the electricity are not ripped off by having all the inefficiencies and unnecessary costs loaded onto their retail tariffs. Since it is these two concerns that, in various shapes and guises, lie at the heart of this book's critique of the orthodox development paradigm (outlined in Chapter 1 and brought down to earth in the case study chapters), financial engineering can usefully be seen as an integral component – part of the new policy toolkit, as it were – of the new paradigm we are proposing.

Financial engineering

A project is successfully engineered financially, we can say, when it is completed within the initially estimated cost (neither overestimated[3] nor underestimated[4]) and within the stipulated time. Many large construction projects around the world do precisely that; Arsenal Football Club's new ground – the Emirates Stadium in London – came in on budget and on time (Thompson 2008), so this is not some hopelessly unattainable counsel of perfection. For this to happen, however, the structure and content of the contracts for engineering, construction, supply/erection and management need to be streamlined and rationalised so as to ensure that there is no scope for the contractors to claim for variation orders or to delay completion on one pretext or another. Cost overruns, obviously, result in the escalation of costs (perhaps beyond estimation and expectation) but so too do time overruns: loss of revenue, increased interest payments during construction, penalties for late delivery of energy, increased costs due to inflation, the escalation of the contractor's overhead linked to time and fees of consultants (which are usually fixed in terms of person-months involved) and so on.

It is not impossible to control exposure to these kinds of eventualities – the many on-budget and on-time instances, of which the Emirates Stadium is one, testify to that – and there have certainly been hydropower projects in Nepal where this has been the case. The Khimti project, which was conceptualised by Odd to generate 60MW and implemented with the help of Norwegian[5] private-sector investments, was completed within estimated cost and in time (actually 12 days ahead of the 'required commercial operation date'). Similarly, the Bhote Koshi project was also executed with a fixed price as well as guaranteed delivery dates and liquidated damages for delay and underperformance (Head 2000). But this has never happened with projects that have been donor-funded. This is not just bad luck; there has been a consistent pattern, in almost all of those projects that have been implemented with foreign aid, of failing to take due care. Donors and the donorcracy (the bureaucracy associated with the donors) have been consistently indifferent to financial engineering, with results that are the negation of the stated aim: Nepal's development.

This chapter will scrutinise, in financial engineering terms, some of the large 'landmark' projects in Nepal's water resources sector since the 1970s. Some have already been built; others, such as the aborted Arun 3 and the West Seti, still under consideration, have not. Lessons can be learnt from them all, but money can be saved only on those that are still no more than twinkles in the eyes of their proponents.[6]

The 1970s, 1980s and early 1990s

There are three landmark projects that were conceived during the Panchayat era, two of which were built and one aborted. None, as we will see, paid much attention to the financial aspect of their engineering.

Kulekhani 1

Kulekhani 1 is the only reservoir-type hydropower plant in Nepal. Its installed capacity is 60MW, made up of two units each of 30MW. Though designed as a peaking power plant, it has also been used at times for voltage improvement and system stability. The designed annual generation capacity is 16GWh[7] as primary energy and 46GWh as secondary energy. The project was constructed with the financial assistance of a melange of donors: the World Bank, the Kuwait Fund for Arab Economic Development, the Organization of Petroleum Exporting Countries Fund, the United Nations Development Programme, Japan's Overseas Economic Cooperation Fund and the government of Nepal. From the perspective of financial engineering, we need to compare the project's estimated and actual costs (Table 8.1).

This table throws light on a number of failures in financial engineering. First, though estimated to cost US$68 million, the project ended up costing almost double that amount, the cost overrun being a whopping 81.8 per cent. This serious failure in financial engineering derives from either a lack of contracting skill on part of the donors (thereby allowing the contractor to rake in almost double the original estimate) or an inability to make a realistic cost estimate prior to the commencement of construction work. Or both. It is also important not to lose sight of the simple fact that the project might never have gone ahead if the feasibility study's estimate had been realistic. Furthermore, the first generating unit, projected to be commissioned in June 1980, was 21

Table 8.1 Estimated and actual costs of Kulekhani 1

	Cost estimate (million US$)	Actual cost (million US$)
Preliminary works	0.8	1.709
Resettlement	0.6	1.139
Civil works	47.5	89.895
Equipment		
Hydro-mechanical	3.7	2.657
Electro-mechanical	9.1	12.426
Transmission and substation	2.1	2.869
	14.9	17.952
Engineering services	3	5.271
General expenses	1	4.915
Duties and taxes	0.2	2.746
	68	123.627

Source: World Bank (1985).

months late, the loss of revenue amounting to 193GWh, the equivalent of US$15.49 million.[8] This is a serious time overrun – amounting to just under 23 per cent of the original estimated cost – yet it does not figure in any of the multitude of appraisals and assessments that were carried out by or for the donors.

A double jeopardy such as this – serious overruns on both cost and time – would have been unaffordable to a private-sector developer. Yet, with donor financing, scarcely an eyelid was batted, the reason being that, for donors, it is disbursement that is the priority, not the financial soundness of the project. Someone, of course, has to pick up the tab for all this and, with the Nepal Electricity Authority being required by law to operate commercially, that someone is the end user: the Nepalese consumer.

Marsyangdi

The 69MW Marsyangdi hydroelectric project was financed by the World Bank, the Kreditanstalt fuer Wiederaufbau,[9] the Asian Development Bank, the Saudi Fund for Development and the Kuwait Fund for Arab Economic Development. It is a peaking run-of-river project with a designed annual generation of 462.5GWh. Estimated and actual costs are set out in Table 8.2.

Again, we can discern various failures in the financial engineering of this project.[10] To start, at US$4,681 per kW of installed capacity, the estimate was remarkably high, yet it was deemed feasible and the project went ahead.[11] However, from the perspective of the private investor, the cost is much too high. It also transgresses the concept of sustainability promulgated by the donor

Table 8.2 Estimated and actual costs of Marsyangdi

	Cost estimate in million US$	Actual cost in million US$
Preliminary cost and administration	8.6	8.6
Civil works	157.3	109.5
Electro-mechanical equipment	47.7	75.1
Transmission works and local distribution	18.9	29.0
Construction supervision	7.5	21.9
Technical assistance	4.1	5.7
Physical contingency	33.6	–
Price contingency	45.6	–
Grand total	323.3	249.8[1]

Note:
1 The actual total cost incurred does not include the amount spent on Mugling Marsyangdi Road – US$2.5 million – which line item doesn't figure in the original estimated cost.

community itself. The World Bank, in its 'implementation completion report', pats itself on the back, noting that the 'cost was some 20% lower than set forth in the appraisal estimate'. The World Bank, it would appear, has opened up a whole new way of making gratifyingly large savings: just double the estimate and then see if you can come in below it!

Even with this substantial 20 per cent saving, the installed capacity cost that was incurred comes to US$3,620 per kilowatt: far too high, even at today's prices (with steel, for example, having gone through the roof). Much too high also for the Nepalese consumer and for the economic development of his or her country. A quick comparison with Kulekhani will drive this point home. The actual per kW cost of Nepal's largest high dam, Kulekhani, even after a cost overrun of 81.8 per cent, was US$2,060, yet Marsyangdi, which was merely a run-of-river project with just a small diversion weir, ended up costing 75 per cent more per kW than a storage unit.[12] The donors may have been patting themselves on the back but the cost of the project to Nepal was seven billion rupees. Yet the Nepal Electricity Authority, in its book of account, capitalised this asset on its completion at just five billion rupees. One wonders what happened to the whopping two billion rupees. Perhaps they trickled out through the cracks in the project's financial engineering. The World Bank's 'implementation completion report' also mentions that the project was completed in February 1990 after a seven-month delay, but it does not dwell on it. However, if the report had considered the financial engineering it *would* have dwelt on it, since the loss of revenue that resulted from this delay amounts to 233GWh, equivalent to US$18.7 million.[13]

The bottom line in all this, as already mentioned, is that no private-sector developer would have touched this project with a bargepole. It also transgresses the donors' own criteria for sustainability. So why, the ordinary Ram Bahadur might wonder, did they do it? The only plausible answer is that the donors' compulsion to disburse overrode all other considerations.

Arun 3

In the dry season of 2009, load-shedding in Nepal was at record high of 16 hours a day, thanks to the supply of electricity falling way short of the demand. Many people – ranging from the then finance minister,[14] through various economists, electricity experts and energy planners, to a fair proportion of Nepal's intelligentsia – confidently ascribed this crisis to the cancellation of Arun 3 by the World Bank, back in August 1995. Arun 3, they asserted, had been a key component in the country's energy planning, and so it stood to reason that its last-minute cancellation would have profound repercussions further down the line: around the time, that is, when it would have started feeding its electricity into the grid, around 2003/4 (assuming it had been completed on time). 'Well, yes,' is the response to this, 'but only if (a) the planning had accurately anticipated the future demand and (b) nothing else had emerged during ensuing decade to fill (or even exceed) the gap left by Arun 3's cancellation.' Since (a) and (b) can work with or against one another (depending on whether the planners undershot or overshot, and on whether a lot or nothing winged its way in during the interim) it is important to consider them both. The hydropower projects with installed capacity above 10MW[15] that have been implemented in the two decades immediately following the cancellation of Arun 3 are therefore summarised in Table 8.3.

Table 8.3 Projects implemented between 1995 and 2015

Project	Capacity MW	Energy GWh	Total cost million US$	Average cost US$/kW	Year commissioned	Construction period in yrs
NEA						
Modi	14.8	92.5	30	2,027	2000	5
Kali Gandaki A	144	842	380	2,639	2002	6
Middle Marsyangdi	70	398	357	5,100*	2008	7
Total/average	228.8	1,333	767	3,352		6
IPPs						
Khimti	60	350	142#	2,367	2000	4
Bhote Koshi	45	293	98	2,178	2001	4.5
Chilime	22	132	33	1,500	2003	5
Mai Khola	22	128	37	1,680	2015	4
Total/average	149	903	310	2,080		4.375
Grand total/average	378.8	2,236	1,077	2,851		5.07

Note:
* The cost doesn't include interest during construction according to NEA's 2009/10 annual report.

Source: Himal Power Limited, which currently operates Khimti: www.hpl.com.np.

Over this 20-year period the Nepal Electricity Authority, as we can see, added 228.8MW of capacity with an average annual generation of 1,333GWh, at an average cost of US$3,352 per kW and with an average lead time of six years. Over the same period, private-sector independent power producers added a further 149MW,[16] with an average annual generation of 903GWh, at an average cost of US$2,080 per kW and with an average lead time of 4.375 years. What all this means is that, during those 20 years, Nepal's generation capacity went up by a total of 377.8MW – *almost 90 per cent more* than Arun 3 (201MW) would have provided had it not been cancelled. With a total average annual generation of 2,236GWh, and at a total cost of US$1,077 million, this works out at a commendable average cost of US$2,851 per kW, with an impressively short average lead time of 5.07 years.[17]

Had the World Bank decided to continue with Arun 3, the Nepal Electricity Authority would not have been able to build Kali Gandaki-A (144MW) and Middle Marsyangdi (70MW) due to the mutually exclusive nature of ADB and Kreditanstalt fuer Wiederaufbau (KfW) financing,[18] respectively, or Modi (14.8MW) due to the donor-imposed covenant for Arun 3 against the building of a project with installed capacity over 10MW. Nor would the independent power producers have been able to build any projects in excess of 10MW capacity, due to the same covenant. In consequence, only the 201MW Arun 3 (in contrast to the 377.8MW with Arun 3 cancelled, not counting projects with an installed capacity of less than 10MW) could have been added to the system. That addition, moreover, giving an average annual generation of 1,715GWh at a total cost of US$1,082 million, would have resulted in an average cost of US$5,383 per kW and an average lead time of 10 years (in contrast to US$2,851 per kW and 5.07 years with Arun 3 cancelled). By abandoning Arun 3, Nepal gained 176.8MW of extra capacity and 521GWh of energy by investing only US$1,077 million, thereby saving US$5 million!

As the Khimti project turned out be, with due respect to gender sensitivity, a 'trophy wife', with an extremely high return on investment, the private sector developed a herd mentality and became interested to invest in hydropower projects, due to which an additional 122MW were added to the system by projects of installed capacity of 10MW or lower. In this manner, a total of 499.8 MW were added to the system due to the cancellation of Arun 3. Moreover, had it not been abandoned, Nepal would have had to endure severe and ever-worsening load-shedding (with Arun 3 not having come on line until 2005) since only a meagre 9.4MW[19] of installed capacity (aggregate of projects below 10MW commissioned by NEA) would have been added in the interim.[20]

Yet even this scenario is over-optimistic, once one examines the track record of the outfits responsible for all these projects. There is no history of public-sector, donor-funded infrastructure projects in Nepal being completed on time. The Middle Marsyangdi, for instance, stated to be finished in 2004, was 50 months late; and even the much-acclaimed Chilime (which won a number of awards) incurred a 40-month time overrun and a substantial cost overrun (it even had to change the civil contractor half way through the construction process). So, in a more realistic scenario, the ever-worsening load-shedding would have been still more severe and would have lasted until 2009. On top of all that, the historical record suggests that the cost overrun would have led to the estimated US$5,143 cost per kW spiralling to an eye-watering US$8,000,[21] four times greater than the cost of the private-sector electricity that has more than filled the gap left by Arun 3's cancellation.

This, then, is the truly horrendous scenario that was averted, in the nick of time, by the cancellation by James Wolfensohn (at that time the newly appointed president of the World Bank) of Arun 3.

From the 1990s onwards: the liberalisation of the electricity sector

In 1992 came the government of Nepal's Hydropower Development Policy, closely followed by the Electricity Act (1992) and the Water Resources Act (1992), these two acts being the means by which this new, and liberalising, policy was implemented. Almost immediately (and as we have seen in the previous chapter) there came two foreign investment-funded projects: the 60MW Khimti (with funding from Norway) and the 45MW Bhote Koshi (with funding from the United States).[22] The government signed the project agreements, licences were expeditiously issued by the Ministry of Water Resources[23] and the power purchase agreements were signed by the Nepal Electricity Authority. With the commissioning of Khimti project in 2000, the load-shedding that had built up during the late 1990s was effectively mitigated.

The agreed tariffs were 5.94 US cents for Khimti and 6.00 US cents for Bhote Koshi, at 1995 price level (Head 2000). These figures, however, are not directly comparable because the royalty payable by Khimti was borne by the Nepal Electricity Authority, while in the Bhote Koshi case it was borne by the developer. Adjusting for this, the rate for Khimti is 6.09 US cents and the tariff had escalated to 8.088 US cents (without royalty) for Khimti and 8.205 US cents for Bhote Koshi in 2006.[24] The contracting agreements too were somewhat different. With Khimti, all the work – engineering, procurement and erection of electrical-mechanical and civil construction (EPC) – was shared among the promoters/proponents and there was no transparent competitive bidding. The total cost estimate was US$142 million. With Bhoti Koshi, the estimated cost (which was also used as the basis for the tariff negotiations) was US$100 million, and there was a call for competitive bidding that culminated in the full package of works being awarded to one contractor for US$48 million (Head 2000). After adding other 'soft' costs, the project can be estimated to have cost around US$70 million at completion: a substantial saving for the developer.

These two projects, with their interesting differences, were the only foreign direct investments to find their way into Nepal in the mid-1990s. Indeed, Nepal failed to attract any more such projects during the entire decade that followed liberalisation. A full explanation for this manifest policy failure is beyond the scope of this chapter, but it can certainly be ascribed, in part, to the rent-seeking mindset of the hydrocracy.

Within a couple of years of the commissioning of these two projects, officials from the Nepal Electricity Authority (with some support from the wider hydrocracy) began alleging that these independent power producers had got the better of them and of Nepal's economy. Both the project agreements and the power purchase agreements, they claimed, had been unfair and one-sided. In addition, they continued, the agreed tariffs were exorbitantly high and other covenants inequitable; the independent power producers were earning unconscionably high returns on their investments. The hydrocracy (as well as managing to ignore the fact that, despite all these iniquities, the Nepalese consumer was getting a much better deal) had failed to notice that the project documents were not signed by them at gunpoint, nor were they denied the opportunity to read those documents (and, if they wished, consult experts) prior to executing them. Nor could they plead ignorance, there having been many and lengthy rounds of negotiations, sometimes into the wee hours. In other words, they failed to exercise due diligence; their financial engineering left much to be desired. Had they exercised due diligence they would have assessed the current as well as the future impacts of the documents' terms and conditions on the financial health of the Nepal Electricity Authority, on the retail tariff in particular, and on the overall macro-economy of the country. It thus becomes clear, from the litany of their own complaints, that they failed both their own respective institutions and their nation's economy.

There is something else they failed to appreciate: which side they were on. The donors, in all other donor-funded projects, are seen as being on the side of the Nepal Electricity Authority and/or the government of Nepal, rendering financial assistance for the implementing of the project. In the case of private-sector projects such as Khimti and Bhote Koshi, however, the donors (the International Finance Corporation of the World Bank, the Asian Development Bank and so on) are on the other side, since they are rendering financial assistance to projects that are being promoted and developed by the international private sector. Why, we therefore need to ask, did the donors (and their donorcracy) stampede the Nepal Electricity Authority and the government of Nepal into signing these project documents, which subsequently turned out to be, to borrow the hydrocracy's words, blatantly unfair? Again, it has to be the *dharma*-distorting pressures that end up forcing the donors into that fatalistic corner where they face the stark choice: disburse or die!

It becomes clear from the above that sound financial engineering is important for more than just taking up a project for implementation. It is also essential in the process of agreeing to buy the electricity from those projects that are being implemented by domestic and/or foreign investors. On top of that, there is another, and positive, dimension to the financial engineering that deserves close scrutiny.

The Khimti project was commissioned and began commercial operation in July 2000. Initiated with a budget of US$142 million and with a 40-month time frame, the project did not incur any cost overrun and was commissioned 12 days ahead of the stipulated date, thereby earning the contractors a handsome bonus and conferring a windfall gain, in terms of interim energy revenue, on the project's proponents. This demonstrates successful financial engineering from the proponent/developer side and is therefore an example that is worth emulating.

In almost all donor-funded projects, the contractors use defective design as an opportunity to come up with variation orders (claims for money and/or time additional to what has been contracted for), while the engineering consultant, for his part, complains of shoddy workmanship. These two, however, usually work in tandem, increasing the project costs and delaying completion, thereby enabling them both to earn more at the expense of the project owner and the overall economy (including, of course, the ultimate users of the electricity). But with Khimti this trap was avoided by the signing of a fixed price, fixed time, 'turn-key' contract, in which the lead responsibility was reposed in the civil contractor (thereby making them responsible for the engineering design as well as for supervision, gaps and cracks between various contracts for supply and so on). Moreover, specific deliverables were fixed for the contractor in terms of the rated performance of the plant (assuring that the plant will be able, on commissioning, to generate electricity at the designed capacity), including the minimum head and flow of water that needs to be achieved within a fixed time frame and for a fixed cost.

Again, far from eagerly replicating the excellent financial engineering inherent in these two success stories, the attention of both the donor community and Nepal's hydrocracy is elsewhere, as is evident from their more recent projects.

Kali Gandaki-A

This project is a 144MW semi-run-of-river hydropower plant with a daily pondage of 3.1 million cubic metres, commissioned in 2002 and generating an average annual energy of 842GWh. It is designed to operate, during the non-monsoon period, for peaking power of four to six hours a day; during the monsoon period, it can operate at full capacity 24 hours a day. Its estimated and actual costs are summarised in Table 8.4.

As we have already seen with Marsyangdi, this is one of those seemingly amazing projects that come in way below the estimated cost: just short of US$100 million under the estimate of around US$450 million. In order to determine whether it really *is* amazing we need to take a close look at the financial engineering. The estimated cost of US$452.8 million works out at $3,144 per kW, which, though somewhat less than Marsyangdi's actual $3,620, is still way too high. It is therefore a mystery (unless we invoke the aforementioned compulsion to disburse) why this project was deemed feasible. Nor, given this level of over-estimation, is it any wonder that it was possible to save $98 million.

• The total cost, at the time of the awarding of the various contracts, came to just 10 billion rupees, but after completion the Nepal Electricity

Table 8.4 Estimated and actual costs of Kali Gandaki-A

	Cost estimate (million US$)	Actual cost (million US$)
Preliminary works	4.7	–
Civil works	197.1	167.6
Electro-mechanical equipment	88.3	62.1
Construction engineering	15.1	21.0
Project management	8.2	6.2
Environmental mitigation	5.3	3.8
Loss reduction component	3.2	1.7
Taxes and custom duty	18.3	11.0
Contingencies	55.7	0
IDC	56.9	81.7
Grand total	452.8	354.8

Source: ADB (2012).

Authority had to capitalise the project at 23.66 billion rupees, an increase of 136 per cent. A similarly glaring lack of contracting skill is also evident in the civil contract, which was resolved by the board of the Nepal Electricity Authority to be awarded at a price 'not to exceed 7.35 billion rupees'.[25] In the event, 12.18 billion rupees were subsequently paid out to the contractor, without any authorisation from the board, when political instability overtook Nepal after 2005. The completion report of the Asian Development Bank makes no mention of this.

• Though scheduled for commissioning in November 2000, the project was not completed until May 2002, a time overrun of 18 months. This delay entailed the loss of 1,263GWh, which works out to be the equivalent of US$101 million.[26]

Starting from their wildly unrealistic over-estimate of US$452.8 million, the donors have been congratulating themselves for being able to save US$98 million. However, with the benefit of a financial engineering perspective, we can see that the loss of revenue of US$101 million due to the delay has more than wiped out those savings.

Middle Marsyangdi

A run-of-river-type scheme, with a daily pondage of five hours, the Middle Marsyangdi project is designed for an installed capacity of 70MW in order to generate 398GWh of average annual energy. *Kreditanstalt fuer Wiederaufbau* initially provided a grant of €172.963 million towards the estimated cost of €212 million, with the balance to be managed jointly by the government of Nepal and the Nepal Electricity Authority.[27] The donor then imposed a stranglehold on the project by covenanting that its funding could be used only for goods and services sourced in Germany and, even then, only through a German contractor/supplier. In addition, the contract for the civil works could be awarded only to a firm based in the European Union.[28] The estimated and actual (estimated) costs are set out in Table 8.5.

The cost estimate and actual cost do not include the project's liability in relation to interest during construction. The estimated cost per kW was US$2,586 while the actual cost is US$5,100, which is a record high without accounting for interest during construction. Indeed, it is 97 per cent higher than the average cost of the power plants that have been built even by the Nepal Electricity Authority. As the estimated cost itself was on the higher side compared to the sector, but actual cost was way too high, the estimate seems to have been prepared with an eye on making the project 'feasible at any cost'.

With the project commissioned in November 2008, with a delay of some 50 months, the project has lost 1,658.33GWh of electricity as a result of the delay, which equates to US$133 million.[29] This, together with the record price, represents a massive setback to the country, but there is no acknowledgement of this in the donor's appraisals and evaluations. If all related costs are to be accounted for, the total cost would come close to US$6,000 per kW – a staggeringly high cost – forcing one to wonder why the donorcracy rammed such a project down the unsuspecting throat of a least developed country.

The owner of the project, the Nepal Electricity Authority, also called 'the client', appointed a consulting engineer (Fichtner Joint Venture) to represent it in relation to the design and supervision of the works. A High Level Investigation Committee was set up by the government of Nepal after the political changes of 2006 to investigate the wrongdoings of this project. It scathingly reported that the consulting engineer, far from ensuring the best interest of its client, 'did not even act as a referee'. It went on to add that this particular consultant was selected irregularly, at the insistence of the donor.

So, in this project, we see much of the same failures in financial engineering as in the other donor-supported projects we have looked at: an all-time record cost increase, the donor getting bogged down, and then acting irregularly, in the micro-management of the construction works. That there is development

Table 8.5 Estimated and actual costs of Middle Marsyangdi*

	Estimated		Actual#	
	million €	*million* $	*million* €	*million* $
Cost	212	181.27	274.72	357.14

Notes:
* Information related to detailed breakdown of estimated and actual cost has not been made publicly available; these figures have been gleaned from discussions with key informants within the government and donor agencies.
# Conversion rate of the estimated cost was €1.17 per US$ in 2000 while that of the actual cost was €0.769 per US$ in 2008.

aid aplenty is not in doubt, but it is by no means certain that it is *from* Germany *to* Nepal: if one looks at who really made the money from it (consultants and contractors) and who is now paying for it (Nepalese government and consumers), it is, one might say, the other way around.

Remittance hydro and carbon credits: is this really the future?

Nepal is now very much a remittance economy, with almost one out of 10 Nepalis working in places like the Gulf States and East Asia and sending home a sizeable proportion of their earnings. The same, it is now proposed in relation to a whole cohort of very large projects, should happen with the country's hydroelectricity: it should be sent abroad, even while more than half of Nepal's citizens still have no access to it and those privileged to have electricity are suffering from almost 15 hours of power cuts every day. Without even thinking of ensuring energy security for the country,[30] there is a mindless rush to export so that it can then remit its earnings to the ol' country. A financial engineering analysis of the most imminent project in the cohort, West Seti, suggests that this is not such a marvellous idea.

The 750MW proposed West Seti was[31] an export-oriented reservoir project to be undertaken by the Australian firm, the Snowy Mountain Engineering Corporation. Its supporters – the donor community[32] and the hydrocracy as well as many Nepalese politicians and intellectuals – have shared an almost utopian view of this project; it would, they are convinced, transform the prospects for the Far-Western Development Region, the currently impoverished part of the country where the project was located. Although the licence of that avatar of a project has been cancelled, the site remains highly popular and the project will be implemented sooner or later. Hence an analysis of its failure

Table 8.6 Estimated costs of West Seti

	Estimated cost (million US$)★
Civil works	469
Electro-mechanical	180
Transmission	22
Resettlement	25
Project management	67
MIGA	34
Interest during construction and other financing cost	255
Legal costs	18
Development cost	27
Total initial investment in million US$	1,097

Note:

★ The amounts quoted are inclusive of contingency at a rate of 15 per cent for the civil works and 10 per cent for equipment, project management and resettlement (as provided for in the project's 'Detailed Engineering Report').

Source: SMEC (1997).

of financial engineering from a macroeconomic perspective embodies valuable lessons. Since the project is still at the proposal stage, there are no actual costs, but the estimated costs are set out in Table 8.6.

An analysis of financial engineering from a macroeconomic perspective entails an assessment of the various linkages of this project, and hence of its contribution to the nation's economy. These linkages, which I will now explain, can be traced along a number of 'dimensions': backward, forward, investment and fiscal.

Backward linkage

Hydropower projects, being capital-intensive, entail high initial investment. A project's backward linkage can be assessed by determining how much of that initial investment is going to be retained by the national economy, thereby generating employment, achieving a higher level of industrialisation and increasing foreign exchange reserves, as well as enhancing capacity, technology transfer and capital formation. The extent to which all this can happen does, of course, depend on the absorptive capacity of the economy. The contribution in terms of backward linkage will therefore be at its highest possible level if 100 per cent of the initial investment percolates back into the economy; conversely, it will be at its lowest if nothing at all percolates back. A project that scores high on this scale can be said to have been well-engineered financially from a macroeconomic perspective. In order to assess West Seti in terms of its backward linkage we need to examine the structure of its estimated initial investment, as set out in Table 8.6 above.

- Most of the US$469 million total cost of the civil works will be incurred in the procurement of cement, steel bars and other construction materials. Although there are about 10 cement factories in Nepal,[33] they do not have sufficient capacity to meet even the existing domestic demand. The same holds for Nepal's factories that produce steel bars (moreover, since they rely on imported steel, the percolation into the economy, even if these local producers could meet the demand, would be slight). All these demands, therefore, will have to be met by imports, apart from sand and gravel, which *are* available in Nepal, but which are estimated to cost only around $1 million.
- Since Nepal has yet to set up industries for manufacturing electro-mechanical equipment, even for small (i.e. below 10MW) hydropower projects, the entire budget for these essentials – $180 million – will be spent on imports. The same holds for $22 million for the transmission line. However, it is likely that about $1 million will go to Nepalese workers employed in the installation and erection of the electro-mechanical equipment and the transmission network.
- The resettlement entails the purchase of land and the building of houses on it for the population that will be displaced, with the land and

construction materials expected to cost around 50 per cent of the $25 million budget. This, clearly, will percolate into Nepal's economy, but that gain is pretty well wiped out by the land[34] and houses that will be lost by the displacees.

- Project management, however, was to be the responsibility of the Australian Snowy Mountain Engineering Corporation and is therefore expected to be a predominantly expatriate affair, with just 10 per cent or so going to a few selected technocrats from Nepal.
- The Snowy Mountain Engineering Corporation has said that it expects that some 5,000 unskilled workers will be employed over the estimated 5.5-year construction period, with the skilled workers being largely sourced from outside Nepal. The work force will be small in the initial years, peaking in years three and four and then tapering off towards completion with the result that, with an estimated total of 165,000 worker-months, the wages total works out at around $16.5 million.[35]
- The $34 million premium paid to the Multilateral Investment Guarantee Agency – a subsidiary of the World Bank – will be spent overseas. Similarly, since debt financing will be coming from foreign financial intermediaries (foreign banks, multilaterals like the Asian Development Bank and other financial institutions), the interest during construction (along with other financing costs) will not percolate into Nepal's economy. It is expected that around $0.2 million will be paid to lawyers in Nepal, with the balance of $17.8 million going to foreign lawyers. The Snowy Mountain Engineering Corporation was also entitled to a 'development cost' of $27 million for the project's preparation, and it can be reasonably assumed that around 10 per cent of this will be spent in Nepal.

From the above, we can deduce that, out of the total initial investment of $1,097 million, around $28 million will be spent in Nepal: a percolation rate of just 2.56 per cent of investment. Similarly, though the project entails foreign direct investment totalling $1,097 million, the contribution to Nepal's foreign exchange reserve (another form of backward linkage) will be limited to just $28 million, with the rest deserting the country immediately due to outlays in foreign countries. The percolation rate, and hence the backward linkage, would of course be better if only Nepal's absorptive capacity were greater: if it were in a position to manufacture the cement, for instance, and produce the steel rods. West Seti will do little to improve that capacity, and it would seem that the same has been the case with all the aid-funded projects that have preceded it.

Forward linkages

A hydropower project can also benefit the economy through its forward linkage, depending on the extent to which the electricity it produces is used domestically. Electricity use has a multiplier effect on the economy,[36] generating employment, promoting industrialisation, adding to the foreign exchange reserve, enhancing capacity and augmenting capital formation. Once it becomes available, the electricity can be used in all sectors, for instance in agro-processing including tea processing, which is currently processed using furnace oil or firewood. Just one change such as this will benefit the economy by decreasing the import of fossil fuel, which drains hard currency, while also conserving the forest and decreasing environmental degradation. Much the same holds when electricity is substituted for diesel in the pumping of water for irrigation, and farmers (and hence the economy) can further benefit by growing more crops within the year, branching out into cash crops and so on. Hence, percentage of forward linkage will be same as proportion of electricity used domestically.

Currently Nepal is moving in the opposite direction, with the non-availability of electricity stifling its industrialisation and with the industries having to rely on fossil fuels, which, far from being cost-effective, result in higher production costs, thereby impacting both the industries themselves and the consumers of their products. Also, the reserve of foreign exchange is depleted, while greenhouse gases and particulates exacerbate environmental pollution. Much the same holds for the transport sector, with its current heavy reliance on fossil fuels (as we have seen in Chapters 5 and 6), and also for the tourism, health, education and domestic sectors.

It is clear from the above that the in-country use of the electricity from a project results in beneficial import substitutions, while also having a positive impact on the foreign exchange reserve. Many development economists, however, maintain that the exporting of electricity from West Seti to India will help mitigate Nepal's trade deficit with India; it would, they claim, reduce the current balance of trade deficit by 25 per cent. But this is true only if you ignore the project's cash flow subsequent to its commissioning. For the duration of the debt service period (around 15 years) a large portion of the total revenue generated will go towards paying the interest on the debt and the repayment of a part of the principal of loan borrowed from abroad. Anything left after meeting these requirements, together with operation and maintenance costs, will then be distributed as dividend, of which only 15 per cent will reach Nepal as Nepal holds 15 per cent of the equity. Moreover, since the government of Nepal is borrowing the money to invest in the equity of the project company, most of its share in the dividend will be spent in meeting this part of the debt service obligation. The only foreign exchange that will enter and stay in Nepal, therefore, during these first 15 years of operation, are the energy and capacity royalties. These add up to around just 2.66 per cent of the total export revenue, dealt with under fiscal linkage. For the sake of simplicity, and since only 10 per cent of West Seti's electricity is destined to be made available to the Nepalese economy,[37] we can award it a 10 per cent mark on forward linkage.

Investment linkage

The country can also benefit from the construction and operation of a project in terms of the return on investment. The return, once in the hands of the recipient, will either be used as increased purchasing power, which will then result in employment generation, or it will be saved and thus invested again, which will lead to capital formation. If a project is fully financed domestically, then the interest earned by the financial intermediaries on their investment and the dividends received by the equity-holders would remain in the country. The investment linkage mark, in that case, would be 100 per cent.

West Seti, however, falls far short of that mark. All the debt is being sourced from foreign financial intermediaries, and only 15 per cent of the return on investment – derived from the government of Nepal's equity stake in West Seti – will percolate into the nation's economy. Had the government taken up its 15 per cent equity from domestic sources – perfectly feasible, given all the remittances and the current lack of investment opportunities – at least 3.75 per cent of the return would have accrued to Nepal.[38] The government, however, is borrowing the money to take up its equity position and this means that whatever dividend it receives will flow straight back to the lender in debt service. The project therefore gets a very poor mark indeed on investment linkage: less than 0.1 per cent.

Fiscal linkage

A final linkage has to do with the contribution that a project makes to the nation's treasury, in the form of various rates, taxes and duties. In the case of a hydropower project this linkage takes place in two stages: during construction and post-commissioning.

In the construction stage, as we have seen, a lot of material and equipment has to be imported (the ratio of imported to home-produced increasing as we go from micro hydro to small to medium to large). In Nepal, hydropower projects are 99 per cent exempted from customs duty on the import of plant, machinery and equipment (a provision that, inadvertently perhaps, constitutes a hidden subsidy to large-scale projects). West Seti is entitled to value-added tax exemption, too. So the project will end up paying just customs duty, at just 1 per cent: around $2 million. This works out at 0.18 per cent of the total initial investment.

During the operational period a hydropower project is required to pay a capacity royalty of 100 rupees per kW and an energy royalty of 2 per cent of the revenue during the first 15 years of its operation, totalling 2.66 per cent of revenue as described above. Also, under current Nepalese law, it is required to pay income (corporate) tax at the rate of 20 per cent of its net income.[39] West Seti, however, is exempted from paying income (corporate) tax, and will thus, over its first 15 years of operation, pay nothing apart from an export tax of 0.05 per cent of its revenue and royalties. Other projects, while not paying this export tax, have to pay the much more onerous 20 per cent income (corporate) tax and will thus be contributing over 7 per cent of their revenue in the first year, rising to more than 14 per cent from the ninth year onwards. When account is also taken of its exemption from tax on interest paid and dividends distributed, West Seti will be contributing to the treasury rather less than 25 per cent of what other projects pay.

Furthermore, since this is a reservoir-type project, it will be augmenting the dry season flow downstream in India by 7,770 million litres per day: an enormous benefit to India's agriculture. At the same time, Nepal will be sacrificing 2,750 hectares of its land to create the reservoir and also helping to alleviate flooding downstream in India during the wet season by holding back some of the monsoon-generated flow. No arrangements have been made for Nepal to be recompensed for all this, despite the precedent set by the Colombia Treaty between Canada and the United States.[40] The message is clear: the larger the project the weaker the fiscal linkage. And West Seti, being far and away the largest, will contribute just 7.79 per cent of what other projects pay during the construction stage, and less than 25 per cent during the operational phase.

The overall mark sheet

West Seti will contribute 2.56 per cent in backward linkage, 10 per cent as forward linkage, 0.1 per cent as investment linkage and, when it comes to fiscal linkage, just 7.79 per cent of what other projects pay during the construction phase and 25 per cent of what they pay over the operational phase (and that is without factoring in the non-payment of recompense for the augmented flow to India and the corresponding sacrifice by Nepal). This means that, out of a possible maximum score of 400, West Seti's tally is a pathetic 20.44.

In conclusion

The full extent of the technical soundness of each of the projects dealt with in this chapter will only become apparent in a decade or two's time. Only then will we have an adequate picture in terms of its performance, the frequency and severity of unscheduled outages and so on. But it is not at all difficult to test the soundness of the financial engineering from the owner's perspective of each of these projects and from the macroeconomic perspective in terms of economic linkages, nor do we need to wait. Negotiators from Nepal, it is evident from the above analyses, have been consistent in one thing: failed financial engineering. That fatalism has become all-pervasive is evident from the near-universal inability to learn from past mistakes – and past successes. How else can one explain the steady progression (even after Arun 3's cancellation) to projects with ever more expensive electricity? And how else can one account for the failure to replicate the glaringly successful private-sector models, of which Khimti is perhaps the prime example?

Nepalese hydrocrats, however, do not have a monopoly over failed financial engineering. Indeed, they are outdone by the donors and their donorcracy, imposing covenants and conditionalities without any consideration of the specific circumstances of the country in which they are working, and remaining wilfully ignorant about how to draw up a proper contract: one in which neither cost nor time overruns are incurred. Such failures, unremedied, do not dissipate; they weigh, heavier and heavier, on those that all these aid efforts are supposed to be benefitting: the Nepalese citizens (both those who are paying through the nose for their electricity and those who simply have not got any). And, at the other scale extreme, it is their nation's economy that suffers. Yet each specific donor official feels that he or she is doing a difficult and excellent job. Tasked with this or that specific project, these officials scrupulously ensure that they meet their disbursement targets, and then move along, leaving trails of financial engineering failures in their wake. Such achievements do not just happen, they require the inculcation of a host of dos and don'ts:

- Under-estimate the cost of a project so that it can be deemed feasible, thereby paving the way for disbursement, but do not make any effort to ensure that the project gets implemented at the estimated cost.
- Alternatively, over-estimate the cost so as to be able to claim to have made a saving (all the while twisting the host country's arm so as to divert attention from the cost being way too high). The bottom line, again, is disbursement, but fine judgement is needed in deciding whether to under- or over-estimate.
- Never bother about time overruns – someone else will pick up that tab – but take care not to mention them in your completion reports (if you're still around by then, that is).
- Never practise what you preach about sustainability; just ram the dodgy projects down the throat of a poor host country. By the time they've found out, you'll be gone.
- Don't try to ensure a level playing field in connection with negotiations between the Nepalese government, the Nepal Electricity Authority and the independent power producers. The last thing you want is the emergence of a proper market.
- Be firm about getting the Nepalese government and the Nepal Electricity Authority to sign project documents that some troublemakers might deem to be infeasible. You have to be cruel to be kind (and you get a speedier disbursement that way).
- Be sure to undermine the authority of the board of the Nepal Electricity Authority by making payments to contractors in excess of limits they have approved and not telling the board.
- Do force a multipurpose export-oriented reservoir project on the country, instead of ensuring availability of water and electricity for Nepal, but be careful to ensure that the country is unable to secure what it is due by way of various linkages and downstream benefits.
- Make sure you give away Nepal's right to carbon offset when it exports its hydropower to India.
- And, finally, make sure you never allow pesky social and environmental activists to derail gravy trains like Arun 3 ever again by buying out journalists and politicians well in advance ('small potatoes' compared to the huge profits to be made in such projects).

Notes

1 Presently the capacity is 1,024kW after a couple of upgrades.
2 Unlike other NGOs or incorporated institutions, UMN isn't a legal entity entitled to own landed property,
3 The type of estimate in fashion now with donorcracy, which affords an opportunity to crow that project has succeeded to save by completing the project at cost lower than estimated.
4 A lower estimate designed to persuade proponent to implement the project just to end up paying more by way of time and cost overruns to commission the project.
5 It was led by Statkraft SF, an undertaking of the Norwegian government.
6 And, even then, there are considerable sink costs: feasibility studies have been commissioned, carried out and paid for, as have various appraisals and evaluations. There may also be penalties payable in the event of cancellation.
7 One GWh equals one million kWh.
8 At NEA's average price of 8.14 rupees per kWh (for fiscal year 2014/15)
9 An affiliate financing agency of the German donor.
10 The actual total cost incurred of 249.8 million dollars does not include the amount spent on Mugling Marsyangdi Road of US$2.5 million, which line item doesn't figure in the original estimated cost.
11 For the average non-technical reader, it must be remembered that hydropower projects are normally built at costs between 1000 to 1500 US dollars per kilo Watt of installed capacity, although the numbers can shift up or down by ten or twenty percent depending upon the site conditions, but not certainly five hundred percent that we are discussing here. For comparison, Ethiopia (a country comparable in poverty to Nepal in normal GDP per capita terms) is building its 6000 MW Grand Renaissance Dam (begun in 2011 and slated for completion in 2017 without any international donor funding) at just US$ 800/kW.
12 Storage units entail a building a dam with appurtenant negative externalities like inundation and involuntary displacement, which entails investment in resettlement/re-habilitation: they should come out considerably more expensive than run-of-river projects.
13 At NEA's average price of 8.14 rupees per kWh (for fiscal year 2014/15).
14 Recounted in Mahat (2005).
15 Since the donor-imposed covenant restricted implementation of projects of more than 10MW installed capacity if Arun-3 would have been implemented (World Bank, 1994), no project with installed capacity over 10MW could have been built.
16 Excluding 122MW of IPP projects with 10MW or lower installed capacities that too were added to the system in this 2-decade period.
17 But average cost per kW would have been US$2,333 and lead time 4.75 years only if Middle Marsyangdi, failure of financial engineering of which is dealt with in a separate section later, would have been implemented in manner at least comparable to Modi and Kali Gandaki A.
18 See Gyawali (1997) for how Arun-3 was envisaged by the lead donor, the World Bank as a tool for "structural adjustment of Nepal's macro-economy". ADB subsequently diverted fund earmarked for Arun-3 to build Kali Gandaki A and KfW invested in Middle Marsyangdi.
19 Chatara 3.2MW in 1994 and Puwa 6.2MW in 2000.
20 Because of the donor-imposed covenant, no projects of more than 10MW could have been added, leaving just the 6.2MW Puwa by the Nepal Electricity Authority and the odd project by independent power producers.
21 As evidenced by the case of Middle Marsyangdi, the estimated cost of which was just US$181 million (US$2,585 per kW), almost doubling without including interest during construction.

22 The US investors have recently divested their holdings in Bhote Kosi to their local partners associated with the Soaltee Hotel group.
23 Now called Ministry of Energy.
24 According to "White Paper" 2006, published by NEA. No new information has been made public due to confidentiality provision enshrined in the PPA.
25 Full disclosure: this author was then a nominated independent director to the NEA board who conducted this investigation for the board while the ex-officio chairman of the NEA board was one of the editors of this volume as minister of water resources of Nepal.
26 At the weighted average price of 8.14 rupees per kWh (for fiscal 2014/15).
27 NEA's Annual Report for 2010.
28 Fichtner Joint Venture was the engineering consultant, together with TAEC/NESS Nepal and Dywidag – Dragados – CWE Joint Venture, with 14 December 2004 as the completion date. Equipment contractors comprise VA Tech-Hydro, Voith Siemens, Alstom Power Alstom Energie, AREVA Energie and SAG Energie.
29 At the weighted average price of 8.14 rupees per kWh (for fiscal 2014/15).
30 The Indian blockade of Nepal, in the wake of great earthquake in 2015 and the promulgation of Nepal's new constitution that it did not like has finally succeeded in drawing the attention of politicians, bureaucrats, business community and the general public towards importance of achieving energy security.
31 Its license was cancelled by GoN in April 2011 for failure of project proponent to achieve financial closure, after GoN granting many extensions over a decade and a half to achieve financial closure.
32 ADB must be thanked for belatedly appreciating that exporting electricity from such projects doesn't help Nepal achieve energy security and refusing to fund this project, which impelled GoN to cancel the license.
33 These actually manufacture cement, that is. There are others that mainly grind clinker imported from India and then fill it into sacks.
34 A reservoir project uses land twice: once in inundation and once more for resettlement.
35 Assuming an average rate of 10,000 rupees per worker-month.
36 It is believed that use of 1 unit of electricity generates multiplier effect of 2,5.
37 Pursuant to the Parliamentary Natural Resource and Means Committee, the government of Nepal is required to take 10% of the electric energy in kind. This despite the fact that the project agreement (through its eighth amendment) envisages the government receiving money in lieu of energy. I am assuming that the government will succeed in amending the agreement so as to receive the energy itself, so as to conform to the parliamentary committee's decision.
38 Assuming that debt to equity ratio will be 3:1.
39 According to Sub-Section (4) of Section 2 of Schedule 1 of Income Tax Act, 2000.
40 The Columbia Treaty signed on March 29, 1999 between Canada and USA.

9 Biogas

Buoyant or bust?

Saroj Rai

The early years

Father Bertrand Saubolle, who was for many years a teacher at St Xavier's School at Godavari in Lalitpur until he passed away in 1982, constructed Nepal's first biogas plant in 1955. It was made out of two 200-litre metal oil drums, one used as the digester, the other as the gasholder. His research, however, started at a more micro-scale (NBPG 2007):

> I experimented and succeeded in producing cow dung gas in a coffee can, just sufficient to light a flame for five seconds. It was enough to satisfy me. I have grasped the principle. I constructed a small experimental plant outside my window. It gave me two hours work a day. People came to see it in one's and two's and tens and busloads. They asked me questions, took notes and went home and forgot about it.

Father Saubolle's frustration, however, did not last long. The awesomely simple technology, it turned out, had caught on in Nepal's southern neighbour, India, and in 1968 the Khadi and Village Industries Commission (KVIC) – a Gandhian initiative – set out to re-introduce biogas to Nepal by constructing a demonstration plant, with a floating drum design, at an exhibition in Kathmandu.

This biogas technology, with its very obvious benefits to farmers – it is clean, it is environmentally benign, and the residue is a better fertiliser than the cow dung it starts off with – soon attracted some state attention. The Ministry of Agriculture, it so happened, had designated the fiscal year 1974/05 'Agriculture Year' and, with a view to giving that declaration some substance, it supported the construction of KVIC-design biogas plants in 199 households. Interest-free loans from the Agricultural Development Bank – a state-owned bank with an extensive rural network – were also made available to the lucky households. The idea was to promote a small-scale technology that would reduce the use of fuelwood and cattle dung in cooking, improve health by eliminating the smoke from the hearths and provide, as an end-product, a digested slurry that, when used as a manure, would lessen (or even eliminate) the need for imported and costly chemical fertiliser.

The early recognition by the state of the technology's multiple benefits, together with its enthusiastic but modest promotional efforts, certainly helped its introduction to Nepal and set the scene for its expansion. Given the state's penchant (evident in the preceding case study chapters) for large-scale, high-tech and capital-intensive technologies, this is somewhat surprising, but can perhaps be explained by the markedly small-scale nature of Nepalese agriculture and by the major role played by biomass in the country's energy consumption. Even today, after some four decades of industrialisation and urbanisation, more than 80 per cent of Nepal's population depends on subsistence agriculture, and almost 87 per cent of national energy consumption comes from biomass: mainly firewood, agro-waste and cattle dung. So, though the technology itself may be small-scale, its impact, if it proved possible to roll it out across the whole country, would be massive. The new technology certainly appeared to fit very well with the way agriculture is done in Nepal: the household-sized plant matching the way the houses, each with their cattle in adjacent stalls, are dispersed across the landscape, and with the energy need being mostly for cooking (very few households use their biogas for lighting). The input – cow dung – is therefore on site, as too is the by-product – the slurry – which can then be used as it is or composted with other available organic materials (the animals' bedding and so on) before being carried out to and spread on the fields. And, on top of all that, the slurry turns out to be a better organic fertiliser than the farmyard manure that is traditionally relied on.

The first biogas company – Biogas and Agriculture Development Company Private Limited (more popularly known as GGC) – was established in 1977 with joint investment by the Agricultural Development Bank, the United Mission to Nepal (the same INGO that, as we have seen in Chapters 6 and 7, has been so active in small hydropower development) and the Nepal Fuel Corporation (now the Nepal Timber Corporation). The GGC then became the key organisation in the promotion of biogas in Nepal. As a private limited company it is formally a private-sector organisation but, with one of its three investors being a government-owned bank and another an INGO, it is evidently more of a 'hybrid', and this is confirmed by its continued (but not regular) support from both government and various international development organisations. The absence of competitors (in its early days, that is) also makes it somewhat anomalous, competition being a prerequisite for the effective functioning of markets. On the other hand, new technologies are often nurtured in this way: Britain, for instance, entered the new field of biotechnology by way of a government-funded company – the ultimately highly successful Celltech – that made no profits and had no competitors during the first decade of its existence (Cooke 2001).

In much the same way as Celltech, GGC, during its early years, received some investment subsidy and technical assistance for design improvement and dissemination. By 1990 they had finalised as the standard design the all-concrete GGC 2047. This had a fixed dome and was an improved version of a Chinese design (Chinese farming systems, of course, having many similarities with those across the border in Nepal). Initially, they were exclusively cattle dung-fed plants, though the design originally had a provision for latrine connection; later, a gradually increasing number of biogas plants were connected to latrines. So this technology, with its inherent flexibility, has paved the way for one of the leapfrogs we mentioned in Chapters 5 and 6, missing out the entire phase of handling human waste by putting it into the water cycle that all the world's developed countries are currently so deeply locked into.

Besides institutional actors, several individuals played significant roles in development of the technology and in promotion of it in Nepal and beyond. Among these individuals, one name stands out – Dr Amrit Bahadur Karki, who is respectfully and rightfully called 'the Father of Biogas' in Nepal. Dr Karki devoted his life to biogas and remains active in one or another capacity. Among his many, often voluntary, contributions, he initiated and edited Nepal's *Biogas Newsletter* for nearly 22 years, starting in 1978.[1]

Biogas technology and its potential in Nepal

Biogas technology, though simple, requires meticulous design and construction, if it is to operate successfully. Any organic material, when subjected to anaerobic fermentation (in the absence of oxygen, that is) produces a mixture of gases, of which 60–70 per cent is methane and the rest carbon dioxide, along with traces of other gases. The mixture is called biogas, and it burns with a higher calorific value than the biomass from which it is produced, and without producing any smoke or particulates. The residue, as has already been mentioned, is an excellent fertiliser. A biogas plant system has as its main parts an inlet tank, a digester, a gas storage dome and an outlet tank (see Figure 9.1).

In the standard GGC 2047 design, the inlet tank, digester and outlet tank are made of stone or brick masonry and the dome is a concrete casting without reinforcement. The digester and gasholder dome are underground, while the inlet, gas outlet pipe and slurry outlet tank are left visible. Apart from the mixing device in the inlet tank, there are no moving parts, and the design culminates in two pits that are dug next to the plant for collecting the slurry and, if desired, composting it with farmyard waste. A flexible gas pipe brings the gas into the house for cooking on a gas stove and, if required, for lighting from a gas mantle.

It is estimated that, out of a total of some 4.5 million households in Nepal, around 1.01 million are suitable for biogas installation with cattle dung feeding. By 2015 the number of households with biogas plants had reached over 350,000. The technology has thus achieved over 34 per cent penetration, but in a somewhat patchy way. Three districts have over 20,000 plants per district, and 14 districts have more than 10,000 plants. However, 11 districts have less than 10 plants, while 23 districts (almost one-third of the total, and mostly mountainous) have fewer than 500 plants. The aim, therefore, should be to continue increasing the penetration while ironing out the unevennesses.

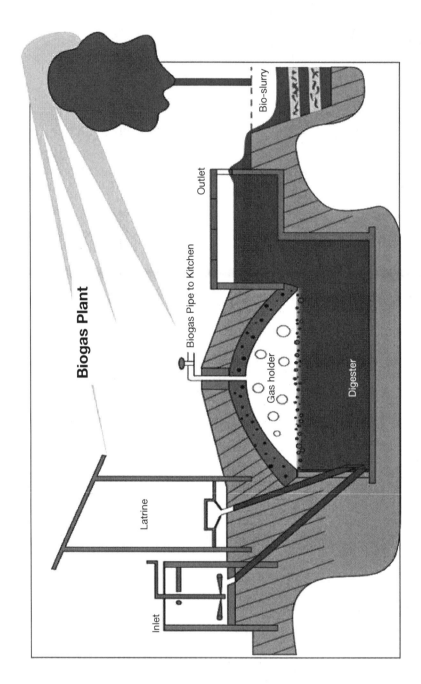

Figure 9.1 Schematic design of a household biogas plant

The achievements and four phases of the Biogas Support Programme

Nepal's Biogas Support Programme was started in July 1992 with funding from the Netherlands.[2] This marked the start of fairly substantial and regular aid for biogas promotion in Nepal. The idea from the start was to promote private companies as 'front runners' in this still quite new industry by providing assistance – for product, market and skill development, quality improvement and so on – while at the same time making available limited subsidies and credit facilities to the customers: farming households with little in the way of surplus funds. There was therefore an individualistic market component, a hierarchical donor community component and an egalitarian (helping low-income households come up with the entry fee for the market) component. No one player was running the entire show, and 'patches' were by no means clear cut and agreed, with the result that there was an inbuilt and three-cornered system of checks and balances.

Phase 1 (1992–94) and Phase 2 (1994–97) were primarily focused on the improvement of quality through market development and regulation. By the end of Phase 2, there were 36 biogas construction companies, mostly very small and run by ex-employees of GGC, the first company. During these two phases, just over 20,000 plants were constructed, mainly in the Terai and the Middle Hills. In 1995, the companies formed a trade association – the Nepal Biogas Promotion Group – which, together with the Biogas Support Programme, was successful in pushing for a specialised government body: the Alternative Energy Promotion Centre. This centre now has several large rural and alternative renewable energy development programmes and projects under its umbrella, including the Biogas Support Programme.

In Phase 3 (1997–2003), the Nepal government and Germany's KfW also started funding the Biogas Support Programme, and by the end of this period 50 biogas construction companies and 11 accessory/appliance manufacturing workshops had been established. A total of over 91,000 plants were constructed during these six years. (Table 9.1 shows the (mostly) rising rate of annual construction since the start of Phase 1.)

In Phase 4 (2003–10), the Alternative Energy Promotion Centre (a government body) became the executing agency, with the Biogas Sector Partnership – Nepal (a non-governmental organisation) as the implementing agency. Biogas Sector Partnership – Nepal was practically created as a national NGO out of the Biogas Support Programme structure, which until that point was part of the SNV Netherlands Development Organisation. It further consolidated and strengthened the various NGO involvements from the earlier phases, thereby keeping the three apices of the triangular interplay roughly balanced. Phase 4 had set itself the target of constructing 200,000 biogas plants during this six-year period, but annual progress has averaged out at around 16,000: hardly surprising, in view of the Maoist insurgency/'People's War', which lasted from 1996 to 2006 and claimed over 13,000 lives, mostly in the rural areas. As can

Table 9.1 Biogas plant construction trend after the establishment of BSP

No. of plant construction in Nepal

Year	No. of plants
1992	0
1993	3,318
1994	3,506
1995	5,115
1996	7,157
1997	8,387
1998	9,869
1999	11,052
2000	13,265
2001	17,857
2002	15,527
2003	16,340
2004	11,259
2005	17,803
2006	16,118
2007	17,663
2008	14,884
2009	19,479
2010	21,158
2011	20,056
2012	18,584
2013	22,110
2014	40,200

be seen from Table 9.1, the rising construction trend continued through the first few years of civil strife before falling off somewhat between 2001 and 2006, after which it has resumed its rising trend.

Many government- and donor-supported rural development projects came to a standstill during the latter half of the decade long insurgency. The Biogas Support Programme was one of the few that could continue, albeit with great difficulty, mainly because the programme was primarily driven by the private sector and NGOs at the implementation level. As the target could not be met and budget was underspent, the programme got a year budget-neutral extension so as to last 7.5 years. Phase 4 achieved a total installation of 113,961, which was a little short of the revised target of 117,500 (RESS 2010). The 18 year-long financial support from the Dutch government through the SNV Netherlands Development Organisation came to an end with the end of Phase 4 in December 2010. With more than 231,000 plants constructed in all 75 districts of the country (RESS 2010) and a functionality rate of over 95 per cent, the biogas market was working well, at least in some districts. The annual average installation during the Phase IV was about 18,000 plants. After a mid-term review in 2005, the Biogas Support Programme revised its overall objective, making it more holistic and better fitted to the future tasks of consolidation and commercialisation (World Bank 2006: 5):

[T]o further develop and disseminate biogas plants as a mainstream renewable energy solution in rural Nepal, while better addressing poverty, social inclusion, and regional balance issues and at the same time ensuring commercialization and sustainability of the sector.

A student of clumsiness would identify three voices within this short mission statement. First, the word 'sustainability', together with the plan about further developing and disseminating this mainstream solution, is very much the hierarchical (state apex) voice. Second, the stress on poverty, social inclusion and regional balance, being all about equalising differences, reveals the egalitarian (civil society) voice. And, third, the stress on commercialisation ensures that the individualist (market apex) voice is not crowded out by these first two. There is, therefore, something *constitutional* about this mission statement, in the sense that it insists that each of these voices is legitimate, it has the right to be heard. The Washington Consensus prescriptions, for instance, are in there – in the stress on markets and commercialisation – but, and this (which will be explained more fully in a moment) is what is crucially lacking with the Washington Consensus, it has to co-exist and contend with the other two sets of prescriptions; it cannot exclude those challenging voices in the way the Washington Consensus did (until, that is, it was officially declared dead – see Chapter 4). However, this is not some cosy three-cornered consensus – how could it be, given the fundamental contradictions of the problems and solutions that each espouses – and there is ample space for argument and disagreement over which voice (and how much of it) needs to be listened to in any particular situation, thereby ensuring the never-ending 'constructive engagement' that is the hallmark of clumsy solutions.

The clumsy arrangement that was the Biogas Support Programme during its first four phases (1992–2010) achieved an excellent macroeconomic track record:

- By July 2010 the programme had reached all of Nepal's 75 districts and (at the more local government level) 2,769 out of the 3,913 village development committees and municipalities. At that time, the total number of plants constructed had reached 231,231. Of these, a survey had shown, more than 98 per cent remain operational. Patchiness, however, remained quite pronounced, despite measures taken right from 2007, including market development interventions and financial incentives with additional subsidy for the poor and other marginalised/disadvantaged communities. The patchiness is basically linked to altitude or temperature, level of people's socio-economic status, and road connectivity. Nepal has the world's second highest penetration level for household-size biogas plants,[3] with China in first place. As of the end of 2010, when the cumulative number reached 231,231 plants, around 63 per cent of the plants also had latrines attached to them, and 74 per cent of the owners used the slurry, in one form or other, as improved manure, thereby substituting chemical fertiliser.
- In the early years of the Biogas Support Programme, almost all the plants were constructed with credit from the Agricultural Development Bank (in addition to a state subsidy). As the momentum built up, more plants were constructed with cash as, due to a demonstration effect, rural households started prioritising biogas in their list of investments. As the cash market started dwindling, linkage to credit again became imperative. With some credit related inventions, the share of biogas plants constructed with credit reached close to 32 per cent in 2009, drastically higher from 17 per cent in 2007. So the market, though still enjoying certain forms of support, is more than holding its own.
- There were over 81 private-sector biogas companies by the end of 2010, with around 200 offices across the country, together with some 16 workshops manufacturing components and appliances (cookers etc.) for the biogas systems. These private companies are registered with an office of the Ministry of Industry and Supplies. Lending from the big banks has also declined as a consequence of the entry into biogas lending of micro finance institutes, of which there were some 160 in 2010. They receive wholesale loans from the Biogas Credit Fund, which is managed by the government's Alternative Energy Promotion Centre, and then pass these loans on to households for biogas plant construction.
- By 2010, over 5,000 biogas masons and some 1,500 supervisors had been trained under the Biogas Support Programme, many of whom moved on to other things, with an estimated retention rate of 30 per cent.

The technicians involved in these private-sector companies, and even the entrepreneurs and managers, come mostly from rural Nepal (in marked contrast, as we have seen in the previous chapter, to how things are in that other part of the energy sector, large hydro). The total direct and indirect employment created by the Biogas Support Programme was estimated to be around 9,000 people in 2010. The programme received a number of international awards,[4] and was increasingly seen as providing a model that can be replicated: both in Nepal (where it is applied to rural electrification by way of solar photovoltaic panels) and abroad (in at least 24 countries of Asia, Africa and Latin America, for the promotion of biogas[5]).

These macroeconomic effects came about due to the excellent microeconomics that the Biogas Support Programme facilitated. A cost-benefit analysis based on 2010 costs brings this out. A six cubic metre plant – the average size – was costing around Rs35,000 (roughly $540) in 2010 and there was a 27 per cent subsidy: Rs9,500 (roughly $150).[6] In terms of product lifetime costs, this is not expensive, but the up-front costs can be a major obstacle for poor households. Users, however, can contribute Rs10,000 (around $154) in kind, by providing the labour for digging, filling mud, collecting stone and gravel and so on. This still leaves them with around Rs15,500 ($238) as a cash requirement and, for the poorer users, the only way to meet that is by way of a bank loan. A Rs12,000 ($185) loan, over just five years and even with interest at 16 per cent, works out at a monthly instalment of Rs292 ($5.50), which equates to the selling of half a litre of milk a day. And, if they had been using kerosene for lighting before they changed to biogas, then the saving on that alone would be 92 per cent of the monthly instalment. With a biogas plant lasting 40 or 50 years and costing barely Rs300 ($4.60) a year to maintain, it undercuts LPG (liquefied petroleum gas), even though it is subsidised, by two-thirds. So, even for poor households, biogas is well worth it, as long as the up-front costs can be met. This analysis has not considered the benefits from bio-slurry, the other product. Some argue that the economic benefit from bio-slurry may outweigh the energy benefit, provided bio-slurry is properly used for improved agriculture yield and reduced use of chemical fertiliser. There is a difficulty in quantifying or monetising the bio-slurry benefits due to the fact that the energy benefit is so obvious and visible, overshadowing the other.

In addition to these economic benefits, the polyrational Biogas Support Programme has also made significant contributions to ecological and health improvement:

- As mentioned above, biogas burns smokelessly and thus has a number of advantages over the traditional alternatives: firewood, agro-waste and cattle dung. Moreover, as well as reducing the incidence of respiratory and eye-related diseases, it relieves the women and children of all the drudgery involved in the collecting and drying of the traditional fuels. Adding in a latrine attachment, besides enhancing biogas and manure production, it significantly improves sanitation, while ensuring that this is not at the cost of putting human waste into the water cycle.

- Bio-slurry and bio-compost improve agricultural yield, while at the same time displacing or reducing chemical fertiliser (and its associated costs and drudgery). Kerosene purchase is dispensed with, and around 2.5 tonnes of firewood per year per household is conserved. On top of that, agro-waste and cattle dung that previously went up in smoke can be diverted into manure and compost production.

These advantages, moreover, are clearly evident to the householders themselves (BSP 2009):

> The biogas technology has made so much difference to us. The neighbours often come to us and ask for advice as they see how easy it is to save money with the help of biogas. They were the same people who had cautioned us not to risk our savings by investing in a biogas plant
>
> (Mrs Jagita Chaudhary, Morang District)

> Cooking has been faster and easier due to biogas. In addition, farming and vegetable production has increased due to the bio-slurry as manure. Thus biogas technology has been a blessing for us – village farmers
>
> (Mr Laxman Ghimire, Lalitpur District)

None of this is to argue that the Biogas Support Programme has been flawless. Apart from its uneven penetration, there has also been the risk, as some critics have pointed out, that biogas will end up locking farmers into cow ownership, thereby reducing their adaptability in the face of economic and climatic change. And, at some stage in the future, biogas may find itself losing out to competition from other technologies: electricity from rural mini-grid or even from national grid extension. Last, but not least, the wonderfully clumsy arrangement that has been the Biogas Support Programme has in recent years become increasingly at risk of being undone.

Integration into the National Rural and Renewable Energy Programme

For a number of years, a comprehensive discussion had gone on among the government, donors and other stakeholders about whether to integrate the Biogas Support Programme into other renewable and alternative energy programmes on micro hydropower, solar photovoltaics, improved cookstoves, water mills etc. In view of this, the biogas programme entered into an interim period (January 2011 to July 2012), where a private-sector association, the Nepal Biogas Promotion Association, was given responsibility for private-sector capacity development. Furthermore, in July 2012, the Biogas Support Programme was integrated into a large, five-year National Rural and Renewable

Energy Programme. The arguments in favour of this integration concerned harmonisation, cost-effectiveness, tapping into a larger pool of fund, better coordination, synergy etc. After so many years of donor support for capacity development, enabling environment and improved performance of actors, there was a strong case for the government to take up more responsibility, particularly at the national steering level through a consolidated single national programme framework. Nevertheless, some partners foresaw problems and stated that there was a risk of existing systems and capacities getting undermined. They thus argued for integration only at the executive level, while leaving the actual implementation to the existing implementing agencies. This arrangement would have avoided an unnecessary rocking of the boat, while making use of current capacities and systems and further strengthening the checks and balances. Given the complexity of the programme, it is important that there is a clear division of role between policy guidance and oversight (by the government) and actual implementation by private-sector and civil society actors.

Under the new, integrated set-up, roles in programme implementation got substantially revised and redefined among the government body involved (the Alternative Energy Promotion Centre), the private sector and two implementing partners (namely the Biogas Sector Partnership – Nepal and the Nepal Biogas Promotion Association, which is a private-sector business association). Except for these outfits, no other NGOs were involved in the implementation any longer, unlike previously, when a number of big or small NGOs participated. In addition, the subsidy rates were almost doubled in 2013, with the intention to reach the real poor and to start earning from the Clean Development Mechanism. The market surged in no time (as is evident from Table 9.1), as it became possible for households to obtain biogas plants in exchange for only some labour (for digging the pit and helping the mason). This surge was intensified by the four-month fuel blockade of the country by India in reaction to the promulgation of Nepal's new constitution in September 2015. This induced business entities, such as dairy and poultry farms, and institutions, such as army and police barracks, to invest heavily in biogas. A news report headline read 'All army barracks to have biogas in one and half years'.[7]

Unfortunately, by now, reimbursement of the subsidy to the biogas companies has become a huge problem for two reasons (a) changes in procedures and paperwork; and (b) limited allocation of the overall subsidy budget to biogas in each fiscal year. (Biogas companies typically pre-finance the subsidy first and only claim after completion of the plant and submission of the necessary documents.) The framework for quality management has become undone as well. This has left rural biogas buyers and users, who often have little knowledge, if any, of the technology, to fend for themselves when confronted with quality problems in construction and after-sale service. As a consequence, there is an increasing incidence of plants having been constructed without the conditions for proper functioning (such as the availability of dung) having first been ensured. The increasingly weak regulation of company licensing and quality monitoring has also created a non-level playing field between companies with institutional and financial might and other firms.

All these problems have negatively affected the credibility and quality of the programme and the possibility to generate money through the Clean Development Mechanism. The biogas market is currently in turmoil. In April 2016, seven associations of different renewable energy companies, including the biogas companies' association, and NGOs working as partners under this integrated programme, submitted a strongly worded letter containing five demands and a seven-day ultimatum. They threatened to stage a series of protests in the event that their demands for timely contract agreements and subsidy reimbursements were not met.[8] This has created not just an unprecedented, but also a highly polarised and dangerous situation. The protesters have expressed their anger and frustration, stating that companies are on the verge of bankruptcy due to the perennial delay in settling bank loans that they have taken out to pre-finance the users' investment subsidy. The agreements and payments from the programme have been halted as management has struggled to address donor demands to clean up mismanagement. All of this has served to justify the fears of those who argued against making the Alternative Energy Promotion Centre solely responsible for execution and implementation of the biogas programme.

On the need to become clumsy again

The history of biogas in Nepal is therefore marked by two distinct periods: a lengthy and highly successful one from 1992 to 2010 and a shorter and much less successful one from 2010 to the present. In the first of these the Biogas Support Programme was developed and implemented. This represented a highly clumsy (or polyrational) undertaking, as it included, from the outset, all three 'voices': the state (both domestic in the form of the Ministry of Agriculture and the Agricultural Development Bank, and foreign in the shape of aid donors), the market (in the form of the GGC and, later on, its private-sector offshoot competitors) and civil society (in the incarnation of the scrupulously egalitarian United Mission to Nepal and other NGOs).[9] Their forever-changing interplay achieved a track record of steady progress – even through the period of civil strife – across various fronts, including poverty alleviation, the founding of micro-credit institutions (through a collaboration with the Grameen Bank), environmental protection and health improvement. Indeed, in some villages in the plain south or Middle Hills, biogas has become the mainstream cooking energy among farmers. Similarly, there are plenty of stories of farmers reaping full benefits from the other product of the bio-digester technology, namely bio-slurry, including for production of organic vegetables and tea. The total number of biogas plants in national biogas programmes supported by SNV reached over 712,000 units by the end of 2015. At a broader level, the modest biogas programme that was first developed in Nepal has been touted as a model for the promotion of biogas and other similar decentralised energy solutions in the developing world, and has been replicated in over 24 countries of Asia, Africa and Latin America.

Not all hurdles were overcome, of course. Even with micro-credit, the poorest households still struggle to meet the up-front costs of a biogas installation and will need additional support. A geographical unevenness also remains: there is a low penetration rate in some remote and higher-altitude districts. Relatedly, the need remains to communicate certain simple modifications of the technology itself. Anaerobic fermentation goes more slowly in the cooler mountain regions and this can be overcome by building a compost heap on top of the digester. Also, the design can be modified so as to work effectively with other feeds: pig manure, for instance. Furthermore, there is the issue of self-regulation of the biogas industry through the various national and regional business membership associations. These associations set and, where necessary, revise codes of conduct for their members. The implementation of these codes is not yet satisfactory, and needs remedying. Finally, biogas, of course, is not free standing; it has all sorts of overlaps and connections with other rural development programmes: some government-initiated, others donor-initiated and still others initiated by a wide range of NGOs. Programmes and projects that are working for livelihood improvement, health and sanitation, forest conservation, improved farming and so on are all helping, as is biogas, to promote cleaner and more environmentally friendly solutions and thus create demands for one another: 'win-win', you could say. In other words, it makes sense for diverse projects and programmes to work together, as and when opportunities arise.

For these challenges to be met, *dharma* may need to be restored first. The integration of the Biogas Support Programme into the National Rural and Renewable Energy Programme in 2012 has distorted the triangular interplay of the government, private sector and civil society. After this move towards more centralisation and regulation, companies have been mistreated and NGOs have been sidelined. In terms of cultural theory, hierarchy has come to prevail over egalitarianism and individualism. As a result, Nepal's biogas programmes have lost much of their shine, and have even sparked intense conflicts among stakeholders. Only by making these programmes clumsier again will these conflicts be resolved.

Notes

1 Author's interview with Dr Amrit Bahadur Karki.
2 From its Directorate General for International Cooperation through SNV Netherlands Development Organisation in Nepal.
3 Author's estimate.
4 Including first prize in the United Kingdom's Ashden Awards for Sustainable Energy.
5 Presentation by SNV Renewable Energy Managing Director, October 2014, the Netherlands.
6 The amount of the subsidy has remained the same since the early 1990s but has been steadily declining, because of inflation, in percentage terms. This is in line with the original principle that it should be gradually phased out.

7 *The Kantipur Daily*, A Nepali Language Newspaper, December 30, 2015.
8 Joint Letter to Alternative Energy Promotion Centre with subject 'seven-day ultimatum', 14 April 2016.
9 The strong egalitarian bias of UMN is evident in the first few pages of the previous chapter, especially in its 'mission statement' and in the personal style of the charismatic Odd Hoftun.

10 Water supply and sanitation

Elusive targets and slippery means

Anil Pokhrel

The United Nations Development Programme published its first Human Development Report in 1990. Since then it has done one every year, each time taking a different and topical theme of global concern and setting out its analysis and its ideas on how best to move forward. The theme of its 2006 report was water crisis, and its analysis highlighted the challenges that are entailed in the efforts to provide safe drinking water, especially in the world's developing countries. Ninety per cent of Nepalis, the report stated, have 'sustainable access to an improved water source' (UNDP 2006: 293). This is a remarkable achievement for one of the world's poorest countries: a country, moreover, that was at that time going through a major transition in its political structure (see Chapter 4). And the achievement becomes even more remarkable when you consider that Nepal only really started its efforts to provide drinking water in the mid-1970s, just a few years before the start of the International Decade for Drinking Water Supply and Sanitation.[1] A few months after UNDP's water report, Nepal's bi-weekly magazine *Himal Khabar Patrika* reported that only 52 per cent of the population had access to drinking water supply, adding that this was the high estimate.

If the UNDP figure is correct then Nepal is on track to meet its Millennium Development Goals well ahead of the target date; if the *Himal Khabar Patrika* figures are correct then Nepal is in a deep hole and there is little chance of it meeting those longed-for goals. The first figure puts foreign aid in a good light; the second does not. In football, if the ball is through the goalmouth and the player who put it there was not offside, then it's a goal; but, with the Millennium Development Goals, it all depends! All of which suggests that these MDGs, like San Goldwyn's verdict on verbal agreements, are not worth the paper they are written on (Vandemoortele 2011). Who would bother to watch, or play, football if there were no way of telling whether or not a goal has been scored?

A different approach is therefore called for: an approach by way of the history of drinking water access and provision in Nepal, an approach, moreover, that takes account of the fact that people can enjoy access to safe drinking water without there being any provision of it. After all, people tend to settle in places where there happen to be reliable sources of safe water. It is only later, when those settlements grow larger, or when the settlers manage to mess up their water, or when people move to places (like Kathmandu) where there isn't any safe water (or isn't enough of it), or when the climate changes, or when earthquakes damage water sources, that provision becomes a consideration.

The ahistorical assumption behind the Millennium Development Goals, by contrast, is that people are just sitting there waiting to be provided with safe drinking water, and that absolutely does not accord with what has been (and still is) going on. Over the past 30 years, for instance, the population of Kathmandu has risen from 200,000 to considerably over two million, much of it in the last two decades coeval with the Maoist insurgency in the rural hinterlands: faster, that is, than Manchester or Leeds grew at the very height of the Industrial Revolution. Providing just a fraction of that increased population with access to safe drinking water would be a truly impressive achievement (it took Manchester and Leeds many decades), yet it would be judged a sizeable step backwards in terms of the Millennium Development Goals. People *chose* to go to Kathmandu – for the economic opportunities, to get away from the Maoists, or whatever – regardless of whether they would have access to safe drinking water once they got there. By and large, in fact, they *do* have access to it, often from traditional stone water spouts (*dhunge dhara*) and open dug wells (*inar*), in bottled or tanker-borne form or via the market, that is, rather than through the pipes and taps provided by the municipal authorities. If it is through the municipal authorities' pipes and taps then it has been *provided*; if it is through the market's bottles and tankers or *dhunge dharas* then it has been *commanded* by the people themselves.

If you count both provision and command then the *Human Development Report*'s figure is fairly plausible; if you count only provision then the *Himal Khabar Patrika*'s estimate is more convincing. All a bit academic, you may think, but, as we will see, it is the provision-based figures that are being used to justify the hugely expensive and environmentally intrusive Melamchi Trans-Basin Water Transfer Project, a project that, if you believe the hype, will solve all the city's water problems, enabling the streets to be hosed down every morning and ensuring that the Bagmati River is full with clean water right up to the *ghats* every day of the year.

History, not goals

When people began living in the hills, mountains and plains of Nepal they did drink water; life would have been impossible without it. But it was, as it were, freely available (a *common-pool good*) and was neither provided (as a *public good*) nor commanded (as a *private good*). We also know, from documented and archaeological evidence, that earlier civilisations – the Harappans, the Romans and others – did build water supply systems to meet the needs of their citizens and to render their cities viable. Later still, largely as a consequence of the Industrial Revolution, Western technology became installed as the engine of well-being and happiness. Even so, the notion that prosperity, well-being and happiness could be enjoyed by all remained a dream − something to be relegated to the next life − for all save a fortunate few. Only in the eighteenth century, with the utilitarian achievements − 'improvement', as they were collectively called − that were ushered in by the European Enlightenment, was the dream gradually brought down to earth. The Western world's material accumulation, and its imperialistic expansion throughout the nineteenth century, then clearly demonstrated that its technology was a most effective instrument for achieving social well-being. And, on a more tangible level, the citizens of those Western countries − even those living in the horrendous slums of Manchester and Leeds − began to enjoy increasing access to safe water, health services and affordable energy (particularly from fossil fuel: coal and gas).

Much less so, however, the further people were away from the Western centres, with the result that the notion of social happiness that reached South Asia during the colonial era came with a considerable amount of ideological baggage. It was the rule of law that the British introduced to South Asia, rather than the glories of individualism, market economics, secularised governance, liberty and equality of opportunity. These ideas, if not entirely alien, had little practical scope within South Asia's autocratic and religion-dominated structure of inequality. The clash of world views ended with the British prevailing and imposing their colonial project on a then-undivided India.

The transplant, however, was not perfect. The poor quality of India's water and sanitation-related public services, for instance, is a reflection of the systemic governance flaws that accompanied this imperfect transplant. And the contradiction in Nepal − until recently a Himalayan (and Hindu) kingdom − was much the same. Nepal's first interaction with the colonising enterprise that swept across South Asia was the Anglo-Nepali War (1814–16). Following Nepal's territorial ambitions being curtailed by Britain,[2] and the subsequent signing of the Sugauli Treaty, relations between the former adversaries improved, to such an extent that in 1850 Jang Bahadur Rana became the first South Asian head of state to officially visit Europe. On his return he brought with him a water pump, which, sadly, never functioned because of the lack of local technological capacity. Indeed, almost 40 more years were to elapse before the technology of piped water took root in Nepal, in the form of the Bir Dhara Works. The 22 November 1885 massacre, in which Prime Minister Ranodweep Singh was killed by his own cousins, marked the demise of the Jung faction of the Ranas and the rise of the Sumsher clan, who went on to rule Nepal until the middle of the twentieth century. And it was Bir Sumsher Rana, who had replaced Ranodweep Singh as prime minister, who took the momentous decision to construct a drinking water system in Kathmandu. This was an act of expiation for his sins, Bir Sumsher Rana having been accused of killing his own kin.

The man chosen for this novel double-act − expiation for a highly placed murderer and the introduction of modern technology into a medieval kingdom − was a Scottish engineer, Matthew Lochard Sinclair. Back in Scotland, at that time, men such as him were being engaged to design and construct the public works that would (and still do) bring copious quantities of safe water to meet the needs of the toiling masses in cities like Glasgow but, in Nepal, Sinclair's remit was somewhat different. The intention was that the Works, far from improving the lives of the lower orders, should serve the lavish palaces of the ruling elite. It was the Rana potentates, not the capitalist–worker nexus that was driving industrialisation in the West, that were the social carriers of this technology once it had made its way to South Asia, and the planning and implementation of all modern technologies in Nepal still bear the mark of that initial mode of importation.

The Bir Dhara Works provided private connections to the Rana palaces and to the homes of the ruling elite. The system also supplied water to Phohora Durbar (which means 'Fountain Palace') – a cinema hall and a venue for the performance of cultural programmes. A series of fountains was installed in its garden and, within the building itself, there was a crystal fountain that was scented with rose water. The Phohora Durbar was sold and demolished in 1960, and the site redeveloped as the American embassy's recreation centre.

In marked contrast to what happened in the cities of Europe, waterborne diseases, such as cholera typhoid and smallpox, remained widespread in Kathmandu right through to the middle of the twentieth century, resulting in a high mortality rate (indeed, in the wake of the 2010 earthquake in Haiti, Nepalese troops who were sent there to help with the relief efforts are believed to have been responsible for a cholera epidemic, the disease until that time having been absent from this Caribbean island).

The sources of water for the majority of the people in the Kathmandu Valley continued to be the traditional stone water spouts (*dhunge dhara*), springs (*mul*), ponds (*pokhari*), water holes (*kuwa*), streams and dug wells (*inar*). The poor health of the people was then made worse by bad sanitary conditions, the lack of education, inadequate nutrition and the absence of preventive health services, deficiencies that, in the increasingly industrialised West, were being consistently, vigorously and, by and large, successfully addressed. However, some standpipes were installed in selected places, with the aim of providing clean water to the public and thereby improving their health. These standpipes, along with all the other traditional sources of water, are still being used.

Supplementary new water systems were eventually installed, in response to the rising population of Kathmandu, and Rana Prime Ministers went on to build similar systems in towns like Dhankuta, Pokhara and Jajarkot. In 1928 the Tri Bhim Dhara system was constructed and the following year Pani Goswara – Nepal's first water bureaucracy – was established in order to administer drinking water services. A few years later, when a hydroelectric power plant was built at Sundarijal, the water from its tail race was tapped so as to supply the residents of Kathmandu. Eventually – from the 1950s onwards – foreign aid agencies began supporting the expansion of drinking water provision, with Sir Edmund Hillary's small aid programme installing drinking water supplies in most of the Sherpa villages below Mount Everest in the 1960s. These latter, which are still working, were probably Nepal's first rural water supply schemes.[3] 'Home-grown' water supply, both urban and rural, thus became the plaything of the donor community at a stage when it had only just got going. Its subsequent trajectory, therefore, was remarkably different from that which was followed in those Western nations where the technology itself had originated. Drinking water and sanitation, in those countries, were seen as essential for the health and well-being of the workers in the cities that had been created by the Industrial Revolution, and also as essential for maintaining the productivity of those workers, and their provision was a largely local undertaking that was suffused with civic pride and social commitment, together with a healthy dose of 'the class struggle'. Nothing like that has happened in Nepal.

In the early 1970s, the World Bank became the main actor in the management of Kathmandu's water supply and, over the following two decades, some 756 million rupees were pumped in. These loans were aimed at improving the drinking water and wastewater services in the city and in a few towns outside Kathmandu (we say 'aimed at' because these improvements have not always materialised; for instance, the scandal-ridden waste water treatment facility at Sundarighat, just opposite the country's first and premier Tribhuban University, has never treated a single drop of wastewater). They were followed by three additional loan packages.

The government, for its part, established the Water Supply and Sanitation Board in 1974, and in 1989 this was reconstituted as the more market-sounding Nepal Water Supply Corporation. It was during the mid-1980s – the heyday of the undemocratic Panchayat system (see Chapter 4) – that the Melamchi project (a massive trans-basin water transfer to Kathmandu Valley via a 30-kilometre tunnel) was selected as the viable solution to what was seen, by those within this hierarchical and hegemonic nexus, to be Kathmandu's looming water crisis.[4]

The same period saw the entry of other foreign aid agencies into the rural water supply sector, with a multitude of donors providing technical and financial support. But, like everywhere else in what was labelled 'the developing world', the provision of drinking water and sanitation was considered to be an engineering- and construction-led undertaking. While the mid-1970s saw what seemed to be a shift of focus to communities within organisations such as UNICEF and Helvetas, the programme continued to be 'construction oriented, and the beneficiaries had a limited role' (Luitel and K. C. 2000). Needless to say, and in marked contrast to what has happening with biogas (see Chapter 9), sanitation was accorded little attention. Only much later did concepts such as 'total sanitation', 'community- (or school-)based total sanitation' emerge and begin to attract attention.

Thus we see Nepal being carved up into patches, with agencies such as Helvetas and UNICEF supporting the development of water supply and (to a more limited extent) sanitation projects in the rural areas, while the World Bank focused on the capital Kathmandu and a few urban centres outside. Subsequently, in the rural sector, the two leading agencies began to involve the beneficiaries in the processes of drinking water project identification, design and implementation (including operation and maintenance) with the objective of building systems that performed better. It was in the context of this institutional transition that the United Nations declared that the decade 1980–90 would be the International Drinking Water and Sanitation Decade. The Nepalese government similarly set lofty goals for reducing the drudgery involved in collecting water, for improving health and for extending the services to almost 70 per cent of the population by the end of the decade. In 1980 – the start of the decade – about 10 per cent had access to piped drinking water.

At the beginning of the decade, the Department of Water Supply and Sewerage and the Local Development Department were the planning and executing agencies for the delivery of drinking water and sanitation services. Bureaucratic and top-down, these two agencies did not yield the expected outcomes. By mid-decade it had become clear that, without major institutional changes, even the halfway points to the goals that had been set would not be reached. This embarrassing realisation helped open the way for other donors to enter the sector and begin providing support for the government. Thus it was that, in the late 1980s, Water Aid (and subsequently other organisations) began working in Nepal. Indeed, by 1995 (five years after all those goals had been missed) there were 25 different organisations working in Nepal's water supply and sanitation sector. It was out of this manifest failure of the top-down, bureaucratic and expert-led orthodoxy, and the subsequent influx of more heterodox, less orderly and less patch-respecting (and therefore somewhat competitive) outfits, that the Community Water Supply and Sanitation (CWSS) approach was born. And, a few years later, in 1989, the Nepalese government, bowing to the inevitable, institutionalised this approach by formulating its Directive on Community Participation.

After the century-long period in which the Ranas were the social carriers of the drinking water and sanitation technology, and the three or so decades in which the World Bank and its kindred organisations took over the baton, things were at last a little more like how they had been back in Europe during the Industrial Revolution. Just who the social carrier now is is much less obvious than it used to be; indeed, a whole range of social actors seems to have their hands on it.[5]

The question of coverage

If, as we have seen, people are already drinking water collected from some source or other, what does *developing* water supply imply? And, if these people are to be *provided* with drinking water, must they first be deprived of the water they already have? The resolution of these conundrums, Sharma (2001) suggests, lies in examining the 'changing configuration of ideas associated with water at the local level'. Such an examination, he goes on, 'brings to the fore how aid processes on water provisioning are as much about modernity as they are about lessening labour or ensuring convenience'. The sources of water that people already have access to, we can now see, are *traditional* sources: sources that need to be moved away from if we are to become *modern*. That, of course, has been the mantra throughout the Age of Aid. The only trouble is that modernity is now terribly old-fashioned; that is why we see students with T-shirts proclaiming 'I'm a Post–Post–Modernist'. And if that is how things now are then those who are intent on *developing* water and *providing* water must be pulling people back. To move things forward we need, therefore, to ask a different question: how can we best improve on the various sources and forms of access we already have? It is in the light of this somewhat disconcerting understanding that the challenges of increasing access, maintaining livelihoods and achieving social inclusion need to be viewed. Whose data, when it comes to the question of coverage, do we believe? And, beyond that, is it coverage that is being measured or is it movement away from the traditional?

Bringing disembodied data down to earth

Data on water supply and sanitation coverage in Nepal appear satisfactory only on paper. Sanitation coverage, the Human Development Report (UNDP 2006) told us, increased from 11 per cent in 1990 to 35 per cent in 2004. And drinking water supply coverage rose from 70 per cent in 1990 to 90 per cent in 2004. These figures, if they were true in the first place, would mean that the Millennium Development Goal to halve, by 2015, the proportion of people without sustainable access to safe drinking water, would have been easily achieved, and that the goal for sanitation could not fail to be reached if coverage continued at the pace mentioned: a rosy picture indeed. The reality in Nepal's rural areas, however, turned out very different, and the same holds for the urban areas.

Anyone walking the 70 kilometres from Laxmipur Village in Rautahat District to Matihani in Mahottari District, to take an example from the Tarai, will get a shocking picture of the state of water supply and sanitation coverage. There is barely a house with a toilet, donor agencies are absent, there is no government support for water supply provision and all the water points that exist in these districts are inundated during floods. Newspapers regularly carry reports of the poor condition of the water supply in towns like Butwal, Dharan, Pokhara, Dang, Silgadhi, Palpa and Birendranagar. And the capital city, Kathmandu, is at the very top of the inadequate service level list. Anyone who believes that Nepal is on course to meet the UN's sanitation goal should take a stroll down to the point (just a couple of kilometres south from the ring road) where the Bagmati River, or what remains of it as a sewer – earning it the sobriquet Dhalmati (*dhal* being sewer in Nepali) – enters the Chobhar gorge. At this picturesque spot the detritus in the sacred river has formed itself into a dam, on which cattle and egrets wander about, with the evil-smelling water somehow finding its way beneath it. And, in the shallows just upstream of this noisome dam, enterprising and bare-legged men and women wade around in the raw sewage laboriously filling sacks with gravel, which is then carted away to nearby construction sites.[6]

The Nepal government's water policy sets out five *indicators of service level* (SL in the following list and in Table 10.1).

SL1:   Fetching time less than or equal to 15 minutes.
SL2:   Quantity greater than or equal to 45 litres per capita per day.
SL3:   No contamination.
SL4:   Reliability of supply during all 12 months of the year.
SL5:   Continuity of supply greater than or equal to six hours every day.

Table 10.1 summarises water supply and sanitation coverage in 18 VDCs (village development committees) located across the Middle Hills: some in the Western region, some in the Mid-Western region and some in the Far-Western region. Collecting data in these often remote places is not easy, and it has not been possible to fully cover all five indicators of service level (which means that the true figure for coverage cannot be higher, and most likely will be considerably lower, than that obtained when using less than all five indicators). Overall, the sanitation coverage for these 18 VDCs is less than 14 per cent, and the water supply coverage (on just the first of the five indicators of service level) is less than 17 per cent.

These figures in Table 10.1 are not easily reconciled with those that were set out in the UNDP's 1990 Human Development Report: 90 per cent coverage for water supply, for instance (a figure that, as we have already seen, was immediately challenged in the pages of *Himal Khabar Patrika*). Indeed, the reconciliation is possible only if we are prepared to accept that national coverage went from under 17 per cent to 90 per cent in just a decade, or if we assume that coverage elsewhere in Nepal (across its Central and Eastern regions, that is) is considerably above 100 per cent. Similar reconciliation problems also arise with data sets that are from the same region and at more or less the same time:

•   Drinking water coverage in Nepal's Mid-Western and Far-Western regions, according to the 2003 National Census, is over 60 per cent. Sanitation, however, with only 25 per cent coverage, is far behind the census's estimation of the national average.
•   SACOSAN's 2006 *Nepal Country Paper* estimates the national average in the rural areas to be 21 per cent and, in the urban areas, 53 per cent.

'There are,' as Winston Churchill famously observed, 'lies, damned lies and statistics,' and that is most certainly true of Nepal. But, that said, some sets of statistics are less worthless than others. Those, like the data that are summarised in Table 10.1, that were gathered by people actually going to the villages and counting what was or was not there (and who, moreover, were honest about the data on some of the indicators of service level that they were not able to determine) are clearly more reliable than those, like UNDP's, that seem to have been simply picked out of thin air by some government bureau. It is

Table 10.1 Coverage of water supply and sanitation in some western, mid-western and far-western regions of Nepal

S.No	Date of study	VDC/district	Total population	Total HHs	Water and sanitation coverage				
					SL1	SL2	SL3	SL4	Toilets
1	Dec–03	Gajari/Doti	2293	351	4	272	73	2	16
2	Nov–02	Khirsain/Doti	3084	557	0	152	204	201	45
3	Nov–02	Chhatiwan/Doti	3532	552	0	188	291	73	47
4	Oct–01	Nirauli/Doti	3279	538	275	143	101	19	11
5	Dec–03	Kaphallekei/Doti	5087	865	303	231	130	201	14
6	Oct–01	Laxminagar/Doti	5046	850	176	400	189	85	51
7	Dec–03	Goganpani/Dailekh	3746	627	39	340	222	26	97
8	Oct–01	Duni/Achham	1970	402	41	213	89	59	16
9	Oct–01	Bhatkhola/Syangja	2938	490	129	306	55	0	191
10	Dec–03	Dipayal-Silgadhi/Doti	22166	4001	257	1396	1592	756	775
11	Dec–03	Ghanteshwar/Doti	2559	541	0	208	306	27	21
12	Oct–01	Sanagaon/Doti	2539	473	27	140	34	272	13
13	Dec–98	Bajung/Parbat	4955	973	613	156	204	0	244
14	Nov–02	Pelakot/Syangja	7299	1140	0	35	44	1061	N/A
15	3–Nov	Chinnebas/Syanja	7539	1081	0	284	653	144	141
16	4–Sep	Gajarkot/Tanahun	7547	1252	371	260	441	180	397
17	1–Oct	Deurali/Kaski	4310	667	230	177	260	0	N/A
18	2–Sep	Rupakot/Kaski	5087	865	266	282	140	177	135
Total			94976	16225	2731	5183	5028	3283	2214

Source: Various Water Use Master Plans (WUMPs) produced by the Water Resource Management–Programme (WARM-P), HELVETAS.

interesting to note that the government of Nepal's report mentions that Nepal exceeded in 2013 the 2015 MDG targets, which were set respectively at 73 per cent and 53 per cent for basic water supply and sanitation facilities.[7] And, if you use these more reliable statistics, then the chances of the Millennium Development Goals having actually been met in Nepal are vanishingly small.

Aid and coverage

Drinking water and sanitation provision, like almost everything in Nepal (the major exceptions being tourism, Tibetan carpets and house construction), has been heavily aid-dependent. In order to assess the effectiveness of that aid, while steering well clear of all those disembodied statistics that, it is claimed, show that Nepal has met the Millennium Development Goals, we now present, for the rural areas, a cost analysis of drinking water supply and sanitation projects and, for urban areas, a multi-perspective look at the Melamchi Trans-Basin Water Transfer Project.

Water supply and sanitation in rural Nepal

Table 10.2 compares the cost-effectiveness of various water supply and sanitation programmes that have been implemented between 1996 and 2000.[8] These programmes are:

- The Fourth Rural Water Supply and Sanitation Project (FRWSS), funded by the Asian Development Bank.
- The Rural Water Supply and Sanitation Fund Development Board (RWSSFDB), funded by the World Bank.
- The Rural Water Supply and Sanitation Project, Phase 2 (RWSSP), supported by Finnish Aid.
- The Self-Reliant Drinking Water Support Programme (SRDWSP), supported by Helvetas (Swiss Aid).
- Nepal Water for Health (NEWAH), supported by Water Aid and DfID (Britain's Department for International Development).

This comparison reveals some remarkable differences between these aid-supported undertakings:

- The cost per capita is highest for FRWSS (the Asian Development Bank) and lowest for NEWAH (Water Aid and DFID), with the former being more than twice as costly as the latter, a startling 126 per cent more, to be precise. When broken down into hardware and software costs, the differences are 133 per cent and 115 per cent respectively.
- SRDWSP (Helvetas), RWSSFDB (World Bank) and RWSSP (Finnish Aid) have the second, third and fourth highest per capita costs, respectively: all very considerably more expensive than NEWAH (Water Aid and DfID).

Table 10.2 Cost analysis of drinking water supply and sanitation projects

Description	FRWSS (1996–2001)	RWSSFDB (1996–2001)	RWSSP (1996–99)	SRDWSP (1994–99)	NEWAH (1992–)
Study period	1996–99	1996–2000	1996–99	1994–99	1997–99
Types of scheme	GF	GF	GF/TW/RW	GF	GF/SP
Budgeted cost (in thousands)	1,821,720	1,445,000	267,040	107150	N/A
Targeted population	570,000	550,000	N/A	N/A	N/A
Estimated per capita cost	3,196	2,627	N/A	N/A	N/A
Total actual cost (in thousands)	422,606	417,655	259,340	91,069	217,325
Total beneficiaries	119,555	135,061	102,181	26,827	139,192
Number of schemes	291	275	113	86	135
Total taps	2,738	3,053	N/A	760	2,651
Total households	N/A	21,991	N/A	4,810	24,715
Population per scheme	411	491	904	312	1,031
Per capita cost	3,535	3,092	2,538	3,395	1,561
a) Hardware cost	2,309	1779	934	1581	990
b) Software cost	1,226	1,313	1,604	1,814	571
Cost per tap	154,348	136,801	N/A	119,828	81,978
Cost per household	NA	18,992	N.A	18,933	8,793
Cost per scheme	1,452,254	1,518,744	2,295,044	1,058,946	1,609,814

Note: all costs in Nepalese Rupees

Source: Sharma et al. (2004): Aid Under Stress.

- While NEWAH's cost breakdown – 63 per cent for hardware, 37 per cent for software – reveals a strong hardware bias, it has actually been a pioneer in the mainstreaming of gender and poverty concerns – software par excellence – with its expertise in carrying out gender- and poverty-sensitive surveys-cum-analyses being subsequently sought out by the Asian Development Bank (for its Fourth ADB-Project Preparation Technical Assistance on rural water supply and sanitation).

In the light of these dramatic differences, we can now make a glaringly obvious but seldom-voiced observation, which is that, if these aid providers (together with their water supply and sanitation projects) had been operating in a market system, most of them would have quickly gone bust (or found themselves taken over by NEWAH). But, despite all their pious affirmations of the importance of the market mechanism, these actors are *not* operating in a market system. Indeed, the logic of the essentially hierarchical system of which they are the component pieces works in the opposite direction: it is the economically inefficient ones that have prospered and it is the leanest and meanest that have gone to the wall. The losers in all of this, of course, are the villagers of Nepal, who end up with less than half of the water and sanitation coverage that they could have had.

NEWAH's major donors have been Water Aid and Britain's DfID, with the latter alone supporting its mid- and far-western rural water supply programme for almost eight years, starting in 1999. By that time, it was amply clear that NEWAH was far the cheapest in per capita terms, as well as being 'ahead of the curve' on the difficult business of mainstreaming gender and poverty. Yet, in March 2008, DfID terminated its support for NEWAH. This termination was not preceded by any proper consultation, nor was there any independent assessment of the eight or so years of support, an assessment that, among other things, could have gleaned much about all the learning that had taken place (especially about the software – surveys and analyses – for the mainstreaming of gender and poverty).

What we see here, and as we have seen with some of the other case studies (the Bhattedanda Milkway, in particular), is yet another instance of the chronic inconsistency that characterises the donor community: changing priorities, new modalities, changing personnel, new flavours of the month in development thinking (part of DfID's justification for dropping NEWAH was that, being a rather small player, it did not fit with what DfID was doing in Vietnam, a somewhat mindless bit of standardisation, given that Nepal is a raucous multi-party democracy and Vietnam a one-party communist state). This chronic inconsistency at the level of specific projects and programmes, moreover, is in marked contrast to DfID's admirable consistency (determined, one presumes, at UK ministerial level) in supporting Nepal through all the difficulties entailed in its transition to a liberal democratic political order, difficulties that were entirely absent in the country with which, at the project and programme level, it was being standardised, Vietnam being less than democratic on the Westminster model standard.

To understand this marked contrast – to understand how it was that the procedural rationality at the lower levels of the hierarchy ended up taking things in pretty much the opposite direction to what the higher levels were looking for – we need to look at what has been happening across Nepal's water and sanitation sector, and especially at what have been termed 'alternative arrangements'. In the early 1990s, the Rural Water Supply and Sanitation Fund Development Board (known as the 'Fund Board') was established in an effort to channel World Bank support to Nepal, while bypassing the government departments that had hitherto been the conduits. The justification for this switch was the growing realisation (starting in the mid-1980s, about halfway through the International Decade for Drinking Water Supply and Sanitation) that the reliance on 'hierarchical monism' – channelling everything through the governmental system – was one of the major reasons for the lack of success. The idea was to introduce more pluralistic pathways – alternative arrangements – with the government's role being scaled back to the ensuring (through facilitation) of a 'level playing field' and to the related tasks of monitoring and regulating.

DfID, for its part, formulated its interim Country Assessment Plan, with the aim of developing a strategy of close co-operation among donors, and this did indeed lead to improved coordination, increased synergy and a more optimised use of the resources that were being allocated in the sector. The challenge, however, lay in reconciling this overarching framework for harmonisation with the newly recognised need to provide institutional space for innovation and for the voicing of concerns about equity and social justice. Prior to DfID's interim Country Assessment Plan, small, innovative and close-to-local-communities outfits, such as NEWAH, had been constructively engaged in precisely the sort of alternative arrangements that the Fund Board had been set up to promote, but there was simply no place for them once the commitment to harmonisation had swung the pendulum all the way back to the hierarchical monism that had already been judged to be the main source of the disappointing results. DfID, in its harmonising zeal, had decided, perhaps inadvertently, that it is better to be an elegant failure than a clumsy success.

NEWAH, though squeezed out by a harmonisation exercise that could not distinguish a one-party state (Vietnam) from a precarious multi-party democracy (Nepal), continued to work in the water and sanitation sector where it engaged with government, in order to enhance its regulatory and adjudicatory roles (the hierarchical solidarity), with the private sector, in order to stimulate innovative ways of extending access to drinking water and sanitation (the individualist solidarity), and with civic movements, in order to strengthen their cautionary roles as 'social auditors' (the egalitarian solidarity).

So Nepal's water and sanitation sector displays an interesting, and inherently unstable, tension, with the Fund Board acknowledging the unsatisfactory nature of hierarchical monism and calling for a move towards alternative arrangements, with DfID (which had actually gone quite some distance in this alternative arrangements direction) scurrying back into the very elegance the Fund Board is so set on moving away from, and with NEWAH (with its explicit typology of voices that need to be heard and responded to) moving all the way to clumsiness. And, slap bang in the middle of all this inherently unstable tension, is the massive Melamchi Trans-Basin Transfer Project.

The debate over Melamchi

Seemingly immune to all the controversy it has aroused, this proposed $500 million project to 'quench the thirst' of the residents of Kathmandu continues on its TINA ('There Is No Alternative') way. The technical problems, as predicted by many of the project's critics, are considerable. For instance, the unaccounted-for water is high: 40 per cent overall, though in some sections of the system it reaches 70 per cent. Bad though this is, the leakage of money is worse.

The selection (out of a list of just one) of Severn Trent – a UK-based company – as the management contractor came just as OFWAT (the UK regulator for the now-privatised water sector) published its damning report on its accounting irregularities. Severn Trent was subsequently found guilty of financial fraud and of having overcharged three and a half million of its European customers tens of millions of pounds.

In Nepal, the public water authority – the Nepal Water Supply Corporation – has seen 10 changes to its senior management in as many years of its existence, and the entire undertaking is awash with corruption and with accusations of corruption. The most serious corruption charges, so far, have been in connection with the re-awarding of the contracts for building the access roads for the new source site and for the drilling of the tunnels. The original construction company (a joint venture between a local and an international contractor), having grossly inflated the costs, was not able to get the payment authorised and therefore withdrew, citing losses. The contract was subsequently re-awarded and, sometime later (following the royal takeover on 1 February 2005), a Royal Commission for Corruption Control was established. This commission convicted the then prime minister, Sher Bahadur Deuba, and his minister of works, Prakash Man Singh, of corruption in connection with the re-awarding. Each received a two-year jail sentence and was fined 90 million rupees ($125,000). The Supreme Court in February 2006 revoked their sentences. A secretary of government responsible for Melamchi, Dinesh Pyakurel, committed suicide – it is widely suspected due to fear of being arrested by the Royal Commission.

An internal investigation by the Asian Development Bank (in May 2008) found no evidence of corruption, but by that time both the Swedish and Norwegian donors had pulled out of the project, considerably increasing the funding gap (the Norwegian government alone withdrew the $28 million it had promised). This forced the Asian Development Bank to review its own commitment, with its Resident Representative explaining that 'It is part of our guidelines that if there is a funding gap of this magnitude we have to go back and review the project to see whether it can be implemented or not as effectively as we had intended'. The Asian Development Bank then formed an independent review commission – comprised of expatriate consultants and local experts – to 'study the recent developments and hindrances in the mega-project and find out ways to carry out the work in a better manner'. The commission started its work in October 2005.

Events since then suggest that it has not been too successful in its efforts to find out these ways to 'carry out the work in a better manner', primarily because donors continue to be blind to the 'toad's eye view' of what Kathmandites want and what they are doing anyway, with tankers, bottled water, rooftop water harvesting and a host of other things. Those stuck with only the 'eagle's eye view' persistently fail to see and refuse to allow their institutional arrangements to filter in 'uncomfortable knowledge' (Rayner 2012) that could be saying that the problem is not what it is made out to be but something else.[9] What is more telling is the failure of agencies and departments, both national and international, to design projects along the much-touted 'integrated' manner to follow a nexus approach, which the civic movements were championing. NGO Forum, a loose network of activists, academics and citizen-based organisations took up a campaign around this time under the slogan 'Bigger Melamchi! Multipurpose Melamchi!', which was very unlike what one expects of NGOs critiquing projects.[10]

Their argument was that, if you are going to sacrifice a river to supply water, irrigation or electricity, sacrifice it well so as to get the maximum benefit in different sectors. They proposed making Melamchi not just a water supply project for Kathmandu Valley but, by making the tunnel slightly wider and bringing in a few more snow-fed upstream tributaries, it would also generate about 250MW of electricity, which in turn would power, among other things, sewerage treatments plants that would clean the wastewater and allow 80 per cent of it to flow clean into the Bagmati. This clean Bagmati, in turn, would also help irrigate tens of thousands of hectares of land in the Terai after the Bagmati reached the Indo-Gangatic plants. In this manner, Kathmandu would get cheap drinking water and a clean river, the country would get direly needed electricity (which would also pay for the cost of the tunnel) and the Terai would get irrigation. The Nepalese water supply bureaucracy did not appreciate other sectors muscling into its project, and the donors were not interested in spending any political capital towards promoting a nexus approach (Gyawali 2015b).

Meanwhile, a month after the ADB review commission, political upheaval overtook Nepal which ended with the sidelining of the monarchy and the coming to power of the Maoists. Hisila Yami, wife of the Maoist leader Baburam Bhattarai (who subsequently became prime minister but went on to split off from his comrades and even renounce Marxism), became the minister responsible for water supply in April 2007. One of her first acts was to set up the so-called Kathmandu Upatyaka Khanepani Limited (KUKL – Kathmandu Valley Drinking Water Company) under a public–private partnership model which the ADB had been pushing for.[11] It is responsible for the distribution of water that it will eventually buy from the Melamchi scheme when it is completed. She also cancelled the management contract of Severn Trent International, which previous governments had hired under ADB pressure, defending it by saying that it would not do to place the management of the capital city's water supply under foreign hands. Most instructive is the WikiLeaks cable on this episode reproduced below.[12]

> On May 8, the new Maoist Minister for Physical Planning and Construction, Hisila Yami, refused to award the water utility operator management contract to UK's Severn Trent Water International (STWI) as recommended by the ADB. Yami cited concerns about STWI's record and complained that the contract had been sole sourced. (Note: A few of STWI's misdeeds include: the company was found guilty of overcharging British consumers; the company was expelled from Guyana before completing its contract, and the company's contract in Trinidad and Tobago was terminated due to local public protests. End Note.) In his June 6 meeting with the Ambassador, Paul Heytens, the new Nepal ADB Director, acknowledged that STWI did not have a perfect record, but defended ADB's decision, explaining that STWI had been selected through a rigorous international competition. Heytens told the Ambassador that claims that the contract had been sole sourced were incorrect. Four bidders, who were all international companies, were pre-qualified and short listed. However, Heytens explained, due to the political instability and related economic risk, the other three bidders had pulled out of the competition. Moreover, Heytens commented, the negotiations between the government and STWI had been difficult and protracted. STWI had extended the validity of its proposal nine times, with the last extension expiring on May 15.

Reform and counter-reforms

These battles are part of the 'reforms' that the water supply sector was to have undergone a long time ago, indeed starting as far back as 1987 as per the Pokhrel Commission recommendations mentioned below (endnote 4) at a time when the Melamchi project was to be the next water supply project of the World Bank.[13] The latest twenty-first-century incarnation included the restructuring of the NWSC by breaking up its functions into three new entities: the Kathmandu Valley Water Supply Management Board (KVWSMB), an authority responsible for policy setting and asset owning; KUKL, the water utility operator responsible for the operation and management of the water supply and wastewater systems; and the Water Supply Tariff Fixation Commission (WSTFC), a board supposed to regulate and protect consumer interests by approving the tariff to be applied. Although it seems to have placated the ADB's insistence on privatisation as the main driver of development, it is far from clear whether that really is the case or if the water supply hydrocracy still retains all the control with little scope for market forces to work.[14] It is also not clear when the Melamchi project, 30 years past its inception, will be completed.

The TINA refrain – long chorused by the proponents of Melamchi – has its origin in 1980s Britain, in the Conservative government that was headed by Mrs Thatcher. It was her frequent recourse to the 'There Is No Alternative' justification that led to her government being characterised as 'elective dictatorship' (or, in the words of Peregrine Worsthorne, editor of the right-wing *Daily Telegraph*, 'bourgeois triumphalism'). In fact, there always *were* alternatives – it was just that she was not prepared to countenance them – and exactly the same is true of Melamchi. Indeed, there are (and always have been) alternatives to Melamchi itself, and there are (and always have been) alternatives to the particular form of Melamchi that has been steamrollered through.

Whether these drinking water and sanitation projects are environmentally harmful or not is of little immediate concern to the villagers and townspeople. What matters to them is whether there is water flowing from their taps, whether sanitation facilities exist, whether these systems will continue to function during disaster events such as floods and after an earthquake and whether they and their children no longer get sick from consuming bad-quality drinking water. However, drinking water and sanitation projects are usually ecologically sound. The exceptions are those instances where fossil fuel-powered pumps are installed so as to pump water from sources that are below the settlements themselves. Also ecologically harmful are all those urban sanitation projects in which human waste is flushed away through sewers that then discharge into the nearest watercourse, without the intervention of any treatment facility. Indeed, since such projects are more harmful to the environment than the dry/earth-based latrines that they replace, they represent a rather spectacular move in the wrong direction. Worse still, they are locking Nepal into outmoded Western technologies instead of enabling the country to leapfrog over them.

Notes

1 This needs to be qualified with that difficult to interpret word 'modern'. Kathmandu Valley has seen some of the most intricate urban stone water spouts (*dhunge dhara*), some of them operating since they were built by the Lichhavi rulers some 1,500 years ago. The first 'modern' piped water system was introduced in a very limited way to his own palaces with a public standpost or two thrown in for the public along the route of the pipe by Rana ruler Bir Sumshere in 1891.

2 Nepal avoided being incorporated into British India, but she had to acknowledge Britain's superior power in a subsequent settlement.

3 These villages tend to be sited in places that are not exposed to natural hazards – avalanches, GLOFs (Glacier Lake Outburst Floods), rockfalls and so on – and, in consequence, are often some considerable distance from the nearest springs. Hillary's team simply brought the water from these springs to the villages through 'alkathene' piping (which, along with its other virtues, does not burst in the frost).

4 Many of these pathologies are described in detail in an investigative commission report, known as the 'Pokhrel Commission' set up by the government and headed by a member of the then parliament.

5 For a description of what actors are at work in Kathmandu's urban water sector reform, see Chapagain (2013).

6 The dam is usually swept away during the monsoon, only to re-form once the monsoon has ended.
7 Government of Nepal, National Water Supply and Sanitation Sector Policy 2014.
8 For a more detailed account see Sharma *et al.* (2004). In the chapter 'Cost effectiveness of rural water programmes' Sharma presents an in-depth cost analysis of drinking water projects in Nepal.
9 Colopy (2012) describes how an unbridled hierarchism cannot see the problems on the ground, with locals and their economy dependent on the river, and comes only afterwards to provide 'mitigation measures'.
10 Southern NGOs, unlike most of their global northern counterparts, do not take up the slogan 'No Dams!': rather their slogan is 'No Bad Dams!' (See Gyawali 2003).
11 Technically, it is a 'public company' registered under the company act as the shareholders of the company, with relative initial shareholdings, are: the government of Nepal (30 per cent), municipalities in the valley (50 per cent), private-sector organisations (15 per cent) (which include the Federation of Nepalese Chamber of Commerce and Industry (FNCCI) (3 per cent), Lalitpur Chamber of Commerce (1.5 per cent), Nepal Chamber of Commerce (9 per cent), Bhaktapur Chambers of Commerce (1.5 per cent)) and an employee trust to be paid by the government (5 per cent). The Chambers of Commerce are registered as non-profit associations formed to further the interests of the commerce its members are engaged in.
12 Wikileaks cable of Monday, 11 June 2007, 1:10 pm (Cable: Ref: 07KATHMANDU1142) entitled 'Cablegate: Melamchi: Adb's $350 Million Dream in Jeopardy'. Available at https://wikileaks.org/plusd/cables/07KATHMANDU1142_a.html.
13 Melamchi was to be the World Bank's fourth water supply project and was meant to have started in 1986. However, the then government was unwilling to implement its major conditionality of massive tariff increase since the benefits promised in its previous three projects since 1974 (inter alia, 24-hour safe water supply in 12 major towns of Nepal, which was literally a 'pipe dream', with only a couple of hours of intermittent and polluted water supply a day, no functioning sewerage or treatment plants etc.). The Pokhrel Commission was set up to find out why. The World Bank spent the next four years trying to suppress the report and its criticism that Melamchi was not the solution to Kathmandu's water woes, which lay primarily in a massively leaking distribution and unaccountable management system. Ultimately it pulled out of the Melamchi project in the mid-1990s, at just about the time that the Maoist insurgency started, and ADB jumped in, picking it up in a classic demonstration of donor competition despite all the talk of 'donor harmonisation'.
14 The local Nepalese market is currently concentrated in the bottled water and tanker supply businesses quite lucratively, whereas the market forces represented in Melamchi are the international consultants and contractors. Indeed, Hanninen (2014) describes in graphic detail in her PhD dissertation on rural water supply policy how, in the dynamics between the donors and the Nepalese water bureaucracies in policy making, the donor is not all-powerful and the recipient is not all-powerless. They are both locked in a state of mutual dependency under permanent negotiation, where donor headquarter interests are directed at furthering their ongoing business and Nepalese hydrocrats are engaged in out-manoeuvring them, oftentimes quite successfully.

11 Community forestry

Thwarting desertification and facing second-generation problems

Hemant R. Ojha

'Nepal', a 1979 World Bank *Country Study Report* asserted, 'has lost half its forest cover within a thirty-year period'. And it went on to predict that 'by AD 2000 no accessible forests will remain' (World Bank 1979). That date came, and is now long-gone, but the forests are still there. Indeed, most of them – the accessible ones in particular – are in very much better shape than they were back in 1979. In 2004, a Himalayan scholar noted in an oft-cited book (Ives 2004: 44):

> Shrublands and grassland have been converted to more productive forest land while some of the least productive *bari* (gently sloping, rain-fed) terraces on steeper slopes have been abandoned and allowed to revert to shrubland and forest. Within the formerly degraded forests at lower elevations, qualitative improvements have occurred to the extent that the locally extirpated leopard and other animal species have returned, or increased in numbers. However, it is the areas closest to population centres [the most accessible, in other words] that have seen the most positive change. Here the efforts to foster community forestry have been most successful, partly the result of the long-term partnership between the local people, the Nepal–Australia Forestry Project, and the Nepalese Department of Forests.

Ives was referring to a community-based approach to forest conservation, with surrounding villagers as partners rather than a problem, whose subsequent nationwide success is now celebrated as a globally valid innovation in natural resource management. It encompasses significant improvements in legal and regulatory development as well as institutions of participation for the sustainable and equitable management of resources (Kumar 2002; Ojha *et al.* 2008; Ostrom 1990; Pokharel *et al.* 2008; Ojha *et al.* 2009). Clearly, this alternative possibility of a future development had not crossed the World Bank's collective mind.

By December 2015, nearly 18,000 community forest user groups (usually niched at one or multiple villages) had been registered nationally, along with legally defined rights to manage, in total, something over 1.6 million hectares of forest areas. This has brought about one-third of the country's population into community forest user group membership, with over 27 per cent of the nation's forest being under their management.[1] Over the past four decades of its rejuvenated life, community forestry has become much more than just a formal, aid-assisted programme of intervention. It nurtures democracy at the grass roots (Ojha and Pokharel 2005) and it has been able to sustain itself through the prolonged insurgency and political turbulence of the past 15 or so years (Rechlin *et al.* 2007; Karna *et al.* 2010). There is now ample evidence to confirm its success in enhancing the flow of forest products: fodder, fuelwood and constructional timber, most obviously, but also a host of 'non-timber forest products' (Gauli and Hauser 2009), ranging all the way from fungi, honey and medicinal ingredients to 'ecosystem services' such as enhanced biodiversity (Shrestha *et al.* 2010, Khadka and Schmidt-Vogt 2008), reduced erosion and safe drinking water, along with all the tourism-derived income that is safeguarded and enhanced by these improvements. Various studies show that community forests have also improved the livelihood opportunities for forest-dependent people (Pokharel and Nurse 2004; Subedi 2006; Chapagain and Banjade 2009), transformed both institutions and their associated 'social capital' (Bhattarai *et al.* 2009) and enriched the ecological conditions of the forests (Gautam *et al.* 2002). This achievement, resonating with the distinction between 'elegant' and 'clumsy solutions' set out in Chapter 1, cannot be attributed to a single factor. There are conducive forces from all spheres: from national politics, through local social systems to international development assistance, as is evident from the above-mentioned 'long-term partnership' between Nepal's Department of Forests, the local people and the Nepal–Australia Forestry Project. It is this sort of three-cornered, and often contentious and argumentative, engagement that has been responsible for the transformation.

With Nepal's community forestry now being publicised as a sustainable development success story, questions as to how exactly it happened, how it is currently evolving and who has contributed (and is contributing) and in what ways have become of interest to many, both within Nepal and in the wider world. The big question in all of this is: how, and to what extent, has foreign aid contributed to community forestry in Nepal? Since donors not only invest in carefully designed and targeted interventions but also in the production of success stories about those interventions (Mosse 2005), and since community forests present them with such a great opportunity for that it is important to decouple what is actually happening on this contested social field[2] from the claims that are being advanced in those donors' self-sponsored evaluations and analyses. Such a decoupling will demonstrate that aid has indeed made a substantial contribution to catalyse community forestry, while also making it clear that aid has served (unintentionally, for the most part) to sustain inequality and at times to distort locally grounded visions of change. But one should note that donor engagement is just one part of the community forestry development story – contributions from other actors have always been an essential part of community forestry evolution in politically turbulent Nepal.

In choosing to set off from the upsurge of concern – typified by the Nepal–Australia Forestry or other similar projects and stimulated by the alarmist predictions (the World Bank's among them) that became rife in the 1970s – I have omitted from the story all the interventions and institutional reforms that, starting way back around the 1960s, were responsible for the serious degradation of Nepal's forests.[3] Nepalese society (as is explained in different chapters) has long been built on inequalities (Anon 2006) – of caste and gender, in particular, but also on those perpetuated by patron–client and donor–recipient relationships. In consequence, it is predisposed to all sorts of shortcomings in its avowed quest for democratic governance. Nepal's community forestry – both its policy and its practice – provides some valuable insights into the sort of institutional dynamics that may or may not lead to varying degrees of inclusive development.

There are plenty of academic analyses of community forestry policy and practice, but here I will primarily reflect on my own experiences over the past 20 years. I have played multiple roles in the field of community forestry: from being a community forester working with the government to acting as a critical policy analyst and lobbyist on the civil society side. In my early involvement with a Nepal–United Kingdom project in the Koshi Hills, I worked with local communities, helping them to organise as community forest user groups, drawing up forest management plans and offering technical and institutional advice. In 2000, I moved into the domain of independent research and policy activism, becoming a lead founder of a now well-established think tank in Nepal, ForestAction. This involved research and policy engagement across various aspects of community forestry: social learning (Ojha and Bhattarai 2003), adaptive management (Ojha *et al.* 2008), science and democratisation (Ojha *et al.* 2010) and advising community networks at the research–policy interface (Ojha 2009), much of which has been synthesised as critical action research (Ojha *et al.* 2015). On the one hand, I have been a 'knowledge broker' between the community movement and the policy networks; on the other, I have tried to link these practical developments with the wider theoretical debate as part of the critical action research programme (Ojha *et al.* 2016). From all this, one thing is now clear to me: the participatory debates, far from being equalised two-way exchanges between those in the communities and those who formulate and implement policy, have increasingly become a more complex field of contestation among the elites from all sides – bureaucracy, civil society organisations, donors and community associations. A 'battlefield', you might say, in the political centre of the field of community forestry (which is assumed to be knowledge-rich), with too limited 'conversation' with the periphery of less powerful actors in all corners of the field.

This imbalance is important because community forestry, contrary to the view from the centre, is very much more than a government programme. Rather, it is played out on the aforementioned contested social field, as is all too evident from the unhappy history of Nepal's forests and people throughout the first four or so decades since development aid began to arrive, the years during which expatriate experts were able to get away with the assertion 'the only way to get a forest to grow in Nepal is to put a barbed wire fence around it and post armed guards at 50 yard intervals'.[4] But the seemingly simple 'ground-level' practices of community forestry – forest harvesting, drawing up plans, holding village-level meetings etc. – are actually the result of the complex web of relationships among a wide range of actors who are located across different social 'layers'. In consequence, it is not possible to understand who controls and/or benefits from the local practices by focusing the analysis at just the local level. A wider world reaches into these communities and they, for their part, reach out into it. Nor is the knowledge that is so crucial in these local-level practices only local in its nature; much is formed by the often global and invariably dominant discussions of development and environmental conservation, and these are primarily nurtured and promoted by the donors and the donor-funded international institutions. In other words, experience of, and immersion in, everyday practices and politics are essential. With transactional processes going up and down, inside and outside, snapshot 'scholastic' studies will always be inadequate.[5]

The birth (or was it the rebirth) of community forestry[6]

Efforts to share power with the local people started in 1978, when Panchayat forest regulations were instituted.[7] The realisation within the government was that the 'barbed wire and armed guards' attitude was counter-productive and that the forest bureaucracy would be unable to protect the forest without engaging the local people. Resistance to the Panchayat system – or 'assertive monarchy', as termed in Chapter 4 – was mounting at that time and the hope was that these new regulations, by offering some economic and symbolic spaces at the village level, might also go some way towards thwarting that threat. At the same time, 'decentralisation' had become the flavour of the month within the donor community, and so this move towards village-level involvement also enabled the government to signal to its paymasters that it was doing the newly designated right thing. In 1989, 11 years later, the Nepalese government, assisted by several donors, formulated the Master Plan for the Forest Sector after a few years of homework and analysis. This plan stipulated strategies for the conservation and management of the country's forest resources, and it explicitly set out the participatory and decentralised measures that were seen as essential for development. Community forestry was identified as a priority programme area, so as to 'meet the basic needs' (the latest flavour of the month) of the local people on a 'sustainable' basis' (MFSC 1988: 111). This master plan, which had been 11 years in the making, actually turned the earlier 'barbed wire and armed guards' approach upside down, with the local people – previously demonised as 'ignorant and fecund peasants' – now at its very centre. From being the problem they had become the solution.

As luck would have it, by the time this master plan was finalised and formally adopted by the government, the people's movement had brought an end to the 30-year period of 'assertive monarchy', replacing it with multi-party democracy in a constitutional monarchy: 'Westminster-on-Bagmati', as it was dubbed. Subsequent governments were therefore able to adjust and adapt the ongoing practices of Panchayat forestry, thereby bringing forest policy into line with democratisation and involving the users of the forests even more directly in their management. Where the Panchayat regulations had transferred rights only to the local politicians, the Forest Act of 1993 (passed by the first elected parliament following the 1990 people's movement) provided local communities, for the first time, with legally guaranteed rights to forest management.[8]

This Forest Act, in consequence, was a landmark achievement. It recognised forest user groups as perpetually self-governing institutions with a 100 per cent claim to the benefits of the forests that have been handed over to them (see Box 11.1: Communities and Forests).

Unsurprisingly, there was an explosion of civil society activity across Nepal, with the resulting organisations playing a significant and proactive role in the movement towards community forestry. Bilateral projects and international organisations also found this to be a conducive environment and community forestry quickly became a key component within the overall rural development agenda.[9] Reflections on Nepal's community forestry soon became a truly international enterprise – through research, networking and collaborative activities – among a wide range of actors, beyond forestry, beyond Nepal and beyond disciplinary and institutional boundaries. And local communities, far from limiting themselves to the 'grateful recipient' role, have organised themselves into networks and federations (Ojha 2012). The nationwide Federation of Community Forest Users (FECOFUN), which was established in 1996 and now has in excess of 18,000 users group members, has become a key player in the forest policy debate.

Nepal's community forestry can be judged a development success on several important counts:

- More than half a century after the ill-judged nationalisation of Nepal's forests, local communities have now come back to exercise their rights and take over management responsibilities. With more than 18,000 community forest user groups (encompassing roughly one-third of the country's 26 million people) involved directly in looking after and utilising forests across the length and breadth of the nation, community forestry is now the largest domain of participatory governance (in terms of both natural capital and population) – far surpassing even the largest of the political parties (in terms of votes cast, that is, not party membership).
- These forests are now much more effectively and sustainably managed; indeed, they have largely reversed the serious degradation most of them suffered during the years (1950s–1980s) when the local communities were deprived of their rights. And community forestry, in bringing more than 1.6 million hectares into this sort of participatory governance, has made a massive contribution to the conservation of biodiversity. This has been

BOX 11.1 COMMUNITIES AND FORESTS

The Forest Act 1993 provides those Nepali citizens who depend on forests, and are willing to be members of a community forest user group, with the following:

- The right to get organised with perpetual succession.
- Entitlement to the growing forest stock.
- The right to all of the benefits resulting from the forest's sustainable yield.
- Inalienable citizen rights, even in the event of a particular community forest being withdrawn by the government because its user group's executive committee is failing to meet the standards for sustainable management.

A community forest user group comprises the people who use a particular forest (or forests). It can include everyone in a village, or just some of them, or even some from another village. The institution is inclusive, and in practice all the households in one or more villages become members. 'The term users group,' as King *et al.* (1990: 6) explain, 'is really descriptive of a category of people rather than a group.' A user group therefore comprises households with diverse interests in the forest, and interest-based sub-groups are often formed so as to ensure that those diverse interests are given due consideration in the decision-making process. Other modes of participation can include decision-making at the level of the hamlet (*Tole*), an elected executive committee, the development of a group constitution, annual assemblies, arrangements for the development of forest management plans and sometimes women-only groups.

The governance of a user group is defined by its *constitution* and by its *operational plan* for the management of the forest.

- The constitution is registered in the District Forest Office. While there are certain standards, guidelines and norms, each user group is free to define the social arrangements, rights and responsibilities in a way that respects local traditions, culture and practices (e.g. farming methods).
- Similarly with the operational plan, which specifies how the forest is to be managed and utilized and which then serves as an agreement between the user group and the Department of Forests.

To take care of the daily activities and to co-ordinate between the users, the group then elects some members to its committee, assigning responsibilities in accordance with its constitution. Committee members serve specified terms (ranging between one and three years) and, if needs arise, sub-committees can be formed to deal with specific issues.

Community forest user groups are therefore *commons-managing institutions* and have many of the characteristics of all those local institutions that perform the same sort of role elsewhere in the world: the *Waldgenossenschaften* of Swiss alpine villages, for instance (Price and Thompson 1997).

– DoF (2008), GoN/MFSC (1995) and GoN (1993)

confirmed by both anecdotal observation and quantitative studies. For instance, the extensive hillsides below the town of Dhulikhel (on the road from Kathmandu to Lhasa), which trekkers used to remark on as being almost uniformly red, because of the exposed earth, are now almost uniformly green. And a 2004 study reported that 74 per cent of the forest area managed by user groups was in 'good condition', with just 19 per cent being still in a 'degraded condition' (Kanel and Kandel 2004). Others have reported that community forests compare favourably to government forests (forests that have not been handed over to user groups) in terms of their positive change in condition (Nagendra *et al.* 2008).

• Institutional innovations, likewise, are profound and diverse. Community forestry has become institutionalised in the state legal system, along with the development of policy and regulatory frameworks (Pokharel *et al.* 2008). And this strong legal and regulatory framework is supported politically, having won the confidence of all the major political parties. At the same time, there are strong networks within civil society, with public intellectuals supporting and extending those networks from the local all the way up to the global level. Increasingly, there are attempts to link community forestry with the market, and a number of community-based forestry enterprises have emerged, some creating significant income and employment opportunity to the rural poor (Pandit *et al.* 2009; Subedi 2006). Over 100 forest products are exported to local, Indian and (in the case of products such as tea and handmade paper) global markets.

• Indeed, community forestry has evolved as a self-sustaining system, thanks to its involvement of diverse and often contending actors, who collectively exert pressure against inaction and also unreasonable deviations. There are, for instance, multiple actors who perform multiple functions: research, activism, knowledge brokering, advocacy, critical reflections and so on. Nepal's Community Forestry Programme, therefore, is not just a government programme offering some services to the people; rather, it is owned and actively sustained by a wide variety of players, only some of which can be labelled 'government'. ForestAction, for instance, which was founded in 2000 at a time when community forestry was expanding rapidly, was a response to the potentially unconstructive polarisation that was at that time building up between community rights activists and forest technocrats. In providing critically engaged and action-oriented research, ForestAction was able to mediate (through more than 20 policy-oriented projects over a span of 10 years) between these two divergent groupings. This critical action research, by unravelling the complex power dynamics in which they were caught up, thereby revealing innovative pathways towards more democratic and equitable governance, enabled these polarised actors to become responsive to one another, rather than just talking past one another (Ojha 2013).

- Community forestry, above and beyond all the formal and informal institutional arrangements and processes that are involved, is sustained by a dynamic balance of active community surveillance and strong discursive engagement. Unlike in the old days, when the forestry officer in charge could not see what was happening in the forests he was responsible for, a villager can clearly see who is doing what in his or her particular neck of the woods. Moreover, s/he can, if s/he feels it is untoward, do something about it. Surveillance is thus continuous, low-key, face to face and effective, the opposite of how it used to be. The other side of this coin, of course, is discursive engagement: symmetrical between similarly situated actors (for instance, villagers); more asymmetrical between differently situated actors (users group representatives and forestry officials, for instance, or engaged researchers giving presentations at World Bank seminars). On a personal note, I see my role within ForestAction as having shifted more towards the discursive framing of community forestry in the later years (before I discontinued active engagement in 2011). One important part of that has been the founding of the *Journal of Forests and Livelihoods* (www.forestaction. org). This has provided a forum where researchers, professionals and policymakers can share their findings and their critical reflections: something that, as they have discovered, is not possible in the more technically-framed journals of the forestry and community development sectors. Without the discursive opportunity of this type – engaging local experience with the semi-academic media, thereby countering the ever-present tendency towards a technocratic regime – community forestry might well have found itself knocked off course. There are several other research groups and expert service providers that have come into being after the advent of the climate change agenda in 2008, further contributing to the discursive politics around community forestry policy and practice.

What (and whose) exactly is the success?

With so many diverse actors, with so much criticism and discursive engagement and with so many levels – all the way from the local (the *Tole*) to the global (the World Bank and the United Nations Framework Convention on Climate Change) – all reaching up and reaching down into one another's affairs, it is clearly impossible to give a single and definitive answer to the question: to what (or to whom) can we attribute this success? Many actors and forces (often acting at what, on the simple view, would appear to be cross-purposes) have contributed, in different ways and at different times, to the dynamic and continuing evolution of community forestry. Small wonder, then, that different studies attribute success to a wide range of conditions, factors and actors. And all, in all probability, have played their part, at times and in places, in this complex, dynamic, contentious and still-evolving system.

- Some (for example, Guthman 1997) credit the projection by the media of the deforestation crisis (the Theory of Himalayan Environmental Degradation also mentioned in Chapter 1) and the subsequent mobilisation of international assistance: a case, one could say, of doing the right thing for the wrong reason. Certainly, it could well account for the launching of the Nepal–Australia project that did so much to set the community forestry ball rolling (but not for that project's dramatic volte-face when, instead of seeing the hill farmer as the problem, it chose to see him as the solution) (Gilmour and Fisher 1991).
- The fact that these forests (unlike their counterparts further west in India) were inaccessible for commercial exploitation was clearly conducive, especially when combined with the increasingly evident inability (especially in the hills and mountains) of the Department of Forests to manage them directly (Pokharel 1997).
- The breaking out of democracy in 1990 was (as already mentioned) a crucial factor, thanks, in particular, to its opening up of civil society 'spaces' (Ojha 2006).
- This expansion of the public sphere, however, was not in itself enough to place the user at the centre of community forestry. That was made possible by the willingness of the elected government at that time to legally empower local communities to manage the forests (Ojha 2006).
- The other side of this empowerment, as the Australian foresters Gilmour and Fisher (1991) have stressed, was the way in which the forest-based livelihood systems in rural Nepal (even under nationalisation) were already providing the incentives for local people to participate in, and themselves benefit from, forest management.
- Others (Fisher 1989; Chhetri and Pandey 1992) have gone on to explain this incentive structure in terms of the presence of deep 'social capital', as embodied in the traditional (i.e. pre-nationalisation) models of collective action across a number of common-pool goods, not just forests: pastures, for example, and even field labour (*ngalok*).
- More recently, and as is only to be expected with a complex and evolving system, other factors have emerged. These can be seen as now constituting a tradition of piloting and reflecting among all the Community Forestry Project's shareholders. Five-yearly national workshops, for instance, have been held since the 1980s (Pokharel *et al.* 2008). At the same time, there has been mounting research on (and a matching increase in scholarly interest in) community forestry: the *Journal of Forests and Livelihoods*, for instance.

Also, there has been a considerable breaking down of the sort of 'structural inequality' that has long underpinned power relationships (of caste, of patron–client transactions and so on) in Nepal. Within community forestry, this has been achieved by various political movements (including the Maoist insurgency and its eventual transition into a political party) and by the emergence of 'subaltern' groups – such as the Dalit Alliance for Natural Resources Nepal (DANAR)[10] and women-only forest user groups (Buchy and Rai 2008).

Gauging the relative importance of these factors would be a difficult, and quite likely pointless, undertaking. But it is probably fair to say that it was the piloting work of donor-led projects (such as the Nepal–Australia one) that provided the initial impetus, and that much of the subsequent momentum came from the opening up of the spaces for civil society in the wake of the 1990 restoration of democracy, an event that, as we have seen in Chapter 4, enjoyed considerable support from some of the providers of foreign aid.

What contributions have donors made?

Donors have contributed in a variety of ways. But, that said, it is important to remember that others too have contributed, and contributed more. Even in the Middle Hills – the zone where aid effort has been most concentrated – the donor contribution has been less than one-quarter of what the user groups themselves have invested (Pokharel *et al.* 2008).[11] Specific ways in which donors have contributed to community forestry development in Nepal include the following.

First, in the early 1980s, when the first of the community-based forest management schemes were being piloted, government officials were reluctant to transfer any rights to the local communities. It was the donor project staff, who found themselves working with both the local communities and the government officials, who, in a variety of formal and informal ways (though reports about their prodigious consumption of *chang* may have been a little exaggerated), were able to persuade these actors across to community-based models of forest governance (Gilmour and Fisher 1991; Gronow 1991). The contributions by Australian, British and Swiss forestry projects during the early stage were particularly noteworthy.

Subsequently, these crucial piloting experiences were promoted horizontally (in extending community forestry to other rural communities, that is) and vertically (into policy uptake at government and donor levels, that is). For instance, between 1991 and 1993, when I was working in the Nepal–UK Forestry Project in the Koshi Hills area, we piloted a range of institutional and forest management modalities at the community level. Government officials, project-based experts and local community leaders were all engaged in this process, and it was fundamental in changing the outlook of the professional foresters, both Nepalese and expatriate.[12]

The donors also created a range of incentives for forest bureaucrats to become involved in, and comfortable with, participatory and community-based forest management. Among these were scholarships for higher studies, short course awards, field allowances and equipment grants. These helped create a critical mass of government foresters intent on moving towards a community-oriented career. At the same time, they were able to act as 'change agents' among their more traditionally oriented colleagues. It is now believed that this critical mass, and its persuasiveness concerning the desirability of participatory involvement, has made it highly unlikely that the forest sector will ever 'regress to the old paradigm of forest management' (Kanel and Acharya 2008).

Furthermore, Nepalese professionals, through their involvement in donor-funded projects, have received training and practical experience in an enterprise that gives equal attention to the trees and the people, thereby reframing forestry as a social as well as a technical discipline/vocation. Indeed, there are technical foresters who, thanks to their work in Nepal, have now become social science professors at Western universities. So the donors, along with the Nepalese and Western pioneers that they funded, can take the credit for breaking open one of academia's notorious 'silos' and creating the new field of social forestry.

Forestry donors, in contrast to the aid industry norm, have committed themselves to the longer term. They have developed successful projects, rather than adopting the more typical 'quick in-and-out' in which most of the results and knowledge generated within a project are lost once it is abruptly terminated. That trees take a long time to grow is, no doubt, part of the reason for this – evidence of what has been achieved by a forestry project takes a while to emerge – but, whatever the reason, the results have been beneficial across a number of fronts. Hopping from one development 'flavour of the month' to another has been stopped before it can start, lessons have been given enough time to emerge and then been drawn on in subsequent projects; and all of this has enabled a 'cadre base' to build up, thereby maintaining the momentum that is needed for the sustained institutionalisation of community forestry.

Last, donors, thanks to their commitments to local participation and the longer term, have helped to create a culture of review and reflection – a rich discursive mix of sharing, arguing, communicating, criticising and responding – that hitherto had not been a feature of Nepal's forestry sector (or, indeed, of its foreign-aided development efforts in general).[13]

However, though much has been achieved by this novel form of donor engagement – a shift that could be characterised (in terms of this volume) as the 'clumsification of aid' – community forestry is not without its problems, many of which, as we will see, are largely the products of its success or the emergence of what is sometimes called 'second-generation problems'.

Continuing challenges – and pointers to the future

Nepal, after nearly 40 years of travelling down the community forest road, is faced with a host of challenges. Alongside all the optimism and claims of success, justified though they mostly are, there is growing evidence that community forestry is not an unalloyed good, either for livelihoods or for ecological systems (Malla 2000; Malla 2001; Acharya 2002; Acharya 2004; Thoms 2008). Community forestry, it is clear, has now run into a number of 'second-generation' and even 'third-generation' issues in forest governance. Scholars and practitioners are therefore grappling with these so as to develop an adequate understanding of them and thereby identify suitable interventions to cope with them.

As community forestry, after its successful piloting, was busy multiplying the number of registered user groups across the country, Nepal entered into a veritable slew of conflicts and political turmoil, the most troublesome and violent of which was triggered by the Maoists' declaration, in 1996, of its 'People's War'. At the heart of this declaration was the Maoists' contention that it was multi-party democracy, together with international development assistance, that was responsible for an intolerable level of social exclusion across the whole of Nepal. This social exclusion, they further argued, being systemic, historically engrained and rooted in the then-current political structure, justified their call for revolution. To what extent, then, does community forestry support or negate this call? Is it perpetuating intolerable social exclusion or is it getting rid of it?

There is certainly evidence to suggest that, as user groups have been largely captured by local elites, marginalised groups have too often lost their legitimate share (Paudel 1999; Ojha *et al.* 2002; Adhikari 2005; Iversen *et al.* 2006). And this has been despite all the rhetoric, by government and donors, about community forestry strategies being 'poor focused'. This loss of legitimate share is evident across a number of domains: the distribution of benefits in terms of forest products and income (Adhikari 2005), the exclusion and marginalisation of traditionally disadvantaged groups as a result of elite capture of benefits and of decision-making processes (Paudel 1999; Iversen *et al.* 2006), and inadequate transparency in the management of user groups' funds (Kanel and Kandel 2004; Chhetri 2006). Underlying all these critiques is the contention that it is equitable, rather than equal, distribution that is crucial. This is because the poorest households, having little or no land of their own from which they can obtain products and other benefits, are more dependent on the forest for their livelihoods (Shrestha and McManus 2008).[14]

In addition, community forests management has tended to be 'over-protectionist', with insufficient attention being paid to a more optimal (yet still sustainable) utilisation of forest products, from both subsistence and market perspectives (Pokharel and Nurse 2004). This is because the management models, operational plans and implementation processes that were initially adhered to were provided by the Department of Forests and, in consequence, focused more on forest protection than livelihood improvement (Dougill *et al.* 2001). Moreover, regulatory instruments gradually increasing in technical complexity have become more restrictive and increasingly contrary to the spirit of the Forest Act of 1993 (Paudel *et al.* 2009). While the addition of complexity in regulation may be desirable (Gilmour 2007), the modified guidelines and procedures have often undermined the legally defined rights of the user groups (Paudel and Ojha 2008).

Furthermore, despite its participatory rhetoric, community forestry has often been used as a mechanism for extending the technical and centralising ideologies of government and development actors. This has resulted in a creeping disempowerment of local actors, especially those who are already poor and marginalised (Nightingale 2005; Ojha *et al.* 2009; Devkota 2010). The policy process, despite the circulation of critical knowledge and the emergence of active civil society networks, has retained much of its technocratic character (Ojha *et al.* 2014). This technocratic emphasis then tends to hide the inherently political nature of both policymaking and local-level forest management, thereby restricting opportunities for deliberation and participation (Nightingale 2005; cf. Douglas 1997). For instance, only two out of 15 forest policy decisions during the period 1998–2004 actually involved any deliberation with concerned civil society groups (Ojha 2006). This technocratic bias, though it has been consistently challenged, especially by the community forestry movement in the Middle Hills, still persists. Indeed, the power difference between the forest users and the foresters (*hakim*) has often increased (Ojha *et al.* 2007). The government, in recent years, has sought to engage diverse actors in the policy process, through both task forces and working committees, but, while this does give the forest users an opportunity to voice their concerns, they are still not allowed to participate in the setting of agendas or the design of frameworks for consultation.

An alliance of officials, politicians and community leaders – known as the 'iron triangle' (Kanel and Kandel 2004) – has begun to subvert the expansion of community forestry into those forest areas that have commercial potential. Indeed, elite and bureaucratic interests readily converge in the appropriation of these valuable resources, thereby undermining democracy by converting what are intended to be common-pool goods into club goods. According to journalist Krishna Murari Bhandari (2011), it is an open secret that forest ministers recoup their 'election expenses' through forest officials who compete in offering bribes to secure transfers to resource-rich districts.

There are also doubts as to the contribution that, it has been claimed, community forestry has made to biodiversity. Yes, there has certainly been an impressive increase in 'greenery', and in sequestered carbon, but the long-term sustainability of the flow of benefits is another matter. Neither the protectionist nor the utilitarian (i.e. timber-oriented) approaches – both of which are present, to varying degrees, in the current management practices – can guarantee the improvement of biodiversity (Acharya 2004). Leopards, and other 'indicator species', such as pheasants and musk deer, may be on the up-and-up but the long-term viability of their supporting ecosystems is by no means assured. And, on top of all that, there is (or may be) climate change. Himalayan ecosystems may be in for a rough time whatever we do (or don't do) to keep them in place. In the face of that level of uncertainty, we will need to promote adaptability by pushing institutional arrangements even further in the sort of clumsifying direction that has been taken by community forestry.

Finally, the future of community forestry is shaped by a few important drivers unfolding in Nepal. As the country aims to move through federalising the structure of governance following the promulgation of the new constitution in September 2015, the community forestry system is likely to experience extra pressure from regional political elites who are keen on adding layers of regulation and government oversight to community forestry. Advocates of community rights are also likely to go defensive, as they are not so willing to explore options for linking community practice with wider local democratic governance (Ojha 2014). The agenda of climate change in the post-Paris scenario will also gain traction, on both adaptation and mitigation sides. On the adaptation side, aid projects are poised to lure forest groups into the adaptation business and away from the core forestry works. Reducing emissions from deforestation and forest degradation – a key mitigation initiative which is centrally about forestry – has already enticed community forestry players to lock forest carbon into global 'compliance markets', thereby undermining community rights (Sandbrook *et al.* 2010; Ojha 2013).

Conclusion

In this chapter, I have drawn on my 20 years of work to highlight the trajectory of Nepal's community forestry, showing how donors, government actors and civil societies have engaged in the game. The consequences of the programme, so invisible at the beginning, have proved wrong a well-conceived but alarmist World Bank analysis which predicted that Nepal would soon become a desert. Thousands of forest user groups, with rights secured in the landmark Forest Act of 1993, have now reversed the trend of forest degradation, alongside the proliferation of forestry civil society in the post-1990 period. Despite such success, the future of community forestry in the new federal democratic republic of Nepal hinges around several issues.

To start, 'structural inequality', clearly, still exists. Indeed, it may well be that community forestry has made no inroads into it; it may even, as the second and third generations kick in, be making it worse. But, for all its importance, community forestry is only one component in the livelihoods of the forest users. The forest is, as it were, an input to all the other components of their farming systems: their fields, their crops, their livestock, their trading, their migrant labour and so on. If structural inequality has been diminished in these non-forest livelihood components, then the current picture, when we stand back from it, may not be so bleak.

We also need to consider whether there has, in fact, *been* a revolution. Not the sort of sudden overthrow of the *status quo* that was envisaged by the Maoists, but the more gradual, but profoundly *transformative*, sort of process that gave rise to the Industrial Revolution, for instance, and, before that, to the Neolithic revolution. The rapid, massive and still continuing movement of Nepal's population from the countryside to the cities and towns in Nepal and outside, together with the massive inflow of remittances from villagers who have sought employment in the Gulf States – both of which were given a considerable boost (inadvertently, of course) by the Maoists – suggest that Nepal is indeed in the midst of such a revolution. Perhaps, having not had the Industrial Revolution, it has now stolen the lead by leapfrogging straight from the Neolithic to the post-industrial (or whatever it eventually ends up being called). Community forestry would play its part in such a revolution – by fostering democratic governance at the grass roots, for instance, and by enabling Nepal to receive substantial transfers of funds from the wider global community in recognition of all the carbon it is tucking away in its trees. However, it does not provide an adequate vantage point from which to ascertain whether the revolution is happening, as the community level is increasingly driven by powerful actors contesting with each other, and being located outside of the community but still claiming to serve the local people. The future lies in how the cross-scalar politics unfolds as the country moves through federal democratic reform after the 2015 constitution and the post-Paris Climate agreement.

Notes

1 Source: http://dof.gov.np/dof_community_forest_division/community_forestry_dof. Accessed 1 January 2016.
2 Such fields, following Pierre Bourdieu (1991, 1998) are arenas where social agents contest for diverse resources as they engage in practices and discourses. This is similar to the notion of 'contested terrains' coined in Chapter 1 of this volume.
3 Though these have been outlined in Chapter 1; see Malla (2001) and Ojha *et al.* (2014).
4 Two laws – The Forest Act 1961 and The Forest Protection Special Act 1967 – reflect this attitude. The latter even authorised local forest guards to shoot people who were using the forest illegally.
5 This criticism of the 'scholastic view' comes from Bourdieu (1991, 1998) and resonates with Karl Polanyi's insistence on seeing the economy as being structured within a political system (Polanyi 1944).
6 There has been much debate as to whether the system for managing the community forests is something entirely new or the revival of the traditional commons-managing institutions that were swept away by the nationalisation that followed on the overthrow of the Rana regime. There is, however, no need to go into this here.
7 The Panchayat system was headed directly by the king (see Chapter 4). It had three tiers, each with its elected body of Panchayat politicians: village, district and national. Real power, however, remained with the monarchy.
8 See Clause 25. Clause 27 stipulates that a community forest can be taken back if its users group causes significant adverse effects on the environment or does not comply with terms and conditions. But Clause 28 requires the local authority to reorganise the group and then hand the forest back.
9 For instance, a 1997 national-level workshop on community forestry and rural development was instrumental in persuading INGOs (international non-governmental organisations) of the potential of community forestry for Nepal's development.
10 See: http://danarnepal.org.np.
11 Of the estimated running cost of 119,100 rupees per year for a users group, 71 per cent is borne by the users themselves, 16 per cent by donors and 13 per cent by the

government. Users group contribution is primarily labour costs (76,500 rupees, or 64 per cent) plus a small proportion of cash (8,000 rupees, or 7 per cent) (Pokharel *et al.* 2008).

12 While pretty much all the young expatriate foresters who were working in Nepal were enthusiasts for community forestry, the same cannot be said for their more senior counterparts 'back home', some of whom eventually found themselves members of the teams dispatched to evaluate the bilateral projects. Indeed, many of them were horrified by what they found. But, by then, it was too late (Gilmour and Fisher 1991).

13 For instance, there are now regular five-yearly national workshops. The first (in Kathmandu in 1982) showcased early field experiments in community forestry; the second (in 1987) made important contributions to the new Forest Act 1993 and to the Forest Rules 1995.

14 In South Asia, rural poor are highly dependent on common property natural resources, as exemplified by a well-cited study by N. S. Jodha, who, based on the study of 80 villages in 21 districts in the dry regions of seven Indian states, showed that contributions of such natural resources to the rural poor is highly significant: higher than benefits from anti-poverty development programmes (Jodha 1986).

Part 3

Beyond the Age of Aid

12 Nepal's experience of foreign aid, and how it can kick the habit

Prakash Chandra Lohani

Foreign development aid, as the preceding chapters have made clear, is a controversial issue. In order to alleviate poverty on a global scale, strong arguments have been put forward, and are still being put forward, for increasing the level of development aid. It was (and is still being) argued that, if the Millennium Development Goals (and now, since 2015, the Sustainable Development Goals) are to be met, there will have to be a larger volume of aid, together with a change in its focus.[1] However, there are other voices that take a rather dim view of increased levels of development aid, pointing to its lacklustre performance in terms of both poverty alleviation and sustained economic growth over the past six decades (Easterly 2006b; Verweij and Gyawali 2007). Even in Nepal, a country that relies heavily on development aid for capital investment, foreign aid (both bilateral and multilateral) is being seen as a mixed blessing. To put this issue into proper focus from the perspective of a Nepalese citizen, I will proceed in four distinct steps. First, I will outline the relationship between aid and development as it has evolved over the past 60 years. Second, I will set out a 'multiple perspective model' with which to analyse the conditions for aid effectiveness. Third, I will use that model as a heuristic device in order to discover where we have succeeded and where we have failed in achieving the oft-stated goals of national development. Fourth, I will make some suggestions for Nepalese planners on a strategy for getting off the aid bandwagon in the years to come.

Step 1: 60 years of aid and development

Since the end of the Second World War, the economic development of what we still call the Third World (even though the Second – the Soviet Union and its satellites – has now disappeared) has been an important part of the international economic agenda, and aid has been seen as an instrument of great potential. Aid, it was reasoned, would supplement the resources necessary for a 'take-off' to sustained growth and economic prosperity. The theoretical underpinning for this early line of thinking was provided by the economists of the 1940s and 1950s (e.g. Rostow 1960). The focus, back then, was on industrialisation through import substitution, state intervention and the mobilisation of savings for increased investments. Since poor countries had low savings rates and were stuck in a low equilibrium trap, it was assumed that aid would be one of the instruments that would enable them to break out of this vicious circle. Aid programmes, in line with this thinking, started out from the optimistic assumption that there is a one-to-one correspondence between the aid dollar and the level of investments. Naturally, under this assumption, increasing investments through aid would boost the rate of growth of the national economy.

This assumption – that foreign aid would play a pivotal role in development and reconstruction – was based, in part, on the effectiveness of the Marshall Plan, which put the European economies back on their feet after the Second World War. We now know, from often bitter experience, that this assumption is not valid in a great many developing countries, countries that, unlike those that were resuscitated by the Marshall Plan, are weak in both institutional infrastructure and skilled human resources. We should also note that during the Cold War years (and as we have seen in Chapter 4) aid to the poorer countries also had a political dimension, one in which the productivity of investments was not necessarily the most important consideration.

The principal–agent framing

In foreign aid, at its simplest, there are two actors: the donor government and the recipient government. Both work together, in the framework of a principal–agent relationship, in the utilisation of aid money. In the donor country, we would have the citizens of that country as the principal and its government as the agent. Both then agree to a set of relationships to produce development in another country, in this case the aid-receiving country. It is in the nature of things that the accountability involved in this type of principal–agent relationship is weak; for the citizens of the donor country, how the aid money is used in some Third World country is unlikely to be an issue of great priority when compared with the pressing domestic problems of employment, health care, education, refugee crises and so on. Naturally enough, they are more interested in their own everyday bread-and-butter issues rather than in the poverty problems of a faraway country. Since it is an issue of lesser concern, there is always a reluctance to allocate budget to this sector, and this is amply reflected in the inability or unwillingness of many wealthy nations to allocate money in line with the international commitments they have signed up to. For example, the world's richest country, the United States, while being committed to allocate 0.07 per cent of its GDP to foreign aid, has never managed more than 0.03 per cent. The record of the European Union is not much better.

Once money has been allocated, the principals tend to lose interest in the way it is being spent. For all practical purposes, they delegate their authority to the agent – in this case, their government, previously a specialised agency but increasingly these days to their foreign ministries – to spend the money in the way it sees fit. This carte blanche delegation of authority by the citizens is seldom objected to by their governments, which then go ahead and exercise it the way they think best. This partly explains why aid money that is supposed to help the poor in developing countries is so easily diverted to buy guns, bombs and mines, or to support projects that ensure that the lion's share of the aid money goes straight back to the donor country: in the purchase of equipment (at a much higher price than that prevailing on the global market), for instance, or by supplying advisors and consultants for each and every aspect of the development process.

The second component in this principal–agent framework is the recipient country. Here, also, if we take the people as defining the principal then the government emerges as the agent and the expected output of this relationship is development. Since foreign aid in many recipient countries is an important component of their development budgets, one would expect both the principal and the agent to be quite serious about the expected outcome, since basic bread-and-butter issues are almost certainly at stake. Yet this is often not the case; the principal–agent relationship is often weak and so too, in consequence, is its impact on the hoped-for output. Indeed, numerous econometric studies have shown that the relationship between aid and development is so weak as to be statistically insignificant, a conclusion that is certainly true for Nepal (Poudyal and Uprety 2006: 55). In fact, the West's aid to 'the Rest' has had very little impact in terms of poverty reduction. For example, $568 billion has been spent on Africa but, in terms of impact, most African countries are as poor today as they were 40-odd years ago (Easterly 2006b). On the other hand, and as will be shown later, there *are* instances where aid money has produced impressive results. The trick, of course, would be to determine just what it is that lies behind these many failures and few successes and to then concentrate all the effort on the latter, and that, you could say, is the trick that this book is trying to pull (by means of its elegance/clumsiness distinction, for instance, and the promotion of its 'new development paradigm' (see Figure 1.1); here the aim is to add the principal–agent framework to that 'policy toolkit').

The principal–agent framing, by itself, is too simple because for it to actually function there has to be a third element between them, a supervisory body created to carry out specific tasks on behalf of the principal–agent, and here that means bureaucracy (and that can include some of the BONGOs, GONGOs, DONGOs and PONGOs that we encountered in Chapter 1, or even a combination of them all). The relationship between the supervisor, the principal and the agent is both complex and fascinating.[2] It is possible that the agent is duped by the supervisor, because the latter may have control over crucial information – the informational asymmetry problem – which can readily lead to bureaucratic corruption. But in a developing country like Nepal, where transparency and accountability to the principal (the people, the electorate) remain weak, it is entirely possible for the agent and the supervisor to collude, so as to extract maximum 'rent' while together providing incomplete information, thereby manipulating the principal: the citizens (who, in any case, are not sufficiently alert to notice the discrepancies and contradictions).

On top of all of this, a weak incentive scheme – both in terms of rewards and punishments, itself a consequence of the weakness of the principal–agent relationship – reduces the transaction costs of corruption to both the supervisors and the agents. We do not have to go very far. Hardly any senior-level politicians in Nepal have been indicted and sent to jail on charges of corruption, even though there is a widespread perception that top-level corruption is the rule rather than the exception. Thus an 'iron triangle' between the bureaucracy, the politicians and a limited business elite has made a complete mockery of the utility and productivity of aid. The latest to join this iron triangle have been the NGOs, largely thanks to many of the donors electing to work more through them than directly through the government. However, we need to be careful here, since there are many NGOs (those that, it is argued in Chapter 1, are genuinely 'of the grass roots') that are performing their supervisory roles in a commendable manner. It is the ever-proliferating BONGOs, GONGOs, DONGOs and PONGOs that are eager to climb on board the foreign aid gravy train, with no concern for the principal: the people. Nor, it should also be noted, have political parties that routinely profess their commitment to the people been averse to riding this gravy train (hence the PONGOs).

The above iron triangle/gravy train exposition is not, however, the full foreign aid story. There are, as I have already mentioned, two sets of principals and agents – one in the donor country, the other in the recipient country – and we need to take account of that totality. The agents in the donor and recipient countries are their respective governments; what can we say about their objectives? Formally, each agent's objective is to serve the interests of its principal. What is crucial here is the ability of the recipient country to articulate its priorities and to then ask the agent of the donor country to organise its aid programme accordingly. When this ability is missing there is the possibility of the supervisory-level actors becoming involved in maximising their own respective interests, leading to various forms of rent extraction, to the inefficient use of aid money and to the implementation of development programmes that are neither sustainable nor replicable. In order to understand why this crucial ability sometimes emerges and sometimes does not we need to look at the differences among the recipient countries.

Aid-receiving categories

We can distinguish country types in terms of whether they have high or low per capita aid and whether they experience high or low (or zero) economic growth (Figure 12.1).

- Nepal started off at A (high aid/low or zero growth) and has been stuck there for decades. It therefore has no trajectory.
- India started off at D (low aid/low or zero growth) and then remained there until the early 1980s. Since then its economic circumstances have changed (though that may not have had much to do with aid), taking it

on a trajectory to C (it still receives some aid, from the UK, despite being a nuclear power and having its own space programme, causing some outrage among those British citizens who are aware of this).[3]

• South Korea started off, like Nepal, at A but then, unlike Nepal, began to move, following a curving trajectory to B and ending all its bilateral aid linkages by the early 1970s.

The nature of the various trajectories (and, in the extreme case, the absence of any trajectory), this figure suggests, must derive from differing interaction dynamics between principal, agent and supervisors (at various levels) as we go from South Korea to India to Nepal. This, in consequence, is where the main problem lies, and its resolution, in the disappointingly static case of Nepal, will have to be sought by the Nepalis themselves. Unless this is done, aid in Nepal will continue to be a vehicle for agency collusion as well as for friction between donors and recipients. Aid ineffectiveness, and the use of aid to avoid making decisions in favour of the principals (i.e. the people), will continue to be the two sides of this dynamic, but going nowhere, coin.

This was the situation in the Panchayat era (1960–90), when assertive monarchy prevailed, and sadly it did not change even after the restoration of democracy. At the same time, the disconnection between agent and principal

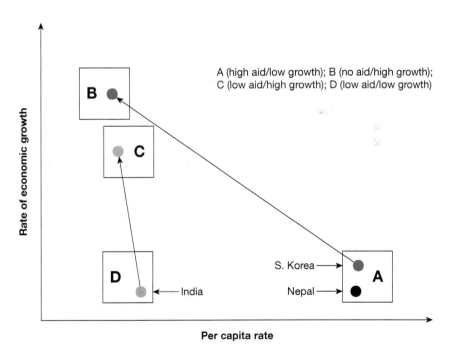

Figure 12.1 National permutations and trajectories

has taken a heavy toll on transparency and accountability. Thus Nepal is now still stuck in a relatively high per capita aid/low growth mode, because the whole host of issues related with the agency problem – the unconstructive dynamics of principal, agent and supervisor – has yet to find a resolution. In the meantime, the country has gone from aid-dependence to aid-addiction, a condition that is both humiliating and distressing. Even in the drafting of an act to be presented to the Nepalese parliament, the tendency now is to give the responsibility to foreigners and to rely on foreign aid for finance. Economic thinking in Nepal so far is simply not willing to envisage the time when we will no longer have to stretch out our hands for bilateral aid: Nepal, we may have to admit, has now become an aid junkie.

Step 2: the multiple perspective model

On the basis of the discussion so far, we can set about constructing what I will call a 'multiple perspective model' for assessing aid effectiveness in any given nation. Aid effectiveness, I will argue, can be viewed as a composite of four different perspectives: the resource augmentation perspective, the resource use perspective, the institutional perspective and the political perspective. Since the first two might be considered as lying within the terrain of economics, while the other two cannot, this model is not inconsistent with the argument (set out, in Chapter 1, in relation to the 'new development paradigm') that development is economic only in its consequences.

The resource augmentation perspective

Foreign aid, in this perspective, is a way of increasing the total resources available for investment. On the logical premise that growth is related to the level of investment, the quantum of foreign aid will increase the level of resources that is available internally and thereby provide a way of closing the savings and foreign exchange gap that might otherwise constrain the growth process. It was this perspective that was the accepted doctrine in the mid-twentieth century.

There are, from this perspective, four important factors to be analysed: the size of the development aid, the terms of the development aid, the nature of the development aid and the absorptive capacity of the recipient country. All four must be carefully considered before asking for aid. In the real world, however, a finance minister in most developing countries is considered successful if he can maximise the size of the aid commitments, without too much concern for either the terms or the nature of that aid (or the question of capacity utilisation). What normally happens is that these issues are handled, for the most part, by the donor countries (and especially by the international financial institutions, such as the World Bank and the International Monetary Fund). They provide the intellectual inputs to all four areas and the recipient countries, often gratefully and sometimes grudgingly, accept that framework.

The inevitable consequence is that the structure of aid reflects the thinking of the international institutions as to the 'correct' route to sustainable development.

Over the years, that development thinking has been changing, and this is reflected in the terms and nature of development aid itself. Until three decades ago, *project aid* was the established wisdom. Then it changed to *programme aid* (or program aid, if it came from the US) because it was felt that government policies needed to be influenced so as to encourage economic reform. Under this new thinking, aid, both for government budgetary support and for foreign exchange, would be available only if the government was willing to undertake the reforms that the international financial institutions considered necessary. 'Here is money available to you, even for budgetary support, so long as you are willing to change your policies in the direction we prescribe' was the message. The logic of *structural adjustment*, with all its terms and conditions, was simply the extension of this thinking, which was then given to the developing countries as their 'own', an indigenous solution to their development problems. In Nepal, we have meekly followed this fatalistic path, becoming ever more unwilling to visualise a time when we can do without aid. It is taken, almost for granted, that aid will be required indefinitely.

The resource use perspective

The successful utilisation of aid resources requires congruence on the objectives, as understood by both the donor and the recipient. Both agents – the donor institution/government and the recipient government – must have the same perception on the utilisation of foreign aid, with programmes tending towards ineffectuality whenever this congruence is lacking. Aid programmes, under congruence, can take shape around any of (at least) three objectives: survival and sustenance, the provision of a lead role in national development and the complementing of national development efforts.[4] For countries, like Nepal, that have been in conflict and/or civil strife for many years, the survival objective has to be uppermost, the reconstruction and rehabilitation of the infrastructure being crucial. The same holds for countries that have suffered major natural disasters or are threatened by widespread killer diseases.

When aid is seen as playing a lead role in development the problems are different. Here, the very meaning and content of development have to be agreed on by both sides, together with a shared willingness to adhere to the norms and values that may be required by that meaning and content. This is far from easy, and donor and recipient countries will often find themselves diverging in the way the problems are conceptualised, leading to coordination and harmonisation difficulties, with each of the recipient's donor countries increasingly following its own strategy. In such cases, aid money for the recipient country readily becomes a reason for avoiding hard decisions on both resource mobilisation and policy reform. Aid then becomes a vehicle for financing government consumption rather than productive investments. The ready availability of aid, along with multiple donor strategies on how that aid should be used, then leads gradually but inexorably to a sense of aid dependency, and even aid-addiction, eventually reaching the point where the tendency, even for minor policy reforms, is to look for donors. However, when aid is clearly visualised as a temporary complement to national development efforts, with the transfers coming to an end after a specified period of time, the chances are that resources will be used more carefully and with a sharper focus on outcome. The lesson, therefore, is that aid should strive all the time, and wherever possible, to work its way from the survival objective to the lead role objective and from there to the complement objective. All too often, of course, the striving (if you can call it that) is in the reverse direction.

The institutional perspective

Effective aid utilisation, for many poor countries, is becoming even more difficult than its availability. There is a persistent complaint in Nepal that aid disbursement is poor and that the country cannot really spend the resources that are available to it. This raises three major issues: the delivery system and the state's role in it; the nation's absorptive capacity for aid; and how these essentials can be monitored and controlled.

The government is the major instrument of the state in the use of aid resources. If that government is weak, partisan or corrupt – and all too often, alas, it is all three – then resource management is going to suffer, and the state's ability to reach the needy will be significantly eroded. This is the state of affairs, discussed earlier, where there is a disconnection between the agent and the principal that is marked enough to give rise to collusion between the agent and the intermediary: the supervisor. Under this scenario, there is every likelihood that a significant portion of the aid money will fall under elite capture – 'suck up', you might say – with little trickling down to the poor. The aforementioned iron triangle – comprised of the bureaucracy, politicians and a segment of the business community that has found its way around the 'invisible hand' – then emerges to extract a maximum premium from aid investments at the cost of the downtrodden and poor. This iron triangle (as is evident in many of our case study chapters) will favour those projects where there is a high possibility of rent extraction (large-scale projects, for instance, especially those involving major construction undertakings and/or the extensive importation of high-value capital goods) while displaying a marked lack of enthusiasm for the sort of 'lightweight' projects (electric *tempos*, for instance and goods-only ropeways; see Chapters 5 and 6) that are designed to cater to the needs and aspirations of those in the poorer city districts, the countryside and the villages. Over time, this leads to the gradual destruction of the bureaucracy's ability to meet (or even to apprehend) the needs of the poor, while encouraging an 'island syndrome': an affluent minority in the midst of a population that is mired in poverty, frustration and disappointment. The delivery system of the state itself becomes an instrument for extracting rent in the name of development. Small wonder, some may say, that Nepal got its Maoist insurgency.

For some donors, the weakness of the state then becomes the justification for bypassing the government in order to reach their target groups, with or without the help of non-governmental organisations.[5] This is a trend that has been under way in Nepal now for several years: yet another manifestation of 'dharma gone wrong' (Figure 1.1 from Chapter 1). While this donor strategy may bring some short-term results, it does not do anything to help resolve any of the systemic (i.e. *dharma*-distorting) weaknesses of the recipient nation. Aid investment cannot have any lasting impact if the role of the state in the direction, implementation and monitoring of foreign-aided projects remains weak. And, without effective monitoring and control (and with an excess of aid and a multiplicity of donors), 'many hands make light work' soon gives way to 'too many cooks spoil the broth'.

The idea of putting the decision makers in the driver's seat of the national economy therefore makes little sense if those drivers become nothing more than a shield behind which the donors can then implement programmes and projects that they decide on their own. In fact, foreign aid is likely to be effective only when the recipient government feels confident enough to interact with the donors on the basis of well-defined priorities. It is never an easy process and it will require continuous dialogue between the two sides as to the appropriate means of delivery, with a focus all the time on the outcome, rather than just the outlay, of resources.

The political perspective

Foreign aid influences the political landscape of the recipient country in a number of ways. Changes in power – both in terms of its amount and its distribution – are the inevitable concomitants of what might appear to be merely technical interventions in the economy, and they can be explored on a number of fronts:

- The link between aid investments and their targeted beneficiaries.
- The participation of stakeholders in decisions: who is to count as a stakeholder and how and to what extent should they then participate?
- The shifting – both anticipated and unanticipated – of the overall balance of power.
- The accountability of the political system.

Aid investments have the potential to create new wealth and income. This means that the mechanisms that link these economic benefits of aid to its beneficiaries will have an impact on the distribution of power within the nation, upsetting many existing balances and creating new ones. For instance, will aid investments benefit primarily those in the rural areas? If yes, how will those benefits be distributed between different ethnic groups, between different income groups, between men and women, and so on? If aid investment is to be urban-focused, how will it affect social stability over time? Beyond these, there are more unsettling questions. For instance, does it make any sense to distinguish rural from urban when so much of Nepal's economic life (especially when it comes to the thriving, informal, grey and black economies) is now located in the sorts of 'rural–urban interlinkages' that, to give just one example (see Chapter 5), now connect the villagers on Bhattedanda to the megalopolis of Kathmandu, a settlement that has grown from around 200,000 inhabitants to almost two million in barely three decades?

Questions like these certainly have an economic dimension, but they have much more. They affect the power balances among and between the different groupings and communities that are spread across the country, groupings and communities, moreover, that are increasingly on the move: from the countryside to the capital, from remote hillsides to the Gulf, on and on. Aid, obviously, is having an influence – a political influence – but so too is all the vigorous and anarchic economic activity that is un-aided. How do these two spheres interact, and what are the political transformations that are set in train by that interaction? These questions, largely unanswerable though some of them are, deal only with what the aid is supposed to be doing. What about the aid leakages, in the form of the rents that are collected by those – the politicians, the bureaucrats and the business elite – that constitute the iron triangle? All of that will be having a significant impact on the overall character of the political system.

What we can say, however, is that, when the institutional accountability of foreign aid utilisation is weak, the probability of external resources being used to finance the consumption of the elite – the 'island syndrome' – or to finance only those projects that benefit that elite, will gain momentum. The result (assuming nothing else is going on, which of course it is) is an increasing bifurcation of Nepalese society, an ever-deepening and antagonistic divide in which the poor, quite understandably, resent the way in which aid resources have been appropriated in the creation of the 'new rich'. If feedback information of this nature is not tapped by the political system for timely correction, social instability and violence are bound to gain momentum. Ironically, it is foreign aid that has become one of the major causes of this phenomenon.

Step 3: Nepal's experience with foreign aid

Using the four perspectives outlined above, I can now move on to consider Nepal's experience with foreign aid in its efforts to achieve national development. Aid in Nepal, from the resource augmentation and resource use perspectives, is seen as a major instrument for closing the gap between savings and the targeted level of investment considered essential for achieving the projected rate of increase in output. In this process, the volume of development aid is such that it dominates the country's capital investment portfolio. This was the situation in the Panchayat era – 1960 to 1990 – when the king was the leader, and it still has not changed even 20-odd years after the restoration of multi-party democracy. As for the underlying philosophy of foreign aid composition, in terms of both policies and programmes, it has been primarily guided by the evolving intellectual inputs of the World Bank and the International Monetary Fund, the cornerstones of the Age of Aid that were put in place at Bretton Woods in 1945. So, over the years, we have travelled all the way from project financing to programme financing (including poverty alleviation), to the Washington Consensus and now to the 'post-Washington Consensus' in the form of second-generation reforms aimed at good governance, fiscal devolution, transparency, accountability and so on.

In this process we have been told that we 'own' this new strategy and, as good customers of aid, we have willingly accepted this, while happily ignoring the sociopolitical norms and values that may be part and parcel of such a form of ownership (only if we move on to the institutional and political perspectives can we rid ourselves of that 'happy ignorance'). In this setting, naturally enough, foreign aid in Nepal is not seen as a complement to national efforts towards the goal of standing on our own feet after a specified time period. Even now, after the Tenth Plan, we are not willing to envisage such a time frame: the not-far-distant moment when bilateral aid will no longer be needed. The general attitude is still to see aid as the easy way to prosperity, even though there is ample and mounting evidence to the contrary. Indeed, the psychology of aid-dependence has deteriorated into a form of aid-addiction, with the result that, even for simple studies and projects that can easily be undertaken in the country, the tendency is to look for a donor: a fix.

And, in the other direction, the donors – or perhaps we should call them aid-pushers – are often only too willing to oblige. This has now led to a proliferation of technical assistance: all the way from gender studies to the installation of information technology systems in the office of the prime minister. Technical assistance programmes, it seems, have their own special features that make them as attractive to the donors (the pushers) as they are to the recipient. They provide new job opportunities for international advisors (they being very much a part of the international aid bureaucracy) and also lucrative moonlighting opportunities for members of the national bureaucracy (either as individuals or in an organised manner, through the establishment of local partner companies). This, though general, has become most pronounced in the area of technical aid, because this is where the lion's share of the money goes to pay for expatriate consultants, with the local counterparts coming a distant second. In this setting, aid-addiction is the norm, and the sidestepping of governmental rules on aid spending is increasingly accepted as a part of the system. Indeed, many development programmes in Nepal are now launched by donors without the government knowing anything about them. The government, for its part, does not even have the courage to tell donors that it needs to be consulted before projects are undertaken.

The idea of having the national decision makers in the driver's seat on aid utilisation – which is what the notion of 'ownership' entails – can, as we have seen, create a host of problems if these drivers somehow manage to ignore the objectives of the passengers, the people. This, of course, is the problem that, as we have seen, arises when the principal–agent linkage is weak, but it is also a political problem, in that it seriously affects both the country's aid absorptive capacity and the private sector's investment atmosphere. In addition, it seriously undermines the government's aid-delivery system (including its ability to monitor projects) and pushes up the transaction costs for businesses in the private sector. This has been our experience in Nepal, and it has been partly responsible for the rise of the Maoist movement across the country. Rising expectations, increasing foreign aid and the decreasing ability of the government to reach the people and create an environment characterised by a favourable risk–return relationship have been a heady political combination conducive to instability and violence.

Step 4: the cold turkey future

Some, looking at the recent and continuing turmoil and confusion, have labelled Nepal a 'failed state'. This is not true; Nepal is a 'fragile state' that is striving to find a way through the fire and fury of Maoist rhetoric, on the one hand, and the democratic aspirations of the people on the other. The institutional arrangements for resource mobilisation, public delivery of services, inclusive politics, control of corruption and the ability to find compromise among competing claims and perceptions remain feeble even more than a decade after the end of the Maoist rebellion.

At the macro level, Nepal's economy is increasingly dependent on remittances (30 per cent of national income) sent by its young people working primarily in Malaysia and Gulf States. Over the past decade, remittances, along with an ever-increasing reliance on foreign aid, are taking the character of the 'Dutch disease'. The government has virtually given up on attempts to transform its subsistence agriculture-based economy. The implicit strategy of development, as opposed to the formal one that is outlined in periodic plans, consists of three distinct steps. First an increasing number of young people entering the labour force are encouraged to go abroad, particularly to Gulf States, as unskilled labourers. Second, there are few employment opportunities to absorb new entrants in the labour market because periodic plans have failed. With agricultural and infrastructural development having remained far below the planned level, a large pool of the young rural population has been forced to migrate to urban areas in search of employment. The special characteristics of this migration are that it is not confined to Nepal but extends to the urban areas in the Middle East and beyond. Third, remittances are used primarily for consumption; the government has not been able to channel it for capital investments.

Rajan and Subramanian (2005) have argued that there is very little evidence that decades of official transfers have contributed much to the growth of developing economies. Barajas *et al.* (2009) take that argument even further and show that 'private income transfers – remittances – have contributed little to economic growth in remittance-receiving economies and may have even retarded growth in some' primarily because they are not 'intended to serve as investments but rather as social insurance to help family members finance the purchase of life's necessities'. Remittances have temporarily relieved the government of the balance of payment problem, but they have also been instrumental in postponing important policy changes conducive to competition, meritocracy and performance-based metrics in public spending. The outward signs of prosperity and modernity based on remittance and foreign aid hide the hollowing-out of the manufacturing sector, a loss of competitive strength and the growth of corruption and cronyism. The fragile state is thus becoming increasingly unable to discharge even the minimum delivery functions that its citizens expect.

The two most recent indicators of state fragility are the government's performance after the devastating earthquake in April 2015 and the response to mass agitation and protests after the promulgation on 20 September 2015 of the new constitution. The massive earthquake (7.8 on the Richter scale) that hit Nepal claimed over 9,000 lives and an estimated seven billion dollars' worth of destruction of private property and public infrastructure.[6] Immediately after the earthquake, youth and civil society groups were active in the field with whatever relief materials they could procure. The resilience of the people in the face of adversity and the eagerness of youth organisations and civil society were heartening. They indicated an untapped reservoir of social capital that, under right circumstances, could be harnessed for national reconstruction.

The response of the government, however, has remained disappointing. Even a year after the disaster, the quake victims have remained ignored by the government and left on their own to face the monsoon rains as well as the subsequent harsh winter. The earthquake reconstruction programme has yet to be launched even while foreign donors are threatening to withdraw funds earmarked for reconstruction because of delay on the part of the government. The lethargy to kick-start the reconstruction programme indicates the fragility of a state that is trapped in a structure – a 'distribution coalition' – that favours the interests of the political elites ruling the country and therefore is unable to connect to the needs and requirements of the people.

The second elected Constituent Assembly (CA) promulgated a new republican constitution based on the principles of federalism, republicanism and secularism. Over 90 per cent of the CA members ratified it, but it was still a source of dissatisfaction and street violence for almost five months for a significant minority of citizens of the nation living in the southern plains, known as Terai-Madhesh. At the time of writing, an uneasy political truce between the Terai-Madhesh-based regional political parties and the government continues. A compromise solution still remains elusive even while it has been causing serious damage to the economy. Both exports and imports have suffered and for the first time in more than a decade Nepal's rate of economic growth could turn negative. On top of that, Nepal's bilateral relations with India continue to deteriorate and the Nepalese government views Indian government policy as the cause of the 'unannounced blockade' of landlocked

Nepal.[7] Worse still, there is now increasing concern about inter-ethnic and inter-regional harmony. These symptoms can no longer be shrugged off with the excuse that the country is in a 'transition' stage.

In the scenario Nepal faces today, the resource use perspective on foreign aid has to focus primarily on survival and sustenance. Otherwise, the serious and pressing economic problems may derail the transition. But, once the country has found its political feet, it must firmly resolve to get out of the aid-dependence syndrome and be free of bilateral aid and grants within the next 12 to 15 years. This – the nation's 'cold turkey' – is possible, and not too unpleasant, provided we are able to exploit the new 'economics of neighbour-hood'. Nepal now finds itself the 'link nation', rather than just the age-old yam, between the same pair of boulders, which, however, have suddenly turned themselves into the two most economically dynamic nations on the planet. The trio, Nepal, India and China, are no longer what they were.

The trick here will be to drive the transition from foreign aid to foreign investment by means of the vigorous participation of the private sectors of both China and India, and beyond. Nepal should aim to attract around 3 to 4 per cent of its Gross Domestic Product in the form of foreign investments: in hydropower, tourism, horticulture and related industries, and in the burgeoning information technology sector. This is possible and it should be the government's focus. For this to actually happen, as Dani Rodrik (2003) has already indicated, we must identify the binding constraints at each stage in the process. At present, of course, it is the political problem (contested constitution, unstable government, a distributional coalition that borders on 'roving banditry' etc.) that is the binding constraint. Once this phase is over, and the binding constraint has become more economic than political, the government will have to have two new priorities. The first is those areas (e.g. health, education, infrastructure) where social returns are high; the second is the shaping of an investment atmosphere in which (in marked contrast to how things are at present) the risk–return relationship is favourable to the private sector, both the national private sector and the foreign private sector. Foreign aid, for its part, should do two new things: it should refocus on these two basic principles and it should put its weight behind the national determination to end bilateral aid within the next 12 to 15 years.

Notes

1 Jeffrey Sachs, in a piece entitled 'The Case for Aid' in *Foreign Policy* on 21 January 2014, made the counterargument for more aid against those who say aid has failed: http://foreignpolicy.com/2014/01/21/the-case-for-aid/. Former UK prime minister Gordon Brown had an opinion piece in *The Guardian* of 9 September 2015 titled 'Cut Overseas Aid and You Force Even More People into the Boats': www.theguardian.com/commentisfree/2015/sep/09/overseas-aid-syria-lebanon-gordon-brown.

2 In going from two to three we go from simplicity to complexity (in the technical senses of these words; *simple systems* are deterministic, predictable, insensitive to initial conditions and so on; *complex systems* are not). Much of the current development paradigm's

problems, we are arguing, stem from it assuming that the system with which it is dealing is simple when it is in fact complex.

3   So the principal–agent linkage in the UK may no longer be as weak as it used to be. Certain major revisions in the UK's pattern of aid disbursement, in 2011, may be a response to this linkage-strengthening (though that could also be attributed to a then change of government). The total amount of UK aid to India is still large (because there are so many capita in India) and that may contribute to the outrage.

4   In the first, the concern is to stop things going backwards; the other two are concerned with going forward, and are each out towards one or other of two extremes. At one extreme aid does it all and there is not even a supporting role for the recipient nation; at the other, the recipient does it all and there is no role for aid. The latter, of course, would mark the end of a successful aid process; the former, to which Nepal has now come perilously close, would make something much less welcome: the end of the recipient's sovereignty.

5   When the NGO route is taken, we often find NGOs forming themselves with the express purpose of them performing this role for the donors. Sometimes the donors actually create them. Either way, these are not 'grass roots' NGOs; they are DONGOs.

6   National Planning Commission *Post-Disaster Needs Assessment,* Government of Nepal, 2015.

7   70 per cent of Nepal's external trade is through the Birganj customs bordering India. For almost five months it remained virtually closed, with Nepal claiming that India was using the political agitation in Nepal as a pretext to impose an 'unannounced blockade of trade'. India denies the allegation, but the plausibility of this denial has frayed over the months as even some within the agitating Tarai-Madhesh parties have now claimed they were coerced by India into owning the blockade.

13 Afterword

The lessons from Nepal

*Dipak Gyawali, Michael Thompson
and Marco Verweij*

Chapters 3 to 11 of this volume presented case studies of numerous efforts to
bring about development in Nepal through initiating technological change.
Particular attention was paid to the (constructive and destructive) roles that
have been played in these processes by Nepal's aid donors. This afterword sets
out the simple, yet vital, lessons that can be drawn from these case studies of
technological change for how to aid development – anywhere.

First, although many development projects end in failure – thus often making
poor people poorer and corrupt states even more corrupt – some development
projects have beneficial impacts on poverty alleviation, the accumulation of social
capital, environmental protection and the improvement of people's health and
general well-being. This is perhaps an unsurprising conclusion, but still worth
noting given the current policy debates about development aid around the world,
which range from 'close the [World] Bank!' on the one hand to 'triple
development aid!' on the other (Verweij and Gyawali 2006). Nepal is strewn
with highly expensive development failures that have lined the pockets of
Western consultants and companies, as well as less-than-honest domestic
decision makers (see Chapters 3, 4 and 10). These include the infamous Arun
3 dam and similarly large hydro projects, often pushed by the World Bank and
other aid donors (Chapter 8). They also include the ill-fated privatisation of
Bara Forest, foisted upon local communities by a Finnish logging company and
the Finnish International Development Agency in the 1980s (Chapter 1).

But development aid has sometimes acted as a force for good. The
Bhattedanda Milkway, for instance, was proposed by local Nepalese experts
with the Bagmati Watershed Project, but was also strongly supported by the
European Union (Chapter 5). The groundwork for the introduction of electric
vehicles in Kathmandu was laid by an INGO, the Global Resources Institute,
in tandem with USAID and Nepalese entrepreneurs and activists. And when
this roll-out stalled, the Danish international development agency pushed it
onwards (Chapter 6). Another INGO, the United Mission to Nepal, pioneered
the construction of small hydro and biogas projects in Nepal, at one point with
the help of a grant from the Norwegian government (Chapters 7 to 9). The
successful scaling-up of biogas benefited from 18 years of steadfast support by
the Dutch government (Chapter 9). And the first steps towards the internationally

lauded formation of community forest user groups were taken with the assistance of a grant from Australia and the United Kingdom (Chapter 11). Hence, although it is vital for poor countries not to become, or remain, 'aid junkies' (Chapter 12), the overriding question is how to ensure that development aid promotes, rather than threatens, poverty alleviation, social inclusion and environmental protection.

One way in which to do so – and this is the second lesson that we draw from our case studies – is by deploying development assistance such that it allows poor countries to leapfrog to the latest technologies, while avoiding, if at all possible, technological lock-in. Nepal, as we have seen, is not locked into the technologies of sewerage and wastewater treatment that, in the developed world, get human waste safely out of the city by putting it into the water cycle, a solution that is increasingly being seen as problematical (Thompson and Beck 2014). Nor is its landscape everywhere festooned with telephone poles and wires, or with lines of electricity pylons radiating out from vast power stations. Yes, there is gas, but there are no gas pipelines and, perhaps most encouragingly of all, there is renewable energy everywhere: biogas, hydropower in its various forms, solar in its various forms and, of course, biomass – from yak-dung to briquettes made from old newspapers, to charcoal and the time-honoured firewood and *banmara*, the forest weed – all cheaper, or rapidly getting cheaper, than fossil fuels (even when they are subsidised). No need, then, for Nepal to follow to the letter the technological paths that have been taken in the countries of the aid providers; it could leapfrog straight over to the new technologies – characteristically green, decentralised and flexible. Indeed, in many instances and as we have seen, it is already doing this, to such an extent that its experts in these new technologies are increasingly in demand around the world. 'Why learn from your mistakes,' as they say in business schools (but not, it would seem, in schools of development studies), 'when you can learn from other people's?'

Third, it is imperative that stakeholders, including foreign governments, realise that development assistance is not always (or even often) the solution, and can be very harmful. Aid has to be handled carefully and aid agencies have to restrain their institutional compulsion to equate mission success with having doled out lots of money. For instance, in Nepal, remittances have reduced poverty (and increased the government's budget) to a far greater degree (and in a much more decentralised manner) than development aid has over the last 10 years (Chapters 3 and 4). Hence, the governments of rich countries that are willing to help should consider a wider set of options (including a greater influx of goods, services and labour from poor countries) than the Pavlovian reaction of offering development aid.

Fourth, it is hard to exaggerate how important it is to get the details – financial, environmental, geological, technical and social – as accurate as possible when planning development efforts. The construction of a road in a remote, mountainous region may offer poor farmers access to city markets, but only very temporarily if there are regular landslides in that area (Chapter 5) and trucking cartels subsequently extort profits out of them literally to death. To understand the eventual success of small farmer co-operatives (Chapter 3) it was necessary to burrow all the way down to the household level – Mr and Mrs Bhattarai and their fellow group members. And an awareness of the '*khuwa* line', and of the Bhattedanda villages being on the wrong side of it (Map 5.1), was crucial to the economic and environmental transformations that have been effected by the various goods-only ropeways. Many development projects appear financially attractive on paper, but only because their costs have been significantly understated, while their benefits have been overstated (Chapter 8). Other development projects are finished on time and within budget – but primarily because their timeline and cost estimates had been inflated (as is documented in the same chapter). Increasing the water supply of a city can be a splendid undertaking, but not if the pipelines into which that supply is pumped are full of holes (as is the case in Kathmandu – see Chapter 10). To paraphrase US election campaigner James Carville, for development aid efforts the motto should be: 'it is the details, stupid'.

Fifth, it is high time that aid donors stop imposing, in a unilateral fashion, their forever-changing priorities and fads on unsuspecting aid recipients. Over the last six decades, Nepal has been made subject to every new development fad – from import-substituted growth to export-oriented growth, from 'take-off' through massive investment in infrastructure to the satisfaction of people's basic needs (and back), from state-led, via market-led, to NGO-led development, and so on and so forth (Chapter 4). The latest imposition concerns adaptation to, and prevention of, human-made climate change, which almost all aid donors are now prioritising in their policies – even though Nepal is far too poor and small to contribute to climate change to any significant degree, while knowledge of possible climate change impacts on the country is rudimentary at best. For instance, in one recent study (NCVST 2009) some 15 Global and Regional Climate Models were examined for what they projected for Nepal. Their predictions for precipitation levels in 2090 (and thus for snow cover and glacier formation) ranged from a 52 per cent decrease to a 135 per cent increase. Nevertheless, for most aid agencies climate change has become of overriding importance. From a Nepalese point of view, other issues appear more pressing. These problems include: daily electricity blackouts of up to 16 hours; insufficient water supply and sanitation; severe air pollution in Kathmandu; the need for reconciliation after a deadly civil war; the struggle against corruption and rent-seeking; and the recovery from the destructive earthquakes that struck in April 2015, to name but a few.

Sixth, and most importantly, all these lessons point in the same direction: towards the need to pluralise and democratise the planning and implementation of development strategies and projects. As explained in Chapters 1 and 2, and illustrated in all the case studies of this volume, development – economic, social, political and ecological – is spurred on by synergies created through the constructive interaction of market, government and civil society actors – at all levels of society. Hence, development aid can only be successful to the extent that it facilitates, rather than undermines, such interaction. Effective development projects are therefore creative, flexible combinations of entrepreneurship, (inter-)governmental regulation and civil society mobilisation (Gyawali and Dixit 2001). To highlight that such combinations tend to be forged in never-ending debates about how to define, and resolve, the problems at hand, we have called these combinations 'clumsy solutions'.

As mentioned in Chapter 2, clumsy solutions resemble Cass Sunstein's (1995) notion of 'incompletely theorised agreements', i.e. solutions that all stakeholders can agree to (or at least do not object to), albeit for very different reasons and from alternative moral viewpoints. As market, governmental and civil society actors tend to favour and replicate their own institutional settings, the solutions on which they can find common ground typically combine entrepreneurship, bureaucratic regulation and citizens' mobilisation. The promotion of clumsy solutions automatically puts into practice all the other lessons listed above. As they are based on competing perspectives on what the problems at hand are, and how these should be resolved, they tend to keep technology flexible, are based on a consideration of policy alternatives and contain details that have been carefully scrutinised. Moreover, as the notion of clumsy solutions entails that all competing policy perspectives are valuable, and need to be listened to, they are incompatible with a hegemony of the aid donors.

In our view, therefore, the main challenge for aid agencies and their partners is to develop ways in which to allow stakeholders in poor countries to generate clumsy (or polyrational) solutions – and then to support these solutions. In this, they need not start from scratch. Back in 1994, cultural theorist Aaron Wildavsky spelt out how the World Bank and other donors could employ a 'cultural audit' to capture the competing perspectives that stakeholders in developing countries hold regarding particular social ills. More recently, Bruce Beck et al. (2011) and Steven Ney and Marco Verweij (2015), as well as Anna Scolobig, Michael Thompson and Joanne Linnerooth-Bayer (2016), have outlined which deliberative and participatory methods can then be used to forge polyrational solutions from the cauldron of hotly disputed perspectives. These (and similar) methods have long been practised by governmental agencies and other organisations in Denmark, the Netherlands and the USA (where the Environmental Protection Agency now deliberately structures its stakeholder engagements so as to produce clumsy solutions),[1] among many other places. It is high time that the aid agencies start to do so as well.

These are the lessons from this volume.

Note

1 See: www.epa.gov/risk/multi-criteria-integrated-resource-assessment-mira (accessed 25 May 2016).

References

6, P. and Mars, G. (eds) (2008) *The institutional dynamics of culture: The new Durkheimians*. Farnham: Ashgate.

Acharya, K. (2004) Does Community Forest Management Support Biodiversity Conservation: Evidences from Two Community Forests from the Middle Hills of Nepal. *Journal of Forest and Livelihood*, 4(1).

Acharya, K. P. (2002) Twenty-four years of community forestry in Nepal. *International Forestry Review*, 4(2), 149–156.

Acharya, L. and Acharya, K. P. (2004) *A Review of Foreign Aid in Nepal*. Kathmandu: Citizen's Poverty Watch Forum and Action Aid Nepal.

ADB (2012) *Performance Evaluation Report: Nepal: Kali Gandaki 'A' Hydroelectric Project*. Manila.

Adhikari, B. (2005) Poverty, property rights and collective action: Understanding the distributive aspects of common property resource management. *Environment and Development Economics*, 10(1), 7.

Anon (2006) *Unequal Citizens: Gender, Caste and Ethnic Exclusions in Nepal*. Kathmandu: DfID and The World Bank.

Arthur, W. B. (1996) Increasing Returns and the New World of Business. *Harvard Business Review*, July–August, 100–109.

Arthur, W.B. (2009) *The Nature of Technology: What It Is and How It Evolves*. New York: Simon and Schuster, Free Press.

Ayodele, T., Cudjoe, F., Nolutshungu, T. A. and Sunwabe, C. K. (2005) African perspectives on aid: Foreign assistance will not pull Africa out of poverty. *Economic Development Bulletin*, 2, 1–4.

Bakker, K. (2007) The 'commons' versus the 'commodity': Alter-globalization, anti-privatization and the human right to water in the global South. *Antipode*, 39(3), 430–455. doi: 10.1111/j.1467–8330.2007.00534.x

Banerjee A. V. and Duflo, E. (2011) *Poor economics: A radical rethinking of the way to fight global poverty*. New York: PublicAffairs.

Barajas, A., Chami, R., Fullenkamp, C., Gapen, M. and Montiel, P. (2009) *Do Workers' Remittances Promote Economic Growth?* IMF Working Paper WP/09/153, July.

Batra, A. (2010) *When Villages Plug In*. Delhi: Down to Earth.

Bauer, P. T. (1972) *Dissent on development*. Cambridge, MA: Harvard University Press.

Beck, M. B., Thompson, M., Ney, M., Gyawali, D. and Jeffrey, P. (2011) On governance for reengineering the city infrastructure. *Proceedings of the Institution of Civil Engineers – Engineering Sustainability*, 164(2), 129–142. doi: 10.1680/ensu.2011.164.2.129.

Bhandari, K. M. (2011) Chinara Sammelan [In Nepali: Wood Workers' Meeting]. *Annapurna Post*, 23 March.

Bhattarai, S., Kumar Jha, P. and Chapagain, N. (2009) *Towards pro-poor institutions: Exclusive rights to the poor groups in community forest management.* Discussion paper. Kathmandu: ForestAction Nepal and Livelihoods and Forestry Program.

Blaikie, P., Cameron, J. and Seddon, D. (1980) *Nepal in Crisis: Growth and Stagnation at the Periphery.* Delhi: Oxford University Press.

Bourdieu, P. (1991) *Language and Symbolic Power.* Cambridge and Oxford: Polity Press.

Bourdieu, P. (1998) *Practical Reason: On The Theory of Action.* Cambridge: Polity Press.

Bruggemann, J. H., Rodier, M., Guillaume, M. M. M., Andréfouët, S., Arfi, R., Cinner, J. E., Pichon, M., Ramahatratra, F., Rasoamanendrika, F., Zinke, J. and McClanahan, T. R. (2012) Wicked social–ecological problems forcing unprecedented change on the latitudinal margins of coral reefs: The case of southwest Madagascar. *Ecology and Society*, 17(4): 47. doi: 10.5751/ES-05300–170447.

BSP (2006) *Multi-Annual Plan.* Kathmandu: Biogas Support Programme [BSP-Nepal].

BSP (2009) *Profile & Stories.* Kathmandu: Biogas Support Programme [BSP-Nepal].

BSP (2011) *Annual Progress Report 2010.* Kathmandu: Biogas Support Programme [BSP-Nepal].

Buchy, M. and Rai, B. (2008) Do women-only approaches to natural resource management help women? The case of community forestry in Nepal. *Gender and natural resource management: Livelihoods, mobility and interventions*, 127–147.

Burke, E. (1790/1986) *Reflections on the French revolution.* London: Penguin.

Caliari, A. (2014) Analysis of Millennium Development Goal 8: A global partnership for development. *Journal of Human Development and Capabilities*, 15(2–3), 275–287.

Carothers, T. and de Gramont, D. (2013) *Development aid confronts politics: The almost revolution.* Washington, DC: Carnegie Endowment for International Peace.

CBS [Central Bureau of Statistics] (2004) *Nepal Living Standards Survey, 2003/04*, 2 vols. Kathmandu: CBS.

Chapagain, D. P. (2013) Urban Water Supply Sector Reform in Kathmandu Valley. *Journal of the Institute of Engineering*, 9(1), 130–141.

Chapagain, N. and Banjade, M. R. (2009) Community forestry and local development: Experiences from the Koshi Hills of Nepal. *Journal of Forest and Livelihood*, 8(2), 78–92.

Chenery, H. B. and Strout, A. M. (1966) Foreign assistance and economic development. *American Economic Review*, 56(4), 679–733.

Chhetri, R. B. (2006) From protection to poverty reduction: A review of forestry policies and practices in Nepal. *Journal of Forest and Livelihood*, 5(1), 66–77. doi: 10.3126/jfl.v5i1.1982.

Chhetri, R. B. and Pandey, T. R. (1992) *User Group Forestry in the Far-Western Region of Nepal: Case studies from Baitadi and Accham districts.* Kathmandu: ICIMOD.

Christie, R. (2015) Millennium development goals (MDGs) and indigenous peoples' literacy in Cambodia: Erosion or sovereignty? *Nations and Nationalism*, 21(2), 250–269. doi: 10.1111/nana.12096.

Collier, P. (2008) *The bottom billion.* Oxford: Oxford University Press.

Colopy, C. (2012) *Dirty Sacred Rivers: Confronting South Asia's Water Crisis.* New York: Oxford University Press.

Commission on the Measurement of Economic Performance and Social Progress (2009) *Report.* Available at www.insee.fr/fr/publications-et-services/default.asp?page=dossiers_web/stiglitz/documents-commission.htm.

Cooke, P. (2001) Biotechnology clusters in the UK: Lessons from Localisation in the Commercialisation of Science. *Small Business Economics, 17*(1), 43–59.

Cox, R. W. (1979) Ideologies and the new international economic order: Reflections on some recent literature. *International Organization, 33*(2), 257–302.

Cruz, M., Foster, J., Quillin, B. and Schellekens, P. (2015) *Ending extreme poverty and sharing prosperity: Progress and policies* (Policy Research Note). Washington, DC: World Bank Group.

Danaher, K. (1994) *Fifty years is enough: The case against the World Bank and the International Monetary Fund.* New York: South End Press.

Dasgupta, P. S. (1993) *An inquiry into well-being and destitution.* Oxford: Clarendon.

Davy, B. (2012) *Land policy: Planning and the spatial consequences of property.* Cheltenham: Edward Elgar.

De Haan, A. (2015) Inclusive growth: Beyond safety nets? *European Journal of Development Research, 27,* 606–622. doi: 10.1057/ejdr.2015.47.

Della Porta, D. (ed.) (2016) *The global justice movement.* London: Routledge.

Devkota, J. (2014) Impact of Migrants' Remittances on Poverty and Inequality in Nepal. Forum of *International Development Studies, 44,* 36–53.

Devkota, R. R. (2010) *Interests and power as drivers in community forestry.* Gottingen: University of Gottingen Press.

Dietz, T., Ostrom E. and Stern, P. C. (2003). The Struggle to Govern the Commons', Science, *302,* 1907–1912. doi: 10.1126/science.1091015.

Dijkstra, G. (2013) *The new aid paradigm: A case of policy incoherence* (DESA Working Paper No. 128). New York: UN Department of Economic and Social Affairs.

Dixit, K. (2002). Hari the Hydro Entreprenneur. *Nepali Times,* 82, 22 February. Available at http://nepalitimes.com/news.php?id=6719

DoF (2008) *Guidelines for Community Forestry Development.* Kathmandu: Department of Forest.

Dougill, A. J., Soussan, J. G., Kiff, E., Springate-Baginski, O., Yadav, N. P., Dev, O. P. and Hurford, A. P. (2001) Impacts of community forestry on farming system sustainability in the Middle Hills of Nepal. *Land Degradation and Development, 12,* 261–276. doi: 10.1002/ldr.438.

Douglas, M. (1966) *Purity and danger.* London: Routledge.

Douglas, M. (1978) *Cultural bias* (Occasional Paper No. 35). Royal Anthropological Institute.

Douglas, M. (ed.) (1982) *Essays in the sociology of perception.* London: Routledge.

Douglas, M. (1987) *How institutions think.* London: Routledge.

Douglas, M. (1997) The depoliticization of risk. In R. J. Ellis and M. Thompson (eds) *Culture Matters: Essays in Honor of Aaron Wildavsky.* Boulder, CO: Westview, pp. 121–132.

Douglas, M. (2004) Traditional culture: Let's hear no more about it. In V. Rao and M. Walton (eds) *Culture and public action: A cross-disciplinary dialogue on development policy.* Stanford, CA: Stanford University Press, pp. 85–109.

Douglas, M. and Isherwood, B. C. (1996) *The World of Goods.* London: Routledge.

Douglas, M. and Ney, S. (1998) *Missing persons: A critique of personhood in the social sciences.* Berkeley, CA: University of California Press.

DST (2008) *Re-imagining the Rural–Urban Continuum: Understanding the role ecosystem services play in the livelihoods of the poor in Desakota regions undergoing rapid change.* Kathmandu: Institute for Social and Environmental Transition-Nepal (ISET-N). Available at www.nerc.ac.uk/research/funded/programmes/espa/final-report-desakota-part1.

Dunning, T. (2004) Conditioning the effects of aid: Cold war politics, donor credibility and democracy in Africa. *International Organization, 58*(2), 409–423. doi: 10.1017/S0020818304582073.

Durkheim. E. (1893/1997) *The division of labor in society*. New York: The Free Press.

Easterly, W. (2006a) *The white man's burden*. London: Penguin.

Easterly, W. (2006b) *Why Aid Doesn't Work*. Available at www.cato-unbound.org/2006/04/03.

Emmerij, L. (1976) *Employment, growth and basic needs: A one world problem*. Geneva: International Labor Organization.

Esser, D. E. and Ha, Y. (2015) Sustaining development as we know it: Limits to downward accountability in post-2015 international development policy. Available at http://papers.ssrn.com/sol3/papers.cfm?abstract_id=2640297##.

Evans, P. (2004) Development as institutional change: The pitfalls of monocropping and the potentials of deliberation. *Studies in Comparative International Development, 38*(4), 30–52. doi: 10.1007/BF02686327.

Fatehpur SFCL (2006) *Fifth Annual Report 2063*, Bara: Fatehpur SFCL.

Fechter, A. M. and Hindman, H. (eds) (2014) *Inside the everyday lives of development workers: The challenges and futures of Aidland*. Boulder, CO: Kumarian Press.

Fehling, M., Nelson B. D. and Venkatapuram, S. (2013) Limitations of the Millennium Development Goals: A literature review. *Global Public Health, 8*(10), 1109–1122. doi: 10.1080/17441692.2013.845676.

Fisher, R. J. (1989) *Indigenous Systems of Common Property Forest Management in Nepal*. Honolulu: Environment and Policy Institute.

Forsyth, T. and Walker, A. (2008) *Forest guardians, forest destroyers*. Seattle, WA: University of Washington Press.

Foss Hansen, S. and Baun, A. (2015) DPSIR and stakeholder analysis of the use of nanosilver. *Nanoethics, 9*(3), 297–319.

Franks, J. (2010) Boundary organizations for sustainable land management: The example of Dutch environmental co-operatives. *Ecological Economics, 70*(2), 283–295. doi: 10.1016/j.ecolecon.2010.08.011.

Frey, B. S. (2007) 'Evaluierungen, Evaluierungen . . . Evaluitis'. *Perspektiven der Wirtschaftspolitik, 8*(3), 207–20.

Frey, M., Kunkel, S. and Unger, C. (2014) Introduction: International organizations, global development and the making of the contemporary world. In M. Frey, S. Kunkel and C. Unger (eds) *International organizations and development, 1945–1990*. London: Palgrave Macmillan, pp. 1–22.

Fukuda, S. Murakami, M., Noda, K. and Oki, T. (2016) How achieving the Millennium Development Goals increases subjective well-being in developing nations. *Sustainability, 8*(2), 189. doi: 10.3390/su8020189.

Fukuda-Parr, S. (2006) Millennium Development Goal 8: Indicators for International Human Rights Obligations? *Human Rights Quarterly, 28*(4), 966–997.

Fukuda-Parr, S. and Yamin, A. E. (2015) *The MDGs, capabilities and human rights: The power of numbers to shape agendas*. London: Routledge.

Fukuda-Parr, S. Greenstein, J. and Stewart, D. (2013) How should MDG success and failure be judged: Faster progress or achieving the targets? *World Development, 41*, 19–30. doi: 10.1016/j.worlddev.2012.06.014.

Fukuyama, F. (1989) The end of history. *The National Interest, 16*, 3–18.

Gasper, D. (2006) Culture and development. In D. A. Clark (ed.) *The Elgar companion to development studies*. Cheltenham: Elgar, pp. 96–101.

Gauli, K. and Hauser, M. (2009) Pro-poor commercial management of non-timber forest products in Nepal's community forest user groups: Factors for success. *Mountain Research and Development, 29*(4), 298–307.

Gautam, A. P., Webb, E.L. and Eiumnoh, A. (2002) GIS assessment of land use/land cover changes associated with community forestry implementation in the Middle Hills of Nepal. *Mountain Research and Development, 22*(1), 63–69.

Gilmour, D. (2007) *Regulatory Frameworks for Community Forestry with particular Reference to Asia.* International Conference on Poverty Reduction and Forests. Bangkok: International Center for People and Forests.

Gilmour, D. A. and Fisher, R. J. (1991) *Villagers, Forests and Foresters: The Philosophy, Process and Practice of Community Forestry in Nepal.* Kathmandu: Sahayogi.

Gitlin, T. (2012) *Occupy Nation: The Roots, the Spirit, and the Promise of Occupy Wall Street.* New York: HarperCollins.

Gold, B. (1981) Changing Perspectives on Size, Scale, and Returns: An Interpretive Survey. *Journal of Economic Literature, 19*(1), 5–33.

GoN (1993) Forest Act 1993. Kathmandu: Government of Nepal.

GON/MFSC (1995) Forest Act 1993 and Forest Regulations 1995. Kathmandu: Government of Nepal.

Gray, J. (2007) *Black mass: Apocalyptic religion and the death of utopia.* New York: Farrar, Straus and Giroux.

Gronow, J. (1991) Shifting power, sharing power: issues from user-group forestry in Nepal. In N. Nelson and S. Wright (eds) *Power and Participatory Development: Theory and Practice.* London: Intermediate Technology.

Guthman, J. (1997) Representing crisis: The theory of Himalayan environmental degradation and the project of development in post-Rana Nepal. *Development and Change, 28*, 45–69. doi: 10.1111/1467-7660.00034.

Gupta, J. and van der Grijp, N. (eds) (2010) *Mainstreaming climate change in development cooperation: Theory, practice and implications for the European Union.* Cambridge: Cambridge University Press.

Gurung, O., Tamang, M. S. and Turin, M. (eds) (2014) *Perspectives on social inclusion and exclusion in Nepal.* Kathmandu: Central Department of Sociology/Anthropology, Tribhuvan University.

Gyawali, D. (1997) Foreign Aid and the Erosion of Local Institutions: An Autopsy of Arun-3 from Inception to Abortion. In C. Thomas and P. Wilkins (eds) *Globalization and the South.* London: Macmillan and New York: St. Martin's Press.

Gyawali, D. (2003) *Rivers, Technology and Society: learning the lessons of water management in Nepal.* London: Zed.

Gyawali, D. (2004) Water, sanitation and human settlements: Crisis, opportunity or management? *Water Nepal, 11*(2), 5–18.

Gyawali, D. (2013) Reflecting on the chasm between water punditry and water politics. *Water Alternatives, 6*(2), 177–194.

Gyawali, D. (2014) How to Energize Women: the Nepali response. *Bulletin of Atomic Scientists, 70*(2), 9–12. Available at http://thebulletin.org/expanding-energy-access-improving-womens-lives.

Gyawali, D. (2015a) Nepali resilience, the Duryog Nivaran way. *Spotlight, 8*(21). Available at www.spotlightnepal.com/News/Article/Nepali-Resilience-the-Duryog-Nivaran-Way.

Gyawali, D. (2015b) *Nexus Governance: harnessing contending forces at work.* Nexus Dialogue Synthesis Papers. Gland, Switzerland: IUCN.

Gyawali, D. and Dixit, A. (2001) Water and science: hydrological uncertainties, developmental aspirations and uningrained scientific culture. *Futures, 33*(8–9), 689–708. doi:10.1016/S0016-3287(01)00014-3.

Gyawali, D. and Dixit, A. (2010) Construction and Destruction of Scarcity in Development: A Case Built from Water and Power Experiences in Nepal. In L. Mehta (ed.) *The Limits to Scarcity: Contesting the Politics of Allocation*. London: Earthscan.

Gyawali, D., Dixit, A. and Upadhya, M. (2004) *Ropeways in Nepal: Context, Constraints and Co-evolution*. Kathmandu: Nepal Water Conservation Foundation and Kathmandu Electric Vehicle Alliance.

Gyawali, S.P. (2000) Reflecting Back on the Peace and Friendship Treaty with India. *Kanoon*, 20.

Hancock, G. (1989) *Lords of poverty: The power, prestige, and corruption of the international aid business*. Boston: Atlantic Monthly Press.

Hanninen, E. (2014) *Legimating Aid: Donors and Policy Making in the Rural Water Supply and Sanitation Sector in Nepal*. PhD thesis. Available at http://kirjakauppa.unigrafia.fi.

Harper, I. (2011) World health and Nepal: Producing internationals, healthy citizenship and the cosmopolitan. In D. Mosse (ed.) *Adventures in aidland: The anthropology of professionals in international development*. New York: Berghahn, pp. 123–138.

Hartmann, T. (2011) *Clumsy floodplains: Responsive land policy for extreme floods*. Farnham: Ashgate.

Head, C. (2000) *Financing of Private Hydropower Projects*. World Bank Discussion Paper No. 420. World Bank.

Hendriks, F. (1999) *Public policy and political institutions: The role of culture in urban policy*. Cheltenham: Edward Elgar.

Hendriks, F. (2010) *Vital democracy: A theory of democracy in action*. Oxford: Oxford University Press.

Hirschman, A. O. (1967) *Development reports observed*. Washington, DC: Brookings Institution.

Hood, C. (1998) *The art of the state*. Oxford: Clarendon.

Hood, C. (2012) Public Management by numbers as a performance-enhancing drug. *Public Administration Review*, 72(1), 85–92. doi: 10.1111/j.1540-6210.2012.02634.x.

Hout, W. (2012) The anti-politics of development: Donor agencies and the political economy of governance. *Third World Quarterly*, 33(3), 405–422. doi: 0.1080/01436597.2012.657474.

Hulme, D. and Fukuda-Parr, S. (2009) *International norm dynamics and 'the end of poverty': Understanding the Millennium Development Goals* (Brooks World Poverty Institute Working Paper 96). Manchester: University of Manchester Press.

Hyden, G. (2008) After the Paris declaration: Taking on the issue of power. *Development Policy Review*, 26(3), 259–274. doi: 10.1111/j.1467-7679.2008.00410.x.

IMF and World Bank (2003) Nepal: Poverty Reduction Strategy Paper. Washington, DC: International Monetary Fund and World Bank. Available at www.imf.org/external/pubs/ft/scr/2003/cr03305.pdf.

International Financial Institution Advisory Commission (2000) *The Report of the International Financial Institution Advisory Commission*. Washington, DC: US Congress.

Iversen, V., Chhetry, B., Francis, P., Gurung, M., Kafle, G., Pain, A. and Seeley J. (2006) High value forests, hidden economies and elite capture: Evidence from forest user groups in Nepal's Terai. *Ecological Economics*, 58(1), 93–107.

Ives, J. D. (2004) *Himalayan perceptions: Environmental change and the well-being of mountain peoples*. London: Routledge.

Ives, J. D. and Messerli, B. (1989) *The Himalayan dilemma*. London: Routledge.

Jerven, M. (2014) *Data for development benefits and costs of the data for development targets for the post-2015 development agenda* (Working paper). Copenhagen: Copenhagen Consensus Center.

Jodha, N. S. (1986) Common property resources and rural poor in dry regions of India. *Economic and political weekly*, 1169–1181.

Kanel, K. R. and Acharya, D. (2008) Re-Inventing Forestry Agencies: Institutional Innovation to Support Community Forestry in Nepal. In P. Durst, C. Brown, J. Broadhead, R. Suzuki, R. Leslie and A. Inoguchi (eds) *Reinventing forestry agencies: experiences of institutional restructuring in Asia and the Pacific*. Bangkok: Food and Agricultural Organization (FAO), 133–156.

Kanel, K. R. and Kandel, B. R. (2004) Community Forestry in Nepal: Achievement and Challenges. *Forest and Livelihood*, 4(4), 55–63.

Karna, B. K., Shivakoti, G.P. and Webb, E.L. (2010) Resilience of community forestry under conditions of armed conflict in Nepal. *Environmental Conservation*, 37(2), 201–209.

Kaufman, D. (2009) Aid effectiveness and governance: The good, the bad and the ugly. *Development Outreach*, February, 26–29.

Khadka, N. (1997) *Foreign Aid and Foreign Policy: Major Powers and Nepal*. Delhi: Vikas.

Khadka, N. S. (2004) 'Divided Donors: It's Just Not Nepalis Who are Not United'. *Nepali Times*, 194, 30 April – 6 May 2004, p. 1.

Khadka, S. R. and Schmidt-Vogt, D. (2008) Integrating biodiversity conservation and addressing economic needs: An experience with Nepal's community forestry. *Local Environment*, 13(1), 1–13.

Khanal, Y. N. (1977) *Nepal's Transition from Isolationism*. Kathmandu: Sajha Prakashan.

Kim, S. and Kim, S. (2010) Cultural Construction of what?: Stakeholders' Cultural Bias and its Effect on Acceptance of a New Public Information System. *International Review of Public Administration*, 14(3), 71–96. doi: 10.1080/12294659.2010.10805162.

King, G. C., Hobley, M. and Gilmour, D. A. (1990) Management of forests for local use in the hills of Nepal, II: Towards the development of participatory forest management. *Journal of World Forest Resource Management*, 5(1), 1–13.

Klein, N. (2007) *The shock doctrine: The rise of disaster capitalism*. New York: Knopf.

Koch, E., Grossmann, H. and Shrestha, B. K. (2003) *Rural Finance Nepal Project Progress Review*, March 2003. Kathmandu: GTZ.

Kuhn, T. (1962) *The Structure of Scientific Revolutions*. Chicago, IL: University of Chicago Press.

Kumar, N. (2002) *The Challenges of Community Participation in Forest Development in Nepal*. World Bank Operations Evaluations Department. 27931.

Levin-Keitel, M. (2014) Managing urban riverscapes: toward a cultural perspective on land and water governance. *Water International*, 39(6), 842–857. doi: 10.1080/02508060.2014.957797.

Loyens, K. and Maesschalck, J. (2014) Police–public interactions: A grid-group cultural theory perspective. *Policing*, 37(1), 144–158.

Luitel, A. and K. C., S. (2000) Local Level Water Management: The Experience of Helvetas Nepal, *Water Nepal*, 7(2), September–February 2000, 87–94.

McArthur, J. (2013) Own the goals: What the Millennium Development Goals have accomplished. *Foreign Affairs*, 92, 152–162.

McCormick, D. (2008) China and India as Africa's new donors: The impact of aid on development. *Review of African Political Economy*, 35(115), 73–92. doi: 10.1080/03056240802011501.

Mahat, R. S. (2005) *In Defence of Democracy*. New Delhi: Adroit.

Malla, Y. B. (2000) Impact of Community Forestry Policy on Rural Livelihoods and Food Security in Nepal. *Unasylva*, 51(202), 37–45.

Malla, Y. B. (2001) Changing Policies and the Persistence of Patron–Client Relations in Nepal: Stakeholders' Responses to Changes in Forest Policies. *Environmental History, 6*(2), 287–307.

Mars, G. (1994) *Cheats at work.* London: Allen & Unwin.

Maslow, H. (1943) A theory of human motivation. *Psychological Review, 50*(4), 370–396.

Mawdsley, E., Savage, L. and Kim, S. M. (2014) A 'post-aid world'? Paradigm shift in foreign aid and development cooperation at the 2011 Busan High Level Forum. *The Geographical Journal, 180* (1), 27–38. doi: 10.1111/j.1475–4959.2012.00490.x.

Mehrotra, S. and Jolly. R. (2000). *Development with a Human Face.* Oxford: Oxford University Press.

MFSC (1988) Master Plan for the Forestry Sector. Kathmandu: Ministry of Forest and Soil Conservation.

Mihaly. E. B. (2003) *Foreign Aid and Politics in Nepal.* Kathmandu: Himal.

MoF, (2015) *Economic Survey of Fiscal Year 2014/15.* Kathmandu: Ministry of Finance, Government of Nepal.

Mosse, D. (2005) *Cultivating Development: An Ethnography of Aid Policy and Practice.* New Delhi: Vistaar.

Mosse, D. (ed.) (2011) *Adventures in aidland: The anthropology of professionals in international development.* New York: Berghahn.

Moyo, D. (2009) *Dead aid: Why aid is not working and how there is a better way for Africa.* New York: Farrar, Straus and Giroux.

Nagendra, H., Pareeth, S., Sharma, B., Schweik, C. M. and Adhikari, K. R. (2008) Forest fragmentation and regrowth in an institutional mosaic of community, government and private ownership in Nepal. *Landscape Ecology, 23,* 41–54. doi: 10.1007/s10980-007-9162-y

NBPG (2007). *Biogas Sector in Nepal: Highlighting Historical Heights & Present Status.* Kathmandu: Nepal Biogas Promotion Group [NBPG].

NEA (2015) *A year in review – Fiscal Year 2014/15.* Kathmandu: Nepal Electricity Authority.

Nepal Climate Vulnerability Study Team (NCVST) (2009) *Vulnerability through the eyes of the vulnerable: Climate change induced uncertainties and Nepal's development predicaments.* Boulder, CO and Kathmandu: ISET International. Available at http://i-s-e-t.org/resources/major-program-reports/vulnerability-through-the-eyes-of-vulnerable.html.

New Era (2006) *Nepal Population Perspective Plan 2002–2027.* Kathmandu: New Era.

Ney, S. (2009) *Resolving messy policy problems.* London: Earthscan.

Ney, S. and Verweij, M. (2015) Messy institutions for wicked problems: How to generate clumsy solutions. *Environment and Planning C: Government and Policy, 33*(6), 1679–1696.

Nightingale, A. (2005) 'The Experts Taught Us All We Know': Professionalization and Knowledge in Nepalese Community Forestry. *Antipode,* 581–604.

NSAC [Nepal South Asia Centre] (1998) *Nepal, Human Development Report, 1998.* Kathmandu: NSAC.

Ojha, H. (2009) Civic Engagement and Deliberative Governance: The Case of Community Forest Users' Federation, Nepal. *Studies in Nepalese History and Society (SINHAS), 14*(2), 303–334.

Ojha, H. (2012) Civic Engagement and Democratic Governance: The Case of Community Forest User Groups in Nepal. In A. Deniere and H. Van Luong (eds) *The dynamics of social capital and civic engagement in Asia.* London and New York: Routledge.

Ojha, H. (2013) Counteracting hegemonic powers in the policy process: critical action research on Nepal's forest governance *Critical Policy Studies*, 7(3): 242–262.

Ojha, H. (2014) Beyond the 'local community': the evolution of multi-scalepolitics in Nepal's community forestry regimes. *International Forestry Review*, 16(3), 339–353.

Ojha, H., Persha, L. and Chhatre, A. (2009) *Community forestry in Nepal: A policy innovation for local livelihoods and food security*. IFRI Working Paper No. W091-02. Ann Arbor, MI: International Forestry Resources and Institutions Program.

Ojha, H. and Pokharel, B. (2005) Democratic innovations in community forestry: What can politicians learn? *Participation*, 7(7), 22–25.

Ojha, H., Timsina, N. and Khanal, D. (2007) How are Forest Policy Decisions Made in Nepal? *Journal of Forest and Livelihood*, 6(1), 1–16.

Ojha, H., Timsina, N., Kumar, C., Belcher, B. and Banjade, M. (eds) (2008) *Communities, Forests and Governance: Policy and Institutional Innovations from Nepal*. New Delhi: Adroit.

Ojha, H. R., Banjade, M. R. and Shrestha, K. K. (2015) 20 Critical action research and social movements: revitalizing participation and deliberation for democratic empowerment. *Handbook of Critical Policy Studies*, 380.

Ojha, H. R., Banjade, M. R., Sunam, R. K., Bhattarai, B., Jana, S., Goutam, K. R. and Dhungana, S. (2014) Can authority change through deliberative politics?: Lessons from the four decades of participatory forest policy reform in Nepal. *Forest Policy and Economics*, 46, 1–9.

Ojha, H. R. and Bhattarai, B. (2003) Learning to Manage a complex resource – a case of NTFP assessment in Nepal. *International Forestry Review*, 2, 118–127.

Ojha, H. R., Cameron, J. and Kumar, C. (2009) Deliberation or symbolic violence? The governance of community forestry in Nepal. *Forest Policy and Economics*, 11(5–6), 365–374.

Ojha, H. R., Khatri, D. B., Shrestha, K. K., Bhattarai, B., Baral, J. C., Basnett, B. S., Goutam, K., Sunam, R., Banjade, M. R., Jana, S., Bushley, B., Dhungana, S. P. and Paudel, D. (2016) Can evidence and voice influence policy? A critical assessment of Nepal's Forestry Sector Strategy, 2014. *Society and Natural Resources*, 29(3), 357–373. doi: 10.1080/0894 1920.2015.1122851.

Ojha, H. R., Paudel, N. S., Banjade, M. R., McDougall, C. and Cameron, J. (2010) The deliberative scientist: integrating science and politics in forest resource governance in Nepal. In L. German, J.J. Ramisch and R. Verma (eds) *Beyond the Biophysical: Knowledge, Culture and Politics in Agriculture and Natural Resource Management*. Dordrecht: Springer, pp. 167–191.

Ojha, H. R., Pokharel, B., Paudel, K. and McDougall, C. (2002) *Comparative Case Studies on Adaptive Collaborative Management: A Review of Eight Community Forestry Sites in Nepal*. Kathmandu and Bogor: ForestAction and CIFOR.

Ojha, H. R., Timsina, N.P., Chhetri, R.B. and Paudel, K.P. (eds) (2008) *Knowledge Systems and Natural Resources: Management, Institutions and Policy in Nepal*. Delhi: Cambridge University Press and IDRC.

Ojha, H. R., Timsina, N. and Khanal, D. (2007) How are Forest Policy Decisions Made in Nepal? *Journal of Forestry and Livelihoods*, 6(1), 1–16.

Organization for Economic Cooperation and Development [OECD]. (2008) *The Paris declaration on aid effectiveness and the Accra Agenda for Action*. Available at www.oecd.org/dac/effectiveness/34428351.pdf.

Ostrom, E. (1990) *Governing the Commons: The Evolution of Institutions for Collective Action*. Cambridge: Cambridge University Press.

Ostrom, E. (2010) Beyond markets and states: Polycentric governance of complex economic systems. American Economic Review, *100*(3), 641–672. doi: 10.1257/aer.100.3.641.

Ostrom, E., Janssen, M. A. and Anderies, J. M. (2007) A diagnostic approach for going beyond panaceas. *Proceedings of the National Academy of Sciences*, *104*(39), doi: 10.1073/pnas.0702288104.

Panday, D. R. (1999) *Nepal's Failed Development: Reflections on the Mission and the Maladies.* Kathmandu: Nepal South Asia Center.

Pandit, B. H., Albano, A. and Kumar, C. (2009) Community-based forest enterprises in Nepal: An analysis of their role in increasing income benefits to the poor. *Small-scale Forestry*, *8*(4), 447–462.

Paudel, D. (1999) *Distributional Impacts of Community Forestry Programmes on Different Social Groups of People in the Mid-Hills of Nepal.* Cambridge: University of Cambridge.

Paudel, K. P. and Ojha, H. R. (2008) Contested Knowledge and Reconciliation in Nepal's Community Forestry: A Case of Forest Inventory Policy. In H. R. Ojha, N. P. Timsina, R. B. Chhetri and K. P. Paudel (eds) *Knowledge Systems and Natural Resources: Management, Institutions and Policy in Nepal.* Delhi: Cambridge University Press and IDRC.

Paudel, N. S., Banjade, M. R. and Dahal, G. R. (2009) *Community forestry in changing context: emerging market opportunities and tenure rights.* Kathmandu: ForestAction.

Pokharel, B., Branney, P., Nurse, M. and Malla, Y. (2008) Community Forestry: Conserving Forests, Sustaining Livelihoods, Strengthening Democracy. In H. Ojha, N. Timsina, C. Kumar, B. Belcher and M. Banjade (eds) *Communities, Forests and Governance: Policy and Institutional Innovations from Nepal.* New Delhi: Adroit, pp. 55–91.

Pokharel, B. and Nurse, M. (2004) Forests and People's Livelihood: Benefitting the Poor in Community Forestry. *Journal of Forest and Livelihood*, *4*(1), 19–29.

Pokharel, B. K. (1997) Foresters and villagers in contention and compact: the case of community forestry in Nepal. PhD thesis, University of East Anglia.

Polanyi, K. (1944) *The Great Transformation: the political and economic origins of our time.* Boston: Beacon Press.

Poudyal, N. and Uprety, K. (2006) *Regression and Economic Methods.* Kathmandu: Asmita.

Price, M.F. and Thompson, M. (1997) The complex life: human land uses in mountain ecosystems. *Global Ecology and Biogeography Letters*, *6*, 77–90.

Putnam, R. D. (1993) *Making democracy work: Civic traditions in modern Italy.* Princeton, NJ: Princeton University Press.

Rajan, R. and Subramanian, A. (2005) *What Undermines Aid's Impact on Growth?* IMF Working Paper 05/126 and NBER Working Paper 11657, (October). Washington, DC: International Monetary Fund.

Rawls, J. (1987) The idea of an overlapping consensus. *Oxford Journal of Legal Studies*, *7*(1), 1–25.

Rayner, S. (1986) Management of radiation hazards in hospitals: Plural rationalities in a single institution. *Social Studies of Science*, *16*(4), 573–591. doi: 10.1177/030631286016 004002.

Rayner, S. (1992) Cultural theory and risk analysis. In S. Krimsky and D. Golding (eds) *Social Theories of Risk.* Westport, CT: Praeger, pp. 83–115.

Rayner, S. (2010) Foreword. In L. Mehta (ed.) *The Limits to Scarcity: Contesting The Politics of Allocation.* London: Earthscan, pp. xvii-xx.

Rayner, S. (2012) Uncomfortable Knowledge: The Social Construction of Ignorance in Science and Environmental Policy Discourses. *Economy and Society*, *41*(1), 107–125.

Rechlin, M., Burch, W.R., Hammett, A.L., Subedi, B., Binayee, S. and Sapkota, I. (2007) *Lal Salaam and Hario Ban*: The effects of the Maoist Insurgency on Community Forestry in Nepal. *Forests, Trees and Livelihoods, 17*(3), 245–254.

Reddy, S. G. and Kvangraven, I. H. (2015) Global development goals: If at all, why, when and how? Available at http://ssrn.com/abstract=2666321.

RESS (2010) *Final Report. Renewable Energy Sector Support Programme (RESS)*. Kathmandu: SNV Nepal.

Richards, P. (2011) A systematic approach to cultural explanations of war: Tracing causal processes in two West African insurgencies. *World Development, 39*(2), 212–220. doi: 10.1016/j.worlddev.2009.11.030.

Rist, G. (2006) *The history of development aid: From Western origins to global faith*. London: Zed.

Rodrik, D. (2003) *Growth Strategies*. Cambridge, MA: Harvard University Press.

Rodrik, D. (2007) *One economics, many recipes: Globalization, institutions and economic growth*. Princeton, NJ: Princeton University Press.

Roe, E. (2012) *Taking complexity seriously*. Berlin: Springer.

Rose, L. E. and John Scholz (1980) *Nepal: Profile of a Himalayan Kingdom*. Boulder, CO: Westview.

Rosenberg, N. and Birdzell, L. E. Jr. (1986) *How the West grew rich*. New York: Basic.

Rostow, W. W. (1960) *The Stages of Economic Growth: A Non-Communist Manifesto*. Cambridge: Cambridge University Press.

Sachs, J. D. (1996) The transition at mid-decade. *The American Economic Review, 86*(2), 128–133.

Sachs, J. D. (2005) *The end of poverty*. London: Penguin.

Sachs, J. D. (2012) From Millennium Development Goals to Sustainable Development Goals. *The Lancet, 379*(9832), 2206–2211. doi: 10.1016/S0140-6736(12)60685-0.

Sachs, J. D. and McArthur, J. W. (2005) The millennium project: A plan for meeting the Millennium Development Goals. *The Lancet, 365*(9456), 347–353. doi: 10.1016/S0140-6736(05)17791-5.

Sachs, W. (1984) *For the Love of the Automobile: Looking Back into the History of Our Desires*. Berkeley, CA: University of California Press.

Sandbrook, C., Nelson, F., Adams, W. M. and Agrawal, A. (2010) Carbon, forests and the REDD paradox. *Oryx, 44*(03), 330–334.

Schama, S. (1987) *The embarrassment of riches: An interpretation of Dutch culture in the golden age*. New York: Knopf.

Schumacher, E. F. (1973) *Small is beautiful: Economics as if people mattered*. New York: HarperCollins.

Schumpeter, J. (1942) *Capitalism, Socialism, and Democracy*. New York: Harper & Bros.

Schuurman, F. J. (2000) Paradigms lost, paradigms regained? Development studies in the twenty-first century. *Third World Quarterly, 21*(1), 7–20.

Schwarz, M. and Thompson, M. (1990) *Divided We Stand: Redefining Politics, Technology and Social Choice*. Philadelphia, PA: University of Pennsylvania Press.

Scolobig, A., Thompson, M. and Linnerooth-Bayer, J. (2016) Compromise not consensus: Designing a participatory process for landslide risk mitigation. *Natural Hazards, 81*(1), 45–68.

Seddon, D. and Hussein, K. (2002) *The Consequences of Conflict: Livelihoods and Development in Nepal*. Working Paper 185 (December). London: Overseas Development Institute.

Sharma, C. K. (1991) Energy and development in Nepal. *Ambio, 20*(3–4), 120–123.

Sharma, S. (2001) *Procuring Water: Foreign Aid and Rural Water Supply in Nepal*. Kathmandu: Nepal Water Conservation Foundation.

Sharma, S., Koponen, J., Gyawali, D. and Dixit, A. (eds) (2004) *Aid under stress: Water, forests and Finnish support in Nepal*. Kathmandu: Himal.

Shikwati, J. (2007) Molding the middle class. *Harvard International Review*. Available at http://hir.harvard.edu/ethnic-conflictmolding-the-middle-class/.

Shrestha, B. K. (2000): *Good Governance in Nepal: Perspectives from Panchthar and Kanchanpur Districts*. Kathmandu: Rural Development Foundation.

Shrestha, B. K. (2004) *Poverty Alleviation, Governance Improvement and Conflict Transformation of Rural Nepal: Report on the Study of Four Selected Small Farmer Co-operatives Ltd. (SFCL) in Eastern Nepal*. Kathmandu: Rural Finance Nepal (RUFIN)/GTZ.

Shrestha, K. K. and McManus, P. (2008) The politics of community participation in natural resource management: Lessons from community forestry in Nepal. *Australian Forestry*, 71(2), 135–146.

Shrestha, U. B., Shrestha, B. B. and Shrestha, S. (2010) Biodiversity conservation in community forests of Nepal: Rhetoric and reality. *International Journal of Biodiversity and Conservation*, 2(5), 98–104.

SMEC (1997) *Detailed Engineering Report of West Seti Hydroelectric Project*. SMEC.

Smith, A. (1776/2003) *Wealth of nations*. New York: Bantam.

Solow, R. M. (1956) A contribution to the theory of economic growth. *Quarterly Journal of Economics, 70*, 65–94.

Specter, M. (2006) The last drop. *The New Yorker*, 23 October, pp. 60–71.

Stiglitz, J. E. (1989) Markets, market failures, and development. *The American Economic Review*, 79(2), 197–203.

Stirrat, R. L. (2008) Mercenaries, missionaries and misfits: Representations of development personnel. *Critique of Anthropology*, 28(4): 406–425. doi: 10.1177/0308275X0809 8259.

Streeten, P., Burki, S. J., Ul Haq, M., Hicks, N. and Stewart, F. (1981) *First things first: Meeting basic human needs in the developing countries*. Oxford: Oxford University Press.

Subedi, B. (2006) *Linking Plant-Based Enterprises and Local Communities to Biodiversity Conservation in Nepal Himalaya*. Delhi: Adroit.

Sunstein, C. R. (1995) Incompletely theorized agreements. *Harvard Law Review*, 108(7) 1733–1772.

Svalheim, P. (2015) *Power for Nepal*. Kathmandu: Martin Chautari.

Swedlow, B. (ed.) (2014) *Advancing Policy Theory with Cultural Theory*. Special issue of *Policy Studies Journal*, 42(4), 465–697. doi: 10.1111/psj.12079.

Tansey, J. (2004) Risk as politics, culture as power. *Journal of Risk Research*, 7(1), 17–32. doi: 10.1080/1366987042000151188.

The Economist. (2013). Towards the end of poverty. *The Economist*, 1 June. Available at www.economist.com/news/leaders/21578665-nearly-1-billion-people-have-been-taken-out-extreme-poverty-20-years-world-should-aim.

Thompson, M. (2002) Man and nature as a single but complex system. In P. Timmerman (ed.) *Encyclopedia of Global Environmental Change*, 5. Chichester: Wiley, pp. 384–395.

Thompson, M. (2004) Technology and democracy. In F. Engelstad and O. Osterud (eds) *Power and Democracy: Critical Interventions*. Aldershot: Ashgate, pp. 185–208.

Thompson, M. (2008) *Organising and disorganizing: A dynamic and non-linear theory of institutional emergence and its implications*. Axminster: Triarchy Press.

Thompson, M. (2011/12) The quest for 'clumsy solutions' in Nepal's mountains. *Options, Newsletter of the International Institute for Applied Systems Analysis*, Winter, pp. 12–13.

Thompson, M. and Beck, M. B. (2014) *Coping with change: Urban resilience, sustainability, adaptability and path dependence.* Future of Cities Working Paper. London: Foresight, Government Office for Science. Available at www.gov.uk/government/uploads/system/uploads/attachment_data/file/396355/15-1-future-of-cities-coping-with-change.pdf.

Thompson, M., Ellis, R. J. and Wildavsky, A. B. (1990) *Cultural theory.* Boulder, CO: Westview.

Thompson, M. and Gyawali, D. (2007) Uncertainty revisited or the triumph of hype over experience. In M. Thompson, M. Warburton and T. Hatley (eds) *Uncertainty on a Himalayan Scale.* Lalitpur, Nepal: Himal, pp. xv–l.

Thompson, M. and Warburton, M. (1985) Uncertainty on a Himalayan scale. *Mountain Research and Development,* 5(2), 115–135.

Thompson, M. and Wildavsky, A. (1986) A poverty of distinction: From economic homogeneity to cultural heterogeneity in the classification of poor people. *Policy Sciences,* 19(2), 163–199.

Thoms, C. A. (2008) Community control of resources and the challenge of improving local livelihoods: A critical examination of community forestry in Nepal. *Geoforum, 39*(3), 1452–1465.

Tinbergen, J. (1976) Reshaping the international order (RIO). *Futures, 8*(6), 553–556.

Tranvik, T. and Thompson, M. (2006) Inclusive by design: The curious case of the Internet. In M. Verweij and M. Thompson (eds) *Clumsy solutions for a complex world.* London: Palgrave, pp. 204–255.

Tull, D. M. (2006) China's engagement in Africa: Scope, significance and consequences. *The Journal of Modern African Studies, 44*(3), 459–479. doi: 10.1017/S0022278X06001856.

United Nations (2015a) *Transforming our world: The 2030 agenda for sustainable development.* Available at https://sustainabledevelopment.un.org/post2015/transformingourworld.

United Nations (2015b) *The Millennium Development Goals report 2015.* Available at www.un.org/millenniumgoals/2015_MDG_Report/pdf/MDG%202015%20rev%20(July%201).pdf.

United Nations Development Program [UNDP] (2006) *Human Development Report – Beyond Scarcity: Power, Poverty and the Global Water Crisis.* New York: Palgrave.

Vandemoortele, J. (2011) The MDG story: Intention denied. *Development and Change, 42,* 1–21. doi: 10.1111/j.1467-7660.2010.01678.x.

Van Norren, D. E. (2012) The wheel of development: The Millennium Development Goals as a communication and development tool. *Third World Quarterly, 33*(5), 825–836. doi: 10.1080/01436597.2012.684499.

Verweij, M. (1999) Whose behavior is affected by international anarchy? In M. Thompson, G. Grendstad and P. Selle (eds) *Cultural theory as political science.* London: Routledge, pp. 27–42.

Verweij, M. (2011) *Clumsy solutions for a wicked world: How to improve global governance.* London: Palgrave Macmillan.

Verweij, M. and Gyawali, D. (2007) Against More Aid: Why Development Assistance Should Not Be Tripled. *Harvard International Review, 27*(4), 26–30.

Verweij, M. and Thompson, M. (eds) (2006) *Clumsy solutions for a complex world.* London: Palgrave Macmillan.

Wellgraf, S. (2014) Facing contempt: Dealing with exclusion among Berlin Hauptschueler. *Ethnography, 15*(2), 160–183. doi: 10.1177/1466138113480574.

Wildavsky, A. (1987) Choosing preferences by constructing institutions. *American Political Science Review, 81*(1), 1–22.

Wildavsky, A. (1994) How cultural theory can contribute to understanding and promoting democracy, science and development. In I. Serageldin and J. Tabaroff (eds) *Culture and development in Africa*. Washington, DC: World Bank, pp. 137–164.

Wilkinson, S., Van Der Kallen, P. and Phui Kuan, L. (2014) The relationship between the occupation of residential green buildings and pro-environmental behavior and beliefs. *Journal of Sustainable Real Estate, 5*(1), 1–22.

Williamson, J. (2009) A short history of the Washington consensus. *Law and Business Review of the Americas, 15*, 7–23.

World Bank (1979) *Nepal: Development, Performance and Prospects*. A World Bank Country Study. Washington, DC: South Asia Regional Office, World Bank.

World Bank (1985) *Project Completion Report, Nepal – Kulekhani Hydroelectric Project I*. World Bank.

World Bank (1990a) *World development report 1990: Poverty*. Oxford: Oxford University Press.

World Bank (1990b) *Nepal, Relieving Poverty in a Resource-Scarce Economy*.

World Bank (1994) *Staff Appraisal Report: Arun-3 Hydroelectric Project*. World Bank

World Bank (1997) *World development report 1997: The state in a changing world*. Oxford: Oxford University Press.

World Bank (2006) *Nepal – Fourth Biogas Support Program Project*. Washington, DC: World Bank. Available at http://documents.worldbank.org/curated/en/2006/11/10788175/nepal-fourth-biogas-support-program-project.

World Bank (2015) Nepal: Scaling up electricity access through mini- and micro hydropower applications: a strategic stock-taking and developing a future roadmap. Washington, DC: The World Bank. Available at http://documents.worldbank.org/curated/en/2015/06/24601157/nepal-scaling-up-electricity-access-through-mini-micro-hydropower-applications-strategic-stock-taking-developing-future-roadmap.

World Bank (2016) Poverty: Overview. Available at www.worldbank.org/en/topic/poverty/overview [accessed 17 April 2016].

World Commission on Environment and Development (1987) *Our Common Future*. Oxford: Oxford University Press.

Yadoo, A. and Cruickshank, H. (2010) The value of cooperatives in rural electrification. *Energy Policy, 38*(6), 2941–2947.

Yang, H., Acharya, S. P., Liu, P. and Guo, Y. (2014) Development assistance for health given to Nepal by China and India: A comparative study. *Globalization and Health, 10*: 76. doi: 10.1186/s12992–014–0076–6.

Yazdanpanah, M., Thompson, M., Hayati, D. and Zamani, G. H. (2013) A new enemy at the gate: Tackling Iran's water super-crisis by way of a transition from government to governance. *Progress in Development Studies, 13*(3), 177–194. doi: 10.1177/1464993413486544.

Yazdanpanah, M., Thompson, M., Hayati, D., Zamani, G. H. and Monfarad, N. (2014) Policy and plural responsiveness: taking constructive account of the ways in which Iranian farmers think about and behave in relation to water. *Journal of Hydrology, 514*, 347–357.

Žižek, S. (2009) *First as tragedy, then as farce*. London: Verso.

Index

n denotes endnote; t denotes table; f denotes figure

Age of Aid: beginnings of 54, 56; and guided democracy 72n9; and hydropower 118, 123; looking beyond 203–221; and World Bank, International Monetary Fund 213

Agricultural Development Bank: and biogas projects 153, 154, 160, 162; financing electric vehicles 102; and hydropower 115, 116; small farmer project 26, 33, 35, 38, 39, 41, 42, 43, 45–47

air pollution 95–112, 110

air quality 95–96

Alternative Energy Promotion Center (AEPC) 116, 157

Arun 3 project 119, 122, 137–139, 218

Asian Development Bank: 1970s involvement 61; and corruption 180–181; in hydropower project 135, 140; increasing aid 70; one of top providers to Nepal 64–65; in sanitation project 176, 178; and small farmers 34

Bagmati Watershed Project 82–83, 85

Balayar, Bhakta Bahadur 99

Bangladesh 55

Basnet, Bharat 98, 104

Bhattarai, Krishna Prasad 62, 64, 99

Bhattedanda Milkway: about 77–78; benefits of 79–81; case for replication of 91–93, 94n11; closed, reopened 86; development of 83–84; enabling construction 85; improvements to 86–87; lessons of 87; Milkway Committee loans 81; modifications to 82; as positive example 218; results of 85; sustainability of 81–82

Bhote Koshi project 134, 139

Bikasey chihan 9

Bikram Tempos *see tempos* (taxis)

biodiversity: enhanced by community forestry 186, 189–190, 197–198; loss reversed by Milkway project 80, 82; as MDG goal 93n3; *see also* climate change

Biogas and Agriculture Development Company Private Limited (GGC) 153–155

Biogas Support Programme: economic, ecologic, health benefits 161–162; integrated into renewable energy programme 162–164; mission statement of 159; need for return to 164–165; organization of 157; phases of 157–159; track record 160–161

biogas technology: about 155; cost-benefit analysis of 161; design modifications in 165; early years of 153–155; GGC 2047 plant 155; household plants 105, 106, 113; penetration of 155; as positive example 218–219; schematic of 156; *see also* Biogas Support Programme

Bir Dhara Works 169–170

Birendra (king) 59, 60

Brahmans 29, 30
bridges, suspension 93–94n7
Butwal Power Company 119–120, 132

Canada 60
caste system 29, 31–32
Chhetris 29, 30
Chilime project 124, 138–139
China 14–15, 58, 60
Civil War (People's War) 63–64, 196
climate change: and community forestry
    197, 198; determining public good 92;
    and development aid 8, 55, 69, 96, 220;
    recognition of 68–9; *see also*
    biodiversity
colonialism, and technology 168–169
Communist Party of Nepal (Maoists)
    63–64; *see also* Maoists
community development 48–49
Community Education Development
    Electric Company 125
community forestry: Bara Forest
    Management Plan 3–5, 218;
    biodiversity, climate change issues
    197–198; credit for success of 186;
    donor contributions to 194–195;
    exclusion of marginalised groups 196;
    exclusion of marginalized groups 197;
    Federation of Community Forest Users
    (FECOFUN) 189; Forest Act (1993)
    189, 190–191; Forestry Act (1993) 4;
    governance issues in 196; imbalance
    within 187–188; local people responsible
    for 188–189; Master Plan for the Forest
    Sector 188; in Panchayat system
    188–189; spread of 4; state of 185;
    structural inequality in 198; successful
    spread of 185–186; success of 189,
    191–193; user group contributions 194;
    utilisation issues 196–197; workshops on
    193–194, 200n13
Community Water Supply and Sanitation
    (CWSS) 172
consumption 11n3
cultural theory: developing dharma 24–25;
    and development issues 21; and grid,
    group dimensions 18; outlined 17; and
    perception 18; policy implications of 21;
    see also plural rationality theory

Dahal, Hari Bairagi 125, 126
Dalit Alliance for Natural Resources Nepal
    (DANAR) 194
Dalits 29, 30
Danida 101–102, 108, 109
Denmark 60
Department for International Development
    (DfID) 176–180
Deuba, Sher Bahadur 66, 180
development aid: 1960s programmes 58;
    1970s programmes 60–62; 1990s failure
    of 35; 1990s programmes 62–65; 2000s
    programme 65–71; affected by unrest
    67–70; aid-receiving categories 206–8;
    Basic Operating Guidelines (BOGs) for
    74n26; for biogas technology 154;
    careful planning for 219–221; continuing
    after Forum 70–71; corruption in 206;
    cost overruns in 134–139; criticisms of
    15; ensuring good results 219–221;
    future of 213–216; and guided
    democracy 72n9; history of 203–204; for
    hydropower 118–119; increase of 64–65;
    institutional perspective 210–211; lack of
    accountability for 52; and leapfrogging
    to new technology 219; and MDGs 203;
    multiple perspective model 208–212;
    need to escape 216; Nepal's experience
    with 212–214; new insights on 15–17;
    paradigms of 6–7, 13, 14; political
    perspective 211–212; positive examples
    of 218–219; potential for harm 219;
    principal-agent framing 204–206, 217n3;
    replication of projects 91–93; resource
    augmentation perspective 208–209;
    resource use perspective 209–210,
    217n4; supervisory bodies for 205;
    supporting clumsy solutions 219–221;
    for water, sanitation 171–172; *see also*
    donors
development tombs 9, 10, 11–12n7, 82
dharma: and cultural theory 24–25; defined
    5; gone wrong 5–6, 7f; restored 6, 7f
dhunge dhara (water spouts) 168
Dixit, Kunda 105–106
donors: in 1980s unrest 62; to biogas
    technology 154; to community forestry
    194–195; differences with NEA 140;
    differences with regime 70–71; and

electric vehicles 101–102, 108; failed financial engineering 150–151; and large hydropower projects 118–120, 141–144; multilateral 61; and small farmer development 27, 35, 39, 51–52; and water provision 170–171; willingness of 213; *see also* development aid
Douglas, Mary 17, 24

economies of scale 12n8
Eco-Vision 105–106
egalitarianism 5–6, 18–19, 22t–23t
electricity: community 129, 131n18; liberalisation of sector 139–141; outages 7, 113, 129, 137; *see also* electric vehicles; hydropower
Electric Vehicle Company (EVCO) 101–102
electric vehicles: breaking into market 97–98; concessions, obstacles for 101–102; decline of industry 109; donor involvement in 101–102; first attempt at 95; government interference with 103–107; industry expansion 102–103; journalist's experience 105–106; new registration ban 109; opportunities in Kathmandu 109–111; in outlying areas 111; as positive example 218; SAFA Tempo development 97; survival of 110–111; technical problems with 100; technology of 99–100; un-green competition with 108
Electric Vehicles Association of Nepal (EVAN) 108, 109
Environment Sector Programme Support (ESPS) 108
European Commission 61
Explore Nepal Group 98, 104, 112n6

farmers cooperatives: banking services in 42; bulk loans for 42–43; and community development 48–51; credit management for 43–46; difficulties with credit 46–47; exclusivity of 38–39; lack of government support for 51–53; loans by 39; pooling resources in 49; programmes for 33–35; rebirth, operation of 35–37; savings opportunities in 41–42; self-governance

of 37–38; socio-economic context of 27–29; success stories of 26–27; women in 39–40
fatalism: and plural rationality theory 20, 21, 22t–23t, 24; as way of organizing 5–6
financial engineering: backwards, forwards linkages 145–147; on export of hydropower 146–147; failed examples of 134–139, 141–149; fiscal linkage 148–149; investment linkage 147–148; Khimti as successful example of 141; of NEA 140; requirements for failure 150; of water resources 133
Finland 60
flood-drought syndrome 118, 130n11
ForestAction 187, 191–192
forestry *see* community forestry
forests 3, 4; *see also* community forestry
Four Point Program 56, 59, 72n6
Fourth Rural Water Supply and Sanitation Project (FRWSS) 176–177

GGC *see* Biogas and Agriculture Development Company Private Limited (GGC)
Ghimire, Dilli 126
Ghirling 81, 93n4
Global Resources Institute 97, 98, 101–102, 218
Gold, Bella 114
goods classification 11n3
governance corruption 32–33
Great Britain: as aid provider 64; in biotechnology 154; Gurkha regiments of 58–59; in India 71n1; TINA refrain originated 183
Green Economy Development Dialogue 88
grid dimension 18
Gross National Product (GNP) 54–55
group dimension 18
guided democracy 57, 59–60, 72n9
Gyanendra (king) 66

hierarchy: and plural rationality theory 18, 19, 22t–23t; as way of organizing 5–6
hierarchy of needs 13
Hillary, Sir Edmund 170

Himal Khabar Patrika magazine 167
Hoftun, Odd 132–133
Hydroelectric Development Policies 127
hydropower: aid-funded projects 118–119;
    Arun 3 project 62, 119, 122;
    cooperatives benefitting residents
    125–126; cost comparisons for 121t;
    development policy for 117–118;
    exporting for remittance 144–145;
    history in Nepal 114–115; paradigm
    crisis of 123–124; plant rehabilitated 125;
    potential of 110; priority options for
    127–128; in the private sector 119–123,
    122; projects for 124, 126; *see also* large
    hydropower; micro hydropower; small
    hydropower; water, sanitation supply

IIASA 14
inar (open dug wells) 168
India: aid to Nepal 57, 58; blockades of
    60–61, 95, 97, 105–106, 111; British
    water, sanitation services 169; economic
    blockade of Nepal 61–62; low-aid, zero-
    growth status 206–207; politics of
    55–56; relations with Nepal 60–61
individualism: and plural rationality theory
    19–20, 22t–23t; as way of organizing
    5–6
individualist technology 10
infrastructure improvements 50–51
International Fund for Agricultural
    Development 34, 61
International Monetary Fund 13, 213
Israel 59
Ives, J. D. 185

Janjati people 30
Japan 60, 64, 70–71, 183

Kali Gandaki-A project 141–142
Karki, Amrid Bahadur 113, 155
Kathmandu: air pollution in 95–96, 98,
    105; diesel vehicles banned 104;
    drinking water system for 169; electricity
    outages 113, 122; electric vehicles in
    95–112, 97, 109–111; improvements to
    57, 58; population growth 168; rural
    migration to 28, 168; water supply in
    170–171, 173, 181–182, 183n1, 184n13

Kathmandu Upatyaka Khanepani Limited
    (KUKL) 181–182, 184n11
Kathmandu Valley Water Supply
    Management Board (KVWSMB) 182
Khadga, Meena 125
Khadi and Village Industries Commission
    (KVIC) 153
Khimti 1 project: completion of 133–134;
    construction of 119–120; as small hydro
    118; success of 138, 139, 140–141
Khit-Khite 81, 93n4
khuwa (condensed milk paste) 78–80,
    82–83, 86
Koirala, Bishewar Prasad (B. P.) 56, 60–61
Koirala, G. P. 64, 66
Kulekhani 1 project 134–135, 136

land ownership 28
large hydropower: Arun 3 137–139;
    defined 114; Kali Gandaki-A 141–142;
    Kulekhani 1 134–135; Marsyangdi
    135–136; Middle Marsyangdi 142–144;
    West Seti project 144–149; *see also*
    hydropower; micro hydropower; small
    hydropower; water, sanitation supply
leapfrogging: development aid allowing
    219; in hydropower 128–129; over
    Industrial Revolution 219; in sanitation
    155; in water supply 183
legitimacy 5
licence raj 91, 98, 103
liquefied petroleum gas (LPG) power 97,
    103–104

Mahendra (king) 57–58
Maoists: 2000s insurgencies 66–67; agency
    of 68–69; bombing hydropower plant
    125; conflicts with donors 70; and
    farmers' cooperatives 34, 46; insurgency
    failure 8; labeled terrorists 66; overtaking
    democracy 33; splitting of 73n22
Marsyangdi project 135–136, 138
Maslow, Abraham 13
Melamchi Trans-Basin Water Transfer
    Project: corruption in 180; debate over
    181–182; electricity generation at 181;
    justification for 168; plan for 171,
    184n13; reform, counter-reform
    182–183

microbus importation 107–108
micro hydropower: advantages,
    disadvantages 117; defined 114; dual
    uses of 115; extending, linking plants
    127–128; penetration, potential
    116–117; rural uses of 113; turbine mills
    for 115; *see also* hydropower; large
    hydropower; small hydropower; water,
    sanitation supply
Middle Marsyangdi project 118, 138,
    142–144
Millenium Development Goals (MDGs):
    and aid effectiveness 14–15; bottom-up
    achievability 50; condescension
    perspective of 19; controversy of Nepal
    meeting 167–168, 176, 203; Milkway
    helping to achieve 79; and need for
    development aid 203; steps toward 79;
    on water, sanitation supply 167, 173
missionaries 132
Moulton, Peter 97, 101

National Rural and Renewable Energy
    Programme 161–163
Nepal: 1960s programmes 58; 1990s
    reforms, instability 62–63; Civil War in
    63–64, 196; colonialism interaction 169;
    constraints of foreign aid 54; export
    trade 61; foreign aid 8; foreign aid to
    foreign investment transition 216;
    fragility of the state 215–216;
    government spending changes 68t;
    government unrest 65–67; guided
    democracy in 57, 59–60, 72n9;
    high-aid, zero-growth status 206;
    involvement in international politics 58;
    macro economics of 214; monarchy-
    democracy tensions 56–57; need for
    stable government 216; Nepali Congress
    Party 56, 57; Panchayat system 59, 62;
    potential of renewable energy 129; Rana
    regime 55–56; remittance economy of 7;
    royal massacre 65–66; self-efficacy of
    8–11; self-sustainment hopes 95–96;
    Tenth Five-Year Plan 67; trade
    problems with India 215–216, 217n7;
    transformative process in 197–198; *see
    also* development aid; donors
Nepal Aid Group 61

Nepal-Australia Forestry Project 4,
    186–187, 193
Nepal Development Forum 70
Nepal Electricity Authority (NEA) 125,
    127, 138, 140
Nepal Electric Vehicle Industry (NEVI)
    98, 100–103
Nepal Water for Health (NEWAH)
    176–180
Nepal Water Supply Corporation 171
the Netherlands 60
Newars 30
NGO Forum 181
Norway 60, 65

Official Development Aid (ODA) 54–55
Organization of the Petroleum Exporting
    Countries (OPEC) 61
Orthodox Hinduism 29, 30
out-migration, remittances: boosting
    income for farmers 28; economy of 6–7,
    30–31; flooding banking sector 42; and
    GNP 54–55; increasing dependence on
    214–215; slowing of 50; statistics on 29

Pakistan 55, 58, 60
Panchayat system 72n11
pani ghatta 113
Pani Goswara water bureaucracy 170
Paris Declaration on Aid Effectiveness
    (2005) 14, 53n4
People s War (Civil War) 63–64, 196

plural rationality theory 20–21; *see also*
    cultural theory
policy process 5–6
population growth 28
poverty: and Bhattedanda Milkway 86–87;
    broader conception of 15–16; under
    democratic governance 31–33; Douglas's
    definition of 24; flexible institutional
    involvement in 16; mismanagement of
    intiatives for 27; and political power 16;
    systemic inequality in 29
Poverty Alleviation Fund 86–87
Pyakurel, Dinesh 180

Rana, Bir Sumsher 169
Rana, Jang Bahadur 169

Rana regime 55–56, 169, 172
remittances *see* out-migration, remittances
renewable energy 129
roadway expansion: costs of 89–90; as
   development project 13, 19; in
   Kathmandu 57; vs. Milkway 85–87, 90;
   political benefits of 91; in Sri Antu
   50–51; statistics on 88
ropeways: Barpak 93n2; cost-effectiveness
   of 93n6; vs. roads 85–87, 90; *see also*
   Bhattedanda Milkway
Rural Water Supply and Sanitation Fund
   Development Board (RWSSFDB)
   176–177

SAFA Tempo development 98
Saubolle, Fr. Bertrand 153
schooling, literacy 49–50
self-help, and solidarity 37
Self-Reliant Drinking Water Support
   Programme 165–167
Severn Trent 180–182
Sherpas 30, 53n2, 88, 170
Sikkim 71n2
Sinclair, Matthew Lochard 169–170
Singh, Prakash Man 180
Singh, Ranodweep 169
skunk works 100, 111–112n3
Small Farmer Development Project 26–27,
   33–34, 35
Small Farmers' Co-operative Limited
   35–37
Small Farmers' Co-operatives Programme
   33–35
small hydropower: compared to micro
   hydropower 117; defined 114; economy
   of 114; lower cost of 122; as positive
   example 218; *see also* hydropower; large
   hydropower; micro hydropower; water,
   sanitation supply
Snowy Mountain Engineering Corporation
   144, 146
social capital 115, 116, 215
social entrepreneur 113, 116
social forestry 4
South Korea 207
Soviet Union 58
Sumsher clan 169
sunk costs 90

sustainable development 71, 74n28, 79–82
Sustainable Development Goals (SDGs) 14,
   19
Switzerland 59

Tamangs 31
technology, and human development 16
tempos (taxis) 96, 98–99
Tenth Plan 30–31
Thamsuhang, Diptara 125
Theory of Himalayan Environmental
   Degradation (THED) 3, 11n1
theory of socio-cultural viability *see* cultural
   theory
tourism: affected by air pollution 96, 98,
   112n6, 147; and community forestry
   186; enhanced by community forestry
   186; hurt by air pollution 96, 98; part
   of GDP 216; Sherpas engaged in 88;
   women engaged in 53n2
transportation: diesel pollution 95–96;
   emissions policies 103; and government
   corruption 107–108; LPG ruled out 97;
   LPG vehicles imported 103–104;
   microbus importation 107–108, 109;
   prohibition of diesel imports 98–99, 101,
   104, 107; *see also* electric vehicles
Tri Bhim Dhara system 170
Tribuvan (king) 56
Tuladhar, Mohan Bir Singh 97

United Mission to Nepal 132, 218
United Nations 59, 172; agencies in Nepal
   61
United States 58, 60

voting, and caste system 32

Washington Consensus: in the Age of Aid
   213; and biogas mission statement 159;
   in biogas objectives 159; conditions of
   13–14; declared dead 11n2; followup to
   14, 15; mixed traits of 21; privatising
   forests 3
water, sanitation supply: availability of
   167, 174–175; Bagmati River condition
   173; as common-pool good 168; by
   donors 170–171; ecological soundness
   183; examining data on 173–180;

in Kathmandu 170; lack of, Kathmandu and the Terai 173; Phohora Durbar fountains 170; rural data on 176–180; TINA (There Is No Alternative) refrain 180, 183; top-down efforts fail 172; traditional vs. developing sources for 167, 172–173; from water spouts, wells, bottles 168, 170, 184n14; *see also* hydropower; large hydropower; Melamchi Trans-Basin Water Transfer Project; micro hydropower; small hydropower

Water Aid 172

Water Supply Tariff Fixation Commission (WSTFC) 182

West Germany 60

West Seti project 144–149

Wildavsky, A. 25

Winrock 104

women: advantages of hydropower 116–117; in caste system 30; community activities benefitting 49–50; community forestry groups of 190, 193; in electric cooperatives 125–126; electricity cooperatives of 125; in farmers' cooperatives 39–40, 43; and khuwa production 79–80, 83

World Bank: 1970s involvement 61; cancellation of Arun 3 62, 118–119, 137–139; and development aid debate 218; and export of hydropower 146; on forestry 185, 198; funding other power projects 124, 134, 135, 136; one of top providers to Nepal 64–65; postponing aid 71; on poverty decline 14–15; and Poverty Reduction Strategy Paper 51, 52, 86; water, sanitation supply loans 171, 176, 179, 182, 184n13

Yami, Hisila 181–182